T0164777

DSI: Dog Scene Investigation

Life Among the Dog People of Paddington Rec, Vol. III

Anthony Linick

AuthorHouse™
1663 Liberty Drive
Bloomington, IN 47403
www.authorhouse.com
Phone: 1-800-839-8640

First published by AuthorHouse 09/12/2011

ISBN: 978-1-4567-8069-2 (sc)
ISBN: 978-1-4567-8070-8 (ebk)

Printed in the United States of America

This book is printed on acid-free paper.

Other AuthorHouse Books
By Anthony Linick

Strictly Come Barking (2007)

The Lives of Ingolf Dahl (2008)

Have I Got Dogs For You (2010)

A Walker's Alphabet (2010)

INTRODUCTION

When I first began to record my impressions of life among the dog owners in my local park I had no idea that one day my journal might actually reach the point of print. *Strictly Come Barking*, published in 2007, altered this perception. The response to this volume, particularly from many of those whose stories it contained, encouraged me to persist in my observations—and thus we saw a sequel, a second instalment of "Life Among the Dog People of Paddington Rec" in *Have I Got Dogs For You!* (2010). Now we have a third volume, *DSI: Dog Scene Investigation.*

My view of our local dogs is restricted, of course, to the hour or so I see them alone, at play, or in interaction with one another—and there is little I can say about the other hours of the day, when all the loyalty and love we associate with dog ownership holds sway. Indeed, I would not want to leave the impression that any of our Paddington Rec dogs is unworthy of such love. I have continued to use only the first names of dog owners, except for celebrities, major and minor, though in every other way I have tried to make this chronicle a complete and accurate reflection of the times as we experienced them. I have also continued to used British spelling and, for inconsistency's sake, American punctuation.

I need to thank many people for their generous participation in this project: the dog owners themselves and all those who supplied me with photographs—Janet and Dan (whose photo of Winnie decorates our cover) especially. I also wish to thank Rob Taggart for his work with the photographs; his picture of Liam with Pepper and Fritz is also among our illustrations. As well, I need to offer my enduring thanks to all those who have helped to make Paddington Rec the oasis that it has continued to be: the management, the gardeners, the café staff, the wise heads at city hall.

Enough by way of introduction. Let the tale begin again and the tails to wag once more.

Anthony Linick
London
April, 2011

June, 2006

Thursday, June 1:

It isn't exactly warm, but temperatures have moderated a bit and, perhaps because this is the first day of June, there is just a hint of better things to come. As we begin another year's adventure in Maida Vale's Paddington Recreation Ground I suppose it is fair to add that there aren't many surprises, after almost three years in the park, that are likely to surface during our inbound journey. Surly joggers are pounding up behind us, my Fritz, the Schnauzer, is making his usual slow progress—sniffing at the bushes—and other dogs are marching counter-clockwise and need to be investigated and ranked by my dog—who thinks he is in the boss of the park. Arran, the exotic Coton de Tulear, gets a perfunctory growl and we are soon on to Hercules, the often hysterical Cocker, and Skye, the white Alsatian. The endless park refurbishment project seems no nearer to conclusion and a section of fencing is still down at the corner of the picnic ground. This spot usually seduces Fritz into a clandestine entry (dogs are banned here) and so it happens again today. I can see that a gate on the Carlton roadway is open and that Fritz has headed straight for this shortcut—which I now take myself, reassuring myself that, although dogs are banned here, people are not.

I reconnect with my dog on the great village green at the heart of the parkland and here there are a dozen or so owners with their dogs, participating in the morning ritual of exercise and gossip that is the hallmark of our society. Our usual spot at the centre of the green has been abandoned in favour of a perch near the loos—perhaps because one of the gardeners is astride his fast-moving lawnmower elsewhere on the grass. Today we have two Border Terriers, Tilly and Flash, Mozart, the long-haired Jack Russell on his visit from Glasgow, Winnie the Pug, Koko the Shih-Tzu, Bailey and Rosie, King Charles Spaniels, Sasha the Golden Retriever, Roxy the Beagle, and Sparkie the Yorkie. Sparkie decides to chase the speeding lawnmower and I am pleased to see that its driver actually stops his vehicle in order to avoid any tragedy. Soon thereafter, however, most of the owners file into the precincts of the café, not quite used to the later opening hours announced here last week—a tardy 9:30 on weekdays. I keep Fritz chasing his yellow rubber ball for another ten minutes and then join my friends for morning coffee.

I am followed into the forecourt by Jasmine the Shih-Tzu and her owner Faz (not his real name), on a break from his duties as a detective for the Metropolitan Police (he has to testify in court later today). We are all crowded around one table and I manage to start an argument by asking Dan and Davide, Winnie's doting parents, when they are moving into their new flat off the Harrow Road—for they each give a different answer to this question. Hanna has left her dogs home today—since Spadge the ancient Schnauzer, has torn a nail. Kate, Skye's mom, is just back from the Cannes Film Festival and keeps us entertained with tales of her socializing there; she says she most enjoyed meeting Robin Williams. She does *not* tell us how she managed to leave us as a redhead and return to us as a blonde, however. Outside the café's fence, meanwhile, other owners pass with their dogs, occasioning a noisy protest from our animals on the inside. Trouble, the Chow belonging to Angie, is one such instigator, and another is the muzzled Paddy, who arrives with Mary McCartney, daughter of the famous Paul. Our group thins a bit as work or appointments beckon and then the rest of us, after half an hour, begin a slow perambulation toward the exit gates, retracing the steps that Fritz and I have used to enter the park in the first place.

Friday, June 2:

I am actually able to enter the park without my leather jacket this morning, a sunny Friday with blue skies and scattered clouds. Fritz bounces along in a lively fashion (again we meet Arran) and manages to miss the entry into the picnic ground. To my surprise the café is already open at 9:15. This is a fact I mischievously withhold from my dog owner chums, out on the green supervising their dogs in a lively exercise period.

Bouncer, an American Bulldog, and Andrew the Akita join the group this morning. Andrew is always well-behaved but Bouncer is relatively new to the mix and there is some concern about his behaviour. Not to worry, he seems quite gentle too, though Bailey distinguishes himself by lying cravenly on his back while Bouncer has a sniff, then by begging to be taken up into Ofra's arms. A toddler named Harriet brings her scooter onto the hard surface of the cricket crease and deftly glides along. The blonde curly towhead won't be two until next month but she seems especially well-coordinated and totally unafraid of the dogs who scamper about at her feet. Helen is out here with Cleo the Pug; the only dog interested in her feminine aura is, surprisingly, Oscar—yet another Schnauzer. I tell Helen that usually Schnauzers are only interested in food. Cleo is lifted up into Helen's arms and Oscar and his roommate Scamp, the Westie, piss on my shoes in frustration.

When we go in for coffee there are only six of us at table and I am the only male. We have the Scottish sisters, Georgie and Jean, Kate, Helen and Ofra. Ofra tells us that today is a Jewish holiday, Shivous. This leads to a general discussion of such holidays and the foods that are traditionally consumed on them. Kate says, "If there's a holiday where you're supposed to eat chocolate, I'm becoming Jewish too."

After the food arrives and Helen backs up her chair to serve the sausage and toast to the dogs, I tell my friends about last night's adventure with Fritz. It was shortly after 11:00 and I was following my usual route—outside the park on Grantully—when Fritz, having rounded a tree, managed to snag the string of his extendo-lead under the bumper of a parked car. Usually I am able to undo this gesture by pulling the lead in the opposite direction but this time it remained securely wedged. Not wanting to pull the bumper off the car of an innocent motorist I had to detach Fritz from the lead, which I left dangling on the bumper while I improvised a new leash from my belt. When our walk was over—and I had returned the dog to the house—I made my way back to Grantully, this time with scissors, intending to cut the offending object off. I then met Hanna walking along the same stretch of walkway with the elderly George (also known as the Hannibal Lecter of Paddington Rec). When I showed her my problem she had a go at the bumper and this time succeeded in pulling the lead free—leaving the bumper intact as well. After telling this tale I am able attach the lucky lead to my dog and we head for the Morshead gate.

Saturday, June 3:

It's official: summer has come to Paddington Rec. I am in shirtsleeves and tan trousers and dark glasses and balmy temperatures prevail as Fritz and I make our way into the Essendine gate. My dog makes no effort to advance, however, touching noses with Fix (a shortened version of this dog's real name, Idée Fixe) and then pausing to sample the succulent shoots of the grass growing at the top of the running track. At least we don't have any incursion into the picnic ground to slow us down and we can make our way up to the Carlton roadway, where two of our baristas are making their own entrance, idling along in the shadow of the new ridiculously tardy weekend opening hours of the caff—10:00. Even though there is no sign of life outside this establishment customers are waiting half an hour before time and among these is Michael, whom we have not seen in several weeks! As Hannah can be called, in all fairness, the Queen of the Park, so Michael was its acknowledged King—until last December, that is, when illness forced him to give up his beloved Charlie and to retire from his central role as director of doggy operations. We shake hands and he indicates that he has brought along for our pooches a lot of the doggy toys never used by Charlie. One of these is quickly winkled out of its bag by a delighted Fritz, who is mesmerized by the presence of his old pal in our midst.

Near the cricket crease some of the other dog owners have set up headquarters on a blanket—and here they sprawl. The group includes Faz, Dan, Janet, Kate and the Scottish sisters—and most of them have been out partying the night before so that we now have our own version of Hangover Square. Little Lisa has her King Charles Spaniels, Zara and Dash, straining on lead nearby and, pointing to the comatose lot at my feet, I say, "Well, Lisa, here we see the awful consequences of too much drink." She laughs (Ronnie says she was in tears yesterday because her dogs are so wilful). Only occasionally does Fritz deign to make a guest appearance, bringing with him a transparent ball that flashes when it is bounced. Skye the Alsatian likes this too and I have to put it in my pocket to preserve it. (It begins to disintegrate as soon as Fritz gets his teeth into it at home). Eventually the recovering inebriates get up and head in for coffee and I follow them.

Michael, once again at the head of our table, seems to be in better shape than the last time we saw him. He has brought so many goodies in shopping bags that Fritz is beside himself, trying to get his nose ever deeper into the recesses of these treasure houses. Michael says that he owes his recovery in part to not having to get up early on doggy missions. But he hasn't reoccupied his own garden, which last year suffered a fatal blow when council gardeners, freeing garage roofs from the grasp of ancient ivy, dumped all the foliage down into his yard. I now ask what Winnie has in her mouth on the June picture from Janet's famous Paddington Rec calendar (it turns out it is her own tongue) and this raises the issue of whether there will be a sequel for next year. Janet wonders if this time she should pose the animals in the laps of their owners. Dan says that this is good idea—only the owners should be nude with the dogs covering their private parts. Kate has the last word: "Thank God I have a big dog!"

Sunday, June 4:

The beautiful warm weather persists and Fritz makes short work of rounding the corners and heading for the picnic ground. Here, however, we begin a day of quintessentially bad behaviour. He dashes through the gap in the fence and enters the cool precincts of this dog-free area, refusing to return, as he usually does—perhaps because there is already some activity within. Indeed there are three moms, some with toddlers, and they cast baleful looks in our direction as I catch up with my dog and lead him out one of the gates. We are very early for any sign of activity at the café and soon I see my rascal streaking for the centre of the green, where a knot of dog owners is gathered on the grass near the cricket crease.

Unfortunately Natasha, the owner of Leila, the Miniature Pinscher, has brought a squeaky ball with her—and this soon has Fritz entranced. I warn her of my dog's proclivities but the ball remains in play and a few minutes later my scamp has made off with it. I am surprised that it takes so little time to extract this object when the time comes, but perhaps Fritz has even greater mischief in mind. These days cricketers arrive at about this time (we would be long gone from this spot if the café opened at a decent hour, but no one has thought of this). One white-clad chap, waiting for his pals, sits down on the grass on the other side of the crease where, to my horror, his back serves as a target for my dog's lifted leg. Fortunately the chap is unaware of this, but our member of the Met, just coming in with Jasmine, gets a good view. This is the second time that Faz has witnessed a public order abuse here recently—on Friday he and Dan had to chase down a seven year-old who had just thrown a water bomb at Janet. No arrests are made today but I am relieved when it is time to put my dog on lead and head in, still a bit too early, for the forecourt of the café.

Ronnie, hoping for an early entry, has already been thrown out once and we have to wait until 10:00 exactly for orders to be taken. By this time there is a huge queue and orders are naturally slow in coming. The situation in the forecourt is also confused. Georgie and Faz complain of cold and move a big table into the prow of the patio in order to be in the direct sun. Ronnie, whose MS has made him quite weak in the legs these days, refuses to move and so I remain with him. My wife Dorothy, currently sun-phobic, sits here as well and we are soon joined by Hanna and by Hector's owner, Peter. The latter has brought a pulsing boom box—which has already drawn a protest from one of the other customers. Peter offers to put on classical music but I reply pointedly that today's insistent church bells provide quite enough sound for us. Kate is sitting with Faz and Georgie and they are soon joined by a much relieved but dogless Janet—after tummy troubles have lead Koko to an early morning visit to the vet. After a shorter day than usual Dorothy and I drop the dog off on our way to Sainsbury's—which is also undergoing a dizzying reconstruction. Not a restful day of rest.

Monday, June 5:

It doesn't take me long to discover that I am underdressed for an appearance in the park today. The sun is shining brightly and might provide some warmth were it not for a chill wind that raises the goose bumps on the bare arms of those in short-sleeved shirts. Fritz makes a lively enough start to his day, however, and waits for me at the picnic ground corner, where I attach his lead—fearing a repetition of yesterday's incursion. As we pass through the precincts of the café I notice that the senior barista is already here at 9:15, but that no effort is being made to open the doors of our place of refreshment.

The dog owners are lined up near the Grantully entrance, perhaps trying to escape the encirclement of the head gardener—who has chosen this moment to mow the grass. Monty the Cocker, Otw the Bichon Frise, plus Roxy, Rosie, Winnie and Cleo are dashing about as their owners wait sullenly for the café to open. Ronnie is the first to make an attempt on the closed doors of the place, but, at 9:30, they are just bringing out the chairs and tables. I sit with him for a few minutes and then go in to place our orders—I am the café's first customer. Ronnie seems a bit miz these days; his 95 year-old mother is losing focus and he departs early to visit her in her care facility.

Faz, Liz, Dan and Helen soon join me—as we all sit shivering in the breeze. Also present is Rhianne, whose Otw stares in disbelief as a biscuit offered to her is snaffled up by my Fritz. Rhianne, who is a photographer, tells us that her Bichon Frise has been getting some well-paid photo assignments recently. I remind her that Fritz The Dog is at liberty. Otw can twirl on her hind legs in return for a sliver of bacon. She ends up on the shoulders of her mistress, a curly white boa. Rhianne says that the vet has suggested that her dog lose four pounds—"I can feel a layer of fat on these ribs." Dan turns to Liz and says teasingly, "well Roxy's vet says that he can actually feel a whole dog under this layer of fat." I am about to accompany the others on a walkround when I spot Linda and Michaela with their dogs. I wait for them (Fritz and fellow Schnauzer Pepper have a raucous recognition scene) and they trundle around with us as well—after my wilful dog has headed out the Carlton gate in pursuit of Liz and Roxy.

Tuesday, June 6:

Another lovely day beckons us to the walkways of the park. There are lots of dogs who have to be checked out as we head toward the green, Fritz on lead as we near the heavy activity of the building sites. There are lots of lorries about as well and so I do not release my dog until we have reached the grass.

Here we find a lively scene on the opposite side of the cricket crease and, since Helen, Dan and Ofra, are sitting in the grass, I stand behind them—lest young Fritz decides to have a pee on *their* backs too. He does not, and, instead, he gets a lovely cuddle from all three, rumbling with joy and seeing off any other dog who might want some of the same attention. Meanwhile Gus and Oscar add their Schnauzer presence to the play period. I would have liked a longer period in the sunshine but I have arrived late (today being the last moment for the builders in our house) and 9:30 rolls around after only ten minutes or so.

We take a table in the shaded forecourt and the coffee soon arrives. Dan is expecting the birth of a new nephew today and, since today is 6-6-6, everyone speculates on whether to call him Damian—if it's a boy. Helen says that Tanya the animal warden is boycotting the café these days because of all the anti-dog activities—all the signs about dogs on the lead at the café, the changed opening hours—there is even evidence that the police were called over the bad behaviour of one dog the other day. Into our world wanders Hector, the delightful young Spaniel, but his owner Peter wanders over to a table at which Rosemary is reading a book about Kim Philby, and it is obvious that he doesn't want to talk to anyone. As we begin our walkround Dan is fantasizing about wanting to be a doctor. To tease him I suggest that this fantasy is appropriate for the son of—"What profession is your father?" I ask, knowing full well the answer. "A butcher," he replies. We all laugh.

Wednesday, June 7:

The pleasant summer weather is with us again and I bask in the sun as Fritz slowly makes his way around the playing fields. A woman jogger is having a rest in a shady patch of grass just past the cypress trees and so I move my dog along with a gentle nudge—not wanting him to deposit a poo at her feet. Instead he waits until we have reached the red poo poo box and then we are able to continue, on lead, out to the green.

I can see a number of dog owners seated near the cricket crease and here we head. Unfortunately the rarely seen sheepdog, Bob, also has his eyes on this prone group and just as we arrive he lifts his leg and pees on Faz's jacket—which Faz is wearing at the time. I must say our policeman shows a great deal of forbearance, though he is visibly upset, and he waves off any attempts on the part of Bob's embarrassed owner to pay the cleaning costs. Fritz resumes his independent exploration, heading for the loos where Tanya (in spite of what Helen said yesterday) has just parked her van. A second poo follows but this time some of it squeezes through the holes in my Sainsbury's fruit and veg bag and I have to head for the gents—where a curious Fritz follows to see what I am doing. Out on the green again we encounter Yankee the Labrador. His mom has just produced a ball and a squeaky dinosaur for her pet and I tell her not to throw the latter—if she wants it back in a hurry. She throws it anyway, Fritz makes off with it, and I can't extract it until we go in for coffee.

Rhianne joins us with Otw. She says that she has trained the white fluff-ball to curl around her neck because she needs both hands free to unload photographic equipment. Otw can also fetch the mobile phone (texting is next). With pieces of bacon as inducement Otw is lead through some of her tricks and this inspires Helen and Dan to try this routine out with Cleo and Winnie—though they don't seem to have much success. The dog owners have convinced themselves that too much sausage is bad for their pets (Koko has been ill of late) and they have just been ordering a spartan plate of toast. With this meagre fuel Fritz must content himself until it is time for us to make our way through the red-clad teenaged athletes who are exiting the park as well. One of these lasses is explaining why she can't run much of late. "You can talk plenty," is the waspish response from her instructress.

Friday, June 9:

I have missed a day in the park—out walking on the Chiltern Way with the Lees. I return to a wonderful warm and balmy morning in a sunny park and Fritz makes his usual slow progress along the upper reaches of the running track. When we reach the cypresses, however, we encounter a new fence prohibiting further progress. Our park plenipotentiaries have not bothered to post a sign at the Essendine entrance, preferring that innocent pedestrians should get this far in their journey to the Carlton gate, for instance, before realizing that there is an obstacle hidden around an unsighted corner. This is what happens to a flustered gentleman in front of us and I must say that Fritz is mightily puzzled when I turn us around for the long walk over to the Morshead side of things.

Just as we reach the green we encounter Helen walking with Cleo. They are heading for a small group of dog owners, again sprawled on blankets, near the bandstand. I pause here while Fritz ranges widely. I can see him greeting people and dogs way over on Mt. Bannister (as I call the park's only hill) and eventually I decide to see what he is up to. As I near the foot of the walkway up to the peak itself my dog disappears behind the bushes that guard this juncture and the next thing I know one of the orange-clad landscape managers is asking me if I'm not going to clean up after my dog. This is always something I am prepared to do and I have one of Tanya's green bags at the ready, but in this case I didn't even know my dog had done a poo. I ask to be shown where the offending pile is located, get it cleaned up (while getting a lecture about never allowing my dog to escape observation—fat chance) but this is only the insult added to another injury. I have just thrown the yellow ball onto the green, wanting to get Fritz out of the path of a swarm of tennis teenies who are brandishing their rackets as though prepared to smite all dogs (though none are paying them any attention). By the time I have completed my other chores Fritz has fetched the yellow ball, run off with it somewhere, dropped it, and now this prized object can not be found anywhere. I circle one end of the green for several minutes, then give up and head disconsolately for the crowded forecourt of the café,

We are at a table with Natasha, Leila's mom, Georgie, Kate, Dan, Helen, and, soon thereafter, Dorothy. I drink only a bottle of still water while Helen distributes the sausage and toast. The others are holding a learned discussion on use of the word "vagina," which they agree is a silly word—though most of its euphemisms are truly nasty. After a while Dorothy and I depart for our stroll to St. John's Wood—where Fritz has an appointment with the vet. He gets all his shots and is weighed (9.2 kilos), then we march downhill and back through the park. I notice, as we near the picnic ground, that pedestrians coming from this end have been given no warning by our neglectful park staff that theirs will be a wasted journey if they take this turnoff too.

Saturday, June 10:

Another warm day beckons but I am late to the park, this time because I know the café won't open until 10:00. Fritz and I do not take our traditional left turn when we enter but slant off to the right, reaching the green much more rapidly in this fashion. A dozen dogs are milling about but many of these are pupils of the obedience school and none of them belong to our usual group. Finally I spot our pals lying down on the grass at the foot of Mt. Bannister. Here we head, though twice I have to move Fritz along as he begins to raise a leg on the many scattered objects that the Saturday crowd has left lying about.

I have a new toy with me, a kind of red basketball about the size of a tennis ball and it bounces well enough to keep Fritz interested—he even brings it back most of the time. Suki the Vizsla, whose own ball ends up in the bushes near the loos, is accompanied today by young Nicole and by her dad. He offers me his ball sling so I can really get Fritz moving.

After a few minutes my dog is panting and so I decide to put him on lead and I sit with him in a patch of shade where our group is gossiping. I have missed another eruption of testosterone-fuelled Herculean rage. This time the Cocker has had a fight with Humpty (similarly un-neutered) and Humpty's dad has been bitten in the process. Indeed while we are sitting on the grass Jean-Baptiste calls on Dan's mobile phone to see if anyone has a phone number for the victim. Our group is universal in its opinion that Hercules needs the snip.

Georgie emerges from the precincts of the café to tell the rest of us that the café has opened slightly ahead of schedule. A gradual troop movement takes place but when we reach the café the queues are long, naturally, and it takes a while for everybody to get settled. I drink a bottle of peach ice tea. The subject of the World Cup comes up—since this afternoon England have their first match and Michaela now has had to tell her Olivia that the primary school reunion scheduled for Queensway will therefore very likely be minus the boys. Dorothy announces that she is going to Marks & Spencer during the event. And Dan is buying a kitchen at Ikea—having reasoned that only married women and gays will be competing for the attention of the staff today. The forecourt of the café is crowded, there are practically no chairs, and therefore there are lots of witnesses to the yelping distress of the young Schipperke, Kiwi, who gets nipped by Jasper the Water Spaniel. It is time for us to head for home.

Sunday, June 11:

For some reason they have forgotten to unlock the Essendine gate again and so we join the despondent march of still more disappointed pedestrians in changing our direction. Fritz is most puzzled, having been lead up to the promised land—only to be dragged away. Once re-launched on the Morshead roadway we haven't much distance to cover before meeting up with our group, sprawled on the grass at the west end of the green.

Fritz works the crowd, eliciting a cuddle from each of the prone dog owners, growling with delight and then trying to hide behind their bodies to escape the rays of another hot sun. A Japanese chap with no dog nevertheless kneels to add his caresses to the assembled pooches. I stand, trying to cast a shadow for my dog to hide in. The park is not nearly as crowded as it was yesterday and, for once, Fritz does not stray any great distance. Someone notices that the umbrellas are out at the café and, fifteen minutes early, we head for the shadier precincts of the café's "garden."

There are a dozen of us eventually—including Davide, who wanders in as Dan says, "Oh here's my husband" while I am saying, "And here's my wife" to Dorothy. Others present include Georgie, Ofra, Kate, Janet, Jo Lynn, Ronnie, and Michael, who comes dressed in vest and shorts and receives another riotous greeting from Fritz. When Faz arrives we decide to replicate the scene from *Cheers* and shout out, in unison, "Faz!" as he enters. He seems pleased and puzzled by this gesture at the same time. Dorothy and Jo are discussing the anorexic Victoria Beckham—"and I have never seen a leather sofa with that skin colour," Jo adds. Dan and Davide (who served Prince Edward on a recent flight) fall to quarrelling again over details of their move; they have to be out of their flat by Tuesday but their new place is far from finished and it appears that they will have to bunk down with Dan's parents in Essex. We have shoved two tables together in an attempt to get more shade but after half an hour my place is in the direct sun and so I get Dorothy to call it a day.

Monday, June 12:

As Fritz and I bounce down the stairs at the start of our visit to the park we encounter a typical urban tragedy. The clampers, who patrol our streets like ravenous piranhas, have just hoisted a smart black car aboard their flatbed truck. It seems that a young German couple, on a visit to the chaps in the flat downstairs, have missed the start of the hunting season by five minutes and now their rent-a-car is on its ways to some penalty garage under Hyde Park. Not only are their entreaties of no avail with these heartless folk, but these visitors to our shores have rushed out so quickly that the front door of the flat has slammed behind them, they have no money, their luggage and passports are inside, they have an easyJet flight in a few hours and they have no knowledge of the work numbers of their hosts. I haven't a clue how to help them and after commiserating I continue on with my dog, promising to give their predicament some thought.

Once again our small troop is on the grass near the trees at the west end of the green. Fritz runs off to greet a few of the other dogs on the grass and I pause to chat with Helen and Davide. Michaela arrives with Skye and, much to everyone's surprise, the Cairn lifts his leg and pees on a canvas bag belonging to Davide. Then, also uncharacteristically, he also tries to hump Cleo. With such idiocy about it is just as well that we only have to wait for 9:30 to begin our journey to the café.

It is Ofra's birthday and there are gifts and cards and the birthday girl has herself baked a biscuit cake. I drink a bottle of still water on another very hot day, though clouds are protecting us from the worst of the sun's efforts. Michael the Pirate, after a long period of invalidity with a bum leg, has returned to us today, once more accompanying the park's oldest canine citizen, the twenty-year old Doofie. The latter, in spite of his antiquity, still has it in him to shuffle after Cleo; he looks like the Groucho Marx of dogs. Helen and Davide like to sit their Pugs on their laps, facing one another, just to see whether it will be kisses or snarls. It is the latter today, and the two wheezing ladies have to be separated instantly. "You two are as bad as the thugs who bring their fighting dogs into the park in the afternoon," I add.

While we are having our drinks Tanya, Pasha's mum, walks by, pushing baby Isabella. "Don't any of you work?" she jokes. "I'm retired," I reply but, truth to tell, Davide, Georgie and Kate certainly do have work, Ronnie and Michael aren't well enough to be among the employed, only Ofra might count as a slacker—if being the mother of two teenagers fits into this category. As Fritz and I make our move homewards I notice that my dog has again stripped the sheath covering his extendo-lead. This is a minor annoyance compared to the plight of the Germans—but they too seem to be recovered a bit, for they are heading off with their backpacks as I arrive.

Tuesday, June 13:

A hot and humid night has ended with some needed rainfall and, still under grey skies, we enter the park in far more humane temperatures. We take the Morshead roadway and this offers the quickest pathway to the green, though the latter is essentially empty and it isn't until I see a knot of dog owners at the Grantully gate that I realize we are not alone. Hercules is just being dragged away from Cleo and Nicholas and Helen are discussing whether this is still shorts weather.

I have brought Fritz's miniature basketball with me and I keep it in play—in spite of my dog's unwillingness to return it to me or, for that matter, just leave it where he finds it. Instead, he insists on carrying it in his mouth for long distances, ignoring all entreaties on the subject of "Drop it!" Pretty soon I can see that Skye has his eye on this prize and, as Fritz has now dropped it, the Cairn makes off with it and races toward the Morshead exit, where Michaela is walking with Christianne. Eventually the ball ends up in Stella the Staffie's mouth and I have to reach the gate before I am able to retrieve it. A little later Fritz carries the ball into a crowd of dogs near the metal gazebo. But this time I can't tell who has made off with the toy and a search of the adjacent grass is fruitless. My dog has lost two balls in one week.

When I go in to coffee only Georgie is present, though we are soon joined by Helen, Hanna and Ronnie. The latter is in a cheerful mood, all the more surprising since his car was broken into (thieves made off with the car's manual and a pair of Cartier sunglasses). Hanna says that she has discovered two books from the Camden Library, discarded in the park, and that she will have to return them herself. (She says that she has had to renew her own library book, on Shamanism, six times.) Another mission she undertakes regularly is to leave kitchen rejects from the café for the local foxes. All of the dogs, who are snacking on toast only these days, have had a really bad night—panting in the heat and trying to find a cool place to lie down. Sparkie now remedies this problem by lying with his tail in a puddle beneath our table. When we get up to leave he looks like a drowned rat.

Thursday, June 15:

The weather has freshened considerably since the humid inferno that was Monday, and I return to the park with some hope that normality will be restored to our doggy world. Indeed I *was* here yesterday, but on a morning threatened by rain there wasn't much activity. The field had been commandeered for some kiddies' sports day—and so there wasn't any action out here anyway. Most of the dog owners were absent and by the time Dorothy came out to relieve me (it was haircut day) only Hanna was still around.

Today is a lovely morning, temperatures in the 60's and sunny. I have a chat with Michaela while kicking the ball to Skye. When Fritz does a poo I walk up to the collection box near the Grantully exit with this contribution and Fritz, at my heels, seems to disappear. I have a worried look out into the street but we soon discover that my dog has admitted himself to the doggy area nearby, and so Michaela and I spend some time here as well. They have created a little hill with a buried pipe covered in grass and Fritz enjoys standing on the top, king of the mountain. Michaela, however, wants to return to the sun and so we walk back to the green after a few minutes and here there are now lots of dogs dancing about. For some reason Oscar the Schnauzer has picked up his brother's bad habits—it used to be Scamp alone who liked to piss on shoes.

I can see that Ofra has arrived and is walking around the green with Tanya, Pasha the Weimaraner, baby Isabella and Bailey. Cleo, who will be staying with Ofra when Helen goes to Holland next week, is also here, but none of the other veterans is about. When it is time for coffee I head for the café, but the scene is not encouraging. Metty is cordoning off parts of the forecourt and none of the regulars is at table. With workmen expected in the house again today, I decide to skip coffee and head for home.

Frid, June 16:

It's another delightful t-shirt morning as we head for the Morshead gate, excited to see what surprises the day will provide. The first surprise is that Fritz disappears almost as soon as we enter the park. I find him seeking admission to the Morshead doggy area, but I remind him that we prefer to visit this spot in the late afternoon—when the shade of the chestnut trees offers some relief from the heat of the day.

Dan (he and Davide are now staying at Janet's, not in Essex) has again brought out a blanket, and he is sharing it with Georgie, Janet and Kate. Fritz runs in among these people, offering his own unique canine greeting—something that amounts to a request to *pet me!* I have also brought his yellow tennis ball and he does some serious chasing, though once or twice the ball has to be removed from the teeth of competitors. Winnie tries to start a fight with some of these, including three of the park's four Sky(e)s—the Alsatian, the Husky and the Cairn. Tara the Kerry Blue also makes a rare appearance in our midst and, surprising for a female, she decides to keep up the summertime peeing propensity by urinating on the blanket. This isn't too bad in itself but soon the male dogs want to cover the scent and I have to nudge Fritz with my foot, for instance, to get him to desist. It is not surprising that when 9:30 rolls around there is a mass exodus for the café.

Here I can see that the reason they have cordoned off two areas of the forecourt is that they are filling in the deep cracks between paving stones with more cement. They are not wiping away the excess cement and I fear for the aesthetic result. It does mean that when Peter throws rounds of sausages to the dogs in the future that these delicacies won't roll into the cracks—and for this Fritz will be grateful. Today he wants to sit in Auntie Janet's lap and this is where he spends most of the morning, looking like a vulture about to pounce on Dan's scrambled eggs at the next place. When Dan is finished Fritz switches to *his* lap. Dan says that most of the other dogs don't really like to be cuddled but that Fritz is different and this is soon demonstrated. Meanwhile another pair of eyes is focusing on the tabletop, those of Kate's Skye. This huge youngster can stand with her front paws *on* the table, towering above everyone. This is considered cute, and it is, but Skye is in disgrace, having picked every item out of her mistress' handbag before chewing the bag to bits and then hiding the evidence under Kate's pillow. This object is produced for its last rites and then Kate says that Skye once devoured a pair of new shoes—before they had even been out of their box—"I'm getting my own channel to broadcast her mischief of the day. I'm going to call it Skye News."

Friday, June 23:

A week has passed since my last appearance in Paddington Rec, the consequence of a weeklong hiking sojourn in the Lakes. A brief investigation reveals a number of events that have transpired during my absence. Georgie's daughter Lynn has gotten married in St. Lucia; Ofra, who is housing little Cleo while Helen is in Holland, reports that the anxious little madam has peed and pooed in her new home; and Liz now owes Kate another chocolate croissant after Roxy has again made off with this pastry while no one was watching.

The school sports day season has also started in earnest while I was away, and Fritz and I arrive as preparations are made for another one on the green. Fortunately there is still room for the dogs to roam and Fritz has a go at chasing his bright green tennis ball. His chief attentions, however, are devoted to greeting his old pal David—pretty soon my dog is rolling on his back at the dogsitter's feet, chortling in delight. This is by far a more intense greeting than I got on *my* return—I think I was being punished for my desertion but then Fritz had also purloined another rubber ball from one of the other dogs that morning and this lip-smacking treasure obsessed him throughout the day until, after retrieving it from beneath the sofa on a dozen occasions, I had to hide it for good. At 9:30 we head in for coffee, just me, Liz, Hanna and a late-arriving Georgie, whose Sparkie pursues a gaggle of screaming school girls who decide to be menaced by a little Yorkie—not understanding that if they just stood still he wouldn't think it was a game.

There is a large gaggle of sports day mums haunting the precincts of the café and it takes a while for the regulars to be served. I note that Doofie, whom earlier we saw circling the western precincts of the park unattended, has been reclaimed by Michael the Pirate. Also that Gus the Schnauzer has received a short back and sides, eliminating at last his blue rinse. Our dogs have some toast while Liz explains that whoever told her to watch *Big Brother* is responsible for a new addiction: "I used to think that whoever watched *Big Brother* was an idiot and now I discover that I am the idiot in question." Faz arrives with Jasmine and a toothache. His Dianah has also been having tooth problems and Jasmine has been cuddling up to the sufferers as a way of comforting their pain. She and Sparkie now have a wrestling match as we make our way toward the exit.

Saturday, June 24:

These days I have to delay my departure for the park on Saturday and Sunday because of the absurd late opening hours of the café. Fritz doesn't seem too bothered and so at 9:30 we make our way into the Rec via the Morshead gate. It has rained during the night and there are even a few drops now but soon the sun tries to break through and temperatures rise suddenly. The dog owners are well scattered today, with a small knot getting ready for today's obedience lessons, some of our lot standing outside the café gate, and a third group relaxing in the centre.

We join the latter group. David is here with Skye the Cairn, the American woman in University of Georgia garb is here with her Husky, also Sky, and so is Kate with her white Alsatian—also named Skye. Fritz wanders off and soon disappears but eventually I spot him, not emerging from the café precincts where I thought he had gone, but from the Randolph Avenue side, where he is chasing Cleo. The latter is in the care of Ofra's husband Rickie, who also has his Bailey in tow. He joins us at two large tables that have been drawn together in the café patio.

The subject of Cleo's continued pooing and peeing in Ricky and Ofra's household comes up. This reminds Dan that Winnie doesn't do this in strangers' households but that she sometimes gets the blame: "My brother's dog Ella makes a mess, pushes Winnie into it and then reports the infraction to the rest of us!" The subject of dental prices dominates much of the conversation because Faz, Dianah and Kate have all been through the wars recently. Kate says she won't say aloud how much she has had to pay out but, "It would pay for a small terraced house up north." Her shoes have also been through the wars and she produces them in evidence. They are a match in colour to the bag chewed up last week by Skye—and now they have suffered the same fate. "You should have saved the bag; you could dress up now as a bag lady," Dan suggests. "I do already," Kate responds. Today is her Skye's first birthday (and still growing) and she has laid on all the treats for the assembled congregation. She eats her own tomato, cheese and ham panini but somehow the tomato ends up on Bailey's back and this has to be cleaned off before we head for home.

Sunday, June 25:

Once again I emerge at the relatively late hour of 9:30, heading for a green (now turning brown) upon which one group of dog owners is standing near the loos and a second set is sprawled on the grass nearer the bandstand. Georgie is complaining that she has been pissed on by Bob the sheepdog, and Skye the Cairn soon rushes up to piss on a nearby poo poo bag. Janet has brought her friend Lyndon today and he has brought his twelve week-old French Bulldog puppy, Lulu. She is an adorable creature, waddling about with great curiosity and bravery among the other dogs.

Kate and David are discussing the 4:00 kick-off for England's World Cup match against Ecuador and Kate seems to be a nervous wreck over the prospects of the lads. I try to keep Fritz occupied with his yellow tennis ball, following him over to the newly resurfaced courts when he wants to do a poo. As I return I witness a slanging match between an Irishman and Franca, with lots of the F word in evidence, but I can't tell what the source of the difficulty might be—though it clearly involves dogs. Meanwhile Hector is digging a big hole in a bare patch of ground from which a healthy tree has been extracted in the name of progress. I note that the café has actually opened up early and pass this news on to the rest of the troops.

At coffee Lyndon, Koko's original owner, spends a lot of time mocking Janet over a decline in the Shih-Tzu's personality—"When I had her she was a princess. Now look at her—an old bull dyke." Skye the Alsatian is drinking buckets of water from a bowl filled by Ronnie. With every slurp water squirts out of the side of her mouth, quite drenching little Lulu below. Michael the Pirate joins us with the oft-told tale of arguments with park staff over his (therapeutic) use of a bicycle (ordinarily forbidden in the park). Dan says that Davide has the hump and is not coming today. The dogs seem uninterested in the toast they are offered—this new anti-sausage regime is a great disappointment to them. The air is humid, though the sun has still not made its presence felt when, after an hour, I drag Fritz toward the exit

Wednesday, June 28:

Two days have passed since I last made an entry: on Monday it rained throughout the morning session and, under any circumstances, I was only in the park for about fifteen sodden minutes. On Tuesday I was here for an hour but I had no computer on which to record my observations since it, and all of the other furniture in our house, was piled high in every unattainable corner as the carpet layers plied their trade. I can begin therefore with a summary. Helen returned from Holland yesterday and had a reunion with Cleo in the park; the little Pug, out of excitement or too much rich food, threw up on our shoes. Dan and Davide left for a wedding in Barcelona, leaving Winnie behind with Janet. Liz will leave for five weeks on Cape Cod on Saturday—with Roxy going back to the Daisy Hill Puppy Farm during her absence. Helen will leave again for her brother's wedding in Malaysia soon, with Cleo bunking down in a variety of settings during her mom's second absence. We didn't win anything after the dog owners, collectively, spent £11 on the lottery.

Today my heart sinks when I see that a parade of toddlers is being marched into the park, since we had a disruptive sports day here yesterday, but this group heads straight for the running track. Instead Fritz is pursued by a quite ancient part-Poodle named Bear, who evidently has a crush on my dog. She follows him over to the Grantully exit and I have to go there and retrieve them both. Hanna arrives with a shorn Spadge; the ancient Schnauzer is so agitated by the haircutting process these days that he is shampooed a couple of days before the actual snipping. She hands me the lead of George while she fishes something out of her bag. Today we have Sam the Dachshund, a relative newcomer, and Pumbaa the Alsatian—whom we have not seen in a long time. Skye the Alsatian chases balls for Kate, and Fritz wanders off a second time—then returns to touch noses with all the other dogs and to beg for treats. Monty the Cocker pisses on Sam's owner, who is seated on the grass.

When we go to coffee I get in line behind Liz, who is buying a chocolate croissant for Kate. Outside, we are entertained by two large and noisy trucks (labelled highway maintenance) who are depositing gunk for the surface of the children's play area, opposite. The dogs get lots of toast, no sausage, and Winnie attacks Cleo when all the goodies are gone. Kate fails to keep an eye on her new chocolate croissant and Roxy snatches it off her plate a second time! Liz is again mortified, though this time they have run out of the treats. In the expectant hope that I might find my house without any workers in it I head for home with Fritz after an hour in the sunny park. I am disappointed.

Thursday, June 29:

It is a beautiful sunny morning and, for once, the school groups have yet to arrive in our part of the world. Fritz chases his bright green ball and visits all and sundry as the rest of us relax in the warmth. Faz is here with Jasmine *and* Koko, his first day off in some time. He lies down on the grass with Ofra while Fritz tries to lie down in his shadow. At one point I count fifteen dogs at play on the green—quite a large turnout for a weekday. Moster the Cocker has a small World Cup English football and I am surprised that Fritz doesn't make off with it. Sky the Husky is also lying in the shadow of his mom's body. She says that today is too hot for a Husky but I add, "Any day over fifty degrees is too hot for a Husky."

Georgie arrives with Sparkie and Winnie (it's musical dogs these days) and follows the rest of us into the café forecourt. She reports that a security guard has asked her to put her dogs on lead (the first time I have *ever* heard of such a rule being enforced here) but she complains that the same guard did not make this request of Faz, who followed her in. We end up at two tables, Ronnie, Hanna, Farrah (with eleven year-old Poppy) and me at one, Georgie and Faz at a second. I haven't the patience to wait in line for any form of refreshment today. I just take off my cap and bask in the sun.

The dogs have a lot of toast, though Fritz is freed once from his lead to see if the sausages have arrived at Peter and Ellen's table—our lot have abandoned the practice of ordering sausages for our dogs. Spadge gets into his usual state of agitation, barking hysterically, and Hanna picks him up in her lap and comforts him as he subsides into whimpers. When she gets up (all he wanted was a poo) I follow her out and we make slow progress of it toward our gate. Fritz follows Peter and Ellen and we also encounter two Pomeranians, one of whom is actually named Sparkie!

Friday, June 30:

Another warm and sunny morning marks the final day of the month for Fritz and his friends. We head for the Morshead gate, passing the ubiquitous clampers—out prowling our streets like so many basking sharks today. They are about to extract a Mercedes estate wagon from this best of all possible worlds. As we make our way toward the green we are in line with a gaggle of pre-school moms who are setting up a fete for their youngsters on the west end of the grass. I note that the section of rose garden hedge, burned to the ground by some older scholars from St. George's two years ago, has begun the process of regeneration—or that the area has been replanted.

On the green itself we make our way out to a prone Janet and a standing Hanna. The latter is again full of apprehension about the future of dogs (and their owners) in this little semi-privatized corner of Westminster. Dogs will have to go on lead, she fears, or worse, the present manager cares only for sports, important management decisions are being undertaken without consultation or consideration, and all these surveyors with their ubiquitous clipboards are planning something horrendous for the rest of us. She notes that yesterday afternoon a gym mistress asked dog owners to move so that her lot could have a game of rounders—having commandeered this portion of the "village green." Ronnie, meanwhile, has been sent on a mission of discovery among his Tory pals in order to see if any of these fears is true; he is never here on Fridays, so there is no way of monitoring his progress. I keep Fritz on lead—not because of all this gossip—but because Franca has again brought a squeaky toy onto the green for her Chinese Crested Dog, Frank, and I know that Fritz will steal it if given any opportunity. Another temptation is provided by a couple sprawled in comatose stupor amid their champagne bottles on the grass near the Grantully gate. Evidently Skye the Cairn has presented them with his ball, the girl rolling over long enough to say, "Please remove your dog. I'm *sooo* not interested."

We go in for coffee at an outdoor table. Georgie arrives with Sparkie and says that she has had another attack of numbness in her arm. Janet tries to get the Queen of Denial to agree to have this checked out, but you can tell she has no faith that Georgie will do it. Faz arrives with Jasmine, who has a booboo on her chin. Yesterday he took both his dog and Koko for an outdoor lunch in Covent Garden, even succeeding in getting Koko to sing by repeating the woo-woo litany. Liz comes by with Roxy to say goodbye—as she is off to the States for five weeks. She tells us that at the vet yesterday there was a woman in tears because she had to make the awful decision to put her dog down. "I didn't even know this woman or her dog but I cried for the rest of the afternoon too." This is the type of person we want to exclude from Paddington Rec so that some Levantine mom (one of whom is repeatedly slapping her child nearby) can have a dog-free environment.

July, 2006

Saturday, July 1:

I delay my departure for the park as long as possible (a task made easier by my sleeping until 9:00) because it is a hot day and I don't want Fritz to spend too much time in the sun before the café opens at 10:00. On the way to the green we encounter a lovely Samoyed named Fred; Fritz endures a close inspection, then rushes over to receive a cuddle from David, who is here with Pasha. My dog squeals with delight as he gets his tummy rubbed while David, who is wearing a University of Maryland football t-shirt, offers his predictions on the England-Portugal quarter final this afternoon. Fritz then rushes off to check in with all and sundry on Mt. Bannister—and at 10:10 we go in for coffee.

My chair is in the sun and I try to get Fritz to sit in my shadow but he doesn't seem too bothered by the sun's presence. Janet, Georgie, Kate and Hanna are present and Dorothy eventually joins—she and I are both drinking bottled water this morning. We have to hear a report on Jasmine's boohoo (twice to the vet yesterday; a steroid shot). Winnie, who is being pissy with everyone, jumps into Dorothy's lap. Kate tells us that Skye has again eaten one of her shoes—this one intended as part of an ensemble for a ball Kate will attend this evening. Hanna phones Ronnie just to see how he is getting on. The group discusses pollution illnesses—which seem to be common this summer. There is a nice breeze blowing and this encourages us to sit for some time but at last someone makes a move and then everybody gets up.

Winnie sits in the middle of the green and refuses to follow Janet for some time as we make our exit. The latter kneels to attach a harness—"You need a degree in physics to manage that," I say. A number of dogs are dancing beneath the shade trees at the west end of the green. Charlie the Cocker is here, so is Humpty the Basset Hound and Skye the Cairn. Dorothy pauses for a decorating conference with Michaela and I sit on a park bench with Fritz, waiting. When we get moving again we are overtaken by John the window cleaner. He stands to win £70 if England beats Portugal this afternoon.

Sunday, July 2:

We have another scorcher on our hands today and I am glad that I am wearing my sunglasses and cap as I stand in the centre of the parched green while Fritz wanders around. Today we have Monkey, the mostly Pit Bull, who has grown quite a bit since I last saw him. His mistress, Maggie, whom I first met at a garden party in the backyard, says that he has transformed the life of her other dog, Finn, who used to pine when left alone. Little Cleo bravely wrestles with the burly fellow while Jorge plays football with a little boy.

I can see that Fritz has moved on to a group of loungers at the foot of Mt. Bannister and I head here too. Jo is here with her Tilly and also the Lhasa Apso named Jonesie (real name, I learn for the first time, is Bridget Jones). Fritz chases his ball around and follows me uphill while I investigate a tree—which has apparently died. (This is the territory where the afternoon thugs who bring in fighting dogs like to hang their pets by the teeth from low lying branches; two saplings have died up here.) Snowdon, the other white Alsatian, is playing here and at one point Fritz, tennis ball in mouth, follows him down to the parking lot—with me in hot pursuit. At other times it is the mostly Yorkie Fonzie who follows Fritz. When we return to the loungers (Georgie, Kate, Janet, Dianah, Faz) there is an incident. A chap wheeling a pushchair through our midst takes exception when Sparkie gives pursuit (the little Yorkie likes to bark at all vehicles, it would appear). The chap is very upset and keeps waving a book at Sparkie with menace. It is time to head into the café.

Metty has installed some new large awnings and one is in place over our table—this gives the sun worshippers in our gang a cause for complaint. Janet says she has had a run-in (over the placement of the water trough) with Hector's owner, Peter. There is a thorough post-mortem on England's loss to Portugal in yesterday's World Cup quarterfinal. The conclusion: David Beckham is a wuss, Wayne Rooney is out of control, and the entire team is rubbish at penalty kicks. There is also a lot of fashion and shopping chatter, most of which I tune out. Ofra wants to know which is the *best* Primark and how do you get to Waterblue (which turns out to be Bluewater). Dorothy says she is looking for a newer version of her Kurt

Geiger sandals and Kate says, "Watch out, Kurt Geiger is one of Skye's favourite tasty treats." Near the end of our session Michael arrives. He looks well and he is quite tanned after much work in his garden. Fritz climbs onto his lap and covers his face in kisses and then turns around and sits on his chest. The sun is beginning, by this time, to creep under the awning—and this is the signal for a grand dispersal.

Monday, July 3:

The heat wave continues and Fritz has spent a most restless night, his panting subsiding only when he goes to lie down on the cool tiles in the new *en suite* bathroom.

I don't want him to run around and exhaust himself so I delay my departure for the park and head almost immediately, after a half circle around the green, for the shade of Metty's new awnings. Georgie, Kate, Hanna, Dan and Ofra are already present.

The news is not great. Michaela's Skye has been hit by a car and rolled over several times on Elgin Avenue—though he seems not to have suffered any serious injury. Hanna returns to her dire predictions on the future of dogs in the park. She says that the management of the enterprise is entirely in the hands of Courtney's, the gym people, and that she fears they plan on issuing a dogs-on-lead edict (though Tanya, the dog warden, is quoted as saying that she will not enforce it). The dog people are muttering about petitions but there seems to be an air of hopelessness. There are new signs; this time banning water balloons, water fights and barbeques.

At 10:30 Dorothy joins me and we begin a long hot walk to St. John's Wood, repeated a few hours later in the reverse direction. The occasion is Fritz's appointment at the beauty parlour on Allitsen Road and I must say he does look a treat when he emerges from this process—and he should be a lot cooler now too. But we won't be able to judge the reaction of his other fans to his new appearance ourselves—for we are off to Paris for four days while Fritz stays with his Aunty Linda and his cousin Pepper.

Saturday, July 8:

I return to the park after four days in Paris, though Fritz, from all reports, has been a daily visitor to his usual morning scene—shared this time with Pepper. Linda reports that he was an excellent houseguest and that the boys had a wonderful time together. I have brought back for Liam a set of Sao Tome & Principe stamps featuring a variety of dog breeds, including one stamp with a Schnauzer puppy on it.

It is a fairly fresh day—with some sun and high clouds. Fritz makes directly for a group of dog owners sitting on the parched grass. Here he gets his customary greeting, repulsing the efforts of any of the other dogs to get any nearer to their own owners—Fritz considers this a division of energies that should be devoted exclusively to *him*. Koko barks in protest when she is separated from Janet, who is lying with her legs pinched together so that Fritz won't steal a squeaky ball she has hidden there. Fritz's strategy is to lie between her legs as well. When she is not admonishing Fritz, Koko is equally upset at the presence of Winnie, who is also a roommate these days. Ronnie comes onto the green and tries to get everyone moving toward the café.

Some of the dog owners have come up with a new communal scheme for ordering their coffee and croissants—heretofore the first one in has been paying for everybody. I am not a part of this scheme, though I do order some toast for the dogs when I get my bottled still water. These days the toast comes with butter on it—since sausages seem taboo—but this does make for greasy work in the feeding of the canines. Georgie goes off to spend the night with her newly married daughter in Herefordshire. But there is real sadness when everyone realizes that this is Ofra's last day for almost two months—she flies to Israel tonight. Her husband will have Bailey for another three weeks and then he goes to Auntie Georgie. With Sainsbury beckoning I make my excuses at 10:30. Boys in their whites are arriving with their folks for some junior cricket.

Sunday, July 9:

There has been just a little rain overnight but you cannot tell that it has mattered at all on the sere grasslands that constitute Paddington Rec these days. Fritz and I again make our late weekend appearance but there is not much activity going on in our part of the park (boys are foregathering for a day-long soccer tournament on the one surviving pitch). I spot Janet and David out on the grass and here we report as well, Fritz soon into the rhythm of tennis ball chasing and the intimate examination of any other passing dog.

Many members of our group are missing: Georgie is in Herefordshire, Ofra in Israel, and Helen is in Malaysia with Jorge, attending her brother's wedding. I ask what has happened to Cleo and it turns out that she is with Dan's father in Essex (still peeing and pooing indoors)—after someone else backed out at the last minute and Dan, of no fixed abode himself these days, simply couldn't manage the task. While I am getting this recital Ronnie toddles in. He is wearing only an open-throat shirt on a day that is surprisingly chilly and brisk—I am glad I put on a flannel shirt myself.

When we go in to coffee I don't order anything. I've just had a coffee at home and it's too frigid for still water. Fritz nevertheless participates in the doggy feast that is soon produced: biscuits and carrots from Ronnie, pieces of croissant from the diners, an order of toast just for the canines. Winnie proves to be a problem eater: twice she takes a biscuit from Ronnie—only to spit out the delicacy in disgust. Then she jumps into Janet's lap and manages to bite her hostess on the finger. This causes a furious reaction from Dan who anchors his wilful dog to the naughty fence and uses his best growly voice to admonish the little madam—"That was very, very naughty!" Meanwhile Hanna has taken Spadge into her lap to quiet him down—the poor old fellow is essentially blind now and he keeps getting his feet trapped in his lead. There is continuing confusion over the food kitty rules—as laid out yesterday—and even those who have invented it can't keep it straight. "I give this system ten days at the most," I predict.

Monday, July 10:

It is rather grey and overcast this morning but the temperature is comfortable enough and the breezes pleasant. There isn't too much activity on the green but we make our way forward to a patch of grass where Dan, Georgie and Ronnie are seated. Over on one side David is walking the Whippets, Denim and Suede, and Fritz has to check this out so that David and I can compare notes on Italy's victory in last night's World Cup.

I can see the dog warden, Tanya, seated at the foot of Mt. Bannister with Franca, whose Bianca the Boxer is wearing her Italy vest. I have two purposes in paying Tanya a visit. The first is to ask for a supply of green poo poo bags (I end up with a lifetime supply). My second is to ask about the repeated rumours we have been hearing about a dogs-on-lead policy for Paddington Rec. Tanya tells me that a recent change in law *would* permit the Council (or park management) to order such a restriction with immediate effect and without any form of consultation. Recently she has attended a meeting of all interested parties (well, except for any dog owners) where the chief concern seemed to be a strategy for dealing with the dangerous dogs brought into the park by the local thugs in the late afternoon and early evening. (One of these cretins actually threatened to set his dog on Tanya when he was challenged last week). For her part Tanya has told the other officials that she is not prepared to enforce a ban on dogs off-lead—"I'm on your side"—and she has told them that if they think such a ban will be effective against the dangerous dog problem they are mistaken.

The others are heading in for coffee and so a few minutes later I suggest that we try to put our own two cents worth in before facing a *fait accompli*. I also offer to work on the text of such a petition. Behind us hundreds of school children are weaving their way through all the construction vehicles, including one lorry which is downloading portaloos. My heart sinks when I see such an assemblage because I know I will have to endure another day of broadcast misery as gym teachers with microphones begin their ritual bullying of sports day participants. Dan offers to give Ronnie a ride home and they accompany Fritz and me toward the Morshead gate where, as Dan opens his back door for Rosie, Fritz tries to jump in as well.

Tuesday, July 11:

It isn't easy steering two Schnauzers into the park at the same time, but this is my task on a cloudy Tuesday morning. Fritz, of course, is one of these two beasts, but I can let him off the lead as soon as we get through the gate. My other charge is Pepper, whom I don't trust as much, and so he has to remain attached throughout the session. We pass through the green, almost empty, and soon enough head in to the café, where we find Hanna and Ronnie. Ronnie buys me a bottle of still water which I drink while he reads the draft of our petition on the subject of dogs-on-lead.

Petition

Many of us have become increasingly alarmed at persistent rumours concerning the fate of dogs in the Paddington Recreation Ground. In particular, we are fearful that a decision to require that dogs be kept on lead will materially damage our use and enjoyment of the wonderful resource that is Paddington Rec, a space left many years ago to the people of this community.

We understand that there is great concern over the presence of dangerous dogs, brought to the park in the late afternoon and early evening by anti-social elements. We too would like to see this problem addressed, for the presence of such animals is also a danger to us. But punishing the vast majority of dog owners, those who manage to control their animals and pick up after them, is not only unjust but will undoubtedly be ineffective. Those who bring dangerous dogs into the park are unlikely to obey any requirements that interfere with their pleasure in terrorizing the rest of us. Those who live near the Rec. have enough reasons to be concerned about the direction of park affairs—the park as a source of broadcast noise at an ever growing level and the presence of young people who turn the place into a playground long after the gates have been locked being two of these. We don't want to see anti-dog policies added to this list.

In opposing any requirement that dogs be kept on lead we would like to emphasize a number of points:

1. For the health of our local canine population the exercise that results from running free is a necessity. Getting in our cars and driving to distant sites where dogs can run free does not seem to be useful social policy.
2. For many users of the Recreation Ground, particularly the elderly, exercising dogs is their own chief recreation.
3. Many people have determined to live in the local community, investing in property in the process, because of Paddington Rec's reputation as a place where dogs can be exercised properly. Changing the rules after such an investment is manifestly unfair.
4. The prospect of the Rec's many joggers having to leap over dozens of dog leads in the often tight corners of the park defies any concern for safety.

5. Dog owners constitute the most loyal clientele of the park's café—as we are there day in and day out in all weathers. We have already suffered a major disruption to our routine with the decision to postpone until 9:30 the opening of the café on weekdays, 10:00 on weekends. This means that we tend to run into conflict with other users of the "village green" much more often.

For all these reasons we, the dog owners of this community, present and former, and others who want to see Paddington Rec. retain an ancient right and privilege, urge that any suggestion that dogs be kept on lead must be rejected.

Ronnie says we should add something about whizzing cyclists. We are addressing the document to our local council representative, Jan Prendergast, who is a friend of Ronnie's, and he will write a covering note when it is time to send in our materials. Kate comes with Skye and Georgie arrives with Sparkie. Unfortunately Kate obviously has a squeaky ball in her purse and Fritz spends most of the morning session moaning over this lost treasure. Then I have to walk both of my fellows home on lead, not an easy task either.

Wednesday, July 12:

We are obviously going to have a lovely morning in the park—if you don't count the yellowing grass or the new horde of school kids marching toward another noisy sports day. I usually keep Fritz on lead, lest he collide with this incoming traffic, at least until his first poo. Then he is allowed to run onto the green where we can usually find the dog owners sprawled in a heap.

Today we have the owners of Charlie the Cocker and Sam the Dachshund and Dan, after reading the petition draft, passes it on to these ladies. I want Tanya the dog warden to read it but she doesn't make an appearance today. Fritz tries to get a cuddle from all seated parties, again objecting vociferously when the owner's *own* dog interferes in this process. Hector and Winnie are playing an interesting game, one that requires Winnie to stand like a statue on Peter. The other Peter, the one with Holly, also pauses to stroke Fritz's fur—the latter is looking particularly good after his grooming last week.

We go into coffee but Ronnie is sitting with Patricia, on a return visit to the park with her Bruce, and, knowing the numbers still to come, I select a second table where we soon have Hanna, Dan, Davide, Georgie and Kate. Dan and Davide are still discussing bathroom taps, Hanna wants us all to admire the fluffy white coat of the recently bathed George, Georgie says it is too nice to go to work, and Kate announces that she is viewing the house where Gunner lives on Wymering. Her Skye wanders from table to table seeing what is going down, then begins to whine from boredom, and Kate has to get up to give the huge beast some more exercise. It is a signal for the rest of us to depart—but this time Fritz gets to meet a seven year-old female Schnauzer named Molly (and to receive yet more complements on his own spiffy appearance).

Thursday, July 13:

It is a grey morning, though the temperatures are warm enough and we have a large turnout of small dogs in the middle of the green. Just as we arrive, however, there is an aggressive display of bad temper (with Skye the Cairn as the target) from Lola, the French Bulldog. Poor Lola seemed to enjoy the company of other dogs until she came into season some time ago; thereafter she has growled and bared her teeth whenever any other dog is around and as a consequence Kat, her owner, has stopped bringing her to the park. Today was obviously a kind of experiment to see if she had calmed down sufficiently—but the experiment has obviously failed and poor Kat, her face red, now has to lead her snarling pet out of the park once again.

Among the other small dogs we have Flash the Border Terrier, Chilli, a kind of Dachshund, Leila, the Miniature Pinscher, Sparkie, Koko. Winnie, and a return visit from the Bichon Frise, Giant. The latter rushes up to give me an enthusiastic greeting, but Fritz is instantly jealous. I keep my dog busy with his green tennis ball and this fascinates a little Middle Eastern toddler, who is wandering around amid other kids and dogs wearing his own harness with dangling reins. He wants to throw the ball to Fritz and is delighted by his success in launching the dog, a gesture repeated on several occasions. His mother eventually leads him away but everyone is pleased, that, for once, fear of dogs has not been reinforced. For that matter two of the tennis teenies detach themselves from their group and come over to see the dogs as well.

When we go in for coffee we (Kate, Georgie, Davide and I) join an already seated Ronnie and Hanna. I get up at one point to share the petition with Tanya, who later returns it with her endorsement. Davide is off to Delhi later in the day but this morning he also has the care of Koko, who is sitting longingly at the feet of a French couple, hoping for a handout. Pretty soon Winnie is there too. Winnie and Bailey have both discovered an easy egress from the forecourt at a spot where two slats are missing from the fence. This rather makes a mockery of the rickety locks that sometimes keep the gates to this space closed—though they are barely attached at this point. We discuss the need for another kind of closing mechanism. The place looks a bit seedy just now—after some off-the-lead kids have been allowed to cover a number of surfaces with coloured chalk.

Friday, July 14:

The weather is strange this morning, warm in the sun but chilly everywhere else—with a lot of cloud about to make sure that you are never warm for long. I am wearing only a red t-shirt and this hardly seems enough as Fritz and I enter the park just at that poignant moment when Dan has to head off for work and Winnie has to go on lead so that she doesn't follow her daddy (or one of them) out the gate. Today it is Janet's turn to strap the harness on this trouble-making Pug, who does agree to trot on tamely toward the green.

For some reason a heavy woman in sports gear is marching steadfastly toward Fritz, though she keeps addressing him as "Rocky." Fritz doesn't answer to his own name most of the time so it is no wonder that the woman soon gives up. Rocky, it turns out, is another grey Miniature Schnauzer and *he* is soon in plentiful evidence, darting about the green while a gaggle of large ladies exercises. For that matter, with Oscar, Spadge, Gus, Pepper and even a distant Yoyo, seven Schnauzers here sets an all-time record. Hanna says that the breed is so popular because Schnauzers don't shed. She adds that Tim and Lizzie have been told by the vet that they should either spay Yoyo or breed her, but that her occasional health woes (hives, evidently, this week) are a symptom of her inability to thrive in her virginal state. Pepper is off to the New Forest for a week, but Linda has a great deal of trouble extracting him from the mix. Fritz, for his part, disappears for long periods this morning—intent on his own explorations and only occasionally interested in chasing his yellow tennis ball. Nicholas wanders into the park with Monty. He tells me that he had a dream last night in which Fritz and I made an appearance—but he doesn't offer details.

Several more people read the petition draft and then we go in to coffee, though only Hanna, Georgie, Janet, and Kate are present. As we pass the table belonging to Peter, Ellen and Barbara, Ellen says, "Ah Fritz, we were just talking about you"—and hands my dog two slices of sausage on a wooden fork. Skye the Alsatian is bored from the outset and handing her five balls to chew doesn't lessen her impatient whining. Spadge is also here to offer his iterative punctuation. Almost blind now, if you reach out to pet him he backs away in fright. Across the Carlton roadway they are finishing up with the kiddies' playground and there is a new sign containing no less than eight prohibitions: no cycling, no dogs, no adults without kids, no rollerblading, etc. A workman with a huge lawnmower-sized machine is attempting to extract leaf litter from the margins—when a broom would be so much more useful, and infinitely quieter!

Saturday, July 15:

Clouds are lifting as Fritz and I make our way into the park on another pleasant, sunny morning. One group of dog owners is congregating in the centre of the green but I head for a second—where I can see Jo Lynn with Tilly and Cynthia with Sky the Husky. I have come on a mission, for today I have brought with me copies of the famous petition on dogs' freedom in Paddington Rec. We have decided to begin the campaign on a Saturday, when there is usually a good turnout, and this proves to be a good move. Jo, who is a fierce opponent of anyone who would curb freedom, instantly volunteers to circulate a copy of this document, and signs on the dotted line—using Cynthia's back.

Soon I can see her approaching every knot of dog owners on the horizon, including Roland's obedience group—never has it been easier to gather signatures. Sabina, Scamp and Oscar's mother, comes up to me to ask for her own copy of the petition. I also give one to Janet, who sees a different group of dog owners when she is at the café in the afternoon. Many people walk over to thank me for undertaking this initiative and it is just as well that I can trust Fritz to turn up eventually since I lose track of him easily in all this chatter. John comes onto the green with Ché and his new neighbours, Emma and Phillip. They have brought to the park, for the first time, a delightful Jack Russell puppy named Millie. She is let loose to dash about among the other dogs and she has a wonderful time. After about half an hour we head in for coffee—where we join Ronnie and Hanna at a table in the forecourt.

Here it is decided to give Georgie a copy of the petition for the dog lovers at the pub where she work. I tell the others that after checking their signatures I am able to see, for the first time in over two years, what *last* names some of them carry. While we are drinking our liquids Natasha comes to the café with Leila and we beckon her over to sign a copy of the petition. She tells us that she has had a long word with another councillor, who does not seem to be in the mood for pressing a dogs-on-lead rule, and that she gotten the impression that the whole idea may have come from one of the park's many security guards, who is afraid of dogs. "Hiring someone who hates dogs to work security in a park is like hiring someone who hates children to be in charge of a nursery school," is one of her arguments. One bit of progress is taking place behind our backs as kids are at last free to play in the new playground, which has a number of wonderful bits of apparatus in the swing and slide category. After I have been in the park for over an hour I take Fritz and we follow the others toward the gates; I note that I have 33 signatures on my copy of the petition.

Sunday, July 16:

Another warm t-shirt morning in the park. I let Fritz go as I near the green in order to concentrate on signature gathering. People now stop me to ask how the campaign is going or, in the case of Peter (of Peter and Holly), to ask to sign on. Peter (Of Peter and Hector) also signs, asking me when we get out the placards. They are setting out the boundary cones for a game of cricket and I can see that most of the dog owners have congregated in the shade at the foot of Mt. Bannister.

Here I meet an American couple who, ironically, are letting their dogs off lead in Paddington Rec for the first time. The beasts in question are two shaggy Airedales named (wait for it) Eleanor and Rigby. One of them disappears into the bushes at the top of the hill but then so does Fritz. I spend a lot of time calling for him around the margins of the tennis courts, but then, looking back down the hill, I notice that the rascal has somehow returned to the company of his other pals below. He is delighted to see me as I retreat, greeting me as though *I* were the missing party.

We take up our positions in the patio of the café, though I have to change seats once when the sun's rays begin to assault the back of my neck. Once or twice I get up to gather more signatures; Kathy Andon comes in to sign. It is interesting to note that many signatories seem to suspect Islamic objections as one reason for the current discussions about dogs (a small dog *approached* a party of picnicking Middle Easterners yesterday, occasioning another ruckus). Michael the Pirate is soon seen at the gate of the forecourt, only this time he has brought his own screwdriver—which he is using to fix the always troublesome catch. "I ought to send them a bill," he says as he finishes. After signing the petition he says, "Soon it will be Christians who are outlawed in the park." "No," I correct him, "they'll be allowed—as long as they're kept on lead."

A young woman named Jennifer comes in to sign the petition. She has a delightful little Pomeranian named Balou with her. He is very busy in visiting everybody but when he approaches a black man with a toddler there is again objection and this family leaves in a huff. We are just about to break up when Michael the dogfather arrives for a visit. Fritz is again thrilled and spends a lot of time in his old pal's lap. When I get up to leave Michael accompanies us to the Morshead gate and we have a visit that reminds me so much of those treasured times when his Charlie was gambolling around with my Fritz at our feet.

Monday, July 17:

We are heading for another scorcher as Fritz and I enter the park and head for an almost empty green. I find Oscar and Scamp's mum, Sabina, and we walk around a bit, comparing notes on signature gathering. Then I encounter Michaela, who, to our surprise, is pushing a baby carriage. The infant in question is her long-haired nephew from Ireland, Rumo. He seems to enjoy the dogs dancing around at his feet until Sparkie barks at him and he begins to cry. Michaela asks if she can take a copy of the petition down to her son's school and I give it to her.

I head in for coffee at 9:30 exactly, joining Hanna, Georgie and Davide. Ronnie calls to say it is too hot and that he's not coming, which is too bad since Davide has brought some cigars from one of his many trips to foreign climes. Georgie is looking forward to the end of school on Thursday—which means that one of her jobs also comes to an end for a few weeks. Hanna says that she made too much pasta with Sicilian sausage last night, and that Spadge and George enjoyed some of the leftovers—as did the foxes—animals that Hanna feeds in her garden. Her cat, meanwhile, has returned to the house with a live field mouse. Rescued without major injury, the mouse is convalescing on Cheerios and will soon be released.

While we are still at table Michaela returns with some interesting news. She has run into the park manager and decided to share with him her own concerns on the subject of dogs-on-lead. He says we are welcome to work on our petition but such a rule is not on *his* agenda, which is again directed only to those who bring in dangerous or fighting dogs. It is interesting to note how, once we have begun our campaign, no one will admit that the topic is even under discussion, but, on the whole, this is good news—though we will not slacken in our efforts. On my way out I run into a face I have not seen in some time, that of Anthony the Inebriate. He has Ty on lead but he stops to chat and to sign the petition. We are near the doggy area on Morshead Road and here I met another Tyson recently. What are Staffie owners trying to tell us with this name?

Tuesday, July 18:

The sun keeps up its relentless assault on our senses as Fritz and I make our way into the park on a warm Tuesday morning. There is no activity on the green, only a few passing ships making their way toward shadier ports. I cross this vast waste with Fritz and join up with a few dog owners at the bottom of Mt. Bannister. Tanya the animal warden is here as well and I give her an update on our activities while two people, sprawled on the grass nearby, sign on.

I take a look into the café but there is no one about, the heat having driven all but the most hardy away. Eventually I see Georgie with Bailey and Sparkie—and Fritz and I venture out to the centre of the green to make contact. Before long we are seated in the shade of one of Metty's awnings. Georgie is carrying a small lock box in which she has secreted the collective funds of the dog-owner's breakfast club. When one of the baristas makes a delivery to our table (which now includes Hanna)

Georgie asks if they can keep the box behind the counter—since she is not going to lug it to the park every day. There is agreement to this plan (to my astonishment) and just then Dan arrives with the long-lost Helen, back from her brother's wedding in Malaysia.

Jorge soon joins us as well and then it turns out that Metty's wife has sensibly overruled the attempt to make the café into an annex of the breakfast club treasury and the box is returned. Dan describes his holiday in Wales with Winnie, who went swimming in the ocean and seemed ready to attack the jellyfish. Here also she became the favourite toy of a bunch of toddlers, "And she was so good," Dan brags—just as the madam turns viciously on poor Sparkie in the adjoining lap. Helen gives us details of the wedding—but Cleo is still out at Dan's dad's house. Several people stop by to sign the petition and I collar Nicholas, who comes to our table to sign (my ninth signature for the morning). Then, after consuming a bottle of still water, I head off with Fritz as still another school group enters the park—though without loudspeakers for once.

Wednesday, July 19:

Everyday it seems to be a little hotter than the previous day and today is no exception—as temperatures are scheduled to set a record for the hottest July day since 1911 (36.3 degrees at one spot in Surrey). Fritz does a huge, multifaceted poo against a black plastic trash bag while I talk to Jeff. I know he has already signed the petition but he asks me for some information on the origins of the present campaign. He repeats something I have heard a number of times—"A lot people think the Moslems are behind it." I tell him that in the present instance I have not heard this from anyone in the know but since a Moslem mother, fearing any contact with a West Highland Terrier, has yanked her kid across the street on the approach of Elvis this morning, he is not convinced.

Fritz and I make our way across the parched green to the foot of Mt. Bannister, where a knot of dog owners is lolling in the shadows. For some reason Fritz decides to follow Arran toward the Randolph Avenue gates and I have to chase after him. My dog, who lolls around the house panting on these hot days, doesn't seem to mind running around in the sun and he therefore accompanies me as I spot Tim with Yoyo and go over to get a signature. Yoyo is already hiding from the sun after only five minutes in the park—but she needs a haircut and her black fur must absorb the heat.

I go in for coffee at exactly 9:30 (well, these days it is not coffee, but still water that I consume) but it takes a while for Dan, Kate, Georgie and Helen to join me. Helen has at last reclaimed Cleo, who has definitely put on weight at the home of Dan's dad, a butcher. Georgie is passing around photos of daughter Lynn's wedding in the Caribbean, though the news is not all that good: her son-in-law, a soldier, goes on active duty today. I am only at table for fifteen minutes or so and then I have to leave so that Dorothy and I can make an 11:00 rendezvous with the Modernism show at the V & A.

Thursday, July 20:

It is a few degrees cooler today but the park is still rather empty and would be even more so if troops of kiddies weren't being frogmarched onto the green. Shortly after our arrival we are joined by Leila, the Miniature Pinscher, who loves to follow Fritz around—even squatting to piss on his poo. Natasha and I attempt a walk along our former path behind the playing fields but it is still blocked. Helen comes in and joins us with Cleo as we head back to the green. Natasha receives a call on her mobile phone inviting her to Milan—if she can drop everything and be at the airport for a 1:00 flight. She can't do it, though Cleo almost gets a sleepover partner.

I have to put Fritz on lead as we cross the green, since they are setting up some sort of bowling game for the kiddies, one involving tennis balls as the projectile of choice. At the foot of Mt. Bannister I let Fritz off the lead and again he disappears for long periods of time as I check on the progress of petition signing and get the signature of Artemis the Border Terrier's owner. When it is time to go in for refreshments I stake out a table in the centre of the patio and I am soon followed by Natasha, Georgie, Kate and Helen. The latter is outraged, "Did you know they've stationed a bouncer at the entrance to see if your dog is on lead." I've seen security guards do this before but they are quite inconsistent (or they've exhausted their English) and Kate's Skye, for instance, soon enters unchallenged by anyone.

Helen passes around photos of her brother's wedding in Malaysia. She and Natasha begin to worry a bit about the safety of Ofra, who hasn't answered a text sent to her in conflict-ridden Israel. Georgie is celebrating the end of the school year and the end of one of her many jobs—ferrying disabled school kids to classes. Kate says she has to go home and tidy up her place for the cleaning lady. The ladies take several mobile phone calls and I head with Fritz toward the gates.

Friday, July 21:

Once again we enter the park under sunny skies at the beginning of another scorcher. Usually I keep Fritz on lead until we reach the green, hoping thus to be in better position to scoop up my dog's first poo. Today, as we reach the green's circular walkway, I spot Artemis's mom again, and this time she has with her Laurie, who owns Abby the Lab. After Laurie signs the petition both women sign for their husbands as well. By this time Fritz has crossed the hot green himself and has enrolled as a member of Hanna's slow-moving procession with George and Spadge.

I make my way over to the collection of dog owners sprawled at the foot of Mt. Bannister. They are lolling comfortably when an Australian groundsman pulls up on his power mower prior to "mowing" the grass. Sparkie charges his moving vehicle twice but the chap is careful to stop and he actually speaks to us as human beings, apologizing for the fact that he will soon be raising a lot of dust. Someone suggests that there is no grass to mow, since the entire hillside is nothing but parched stubble, but he says, "Got to look busy for the boss," and—with the café now open—we migrate there.

There seem to be a lot of bosses about today and Hanna complains to one of these chaps about the fumes issuing from the nearby leaf blower (emphasis on the singular these day). Quite a few suspicious glances are sent our way thereafter but we soon settle down to our usual chatter under one of Metty's capacious umbrellas. After a few minutes Dorothy comes to replace me at the end of Fritz's lead—as I have an appointment to have my blood pressure checked at the Randolph Surgery. On my way out of the park I encounter Francine with the black Pug Oscar. This is their last time in London—off to Singapore soon—but Francine stops to sign our petition anyway.

Saturday, July 22:

We have actually had a bit of rain during the night and temperatures are not nearly as fierce this morning. I am walking across the green when I see Rowena heading toward me with Chris (of Chris and Roxie fame). Rowena also asks me if the interest in putting dogs on lead isn't a Moslem-inspired agitation. I can only tell her that this hasn't been my impression. Chris has been asked to sign the petition by two friends. I have had to add a fourth page for signatures to my copy of the petition, and that means that I must have seventy names so far.

Kate, Georgie and Janet are sitting in a sunny spot at the foot of Mt. Bannister and I head here with Fritz. Skye is digging a hole in a bare patch of earth once inhabited by a tree (lots of dogs like to do this). When Fritz wanders over near the café entrance I can see that his activities are being closely monitored by a security guard I have never seen before but this chap is smiling (usually we get only scowls) and, indeed, proves to be English. It turns out that he has a ten year-old Miniature Schnauzer at home, and so he asks a lot of questions about my dog before I join Ronnie at an outdoor table.

It has been a week since Ronnie has made it—the heat having had an adverse effect on his MS. Also, he tells us, he has been spending a lot of time at his 95 year-old mom's rest home, sometimes up to five hours a day. It hasn't all been gloom—yesterday he was honked at in Chelsea when he slowed down to have a closer look at a girl with the longest pair of legs he's ever seen. Ronnie is wearing shorts himself today and seems to be in a good mood, though obviously tired. One of the waitresses brings out a tub of water for the dogs and Skye dives in—as much liquid squirts out of the side of her mouth as down her throat and there is soon a swamp under our table. Georgie says she has received a phone call from Ofra in Israel and the latter is well. Hanna arrives without any dogs for once, having taken her panting animals home early. She also reports that her cockatiel, Num-num, has been making mad passionate love to a lamp. The sun gradually overtakes half of the table and when this proves to be too much for those on that side we all get up to leave.

Sunday, July 23:

We enter the park under grey skies and this means that the temperature is marvellously reduced. Perhaps this is only a brief respite—with more hot weather predicted for next week—but people are so grateful that they pronounce the morning "delightful"—even though there is no sunshine. Fritz pauses for his first poo just as we near the green—warning Chubby the Cocker not to get too close while he is concentrating. Then we cross the almost white green to reach a colony of dog owners camped out on a blanket at the foot of Mt. Bannister. Ricky is here with Bailey and he has to answer a lot of questions about Ofra's safety.

Given the more humane temperatures it is not surprising that Fritz is even willing to do a lot of ball chasing on the green this morning. When he is not chasing he is pissing. With a strong West Indian accent a black man sitting on the bench is marvelling at his output—"He come all de way over here to piss on dis bin, den he going to piss on dis tree. How come he has so much water in him? He must be on de beer." After a few minutes Janet's friend Lyndon arrives with a friend of his own and Lulu the French Bulldog. Much fuss is made over this wonderful puppy. She is wearing a camouflage collar and Lyndon, leaning on a cane with his head topped by a Mohican cum Mullet, says, "We tried pink but she just looked silly. So we are going for the bull dyke look." After a while Faz heads in to order food and drink for everybody and I follow him to stake out a table. Next to us is a young man reading a *News of The World*; he has with him a delightful white furball, a Japanese Spitz named Mojo.

We are eleven at table, with Hanna as an outrider at a table of her own. Everybody plays pass the parcel with Lulu but Winnie takes umbrage over this and snaps at the puppy. Sparkie and Skye keep discharging themselves from the café forecourt and someone is always getting up to see where they have gone. During one of Georgie's absences Hector hops into her chair and makes himself at home. The subject of national service comes up. Dan thinks it is a good idea and Davide actually served 18 months in the Italian navy, though he says he worked for the ministry of defence in Rome and never made it onto an actual ship. Lyndon says that he had always wanted to do two things before his fortieth birthday, run the London Marathon and travel round the world. These plans were thwarted when he had a stroke but on his fortieth birthday Janet told him,

"You'll have to *walk* the Marathon route now, but we *have* gotten you that ticket for a roundtrip journey—on the Circle Line."

Monday, July 24:

As I reach the park on a sunny Monday morning I see Jean-Baptiste, wearing a Superman t-shirt. It is the first time I have seen him since we began our signature gathering scheme, and I now hold onto Hercules' lead as he signs. Soon thereafter I retrieve a copy of the petition from Sabina, Scamp and Oscar's mom. I now have 76 names on my copy.

There is still a cool breeze blowing and Georgie (who has forgotten her petition), Davide and Dan are actually seated in the centre of the green. Fritz chases his tennis ball a few times and then I just follow him around to see that he doesn't get into too much mischief. Kate arrives with big Skye, who is also chasing balls. Hanna makes slow progress toward our group. She says that yesterday she went to a christening where her Jewish hosts barbequed a whole suckling pig. She tells us that she took the head home, cut off the ears and cheeks for her dogs, and left the rest for the foxes. Georgie is looking green at the end of this graphic recital and gets up to head in for coffee.

I drink a bottle of still water but the staff manages to confuse most of the rest of the order. I tell Hanna that I know lots of Jews who wouldn't hesitate to eat pork—but "a christening" strikes a sour note. She admits it wasn't a real christening—just a celebration to greet the arrival of a four month-old baby. Nicholas arrives with Monty and tells us that his girlfriend has put him on a no-carb diet and that he has to download a recipe for cabbage soup. Others groan and say they are not walking behind him anymore. "I'm not getting fat," he explains, "it's just that I can't get into any of my clothes," including, he later tells me, an £800 suit from Gieves and Hawkes. Michaela comes in with her Skye because this is the last time she will see Helen—who is returning to the States a week from today. This means that we are seeing the last of Cleo, whose own passage to the States is bedevilled by an airline requirement—they won't accept dogs in their cargo hold if the temperature is above 75 degrees, and we are in the grips of a heat wave. Michaela also returns her copy of the petition to me; it has nineteen names on it, but I notice that many of our enthusiastic if foolish dog owners have signed her sheet—after signing mine first.

Tuesday, July 25:

We are obviously moving back towards a more sultry climate as Fritz and I penetrate the park today. I am looking for one or two late signees and so I approach Arran's mom as she pushes her pram around the playing field. The Coton de Tulear is incredibly white, even though his last bath was Thursday—"But it's been dry since then," is the explanation. I am in for one surprise, however, for Arran's mom is pushing two babies not one, four month-old twins!

Out on the green it is still cool enough for some of the regulars to sit in the burnt grass. I don't join them, heading instead for four women exercising their dogs nearby. Two of them have signed the petition and the other two do so now, though Jonesie's mom is certain that the ban on dogs-off-lead is only going to be enforced in the afternoon. If true, this sounds like another recipe for disaster. Her friend's dog has a bright green tennis ball similar to Fritz's, and there is a bit of confusion in which I think *we* end up with the newer ball.

I join Dan, Natasha, Hanna, Kate and Georgie at coffee. Kate is interested in a 1.6 million pound house, currently containing six flats (well, finance is her profession). Hanna cuddles Spadge, who keeps twisting a nerve in his back when he kicks backwards after every poo. ("Stop being a shitkicker" is the obvious advice.) Georgie returns her copy of the petition—it has 26 signatures, a very respectable effort and one that brings the campaign up to 130.

Wednesday, July 26

It's going to be very hot again today and I delay my departure so that there will be only fifteen minutes before it is time to enter the café. As I reach the green Dan and Janet are just leaving, on their way to work. A few minutes later, however, I see that they have returned and someone says, "One of them must have lost something." Sure enough, Janet has dropped a £20 note during her exit but Dan finds it on the grass—and all is well.

David is in the middle of the green with Skye the Cairn—Michaela's family having left this morning for Sardinia. For once neither Skye nor any of the other dogs seem motivated to chase balls; they lie in the shadows of their owners, panting. David says he has lost *Lost* and I try to bring him up to date. I get another signature while Fritz goes walkabout. I can see him over with Peter and Ellen but after a while he disappears and I spend a lot of time searching the horizon until I see him happily trotting along the pathway at the top of Mt. Bannister—as if he owned it, the park and the world as well.

There is a really small turnout at coffee, just Georgie and Kate. The latter is getting ready for a holiday in Turkey. Georgie describes *her* fear of flying—a phobia that grew with each experience until she stopped flying altogether. Kate has a bag full of cheese and adds this to the dogs' diet after the ubiquitous toast. When I get up to leave I see a new group of dog owners on the green. The Vietnamese woman, the owner of Snowdon the Tibetan Terrier, has been looking for a home for the gentle giant Great Dane, Prince, whose owners can't keep him in their new posting. Now she has decided to keep the beast herself. Her name is usually pronounced "Queen" by the rest of this, though we know this is not quite right. Another owner says, "Everyone is delighted that Queen is keeping Prince"—the unsaid corollary being, "so I don't have to."

Thursday, July 27:

I try to keep an eye on Fritz as we enter the park today, letting him off lead almost immediately and knowing that a poo is coming somewhere soon. He takes his time, darting around behind the clubhouse before venturing onto the green—where David is throwing the ball to Skye the Cairn. Then Fritz heads for the bushes on the south side of the park while I bring Jo Lynn up to date on the campaign. When he disappears in the bushes themselves I follow, only to discover that the rascal has emerged behind me and is looking at me as though *I* had been the one missing. Then he heads for the Grantully exit and I am happy to distract him with an invitation to head into the doggy area on this side.

We are soon followed by Guy—accompanied by the large rescue dog, Hootch. Guy is wearing a t-shirt that reads, "I love to see Arsenal lose." He is interested in my cap, though at first he mistakes Michigan Film Office for Afghan Film Office. I tell him about our petition and he signs the copy I still have with me. He says that he heard recently that someone, complaining to the park manager about a dangerous dog situation, was told that dogs would not be required to go on lead. This is the second time we have heard such an opinion attributed to this source, and this is good news. I share it with Hanna, who is sitting by herself on a bench, her dogs wandering at her feet. She looks exhausted and complains of not being able to get to sleep because of all the heat. At 9:30, however, we start our slow progress toward the café.

We join a table inhabited by Dan, Kate and Georgie. Kate is explaining that she can't stand coffee, though she likes coffee-flavoured confectionary. My bottle of water is so cold that there is ice in it and soon I realize that it is one long block of ice shaped just like a phallus. This amuses everyone as we pass it around. When it is time to go we encounter Linda, Liam and Pepper on the green and the two Schnauzers have a superb roaring reunion. When I get home I get a call from Ronnie, who is supposed to be preparing a cover letter to go with our petitions. His voice is quite slurred today but his message is cheering. He has just talked to Jan Prendergast who has assured him that dogs are going on lead in Paddington Rec "over my dead body." So the day ends with more good news.

Friday, July 28:

A rain front has moved through during the previous evening and, though very little moisture has resulted, the temperatures are still refreshingly diminished this morning. Out on the green there is a much larger than usual turnout today—including a delightful four month-old Jack Russell puppy named Lily. She tries to make up to Fritz twice but he isn't having any of it. For that matter Koko is cross with Fritz too. My dog is receiving an affectionate greeting from Dan, but Fritz has displaced Koko—who was getting similar treatment a moment before. I am about to throw a tennis ball when I find my hand in the mouth of Skye the Alsatian—this really hurts.

When I get it lofted, Fritz chases down the yellow ball and then he begins a long period of wandering, first to see if Peter and Ellen are serving sausages, then across the green and into the doggy area again. Today there is no one else present so we return to the green and he's off to the café again. When I follow him in I can see that Georgie is already present, so I sit down too. The sign on the café door reads "Closed," but after a while we realize that they have just forgotten to turn it over, and Georgie goes in to place orders. It is cool enough for me to request a small black decaf coffee. Janet soon takes a place in the queue but as each of the other owners come in they shout in their requests to her as well—which, I suppose, might be a bit upsetting for those behind her.

Skye purloins Fritz's tennis ball off the tabletop. Kate suggests that I am too kind when I argue that it *does* resemble some of her own balls—so I add that it would be useful if the Alsatian could learn to recognize the difference between ball and hand. Georgie distributes some puppy chocolate drops to the pooches, surprised that Sparkie, who won't touch them at home, seems to enjoy them when all the other dogs line up. Dan, it turns out, is mad at Nicholas because the latter, in hoisting Winnie onto his lap, picked her up by the collar. Kate's phone continues to ring throughout the session; it's as bad as Spadge's barking. When we get up to leave it turns out that Peter and Ellen are *now* serving sausages—so we have to stop for a handout before departing for good.

Saturday, July 29:

Conditions are far fresher this morning as Fritz and I make our way out to the green. Franca is here, trying to get Wolfgang's owner to extract Bianca's ball from his dog's mouth. Over at the foot of Mt. Bannister she tells us that yesterday her Boxer was attacked by a Staffie on Kilburn Lane. The only way she could protect her pet was to lie on top of the thug, even though this gesture was at some considerable risk to her own pregnancy. Why people allow such unpredictable animals to enter public space without a muzzle is a mystery to the rest of us. Meanwhile Franca has had to go to hospital to check on her own health—but the baby's heartbeat is still okay in spite of this incident.

At coffee, which we have to wait for long after the doors have tardily opened, I pass around an article from page 6 of the summer issue of *Wag!* magazine. In it one can see precisely what Tanya the dog warden was talking about when she mentioned a new bylaw giving councils the right to pass legislation requiring dogs to go on lead. This strategy (one of many) comes in a passage of the Clean Neighbourhoods and Environment Act 2005. The matter is left up to the local authority and this will tend to localize effects and place the matter into local politics, one can be sure. One can also see the background for the recent discussion in Westminster Council offices attended by Tanya. Notices do have to be placed in local newspapers before such an action could take place; in the meantime we are already well ahead of matters with our petition campaign, a direct realization of the Dog Trusts' advice, "Write and oppose any ban that you think is unreasonable."

Hanna, who has already parked her dogs at home, tells us that the back passage is again open and so she, John (with Ché) and I head this way when the breakfast session comes to an end. The old playground is still in use, the cricket nets haven't been torn down yet, but there is a thick growth of artificial turf on the older playing field. Elsewhere this is still a building site, not pleasant to penetrate. I see that they have nailed new tops to the fencing around the running track but the wire fence itself is still in terrible shape. Worst of all are the effects of the drought back here. Several more birch trees have died, and there is no evidence at all of our famous pimpernel patch.

Sunday, July 30:

The fresh weather persists for a second day and it is very pleasant to be on the green this morning—if you don't count the green itself, which looks like straw. Our gang is seated around a blanket near the head of the cricket crease, a large group by recent standards. The occasion for this festival is actually a melancholy one, the farewell gathering for Helen, Jorge and little Cleo. Lots of pictures are taken of this trio but there is a second occasion for the blues for also present today are Francine and her family, including the bustling black Pug Oscar. Remarkable that *two* of the park's three Pugs are leaving the country on the same day, tomorrow, though Cleo is heading for Washington and Oscar for Singapore. Dan says he suspects that Winnie has engineered this extraction somehow—her desperate attempt to restore a lost primacy. "She just wants to be able to say, 'I'm the only Pug in this village,'" I add.

Someone brings a red squeaky toy as a farewell present for Cleo but Fritz soon detects its presence and goes mad trying to secure its ownership himself. Jorge puts it in the pocket of his shorts but Fritz can sniff it out there and he wraps himself around the young man's leg, clawing away at the bare flesh until the toy is yielded up. I am afraid I won't be able to collar him when it is time to go in for coffee but he agrees to cross the green as long as he can keep the prize in his mouth.

We are seventeen (a record) at three (also a record) conjoined tables: Francine, her husband and son, Lyndon and his partner, Janet, Georgie, Dorothy, Dan, David, Hanna, Faz, Peter (of Peter and Hector), Helen and

Jorge, me and Ronnie. Ronnie seems to be in much better shape than the last time we saw him. He brings the cover letter we are including in our petition packet to Jan Prendergast, and Helen distributes change of address cards for all of us. Dan presents her with a farewell card that we have all signed. We have a good time but the service is horrendous and people are waiting half an hour for a cheese croissant—this is another consequence of such tardy opening hours; by the time they *do* open the doors there is such a crush that they can't cope.

Throughout the session, however, there is the discordant echo of Fritz—chomping down on the squeaky toy; at last David manages to snatch it away and it remains hidden until we are able to make our getaway. We have one last chance to say goodbye to Helen and Jorge when they return Dorothy's sewing machine later in the afternoon. We will really miss them, though Helen has promised to return for her college graduation in December.

Monday, July 31:

Fresh winds continue to batter the park as the month of July comes to an end; we have just endured the hottest July on record but the last few days have been quite comfortable. Fritz rushes out to join David, who is keeping Skye the Cairn on lead because he has a sore claw. Also present for the first time in quite a while is Suzanne—with her recently reclaimed Springer Spaniel, Sunny. Suzanne, it turns out, has either been in the States (where her father died) or convalescing from a hip replacement operation. She looks well, walks without a limp now, and, indeed, did ten miles on the Thames Path recently.

Tanya the animal warden has brought Frank and Bianca to the park and we chat with her for a while. She has been off for a week after being bitten by some bug, a creature whose sting left the victim with a leg so swollen she couldn't drive. I bring her up to date on our petition campaign (materials go off to Jan Prendergast later in the day) and then I begin the eternal search for Fritz. I last saw him heading for the café but when I get there now Georgie and Hanna report that he has been and gone. I begin my search on the Carlton roadway, noticing that Franca is walking into the park with a Schnauzer I have never seen before. Oh yes I have—it's Fritz, who was found at the turning circle before the park exit and is being kindly returned to me now! Mr. Independent gets a scolding from me, but it doesn't represent my true anger nor is it likely to be effective, coming so long after his escape.

I buy Suzanne some toast while waiting for my decaf coffee. Then we join the others, including Dan. The latter has just returned from Cardiff, where he went to see Madonna dazzle the audience in a show that featured the chanteuse crucified amid images of Blair and Bush. Suzanne isn't used to Spadge's manic barking but she soon realizes that the old fellow is mostly deaf and blind. Hanna discovers that there is an article in the *Metro* about the Kubb wooden toys that David manufactures and she calls him on her mobile to let him know. Suzanne has torn the toast into such tiny pieces that it takes forever to conclude the feeding process and in the end most of the dogs lose interest.

August, 2006

Tuesday, August 1:

It's the first day of August—but I am wearing a sweatshirt as Fritz and I make our way into the park on a breezy Tuesday morning. Ahead of us is Georgie, muttering to herself as she is propelled along by Sparkie and Bailey. When Fritz pauses to poo I fish out not only the official green bag but two Sainsbury fruit and veg bags as well—and the latter set sail across the green. By the time I have finished with Fritz they are well on their way to Brussels but I manage to catch up with them at last. I have an admonitory word with Fritz on the subject of his wandering ways, and then he is freed to gambol across the park.

As a matter off fact he does manage to say a bit closer today, though this may only be the result of my greater vigilance. We are soon overtaken by the speedy Leila, and later we meet up with her a second time—as Natasha is having a walkround with David the dogsitter and the indisposed Skye the Cairn. The yellow tennis ball is in constant use this morning and it is a pleasure to be able to give my dog a workout without worrying about sunstroke or heatstroke.

Ronnie and Hanna are already seated at an outdoor table when Georgie and I enter the precincts of the café. Ronnie is complaining about all the ironing he has to do, and I suggest that he might take his shirts to Harlequin on Maida Vale Parade instead—if he took out a second mortgage on his house to pay their charges first. Hanna says she is allergic to starch and deflects Ronnie's attempt to offload his chores on her. Linda comes in with Pepper and I free Fritz temporarily so that he and his pal can have a proper greeting. Ronnie is discussing recent episodes of *Curb Your Enthusiasm* and you can tell that Linda is offended when he mentions that Larry David has been walking around choking on a pubic hair.

There have been a number of references to the poor health of Georgie's husband, James, but today is the first time I have had a chance to ask her what is wrong; perhaps this is the source of her muttering. She says that he and his mates had too many pints the other night and then decided to ride their bikes home. James said there was no way he was going to ride a bike along the canal—as he would be certain to fall in. The others prevailed, however, and James did, indeed, fall in, injuring himself quite severely when he climbed out, slipped, and fell onto a barge. After listening to this tale Linda and I take the newly restored back passage; there are kids on the new astroturf field for the first time.

Wednesday, August 2:

Under grey skies Fritz and I enter the park, cooler temperatures still prevalent. The green is almost empty—with many dog owners on vacation—and we have the place pretty much to ourselves until we spot a small grouping near Tanya's van. Here I see a dog I have not seen in some time, Nelly, the Mastiff-like destroyer of stuffed toys. Her master is tossing a baby up in the air with one hand, a new sibling for the dog, and there is much cooing over the little fellow, who is beaming happily. Tanya, indeed, brings out a cuddly toy from her van and makes a presentation—only later do I begin to fear that it might fall into Nelly's jaws.

Once again I keep a sharp eye on my own pet, though Fritz seems content to chase his tennis ball most of the time. I can see Georgie heading into the café with her dogs and soon thereafter Fritz heads this way too. I am just congratulating myself on my having escaped another disappearing act when I see him enter the café's forecourt—and just as quickly disappear in pursuit of the black Taz, who is heading for the Carlton gate. This time I am able to retrieve my own dog, whom I march back to our table on lead.

To my surprise we have not only Dan, Hanna and Georgie, but the latter's sister Jean, on a visit from Glasgow with both Billy and Mozart. Billy is still his lively self but he has taken to biting the neighbourhood boys on the bum and he must wear a muzzle. Mozart, the rescued long-haired Jack Russell, is very much the momma's boy, but at least Bailey, also a frequent guest at Georgie's, has lost his antipathy for the stranger. Last night, Jean reports, she had Sparkie, Billy, Mozart and Bailey on her bed at the same time. For some reason there is now a discussion devoted to which dog would stand in for which actor—if there were a canine remake of the *Carry On* films. I don't remember all the castings but Winnie gets to play Barbara Windsor, Bailey is Charles Hawtry, Koko is Hattie Jacques and Fritz somehow ends up as Frankie Howerd. For her part, Winnie is obviously suffering from the lump on her face and, having scratched it, now seems to be covered in blood. Dan is not happy with the vets, who won't issue any antibiotics, and, as we all take the back passage home, he contemplates going back to his old surgery.

Thursday, August 3:

I am a bit late getting into the park this morning but there is no reason to rush proceedings because it is again a chilly, grey, blustery day. I let Fritz off the lead almost immediately and he makes slow progress toward the green. Indeed, he hasn't even parted with his first poo before he spots a cluster of dog walkers at the eastern end and takes off like a shot. Hanna is walking around with Spadge and George—and today they are accompanied by Tim with Yoyo. Seated on a bench over here is Tanya with Franca and her two dogs. Indeed nosy Bianca the Boxer almost gets a poo in the face when Fritz at last parts with his gift.

The tennis ball comes out and we have some spirited chasing on the green. I am almost floored by two freak accidents. First I stumble in my pursuit of the ball and right myself only at the last moment. Hanna, who has just been to the Royal Opera House with Ronnie and Susie in order to see *The Pharaoh's Daughter* ballet, says that my pirouette was worthy of the stage. Next my right ear almost disappears as Yoyo's blue Frisbee whistles past. A cute puppy named named Ziggy, part Bedlington and part Whippet, is let loose and he bravely mixes it up with the much larger dogs, including a second Boxer, Max. When we have had enough ball chasing Fritz and I enter the breezy confines of the café patio and I go in to order my coffee. Tim is ahead of me and wants to know if I know anything about alum—since its addition to the coating of one of his wallpapers in China has just cost him £3000—when it bleached out the background colour.

Only Hanna, Georgie, and Jean have braved the tempest this morning. Mozart, sitting in his mom's lap, growls when Yoyo sticks her head up on Jean's chair but Jean says he is actually growling at Tim, since the little tyke doesn't like men—particularly Scottish men. "Yes," Georgie adds, "he growls at James all the time. Though maybe he learned that from me—since *I* growl at James all the time too." More growling ensues when Fritz is suddenly blindsided by his pal Pepper, but these are actually sounds of pleasure and everyone has learned to ignore them. When no one can stand sitting any longer we have a traditional back passage walkround.

Friday, August 4:

Just as Fritz and I reach the green today we can see a knot of dog owners in a circle near the bandstand. They are discussing the aftermath of a just-concluded incident. It seems that tiny Lily, the Jack Russell puppy, having been spooked somehow by Sam the Weimaraner, has headed at great speed for the exit on Morshead Road. The other owners and their dogs, responding to this flight, have joined a chase aimed at bringing the puppy to heel. Janet has scoffed at this overreaction, suggesting that if they all calm down that Lily will come back of her own accord—but this strategy made sense only until Koko joined the chase as well. Several of the animals, including Bailey, have actually exited the park, though no one has gotten squashed before all dogs are successfully recovered.

Fritz noses around among the panting survivors and in this way he discovers David, who is still in the company of Skye the Cairn. He gets the tummy-rubbing greeting he craves and then we have some spirited ball chasing under grey skies. At the top of Mt. Bannister they are installing another CCTV camera (David says they've just taken it from somewhere else in the park), presumably because this is one of the spots where dog thugs like to congregate in the afternoon. No one believes that these pictures are actually monitored but, I suppose, someone might be able to look at such pictures *after* the next incident.

When I go in for coffee Georgie is still having palpitations after her role in the great chase. The other ladies discuss our famous doggy picnic, now scheduled for 2:00 on Sunday afternoon. It has also been discovered that the senior barista has a birthday coming up and an attempt is made to learn her name from two of the other waitpersons. These girls don't seem to know the answer—or they haven't enough English to understand our questions. Janet says that she has penetrated the mystery of Bouzha's dog-phobia—which goes back to a time when the U.N. warned her family that they were returning to a war-torn village in Kosovo beset by packs of wild dogs.

Saturday, August 5:

As Fritz and I enter the park I am still mulling over the contents of a dream I had last night. In it, all the dog owners received a long list of detailed instructions from the park management on what they could and couldn't get up to with their dogs. It isn't a dream that requires a lot of interpretation. Our group is standing in some shade at the western edge of the green and as I reach them I can see that a subdued Winnie is wearing a clear plastic Elizabethan collar, after having had her infected mole removed yesterday. Her tail has unfurled, a sign of her distress.

She doesn't participate in the hi-jinks on the green but the other small dogs are tearing around in circles: Bailey, Mozart, Sparkie and Jasmine. Fritz doesn't participate in this kind of play anymore either, but he does chase down his yellow tennis ball in the warm air of the weekend morning. Absent is Georgie, who is home with Billy (Jean could only manage to bring three dogs to the park), having a carpenter box-in the boiler in her sitting room. Someone sees that the awnings are already up at the café, so we head there—though without Treasurer Georgie the others have to improvise a payment scheme.

Ronnie, smoking a cigar, is waiting for us and Hanna soon arrives as well. Everyone wants to know if Dorothy is making chicken for tomorrow's picnic but I have to let them know that it won't be tandoori in style this time. Ronnie asks Jean about her significant other but her reply is succinct, "We've parted ways." I tell the others that Fritz threw up last night at 2:00, the consequence, no doubt, of his having eaten a purloined radish at dinnertime. He seems okay today and trots along happily as we accompany Dan and Winnie towards the gates. Dan gets a phone call on his mobile phone from the vet, asking how the patient is doing.

Sunday, August 6:

Another sunny morning arrives and Fritz and I make our way toward a green with almost no customers. Two chaps are beginning a cricket morning and one of them is joking with a retreating Georgie—"Please don't move; it breaks my concentration!" In fact no bat has made an appearance so far this day and the joke is soon on the chirpy cricketer—whose playmate manages to bounce a ball into a very delicate spot. Insult is soon added to injury as his partner lets someone else, a long way away, know that, "Hey, I just hit Michael in the balls!"

The other dog owners have sought a safer position and are lolling in the shade at the foot of Mt. Bannister, where we all encounter a wonderful eleven week-old Westie puppy named Rya. I don't sit down—since this is not the best position from which to launch search missions aimed at keeping track of Fritz. I soon have my work cut out for me since Franca arrives with Frank and Bianca and asks if anyone claims a squeaky rubber ball—which she has found on her in-lap. "It makes such a change," she says, "to *find* a ball after all the ones we have lost." Naturally Fritz suggests that the red ball is *his*, and, the object securely ensconced in his teeth, he heads off onto the green, with me shouting for him to stop. He is obviously suspicious of my intentions and although he pauses every now and then when I get close to him he continues toward the Morshead gate—as though he were prepared to cross the busy street on his way home with the prize. I am naturally anxious, but I am counting on one possibility—that he will turn into the friendly confines of the doggy area over here—and so he does. The gate closed behind him, I am able to corner him and extract the red ball at last. Then, on lead, we begin our return journey, catching up with Franca just as she is about to leave. Then she tells me that I needn't have bothered since Fritz can keep the ball.

At coffee we make final preparations for this afternoon's picnic and I can tell the others that, after all the whining and importuning, that Dorothy *will* be making tandoori chicken after all. We have a large group walking along the back passage and I count ten dogs in our group, a collection we have not seen in quite a while.

Shortly after 2:00 we join the others in the Grantully doggy area for a very nice and relaxed afternoon. The fact that we can close the gate behind us means that the dogs can run free without our worrying about their whereabouts. Today we have Ronnie, Georgie, Jean and her friend Gerda, Dan and Davide, Hanna, Janet, Michael and Ada with her ancient Scamp. Everyone is delighted that Michael has turned out; he seems well enough, though somewhat breathless. There is a mountain of food and the dogs do well out of this surfeit as well. Every now and then there is a brief scrap and a roiling mass of dogs pursuing one another, but we have the place pretty much to ourselves until four teen-aged boys come in to share a joint on a distant bench. The weather clouds over and it becomes quite humid so, fearing (and hoping for) rain we head for home at 4:30.

Monday, August 7:

It is grey and somewhat chilly as we enter the park on a very quiet Monday morning. Ahead of us I can see Dan and the Scottish sisters and so I let Fritz loose so that he can join the other dogs. He checks in with his pack and then sidles off to the side where I dog his footsteps until he has had his poo. Then I hand Dan a cosmetics shopping list for Dorothy—since Davide will be flying into L.A. later this week.

Pepper is out on the green and he and Fritz get a chance to tussle briefly. Yoyo is here with both parents and the blue Frisbee is soon in flight. Fritz runs around in all directions—with me keeping a close eye on his whereabouts and trying to keep him interested in his tennis ball—which he runs down with a speed that impresses the other dog owners. When I return from one of our voyages to the periphery I can see the others heading in for the café—and so can Fritz, who follows them soon thereafter.

The senior barista, Bouzha (not the actual spelling, I'm afraid), has her birthday today and to celebrate it a complimentary plate of sausages is sent out to the dogs—as well as five slices of a kind of home-made Swiss roll. The Scottish ladies look a bit the worse for wear after yesterday's festivities and neither feels up to cake eating so early in the day. Several matters of etiquette are discussed as Peter can be heard in the background growling at his Hector. I suggest that the habit of latecomers shouting in their orders to whichever dog owner is in the line at the café counter is a form of queue jumping, one that is certain to induce resentment. Hanna suggests that it would be rude to leave pieces of birthday cake behind, and so we wrap up the remaining slices and give them to Georgie and Jean. It is spitting a bit so we use the shelter of the trees as we make our way home at last.

Tuesday, August 8:

It is a lovely morning, sunny but not hot and I am almost too cool wearing nothing but my maroon t-shirt. Little Lisa, whom I have not seen in some time, comes up with Dash and Zara, her King Charles Spaniels.

She wants to know why no one seems to be on the green at 9:00 anymore and I tell her that a lot of people are away on holiday while others come later because of the tardy hours of the café. She says she has been on holiday but that she has been taking her dogs to Hampstead Heath lately because Dash doesn't get along with other dogs here. To illustrate this point she picks up the younger dog and hustles him out of the park. "I'd go to the Heath now," she says, "but I can't drive there by myself." This seems sensible—since she is only twelve.

Within five minutes of her departure we have Fritz, Billy, Sparkie, Mozart, Bailey, Sasha and Yoyo on the green. Fritz looks like he is heading out of the park and Lizzie gives chase but I think he just wants to go into the doggy area on the Grantully side, and I am able to distract him with his tennis ball before this. In the middle of the green a small black dog with a diamante collar steals the ball—but we get it back eventually. Over near the loos a louche couple are having an early morning nip from a concealed bottle. They joke with us about keeping an eye out for all these dog owners, "who look more desperate every moment." Ellen mentions the dogs-on-lead issue and the chap says, "No, it's only the big dogs they want to do that to." Ellen is certain all dogs are about to face the noose—here is somebody who has no faith in our campaign.

I join Georgie, Jean and Dan for coffee. Georgie says that at her house having to feed four dogs at the same time is a problem, especially since Bailey and Mozart try to scarf down *all* the food. She says that the dogs tend to follow her around the flat and that the sound of all those clacking toenails on her hardwood floors drowns out the telly. Dan tells an amusing story about being groped by a woman twice his age in the ball pit of a warehouse rave—when he was a teenager. Michaela comes in with Skye and brings us up to date on her Sardinian vacation—which ended with a desperate escape from Luton Airport, where the computer froze, trapping all the cars in the parking lot. Then we have a final walkround and separate at the gate.

Wednesday, August 9:

A cold front, bringing only a trickle of rain, has passed through during the night and it is still grey and chilly as Fritz and I enter the park. I can see a sliver of blue on the western horizon and this means that there is a chance that things will improve before long. There are quite a lot of dogs out on the green, though Fritz isn't greatly interested and soon follows Hanna onto the flanks of Mt. Bannister. Here he disappears into a tunnel in the withered hedge and I have to climb to the top of the hill to keep an eye on him. After chasing the ball down the slopes a few times we join the others at coffee.

Ronnie is already seated and soon we have Hanna, Jean, Georgie, and Dan as well. After a while we can see old Albert heading our way. He's got one of his wife's Yorkies on lead and he takes a chair at our table so that we can catch up on his news. He looks well enough, though the jagged remnant of his last bottom tooth seems more lonely than ever. He is off to Holland soon and this is always something he looks forward to. The little dog is called Saffy and she seems very sweet—Fritz gives her the sniff test as she settles down in the old vet's lap. Ronnie has brought a carrot for Jean, who is spending her last morning with us before returning to Glasgow this afternoon.

Ronnie heads for home with Rosie and the rest of us begin a back passage walkround—there is sun now and in it the temperatures have climbed dramatically. All the dogs pause for at least one poo while Bailey somehow manages to get into the fenced building site where piles of the old astroturf lie piled in a heap. Sparkie is also misbehaving, on a real barking jag today, much to the annoyance of his mistress. I try to keep Fritz from penetrating the cedars while on lead, but I am only partially successful. I bid farewell to Jean, Billy and Mozart as we near the Essendine exit after an hour in the park.

Thursday, August 10:

Conditions remain on the cool side as Fritz and I make our way past David the dogsitter, exiting with the highly-strung pair of Whippets, Denim and Suede. I have just heard that a major terrorist plot against the airline industry has been foiled at Heathrow, and I am wondering how many people in the park also know this. I don't have a chance to find out for Dan, passing us on his way out of the park with Winnie and Koko, tells me that someone is waiting for me in the centre of the green. I can see a familiar grey shape in profile but I am not looking at my own dog, who is somewhere behind me, but at a *new* Fritz, a sixteen week-old Standard Schnauzer puppy, whose presence in our midst I have been hearing about for a week or so. When I get to the cluster of dog owners

I am introduced to Christine and Richard, the puppy's proud owners; they have heard a lot about my Fritz and know that he is "the boss of the park." They are still a bit reluctant to let their handsome boy—still with his puppy fur—off lead, and they soon depart with the others, chilled to the bone by the fresh breezes.

I persist in making the rounds of the park, trying to give my Fritz some exercise. We go up the hill, down toward the tennis courts and back onto the green, the tennis ball in play at all times. When Fritz runs off with this object in his mouth I try to get him to drop it before he disappears into some spot inaccessible to me—but today he drops it into the bushes at the entrance to the café. This would be easy to retrieve were it not for the fact that one of the dog-friendly park keepers, classifying the object as just another piece of trash, uses his stick to snag it and place it in his black sack. I am too far away to protest and when I reach the café myself I have to hunt up my dog—who has run though the area on his way to the Carlton roadway. By this time the ball is definitively lost.

After I order my coffee I sit down with Ronnie, Hanna and Georgie. They have chosen a table under the eaves of the café because it looks like rain. While we are waiting for our drinks Chelsea's mom comes in to tell us that some suspicious food has been found in the bushes behind the café, and Tanya has gone off to have it analyzed for poison after Blake the Doberman has become ill. Someone makes the connection between terrorists at the airport and dog haters in the park, but there is no evidence to suggest who has left this alien material in the park—or whether it was truly poisonous. Albert comes by with Saffy and discusses his trip to Amsterdam tomorrow. He says he likes to take the bus because it passes countryside he recalls from his ordeal at Dunkirk sixty-six years ago. Chelsea, meanwhile, is staring at a large branch that has been deposited in a trash bin. The portly white Jack Russell likes to carry such lumber in her teeth and the presence of the branch in the bin acts as a magnet—better than any dogsitter in making sure that she doesn't move. Soon we begin a final walkround but for once Fritz outpaces all the other dogs and we are the first to exit.

Friday, August 11:

I am still in flannel *and* sweat shirts as Fritz and I make our way into the park on another brisk August morning. There is a small concentration of dog owners in the centre of the green and here we head directly. There seems to be an intense conversation going on here, and I have to pause to listen. The news is just about as bad as any dog owner can hear.

There have been up to seven instances of dogs ingesting poison in this area recently. A number of these cases were in Queen's Park, but the incident reported yesterday, the one involving Blake the Doberman in the bushes behind the cafe, is part of this total as well. The owners are encouraging one another not to let their dogs wander into the park's bushes—but how such advice is of any use to the owner of a scavenging wanderer like Fritz is not easy for me to divine. He is having a very good time with the ball I have chosen as a substitute for yesterday's lost tennis ball—a knobbly red ball with a bell in it—but after he has had some good running I put him on lead and approach Tanya, the animal warden, to see how much of this recent gossip is confirmed. She tells me that Blake's vet is considering this to be a case of poisoning, though Blake, after emetics and antidotes, seems to be okay. She tells me that the police are investigating the matter, and that the Paddington Rec management has cordoned off the bushes where the Doberman picked up the offending matter.

With this unhappy intelligence I next join the others at an outside table at the café. Hanna has brought me a bottle of pumpkinseed oil—which she swears by as a food additive. Dan is worrying that Winnie is showing signs of grey around her muzzle. Georgie reports that she has already had an early morning conversation with Jean in Glasgow. We also learn that Davide, in spite of the chaos at Heathrow yesterday, had only an hour and a half delay on his L.A. flight—and that he successfully took off with Dorothy's cosmetics shopping list. We have a slow walkround, Fritz the slowest ship in the convoy. I always keep him on lead back here—just as well given the dangers that may be lurking in the bushes, but I do have to say that his poo doesn't look so good.

Saturday, August 12:

Blustery conditions prevail as Fritz and I penetrate the park, an umbrella folded in my back pocket. I can see one or two white clad figures out on the green, members of the cricketing fraternity, and this will explain the unusual presence of the Saturday obedience class on the grass outside the Morshead Road doggy compound. To my surprise there is a convention of dog owners sheltering under the trees at the west end of the green as well. I suppose that Mt. Bannister, a much larger and more open space, is being shunned because it is so exposed to the weather—and also because it is in the bushes on its southwest side that the poison scare is located.

Fritz and Pepper have a riot of a reunion since both Linda and Rob are present. I also manage to find flight paths for the red rubber ball that don't impinge on the cricket players (all two of them so far) who have driven a much larger company of dog owners off *their* usual pitch. Janet is here with Koko and Sparkie—since Georgie has gone to the races at Ascot today (Dan has taken Winnie to work). These dogs run around in furious circles with Jasmine—whom an underdressed Faz has brought. A light rain falls for a few minutes but there isn't much to it. When we have at last collared Sparkie we head in to the café—but by this time it is dry enough to sit at an outside table, albeit one with a large umbrella lofted above.

We are joined by Roxy the Beagle and her owner, Tom—neither of whom we have seen in some weeks. He says that he was scheduled to join the rest of his family on Cape Cod yesterday, but that they had to send him home from a security-conscious Heathrow—from which he will make a second attempt this afternoon. I ask Faz if it wouldn't be telling tales out of school for him to comment on the recent anti-terror arrests—from the police's perspective. He says that the media is naturally excited, but that the briefings he has received are indeed chilling. He has also been a visitor to the Kilburn nick recently—they know all about the local poison scare as well. There is a mountain of toast for the dogs, not to mention some sausages and Hanna's scrambled eggs to share out. I don't let Fritz eat any sausage but on our return walkround I note some improvement in his poo. These animals have their poo analyzed with the dedicated intensity once reserved for the faeces of Chinese emperors.

Sunday, August 13:

A light rain is falling as we make our way into the park on a grey Sunday morning. I am wearing my rain jacket and carrying a large umbrella and the park is almost deserted. There is no one on the green and I decide just to walk around the circumference of this empty space and head immediately for home. Fritz obliges with a poo right next to a red poo box and we are just about to begin our homeward leg when I see Dan and Janet heading for the café—Janet is carrying Koko, who dislikes the rain.

Opposite the café entrance I can see that Peter (of Peter and Hector) and Georgie are already seated under the eaves. We three latecomers join them and Hanna, having delivered her wet boys to the warmth of her flat, comes back to join us as well. I draw up a chair for her but Hector, an immensely large puppy at seven and a half months, keeps jumping onto the chair so that he can survey the table top. Many of the other dog owners have their dogs in their laps, Sparkie on Georgie's lap, Koko on Janet's, Winnie on Dan's. Georgie, back from Ascot, tells us that she has again won money on a horse named Dorothy's Friend.

The rain continues to fall for another fifteen minutes, then it stops and the skies begin to brighten. No one complains about the moisture, which is much needed, even though trouser legs are soon coated in mud. Dan says that Davide has been told that his return flight from Los Angeles won't get off until Tuesday. Ronnie shows off his new Barbour jacket—which he picked up at a recent sale. He also passes around pictures on the screen of his mobile phone; we are at last able to see a view of his 95 year-old mother, whom he visits so often for so long. He has also taken a picture of Hector and Peter; the latter says that the Cocker has some cysts in his mouth (one is visible on his lip as well) and that they are under investigation. Both Ronnie and Peter then join us on our walkround. Hanna and I discuss the recent outbreak of gang graffiti in our neighbourhood. Someone has been painting MVM on street signs, entrance gates and even on the tarmac at the foot of park apparatus. There is some speculation on what the initials stand for; someone, half-seriously, suggests "Maida Vale Moslems."

Monday, August 14:

I am wearing my rain jacket again, more as an extra layer of warmth than as a barrier against moisture. Fritz and I approach the green in fits and starts and he goes off lead only after agreeing to part with his gift against the side of a trash barrel. Georgie is the only dog owner brave enough to stand in the centre of the green—where Sparkie and Bailey are cavorting. Fritz heads almost immediately for the margins, where he is followed by a little brown dog, who seems fascinated. Thereafter, the tennis ball failing to amuse, my dog admits himself to the doggy area near the Grantully exit and here we remain for another five minutes, all alone. Fritz does a thorough job of sniffing and I have time to note that the palisade built of twisted tree branches parallel to the wooden fence has produced no foliage of its own, though it does support some greenery that has grown up around it.

As we make our way across the green at coffee time I can see that there is a fine mist falling. Over near Tanya's van I can see Bianca and Hootch—but I don't dare get too close because Bianca has a squeaky toy. An unaccompanied Staffie rushes up and tries to mount Fritz. Soon discouraged, he tries his luck with Bailey and Pepper as well, even when we are at last seated in front of the café. Hanna identifies the owner of this loose cannon as one of the chaps sitting just inside the door, but his pal, whose Corgi-eared mutt is perched outside the door, has already sent Hanna into a tizzy—and I arrive just at the moment when she is finishing up a vehement request to be left alone by this Irishman—who has accosted her several times in the neighbourhood while drunk.

Unfortunately he later emerges from the café to smoke a cigarette and, since he knows Georgie from her role behind the bar at the Windsor Castle (from whose confines she has ejected him more than once for pestering the other topers), he now approaches us with a long harangue. He is trying to sublet two bedrooms in a flat whose sitting room will be off-limits. "I want quality, no trash." He has recently spent eighty-six hours in the knick at the request of two of his own siblings, arrived from Ireland to contest the bequest of a brother, recently deceased. "I'll tell you why he left everything to me," the chap continues, "It's because I stuck a knife into the guy who robbed our parents. Got two years for that. They hung yellow ribbons up when I got out."

Hanna is twitching by this time and so we make a rather early departure from the café, leaving our hectoring intruder to bore someone else with his tales of woe. (Hanna says that when she offered to loan him a poo bag he declined, saying he didn't care how many fines he incurred, he would never pick up his dog's shit.) It is raining lightly and I am really glad I have my rain jacket on as we make our way along the back passage. Her stomach in turmoil, Hanna has the hiccoughs.

Tuesday, August 15:

Again I have donned my rain jacket on a grey, overcast and cool morning. It doesn't rain but I am happy for the extra warmth as Fritz and I approach the green where, to my surprise, there is a very lively scene indeed. It is as if the holiday season were already over and dogs were being returned to their usual routine. Humpty is here, so is Skye the Alsatian, and we have two delightful puppies again, Rya the Westie and Fritz the Standard Schnauzer.

My own Fritz has to be followed closely before he will part with his first poo near the tennis courts. Thereafter he chases his tennis ball, usually managing to snatch it from the skies on the third bounce. He and Fritz II touch noses and then the latter, off lead for the first time, gets spooked when a little Jack Russell named Millie begins screeching. Tanya arrives in her van, the environmental protection officer in tow—according to Hanna. When it is time to go in for coffee I command Fritz to sit at this woman's feet—and he does, much to my amazement.

Rya's owner joins us for coffee. Yesterday she was mugged by a gang of black youths (including one female member) on Malvern in West Kilburn. They not only kicked her but threatened to kill Rya as well. Naturally the subject of local crime comes up. I tell the others that last night at 11:00 no fewer than six police cars answered a call on Grantully. I witnessed this and two wpcs running down the pavement toward the Essendine gate. No one knows what was under investigation but, from the amount of shattered blue glass on our pavements these days, car crime is suspected. Ronnie arrives and tells me that our local councillor, Jan Prendergast, will be dropping by to visit him tomorrow, having received our petition about the dogs at last.

We welcome back Kate, who has been in Turkey for the last two weeks (it took her fifteen hours to complete a four hour journey yesterday). Dan arrives long after his usual hour, having had a very unpleasant morning. The builders had disconnected his alarm clock and he was late rising. Two new members of the crew were marching about his flat without so much as a greeting to their employer. Winnie had to go to the vet to have her stitches out—at which time they also biopsied a growth between her toes and gave her a shot. A chap sitting on the steps of one of the blocks in Morshead Mansions glared at him as he was unloading Winnie and Koko, so unnerving him that, as he turned around at last, he ran smack into a lamppost. Now he calms down a bit over a cup of coffee, but Winnie, on his lap, is really out of sorts and lashes out at a distant Fritz—who responds with vigour. The two are okay once they are both on the ground, however, and run happily head to head as we begin a final walkround.

Wednesday, August 16:

I venture into the park with only two layers on, instead of three—for the sun is trying to make an appearance and there is *some* warmth. I have to follow Fritz for some distance before I can clean up after him—and he can be emancipated. There are a lot of dogs on the green and among them I spot the little white form of Otw the Bichon Frise. Her owner, Rhianne, is having a rant with Dan on the subject of the African Centre, close enough to her place of residence that life has been made miserable by thunderous music, especially on the weekend, when the noise persists well into the unsocial hours range. Rhianne says that neither the police nor the noise patrol seem much interested in addressing the problem ("Everybody is too p.c. to act") and, in consequence, three of the residents of her mews are moving.

Fritz chases his ball when it is not also attracting the attention of a young Alsatian, also named Ryah. At one point he wanders over near the loos, where Franca is seated, and I get an update on the recovering Doberman, Blake. Samples have not come back from the lab yet but the bushy area behind the café is still fenced off—to prevent other dogs from scarfing up the suspect matter. I return to the green to see how Fritz II is getting on. The brave pup is getting repeatedly rolled over by Ryah, but always coming back for more.

I sit down at coffee with Ronnie, Georgie, Kate, Davide, and Hanna. Davide has at last made it back to London, after a long layover in Los Angeles because of the Heathrow crisis. But this has certainly given him time to make purchases at the drug store on behalf of Dorothy and Hanna. The latter is in a tizzy because she has lost her mobile phone—but when she retraces her steps she finds it on the grass. Now all she has to contend with are screeching rug rats at the next table. Tanya comes by and says that she is now gunning for joggers with dogs—since this tribe never bother to stop and clean up after their trailing pets.

I notice that outside our fence a flag ceremony is taking place as, for the third year running, the park has won an award. Park staff are gathering and I also notice the tidy figure of our councillor, Jan Prendergast, in a grey business suit. Since she is scheduled to see Ronnie later this afternoon I ask him if he doesn't want to talk to her now. He summons her over to the café fence, introduces me as the author of the famous petition, and she repeats that there are no plans to introduce dogs-on-lead legislation in the park and that she knows that Paddington Rec is a unique site in this regard. To underline her point she calls over the park manager, Paul, and he repeats this pledge. Jan says that she would like to present our petition to the entire council, which next meets in November, and that, in the meantime, we should continue to obtain signatures. Now they are calling her over to the flagpoles for a few words and Ronnie and I can return to our coffee in a triumphant mood. At least for the time being, we have won.

Thursday, August 17:

We enter the park on a balmy though grey morning and I let Fritz off lead quite early in the process. His tummy has not been that great lately but his first offering doesn't look too bad. I am carrying a new copy of the petition with me and, seeing Lizzie with Yoyo, I head her way—since I remember that only Tim had signed it before. While we are chatting the little brown dog who followed Fritz around the other day returns and, after Fritz and Yoyo have gone over the low hill to visit the precincts of the tennis courts, I approach the owners, mother and daughter, to ask for his name. It turns out to be Georgie; they are eager to sign the petition but they have more to add to the *other* story that dominates our local scene. They say that a family, one of whose members kicked a dog the other day, was told off by other dog owners—and that their retaliation had been to scatter the poison that has everyone so agitated. Another theory that cannot be confirmed by anyone is that those responsible for the health and safety of the food preparation areas (i.e., the café) have scattered the poison themselves, hoping to get rid of rats.

I follow Fritz around, slinging the tennis ball on occasion; it is snapped up by another low-strung brown mongrel. When it is returned to me I tell the owner of Alfie, for so this young Mayhew dog is called, about our petition and he signs it as well. By this time I have lost track of all the other dog owners and so, figuring they must have gone in for coffee, I cross the green with Fritz on lead in order to join them. Dan, Kate,

Georgie, Ronnie and Hanna make up our group but we are also joined by Dorothy and Linda, with Pepper. Fritz and Pepper begin to chew on one another and Dan says, "They really do seem to be joined together as one dog." "Yes," I answer, "joined together at the face." Kate's mobile phone keeps ringing but, since most of this concerns business, she has a brief look at who's calling, refuses to answer, and shoves the phone back into her bra.

Dan then tells an alarming tale about a girl named Vanessa—whose Cairn puppy was fed something dodgy by another group of sunbathers on the green—supposedly Guinness, but causing vomiting. (They also threatened to kill the dog.) While we are digesting (if this is the right word, in the circumstances) this information we are approached by head park keeper, Boyd, who tells us that as responsible dog owners we will be glad to learn that the management now has a new set of signs warning users of the hefty fines they face if their dogs are allowed to foul the park and that, furthermore, park personnel will be able to issue such fines themselves in the future. The others think this is a good idea but I am deeply suspicious; I can well imagine zealous anti-dog personnel issuing fines without warning, without giving owners a chance to clean up the mess—the Paddington Rec equivalent of those parking police vultures who already blight local lives.

Friday, August 18:

After another rainy night the grass is actually turning a pale shade of green, a welcome sight even if it does mean that someone will have to mow it again one of these days. Two puppies are having a spirited wrestling match on the green, Ziggy—the Bedlington-Whippet cross—and a four month-old Fox Terrier pup named Ruby. I get a few more signatures and then follow Fritz around the margins of the green. He has been almost starved the last day or so—after another bout of tummy trouble—and he seems to be uninterested in finding an appropriate poo patch. He does chase down a yellow tennis ball until Skye the Alsatian pinches it. It is time to go in for coffee.

While I am waiting in line for my turn to order I have a nice chat with Barry, the retired electrician who was once my best park pal—back in the days when his Jack Russell, Stumpy, was the best friend of my Schnauzer, Toby. Ironically he has brought with him for another dog owner some of

Stumpy's old leads—he seems to have no interest in getting another dog. I tell him about our petition efforts and he asks to sign on. Again I am in the unique position of learning his last name for the first time after all these years.

We have a jolly table out under one of the new umbrellas—just as well because the wind keeps showering us with the raindrops clinging to the overhead trees. Today we have Hanna, Janet, Georgie, Dan and Davide, and Dorothy. At a nearby table Peter not only has his Hector, but also Jody—an irrepressible pup a few years ago, now calmed to a genial maturity. Rhianne also comes by to visit, asking our assistance in snagging the elusive Otw. We hear the final chapters in Dan and Davide's struggle to get their builders to finish the job—the boys now have a bidet. Janet is describing how her painter had to apply coat after coat in a bedroom that was stained brown with nicotine—while Hanna and Davide are lighting up. It's a Sainsbury morning for us so we take Fritz home, hoping to make it to Ladbroke Grove before encountering the next pulse of rain. We don't make it.

Saturday, August 19:

With another day of scattered showers behind us, it is no surprise that the green continues to live up to its name. I scoop up two rock hard turds from my Fritz and then we head over to Christine and Richard, who are attempting to exhaust their own dog of the same name. There is some confusion when "Fritz" is shouted by either owner/s but then my version likes to visit with everybody and he is soon getting a cuddle from Richard. I discuss the petition with this couple and they sign on. So does Roland's assistant at the obedience classes. She repeats what I had heard before—the park's refusal to let Roland *advertise* his free sessions. The reasons cited are new to me, however—too much construction going on and too many other users of the same space. One wonders why this latter reason is never cited when school groups or cricketers want to use the green. In the meantime Roland seems to be carrying on as before, surviving by word of mouth. Some of his charges are tied to the flagpoles, waiting their turn, and one Alsatian is howling in frustration.

We go in for coffee and there is a large group surrounding one table—Hanna, Ronnie, Janet, Georgie, Dianah, Dorothy, Kate and Dan. Dan says he can't stand the underground but prefers the buses; Dorothy and I disagree. Kate passes around some Turkish delight that she has brought back from Turkey itself. Her Skye is also howling, with boredom. Everyone admires the *new* Fritz, who is at the next table—when he is not escaping through the gap in the fence to pursue his Schnauzer wanderings.

When we begin our walk home we encounter Rowena with her Toby. She tells us that Lulu, the mostly Maltese white fluff ball belonging to Julia, has died. We hear all the details of the fatal illness of this little dog, who once inhabited the margins of our park, and then Rowena continues with a diatribe against the leaf blowers (Lizzie was outraged on this subject earlier this week as well). These chaps spent all afternoon yesterday blowing leaves around in the doggy area across the street from Rowena's flat—the lady unable to make a phone call in her own sitting room because of the noise. In mitigation, one of the park keepers has told her that they have been ordered to do something about the leaves here because people don't pick up after their dogs when there are leaves about (another one new to me). Then, in an interesting footnote to my conversation earlier this week with our councillor and the park manager, this chap also went on to add that *he* has heard that all dogs will soon be put on lead in this park anyway!

Sunday, August 20:

It is cool and grey this morning and I have donned my rain jacket in anticipation of something worse. Indeed a few drops do fall while I am patrolling the green but the rains never come. I am trying to keep Fritz amused with his tennis ball and gather signatures at the same time. Suzanne is sighted and, as she has told me that she wanted to sign during the earlier version of our campaign, I track her down now. Ziggy is out here as well but, when he tries to snatch Sam the Weimaraner's blue ball, he gets nipped. Peter, Sam's owner, signs the petition as well but by now it has gone 10:00 and it is time to head for the café.

I find the others surrounding a table under the eaves of the café and here I anchor Fritz to a leg and take my place in a very long queue. Metty (who is rarely present himself these days) is obviously understaffed and there are just two girls and Elian to serve the multitude, who have been circling like vultures waiting for the place to open. I am in line for fifteen minutes before I get to register my request—by this time Dorothy has arrived and so it's two small black decafs. Elian promises to bring these out to us so I take up a seat at our table, where all the other participants (none of whom has thought of ordering for me) are almost finished. Nevertheless we wait a further fifteen minutes for our coffees—by which time some of the others have already departed.

Kate tells me that her local pocket park, just south of the canal and opposite the Waterside pub, has suddenly gone not to "dogs on lead" but to "no dogs allowed"—this in a space where the chief users are elderly dog owners. The suggestion is made that *I* need to fire off another letter to Westminster Council. This notion—on a morning in which I have gotten far behind the others because I have been out on the green gathering signatures on *their* behalf—draws the inevitable protest: "Why am I the only one who seems to be doing anything about these issues?" The response is deliberately obtuse, as it is when Dorothy asks me if the dogs have had any toast this morning and I reply, "I don't know; I wasn't here." Rya the Westie and Fritz II come in and this lifts the atmosphere somewhat, but I am still out of sorts as we begin a walkround along the back passage.

Monday, August 21:

I am back in my rain jacket on a cool grey Monday morning and, though we never experience a promised downpour, there is enough moisture in the air to drive the dog owners over to the foot of Mt. Bannister, where there is a little metal gazebo that offers some shelter.

Some of the usual suspects are here, including Bailey, Sparkie, Koko, Winnie, Alfie, Fritz II and the tiny Jack Russell puppy, Lily. Alfie plays with her a bit too roughly and she starts to run off—producing a string of pathetic endearments in French—but this time she stays within the park and hides under Dan.

Fritz chases his yellow tennis ball around and I have to follow him up the hillside several times while he goes exploring. As usual I implore him to drop the ball before he ventures into any undergrowth but today he fails to heed my warning and the next time I see him, running along the back of the tennis courts, he and the ball have parted company forever. Soon thereafter we follow the others in to coffee, joining Ronnie and Rosie, who are stationed bravely at an outdoor table. The good news is that Blake the Doberman is back after his poison scare.

Richard joins us, as does Sasha's guardian, Yasmina. The latter is keeping a wary eye out for her son, who might be among the sports kids just entering, since she doesn't want to be caught smoking a cigarette. Richard, it turns out, is a teacher of little ones, in his case a reception class of four and five year-olds at a nearby school. His girlfriend, Christine, teaches the year three class at the same school. I ask him if he plans to bring his Fritz in for "show and tell" and he says he'd like to, though he doesn't know if this is permitted. I hang on to the burly puppy while his master is ordering his coffee—my Fritz shows no sign of jealousy, though he does keep raking my legs so that I will give him puppy treats since the buttered toast has been exhausted early on. Soon we are attempting our slow moving progress along the back passage, with Koko and Bailey bringing up the rear and the dieting Rosie skipping along in lively fashion.

Tuesday, August 22:

We have a lovely sunny morning at last and things do seem sweet and fresh after all the recent rain. I notice that a portion of the grass on the left side of the Morshead roadway is thick and lush and this means that we will soon have yet another reason to introduce a noisy machine to tame its growth. Fritz is under close observation, having ejected his dinner last night, but his poo seems solid enough—so perhaps this was another false alarm.

I let him off the lead as we reach the green and he enjoys chasing his red ball with the rattling bell inside—I have dragged this out of the toy box once again, following the loss of yesterday's tennis ball. There isn't much activity on the grass and when Kate and Georgie head in to the café Fritz follows them—so I do likewise. After tying my dog to a table leg I get in a queue at the just opened counter but the line is so long and the orders so complex that I have to give up and take a seat at our table in hopes of a later break in the action.

Georgie tells us that yesterday Charlie, a workman who has been active in her flat, approached her accompanied by Sparkie on lead—just as she was leaving her noontime pub assignment. While he was arranging his tool bag at the end of the job Sparkie had evidently jumped over this object and out into the front hall. Just at this moment someone opened the building's front door from the outside—and the little Yorkie was gone.

Charlie scoured the neighbourhood, going as far as the park—to no avail. He returned to Georgie's flat (the front door had slammed shut behind him) but this time he spotted Sparkie sitting on a corner, watching all the cars go by. Using the strap on his tool bag as an impromptu lead he now headed for Georgie's pub, seeking a way to get back into her flat and reclaim the rest of his tools. "Aren't you glad you heard this story when it was all over?" I now ask. Georgie seems very relieved and cuddles the rascal in her lap.

Ronnie and Dorothy make late appearances but the queue has thinned a bit and they don't have to wait too long for their coffee. Skye the Alsatian is digging a hole in the earth at the foot of a tree, scattering dirt everywhere. The Alsatian is easily bored and Kate has to keep supplying her with balls—until all four are in play. Someone notes that we haven't seen Hanna in two days but just then she calls Ronnie on his mobile to explain that she has had workmen patching a hole in *her* ceiling. Kate asks to take the petition home with her—so I am happy to surrender it. As we leave I can see she is getting the signature of baby Sabrina's mom.

Wednesday, August 23:

I have donned my rain jacket again, a precaution against the heavy grey skies above. As Fritz and I make our way toward the green I can see a lively scene ahead, some fifteen dog owners are gathered in the centre—while a chap on a lawn mower makes ever widening circles on the back of his lawnmower. I am walking with Michaela who is using her plastic ball sling to keep Skye the Cairn amused. Unfortunately Wolfgang the ball hawk is present and this leads to the loss of this ball on a number of occasions.

I am careful to throw Fritz his own red ball when Wolfgang is otherwise occupied—but my dog does get in a lot of exercise for once. He is also able to visit the periphery of the green and to touch base with a number of the other dog owners, some of whom are sitting on benches at the eastern end. Fritz II is tugging away at his lead, anxious to join this company, and soon he is ducking and diving with the rest of them. Hanna, dogless, tells me to tell Michael the Pirate that she will see him in the park this afternoon. This is a message I can pass on at coffee, a few minutes later.

Today I sit at a table with Richard and Christine, with Dorothy joining us later. Bianca the Boxer is wandering around and both Sparkie and Fritz II are kissing her. At the next table we have Georgie, Ronnie and Dan and Davide. The latter have just watched a program on plastic surgery on one of the Italian channels that Davide can summon with his satellite. Everyone wishes Dorothy good luck at the gym this afternoon, today being induction day for her at the Paddington Sports Club on Castellain Road. She heads for the bank while I make halting progress with Fritz as we head for home. The sun is trying to come out.

Thursday, August 24:

We have had a lot of rain over night and it is not surprising that I enter the park wearing my rain jacket again. Fritz and I are soon followed by Skye the Cairn, who wants me to kick his tennis ball to him—always a tough task because the chap insists on standing right in front of your shoe. I have a go, trying to fake him out by pretending to kick with my left foot; I also manage to kick the ball off his back a few times as well—he doesn't seem to mind. There isn't much of a turnout on the green, just the two Skyes, Cristal the Alsatian, Sparkie and Bailey. I soon have Fritz chasing after his red ball but he disappears into the bushes behind the tennis courts and I have to follow along so that he comes to no harm.

Even though the skies are lowering we choose an exposed table, though one with a large awning raised above it. Hanna, Dorothy and Davide soon join me, Kate and Georgie. The latter is shivering with apprehension as Sparkie, his paws wet from all the damp grass, prepares to jump into her lap. We ask her if her pub customers ever offer to buy her drinks. She says this happens fairly often but she doesn't drink while she is working. Kate says that she has added a dozen signatures to the petition but that the latter has gotten a bit shopworn in the process. I tell her this will just make the object look more authentic.

We begin a traditional walkround, encountering Elvis the Westie as we do so. Spadge is digging in his heels and growling at Kate's Skye—who then begins barking in return. Both Kate and Davide complete much of the walk while talking on their mobile phones. Davide has major plumbing problems in his new flat and this morning he discovered damp. He is telling this to Dan and I hear him add that he is leaving both Winnie and

Koko at Janet's house today. Sometimes, to escape the workmen, he goes there himself—just for a nap.

Friday, August 25:

For the first time in a number of days it doesn't look like it is about to rain. Indeed I am wearing my sunglasses again as Fritz and I walk toward the green on a sunny Friday morning. There is a lively scene here—I count over a dozen dogs at play. One of these is Pepper and he and Fritz have their usual knockabout and growling session. Later my dog begins to wander on the margins, almost heading out of the park on his own at one time. I am trying to keep a special eye on him because he had a bad night yesterday (or we did)—he showed no interest in food (not even ours), licked and scratched himself in bed, and made a retching sound at 4:00 in the morning—waking everybody. He seems fine today and has a lot of exercise before Georgie asks me what time it is—since the clock on the tower of the clubhouse went out of service yesterday. I tell her that it's gone 9:30 and she heads immediately for the café, Fritz following her.

At breakfast we have Georgie, Kate, Hanna, Janet, and Faz. The latter has just received a commendation for closing a creditable number of cases and the conversation naturally turns to crime—especially since the headlines on the papers that Elian has left on our table suggest that shoplifters won't get jail terms now—if the government has its way. Faz thumbs through the papers and sees an article about a chap he has himself arrested. Out on the green there is a "butch fight," according to Franca, one in which Cristal, Rebel, (whom Faz refers to as Rebel Without a Clue) and Skye the Alsatian need to be separated after some furious barking. Kate gets caught up in this incident and gets knocked over—"I've just landed on my tits," she tells us, thereby assuring us that she has made an especially soft landing.

There is also an incident as we get up to begin a final walkround. A queue of young kids is lined up on the roadway outside the café, waiting to begin a summer sports day in the park. Just at this spot Spadge stops to do a poo at their feet. Hanna rushes forward to pick *him* up before he can kick the offending objects onto the kids' shoes—but as she snatches for the old codger he is separated from his collar and begins to run free. He doesn't get very far, since he can't see where he is running, and Janet and I soon have him under control. He is admonished when Fritz manages to do his second poo under the cypresses. "Look at that, Spadgie," Hanna says, "Fritz knows not to do his on the pavement."

Saturday, August 26:

There are a few drops falling as Fritz and I depart the premises on a grey Saturday morning. Seeing the light brighten my bathroom window I have counted on improving weather and, for once, I have no rain protection at all. Fortunately the moisture soon dissipates and by the time we reach the green it has stopped altogether. Not surprisingly there aren't many people about. Kate and Faz are taking turns lofting balls with the red plastic ball sling, while Skye the Alsatian is making magnificent catches and Jasmine is watching Skye.

Another small group of dogs is centred on the metal gazebo at the foot of Mt. Bannister. One of these is young Oscar, the Labrador. The others appear to be foregathering for Roland's Saturday morning training class. Fritz checks all this out and, until I can distract him with his own red ball, follows several other dogs toward the exits. One of these is Suki the Vizsla. She is accompanied by little Nicole and the latter's father. He tells me that Nicole has been doing a mischievous impression of Fritz, growling up a storm.

Our group crowds around one large table outside the café door—eleven in number eventually: Dorothy and yours truly, Ronnie and Susie, Georgie, Janet, Hanna, Kate, Dan, Faz and Peter, whose Hector arrives with a bag of chicken bones he has snaffled somewhere—the occasion for a spirited under-table scramble to recover all these treats before they go down some doggy throat. Hector has just had a surgery for the removal of some warts around his chops, Skye has one on her tongue and Winnie has just recovered from a surgical procedure as well. One theory is that this is a virus—and naturally the finger points to Winnie as the Typhoid Mary of the group (Dan gives her a big kiss of confidence when these allegations are flying). People are telling Dan that it is time for a housewarming party at his new house.

Most of the morning's conversation deals with unpleasant incidents endured by the dog owners while using public transportation. The conclusion seems to be that an integrated public transportation system (like the tower blocks of yesteryear) may be fine on paper—but no one figures in the nature of the public likely to use (and misuse) the system.

Meanwhile Metty (who sends out a bulging plate of sausages on the house) has only one other set of customers, four community policemen who arrive on bicycles (which are banned in the park) plus two who arrive on foot. This leaves the question—who is minding the streets? On our walkround our own cop, Faz, tells us that he saw an army t-shirt in a surplus shop in Notting Hill with the legend, "Don't Panic, I'm Islamic."

Sunday, August 27:

We have a warm sunny morning for once and I am almost too warm in my purple sweatshirt. There isn't too much activity on the green, though we do find David the dogsitter, just leaving with Skye the Cairn. We have a brief conference on his winter schedule—as Dorothy and I are currently planning a holiday abroad. Thereafter I keep the red jingle ball in play, though it proves to be of great fascination to little Fix, who twice pinches it. The ball is returned to me, Fix is put on lead, and by this time it almost 10:00 and time to head for the café.

Unfortunately this seems to be a popular choice today. There are eight bicycles belonging to the community protection police and this lot is having a leisurely breakfast. Let's hope it's a slow crime morning—it won't be so for long, as the sounds of the Notting Hill Carnival are just beginning their daylong roar in West Kilburn. Absent today is Faz, since he and Dianah are off to Sicily today. (Here Faz will be going on a Mafia tour—almost a professional development opportunity for him.) Jasmine is spending the weekend with Janet (Faz has already called once) and then going on to Auntie Georgie's.

Kate is sitting between me and Dan but she has to get up (Dorothy takes her seat) because Skye the Alsatian is barking with great vehemence—as she wants more play on the green. Dan has a squeaky toy secreted in his jumper and every now and then, just bending over, this toy issues a plaintive squeal. Fritz is instantly mesmerised and he won't let Dan alone, jumping into his lap, sticking his wet nose into all of Dan's pockets. Winnie is not happy to share this position with an interloper and there is some teeth gnashing. The Carnival is the chief topic of conversation—our lot not only will *not* attend, but it is hard to find a good word for the event voiced by any of those seated at the table. Ronnie suggests holding it in the Outer Hebrides, Michael the Pirate wants it held on a concrete island in the mid-Atlantic. Our walkround brings us ever closer to the pulsing rhythms but there is a pleasant enough surprise at the end of our wanderings for, near the Essendine Gate, we meet for the first time a delightful six month-old longhaired Dachshund puppy named Gigi. She is a bit overawed by our parade of animals but she gets to touch noses with the lot.

Monday, August 28:

Just as Fritz and I are about to depart for our morning session in the park there is a brief shower. I am in time to put on my rain jacket and, with the skies still spitting a bit, we enter the park at about 9:45 on a grey Bank Holiday Monday. Naturally the scene is rather bereft of characters and the only animal to greet Fritz as he nears the green is Sky the Husky. I walk with her master, who is wearing his Ohio State Buckeyes sweatshirt, and we discuss the impending start of the college football season. Then I cross the green, Fritz still on lead, in order to see if Metty has counted this as a weekend day or a regular Monday.

The café has obviously been open for quite a while since I find Georgie, Janet, Dan, Hanna, Ronnie and Susie seated at a table outside the front door. Dorothy later joins us as well. There is a good deal of talk about the Notting Hill Carnival, scheduled to reach its apogee and conclusion tonight. Janet says that she once got so frightened on All Saints Road (before its gentrification) that she began to run from the scene, rescued eventually by some local kids who took pity on her, saying, "We're black and *we* don't go to All Saints Road." There were 108 arrests yesterday—which isn't too bad given the volume of revellers. The dogs are sitting on parental laps, perhaps to keep their bums out of the wet—when a true downpour begins and chairs are scraped together so that no one is exposed to the moisture. Fritz takes exception to the presence of the latchkey dog, Buster, at our feet. Winnie is sitting benignly on Dan's lap, her chin resting on the tabletop. Koko is in Janet's lap and she soon joins in a chorus of disapproval as an ancient Sheltie named Timmy limps into *her* space.

It looks like there is a brief break in the clouds and Dorothy and I jump to our feet, hoping to make it home before the next wave of rain. Again we don't make it. Just as we are exiting the café Pepper rushes in, Rob in tow, and the two dogs have to mess around a bit. Linda is hiding in the alcove of the clubhouse but it takes me a long time to reach this spot—since Fritz pauses to do a second poo. I put the hood of my rain jacket over my baseball cap but this prevents me from seeing beyond my own feet—splashing through the puddles. Pepper looks poised to rush into the street at one point and everyone tries to get him to come back; he responds to my whistle and he is reattached to his lead. As Dorothy and I continue on our way I note that, uniquely, Fritz has not been off his own lead even for a minute today.

Tuesday, August 29:

We have a lovely morning in the park, with lots of nice warm sunshine beaming down on the rich green grass—a few weeks ago everything was parched and white. Fritz follows Jonesie the Shih-Tzu onto the green and thereafter devotes himself to patrolling the margins and chasing his ball. He is also attracted to a rubber ball with a small squeak, one belonging to Charlie the Cocker, but I manage to return this to Charlie's owner before there are tears. On the hillside of Mt. Bannister the larger dogs have their own conclave: Nelly, Bianca and Max, the Boxers, and Hootch with his thunderball. Fritz II is playing with the smaller dogs but Richard predicts that he will soon want to mix it up with the big boys and girls.

Dan comes in with three dogs—his own Winnie, plus the pair of Jasmine and Koko. Many people walk around the green with their mobile phones in their ears, often conducting some sort of urgent business transaction. As I near Dan I can hear *him* on the phone asking the vital question, "Have either of these dogs had a poo this morning?"

We join Georgie, Ronnie, Kate, Hanna and Michael the Pirate at coffee. Hanna says that the noise from the just concluded carnival was far kinder on our ears this year than last—perhaps we were just lucky—with the wind carrying the sounds away from us. Kate says that down by the canal she met two policemen seconded to the event—and they were fit! Michael tells us that he has been experimenting with a recipe for garlic soup, which he makes by peeling 100 cloves of garlic! Most of the breakfast crowd begin a walkround; I have to carry Fritz's poo in its green bag a long distance because the red box next to the new playing field is jammed and they have taken away the trash bin outside the five-a-side courts. Both Sparkie and Spadge are raising a barking ruckus. "Did you know," I suggest waspishly, "that dogs can survive quite well without their vocal cords?"

Wednesday, August 30:

It is again a sunny morning in Paddington Rec, but there is a chill wind to keep temperatures depressed. I tell Fritz that his Uncle David is on the green and he is soon searching about for his pal, getting the obligatory cuddle while Skye the Cairn looks to others for a kick of the ball. I do not fetch the red rubber ball from my pocket because Wolfgang the ball thief is about. The latter soon has three tennis balls in his mouth and is looking for a quiet spot on the grass where he can spit out his treasure and protect it from other rivals at the same time. Fritz looks like he would just as soon pee on Wolfgang's kneeling owner, who is today wearing a spiv suit, dark glasses, and gloves. I interrupt this gesture with my foot.

Fritz then does a circuit of dog noses—today including the Border Terrier Flash, whom we have not seen in some time. There are two guys tossing a Frisbee about in our midst and the doggy scene is further complicated by the presence of the lawnmower man, narrowing in on the dog owners in ever decreasing circles. To give them credit, the owners do not take the hint, holding their ground until the man on the machine has had to come to a complete halt—or run over Charlie the Cocker. Fritz, meanwhile, has departed this scene to undertake a long investigation of the bushes between the Grantully gate and the bandstand. I follow as we work our way slowly around to the clubhouse—at which juncture Dorothy arrives and we all head in for coffee.

It takes forever for the latter to appear on our table—since the waitresses, several of them quite new to their tasks, have arrived late for work because of problems on the underground. Today we have Hanna, Dan, Georgie, Kate (often absent with the nagging Skye) and Michael the Pirate. The latter smells like someone who has succeeded with his garlic soup recipe. Conversation naturally turns to the local crime blotter. Last night some miscreants set off an explosion and fire next to the recycling bins at the end of Essendine Road. Georgie reports that two chaps have taken advantage of the bank holiday crush to steal £500 from the premises of the Neald pub, and that a friend went missing when he set out for fish and chips on Marylands Road recently. Seems that while he was in the establishment a chap with a baseball bat came searching for an enemy—whereupon the proprietor locked the door, making all his customers prisoners. The police were called and the hostages freed—but they still had to pay for their fish suppers.

Thursday, August 31:

As I have appointments to keep after our morning session in the park, my preparations take on a different character today. I am wearing my best walking shoes, a pair of dark cords neither encrusted in paw prints nor tattered at the cuff, a clean sweatshirt and my pack is on my back. I shove neither ball nor bag of puppy kibble in my pockets (though there are a few dog biscuits) and there is a good deal of rain equipment in my knapsack. We are ready to roll.

The first new face I see on the green is Liz, reunited with Roxy, and back from her summer holidays on Cape Cod. She buys everyone coffee when we sit down a few minutes later. Ronnie comes in after checking on the health of his mother, who was taken to St. Mary's yesterday after passing out. While we are at table he receives a call from Camden Social Services, checking on her recuperation. (Tory Ronnie always has a positive word to say about the level of care offered by this great stepchild of Socialism.) Dan and Davide are both present and I happen to mention that Ryan Air may soon be permitting mobile phone calls in mid-flight. This propels Dan into a furious impression of what we will soon have to put up with from our seatmates—"Hi—I'm on the plane now. We're having chicken sandwiches and we're *soooo* far up."

As I get up to leave I see Ofra, who has has just returned after seven or eight weeks in Israel, that is during the entire length of the war in Lebanon. I don't get a chance to talk to her because she is on *her* mobile phone—and I have to get Fritz moving toward St. John's Wood, where he loses the use of his legs as soon as he realizes that Karen wants to take him downstairs for a beauty treatment at St. John's Pets.

September, 2006

Friday, September 1:

Often, as I approach the Paddington Rec's Morshead gate, I can see other dog owners heading for the same spot. Today, a block away, I can already see the large white form of Skye, bouncing along at Kate's side, and just coming around the corner is Koko, at the end of Janet's lead. The little Shih-Tzu soon squats on a patch of grass for her first pee—my dog's nose two inches from her fluffy tail. Truth to tell, this intrusion is not exactly welcomed—as Fritz soon discovers when the little madam rounds on him in furious protest. He has better luck with a little girl who wants to throw him his rubber ball.

Out on the green there is a lively scene under bright but sunless skies. Fritz II is having a series of running wrestling matches with the indefatigable Ziggy. Richard and Christine, as Schnauzer owners, are well positioned to appreciate the beautiful job that Karen has done with my dog's coat. Fritz exploits this attention by demanding cuddles from all his friends, including Michaela, who is circling the green with her mother and Skye the Cairn. (Not surprisingly, my dog does not get a similar greeting from two park personnel—who are chattering next to the Grantully gate in Arabic.) I must say that Fritz does me proud today. He comes back from the café when I whistle. He impresses Richard and Christine by catching the kibble I toss to him and he does well with snagging his bouncing red ball as well. When some of the others head in for coffee he follows—and when we get to the café we encounter Dorothy, who has just arrived.

There are ten of us at table—including Dan, Kate, Ofra, Janet, Georgie, Dorothy, Liz, Richard, and Christine. Three of those present are on their mobile phones. When Kate finishes with hers she tells me that yesterday there was an incident. A friend was arriving in a black cab when Skye jumped up against the window of this vehicle to say hello to the visitor. The cab driver became hysterical and called the police. A van with six cops pulled up three hours later to check out reports of a "dangerous dog," then determined that this was, in fact, a non-incident and sent everyone away. We accompany Ofra on the final walkround. She has lots of tales to tell about the recent conflict in the Middle East where, fortunately, none of her friends or relatives suffered directly, though there were some close calls.

Saturday, September 2:

Just as Fritz and I hit the streets a light rain begins to fall. Fortunately I have donned my rain jacket and I manage to stay reasonably dry thereafter. I can see that the dog owners are sheltering in a number of small groups: the Saturday morning obedience class is centred on the metal gazebo, a second group is under the trees near the loos and a third, represented by Davide, Janet and Georgie, is seated on a sheltered bench at the top of Mt. Bannister. There is a large black dog, with fringe hiding his eyes, who is waiting for his turn with Roland the dog trainer, and Richard says this hairdo reminds him of his mother. "I think I'm going to call this dog Jill," he says.

There are, in fact, four Schnauzers at play this morning, Fritzes I and II, Pepper and—his family returned from their holiday—Oscar. My Fritz has a number of wonderful noisy encounters with Pepper on the walkway outside the loos, where there is a complex scene of chattering owners, wrestling dogs and joggers playing through. Eventually Pepper and Fritz report to the café (I have to chase Pepper from its interior) and we soon have a large group of owners seated around two adjacent tables outside the front door. Fritz jumps into Linda's lap, managing to get paw prints all over her jeans and her shirt, then works his way around the table, lap by lap, until he reaches Richard. There is a lot of buttered toast to distribute and a complimentary plate of sausages also. Winnie distinguishes herself by rounding on poor Sparkie as these dogs are nestled in their owners' laps.

We begin a walkround, the rain having come to an end. Such processions are always halting affairs, but especially today when Skye manages to get herself trapped behind some temporary chain link fencing and Fritz sneaks under Sparkie's lead so that Georgie has to untangle the ensuing knot. Then Skye takes exception to something Sparkie does and the two have to be separated. I'd like to get inside (and out of my wet shoes) but Linda and Dorothy can't talk and walk at the same time—and I end up standing around at the exit gate like a dummy.

Sunday, September 3:

I am a bit too warm in my rain jacket but it looks like we might have more moisture after a blustery night. Fritz is distracted, as we wait for his first poo, by other dogs nearby. First Winnie comes in behind us and then Skye the Alsatian enters as well. When we are squared away we head for the centre of the green where two large dogs, vaguely Labradorian in size, are rolling Ziggy into a tight ball. There are also three little boys observing this play but, unfortunately, one of these lads suffers Ziggy's fate and ends up on the grass. Dan, having caught up, says it's time to join the *small* dogs, and this we do—Fritz soon veering off to chase his red rubber ball.

When we go in for coffee one of the senior baristas, the one who always brings water to the dogs, tells us that this is her last day at work—as she will be returning to Poland to look after her parents. She presents us with a box of chocolates—when, had we known, it should have been the other way round. It does seem churlish, given the kindness of this gesture, that Dan and Ofra both object to the taste of their coffee—Dan returning to the café to ask for replacements. Now it is time to open the box of chocolates. Georgie says she is claiming the Raspberry Mischief. "You want the Raspberry Mistress?" Ofra asks. John, wearing his House of Blues baseball cap, comes in with the giant Alsatian, Ché. He is full of complaint over the negligent treatment his dog has received from some people who were house sitting. Meanwhile Ché squats for his patented patio poop.

The conversation turns to the recent police swoop on an Islamic school in East Sussex, described by Kate as a "Hogwarts for terrorists." While this is being discussed Fritz has edged from my lap to Dorothy's and has placed two paws onto Dan's lap, a mischievous act of provocation since Winnie is also there. Soon she reacts to this incursion with spirit and Fritz has to be retracted. This is not good news for Bailey, sitting on Ofra's lap, since the Pug now attacks him as a second best option. We get up to begin our walkround. I notice that a young mother is about to suckle her infant at the next table. I tell Kate, "I'm surprised Metty doesn't charge corkage."

Monday, September 4:

It's a grey morning but temperatures are mild enough as Fritz and I make our way toward the entrance gate. Dan, who must have an early work schedule today, is just putting Winnie and Koko into his car. Fritz begins to nose around, passing Elvis and checking in with Sandy and Jack. The green is almost empty and so I begin to circle the central space, Fritz still on lead. Just as I am cleaning up the required poo I encounter Franca, walking with Tanya the dog warden. I ask the latter if the lab report has come back with information about the suspected poisoning incident. She says there has been a delay (which shows just how little such matters count). I then ask her about the proposal that park personnel be allowed to issue citations to dog-foulers. She says she hasn't heard anything about this and storms off to the park offices for a clarification.

There is no activity at all on the green now and Fritz and I have the place to ourselves as we keep the red jingle ball in play. Down the hill comes Kate, using her ball sling to keep Skye amused. She can see that I am heading for the café so she gives me money for her traditional tea. "What size?" I ask. "Large—everything about me is large," she replies.

We have only a small group at breakfast—just me, Ronnie, Kate, Liz, and Georgie. Liz tells us that she has commissioned a watercolour portrait of Roxy. Kate says that her office is near the National Portrait Gallery and I ask whether she knows how to get there anymore—since she seems to do much of her work at home, over lunch, or on the phone. Then she takes out a hairbrush and begins to groom Skye. Naked Frank, the Chinese Crested Dog, pokes his nose into this process. "No wonder," someone says, "he's never seen a hairbrush before." We begin a walkround. Kate says that a rat has been run over by so many cars at the end of her mews that its carcass is embedded like wallpaper on the cobbles.

Tuesday, September 5:

Under muggy grey skies Fritz rushes forward to growl at Skye the Alsatian as the two again reach the entrance gate at the same time. Only Georgie is in place in the centre of the green, and she is being besieged by the Irishman whom Hanna dislikes, and so, after his Murphy twice growls at me, Fritz and I head for a friendlier collection of dogs at the foot of Mt. Bannister. The red ball comes out but after a few tosses I can see that Fritz is in the grips of wanderlust, and so I have to follow him along the Randolph roadway until I can redirect his attention to the ball, which I have rolled in the direction of the café.

When we enter the sacred precincts they are still putting out tables and chairs (the caff will evidently return to its earlier opening hours, at least on weekends, later this month) and Ronnie, Georgie and I sit on a bench—Rosie lashing out at Fritz, who is innocent, for once. When we move to our traditional table we are joined by Kate, Dorothy, Liz and Dan. The latter is trying to organize a social evening for the dog people, but there is no agreement on whether Friday night or Saturday is best. For some unknown reason Winnie again decides to attack Sparkie, seated on Georgie's lap, and when the little Yorkie is snatched to safety, the pugnacious one turns on Roxy as a substitute. Dan tells us that he had a nightmare last night during which he was attacked by a werewolf—whose shaking of the bed caused him to awaken with a cry. As he opened his eyes he discovered Winnie on the bed, scratching herself.

We begin a walkround. Walking opposite the newly carpeted football field I notice that someone has left a large side gate open and I use this opportunity to step inside and touch, for the first time, the synthetic grass. It feels a little like cellophane, with little black rubbery pellets serving to provide friction and verisimilitude—the surface looks like grass from a distance—with muddy patches. Unfortunately my incursion into this forbidden space encourages Bailey and Jasmine to have a go as well. Soon they are dashing about the field in joyous circles. Corralled at last, we continue on our journey. I tell Ronnie that now that we have these nice wooden signposts on the Randolph roadway (pointing to such locations as Tennis Courts, Netball Court, Pavilion) we are now in a position to add our own directional hints: Annoying Leaf Blower, Broken Clock, Non-Working Hand Dryer.

Wednesday, September 6:

I have a headache, a hangover really, the result of an ill-advised sleeping tablet, and I enter the park this morning in a fog. This is a metaphorical fog—the actual weather is sunny and warm and Fritz, for his part, has slept well and is full of beans. As I near the green I can hear (that is the operative sense) that the park keepers will *not* be doing their part to reduce the pounding in my head. A tractor is being pulled past the café, a leaf blower is manicuring the kiddie's play area and ride-em-lawnboy is circling the green itself—though so little time has elapsed since the last mow that it is hard to know why.

There are quite a few dogs about—and their attached owners, of course. Lizzie is hurling Yoyo's blue Frisbee through the heavens, Flash is making off with Fritz's red rubber ball, and Oscar the Schnauzer is renewing his acquaintanceship with all his pals. I have a fear that Fritz wants to make the acquaintance of a chap who is sitting on the grass in the midst of this mix, drinking coffee and talking on his mobile phone. I have a fear, indeed, that Fritz wants to do this by peeing on the stranger's back. I have to keep an eye on my beast, though, for once, I am content to follow him to the margins—since I don't feel up to socializing.

Dorothy joins us when we go in for coffee. I wait in the queue with Ofra, who has not been to her gym class in two months and who won't be going this week either because her teacher is away. (She also has a dance class.) I tell her that it is possible to exercise without a teacher. Once we are all seated there is a long discussion on the subject of coffee. Dan and Ofra have been complaining about the taste of the local offering and today Ofra has switched to decaf, like me. Davide says that our group is always the first to order in the morning and that in Italy first cups are always thrown away until the newly cleaned machine begins to produce an acceptable taste. Everyone wonders where Hanna has been the last few days but someone suggests that she is home with the builders. There is no one to organize a walkround in her absence and so Dorothy and I head, with our dog, for the closest gate.

Thursday, September 7:

I am certainly feeling a lot better today—perhaps the clear air and sunny skies are here to help me. I am wearing a short-sleeved shirt and there *is* a bit of a chill wind when the sun is absent but, on the whole, this is a delightful day. The clouds are thick and fast moving and as soon as we are cold another breeze serves to restore some warmth. There are a lot of dog people about, taking advantage of the lovely atmosphere. Among them is Jean-Baptiste, whom we have not seen in a long time. He and Tony have been in the south of France for three weeks—Hercules barked for the first ten days.

There is a little girl marching about among the dogs. She pauses to pick up a red ball and throw it at the dogs—but she is very small, can't even throw properly yet, and, at any rate, misses them by a wide mile. I become interested in this object, which turns out to be a fairly new cricket ball. There is damage only to one of its surfaces and it would take an umpire at Lords to determine if someone had been ball tampering—or just let their dog get his teeth into it. After Fritz has chased his own red rubber version of this toy around for a while we go in for coffee and I decide to take the cricket ball into the main office in the pavilion, so that it can be returned to the weekend cricketers when next they show up. I explain my mission to the receptionist (who hails from some Slavic province) and she is quite dubious, having *never* seen a cricket ball before. A green-jacketed member of the park team is standing behind her, however, and he seems to think this gesture is okay.

At breakfast we have Hanna, Ronnie, Georgie, Dan, Davide, Kate, Liz, and Dorothy. Hanna explains that the workers in her flat leave all the doors open all the time and that she can't afford to leave her place unguarded—since the dogs will get out and the thieves get in. Georgie says that Faz and Dianah have reclaimed Jasmine after their holiday and that Sparkie actually had to spend a night without any dog pals. A lot of buttered toast is distributed by Dorothy—with Winnie behaving as though each piece is just for her. Dan says that he has a new garden implement which blows and sucks and that Winnie likes to stand in front of this toy and have all the wrinkles sucked out of her face.

Friday, September 8:

Remembering yesterday's chilly winds I am wearing a sweatshirt today, even though it is again bright and sunny—without a cloud in the skies. The pleasant weather has brought out a large contingent of canines and their owners and the green is almost crowded. Fritz does a preliminary inspection, then heads for the far corners, stopping off to visit with Franca's dogs, Frank and Bianca, at the little hill below the Grantully doggy area, then crisscrossing the green in search of new adventures. On the way we encounter the Yorkielike Rizzo, whose mistress, Denise, is trying to get him into shape with a little spirited exercise, and new mom Tanya, who is here with Pasha and baby Isabella, now ten months old. Pasha meets up with another Weimaraner, a slightly older friend named Barley, and these two, both wearing red collars, have a spirited time chasing one another. Also out on the green is the Fritz-like Schnauzer, Monty.

Fritz finally agrees to enter the mix in the centre of the green, much to the amusement of the other owners—as he soon settles into an extended exercise in attention getting and jealousy. It starts off when Ivana, the owner of Rufus, a young Labrador, kneels to give him a cuddle. Fritz accepts this willingly, but not the presence of Rufus himself—chasing the latter away from his own mistress. Then my dog demands the same attention from Dan, lashing out with his fearsome growls whenever another dog gets close to Dan's feet. Finally Dorothy arrives at the western end of the green and Fritz rushes off to greet her. Winnie and Ziggy do as well, but Fritz won't share his mommy's attentions and chases the other dogs away. It is time to go in for coffee.

There is a long queue in the café and it takes a while for everyone to be served. Today is Sparkie's second birthday and I have brought him a card. Georgie is paying for everyone's drinks and food as part of this celebration and the dogs have a pile of toast and sausages to get through. I am sitting next to Liz, who tells me that our Boundary Road hairdresser, Sali, has finally returned from Lebanon—where he was trapped by the recent conflict for weeks. Liz also says that she and Tom have had a bid on another St. John's Wood house accepted, but that she is prepared to lose this one too—having learned from her last experience just how much of a minefield property buying in Britain can be. Dorothy has been admiring a necklace worn by Ofra who, today, brings in an envelope of jewellery samples made by a friend. Before breakfast is over Dorothy has made an expensive purchase—"It looks like you've just bought me an early birthday present," she says to me.

Saturday, September 9:

As we begin our walk into the park this morning I notice that I am not wearing my proper park shoes. This could be a tragedy if it weren't for the fact that we haven't had any rain in days—and there is no threat from the grass of the green to my suede Clark's. Under pale sunshine and mild temperatures we have a very large doggy turnout today. Indeed the park is buzzing with bodies, including a whole legion of stick-wielding hockeyettes. I see quite a few new puppy faces, including another copper-coloured Cocker named Simon and a lovely longhaired Dachshund named Snoopy. Numbers are swollen today by the addition of the canines of the Saturday dog class. Linda has brought Pepper to the park but she tells me that she has already had a quarrel with Roland, the Czech trainer—since she objects to the way he ties his pupils up (whereupon they spend most of the session barking in frustration) while he devotes all of his attention to one student at a time. "It's not training, it's teasing," she has told him and, although he disagrees, he has refrained from this practice this morning—and I must say things are far quieter.

I am surprised to see Fritz pursuing Sparkie in eccentric circles but the mystery is soon solved when I realize that Sparkie has a squeaky toy, a kind of green rubber alien belonging to Winnie. Before long Fritz has made off with this prize and I realize that there is no chance of his getting any real exercise today. What I don't want to do is chase him down—since the last time I did this he took off for home. A few minutes later he happens to pass near my feet and I manage to hook him on his lead. Then he drops the toy for a fatal instant and I hide it in my jumper. When we go in to coffee a few minutes later I return it to Dan, who is sitting on the opposite side of a table crowded with Davide, Dorothy, Ronnie, Susie, Richard, Christine, Janet, Georgie, Faz (tanned by the Sicilian sun), and Kate.

Fritz soon begins his search for the missing toy, starting with a close study of the underside of the table. When Dorothy attaches our dog to the foot of her chair she makes the mistake of allowing an unlimited amount of lead to emerge from the handle of this object. This gives Fritz the chance to reach Dan and pretty soon he has sniffed out the toy, hidden in Dan's sweatshirt. To forestall further investigation Dan gets up and asks Franca, two tables away, if she will take custody of the toy for him. Fritz persists in circling Dan's chair, even though the latter has placed Winnie in his lap as extra protection. The consequence of this pursuit is that Fritz has soon used his lead to tie Dan's chair up in knots. "I knew he was in to rubber," I say, "but I never realized Fritz was into bondage as well." "Do you suppose he'd like to go out with me on Saturday night?" Dan retorts. Meanwhile Franca has left with her own dogs—and the famous toy—because Blake the Doberman is having a wrestling match with a burly Rottweiler named Bo.

Sunday, September 10:

Fritz and I are a bit late getting into the park this morning—a sleepless night has meant that Dorothy has had to get both of us out of our pit at 9:00. I am wearing my sweatshirt again (and I'm back in my park shoes) but it is quite warm in the sun. I am carrying with me a wad of cash which Dorothy has sent over to pay for the necklace she has purchased via Ofra. I find the latter standing next to Faz and so I say, "This must be the first time this much money has been exchanged in this park for a deal not involving drugs." Fritz now wanders off to the metal gazebo where he does his poo, then we put the ball in play until my dog suddenly expresses an interest in a collection of canines near the Grantully gate. As we approach there is a confrontation between Oscar the Schnauzer and a little black dog on lead. The two are separated, with Fritz supervising, and then, as the little black dog is lead out of the park, my bossy boy follows! I am in a trot now, not far behind, and by the time I reach the Grantully pavement my dog is returning, having seen the snarling stranger off—only to receive a severe scolding for this unauthorized exit.

Shortly after 10:00 we all go in for coffee. The other dog owners are a bit subdued this morning, having exited the Little Bay only at midnight, whereupon most of them continued on to Faz and Dianah's for two and a half hours of karaoke. Ofra now produces a bag of beach pebbles that turn out to be chocolate in disguise. These are shared out, getting mixed up with my bag of puppy kibble only once. Dan and Davide finally arrive and last night's group is reassembled. Those not in the shadow of our table's awning are beginning to complain of the heat and Ronnie gets up once to change seats.

Ten of us begin a walkround, not an easy progress under the crowded conditions of Sunday in the park. A toddler, just learning to talk, wants to pet every one of the dogs, though only Fritz holds still long enough. A little Indian boy then does the same thing. As we pass the five a-side courts there is a furious argument in an unknown tongue among some mahogany warriors in yellow vests. Our way, already restricted by all the construction apparatus, is further complicated by the presence of dogged joggers looking daggers at the jumbled dogs. To get even, Skye the Alsatian decides to make a toy of a large coil of black tubing—which she drags along the path before abandoning it in the middle of the walkway.

Monday, September 11:

It's another pleasant sunny morning and I have abandoned my sweatshirt in favour of a short-sleeved shirt. Fritz begins his sniff and squat routine (the first of *four* such occasions) as we make our way onto the green. I can see that we have a new player in the mix, a seven month-old Boxer pup named Martha. She is soon in action with Skye the Alsatian. I also see Suzanne with Sunny and we have a brief conference on how to get to the American School's annual Trustee's Reception, this year scheduled for Friday at the Imperial War Museum. The park looks a little shop-worn after the Sunday crowds, with many of the trash barrels overflowing and the red doggy bins jammed with poo poo bags. Instead of addressing themselves to this urgent problem the park staff are intent on blowing leaves around outside the café's forecourt.

Fritz is kept busy chasing his red rubber ball—when he is not off exploring—with me in fairly close pursuit as we rumble past the foothills of Mt. Bannister, around the perimeter of the green, over to the Grantully gate (no repetition of yesterday's unplanned exit). Finally we cross the green one last time and head in for coffee. Here I discover that Ronnie has already claimed a table shaded by a large canopy and, as the others (Georgie, Kate, Ofra) arrive, I sit it out, waiting for Dorothy to appear before getting my black decaf.

As often happens Kate begins to receive incoming—mobile phone calls in this case. Her usual response is to see who's calling, turn the ring tone off, and tuck the unit itself into her bra strap. When the phone goes off a second time Ronnie stares at her chest and asks, "Which one is ringing now." "The left one," she responds, "the other one plays the Hallelujah Chorus." Hanna arrives, borrowing a chair from the next table—one that Frank the Chinese Crested Dog has been using to make up a fourth at Franca's table. Also present is Doofie, the park's senior citizen, just a few weeks short of his 21st birthday. Hanna complains that they have forgotten her toast order, but the dogs don't go hungry.

Tuesday, September 12:

"Is there any reason why you have Fritz on lead?" This is a question directed to me by Jo Lynn—only a minute after we have entered the park on a hazy Tuesday morning. I explain that I usually like to keep Fritz in close contact until he has completed his first poo and this answer seems to satisfy. Mission accomplished, we overtake Tilly and head for the green—where already the siren call of a squeaky toy is sounding its seductive bleat. I manage to keep Fritz amused with his rubber ball and one thunderous "No!" keeps him inside the park when he nears the Grantully gate. Thereafter he zeroes in on the squeaky toy, which is actually being manipulated by Charlie the Cocker's owner. She puts it away, so as to avoid provocation, but my dog is insistent. First he climbs her leg, then the leg of Celine, here with Ziggy, then Charlie's mum's leg again—his face wide-eyed in anticipation. To keep him from making a complete fool of himself I have to put him on lead and announce an early departure for the café.

The establishment in question has not even opened its doors yet, though staff members are active in bringing out tables and chairs. This is not to say that there is nothing happening indoors—for I can see that the police car that has just pulled up has disgorged two officers who are interviewing Metty behind the counter. It isn't difficult to see why—for a giant heavy glass window on one wall of the cafe lies shattered in ruins, thieves having helped themselves to the tips belonging to staff, some cash (I hear the figure £47) and some Magnum ice cream bars. I leave Fritz with Ronnie while I talk to a WPC. I tell her that last night, as I was out on my late walk with Fritz, I saw four youths climbing over the Morshead gate with their bicycles. I have no idea if this places them in the frame, and the WPC says they will be checking TV monitors and may get back to me.

We sit down at a table in the pale sun with Kate, Dan, Ofra, Georgie, and Dorothy joining Ronnie and me. Ronnie receives a call from Susie reporting that she is stranded at the City Airport since the place is surrounded by motorways and she is afraid to drive on them. Fritz is jumping from lap to lap, finally reaching Dan—from whom he receives a fulsome cuddle. He is on his back, squealing in delight and someone says, "Fritz, you'll never grow up." He is eventually replaced by Winnie, wearing a pink collar and beaming beatifically. Skye is beginning to agitate for attention, whining at Kate's knee with her patented "Mommy, ball!" impression. This is the sign for a mass exodus and the beginning of a leisurely walkround.

Wednesday, September 13:

Dan and Winnie are just entering the park as Fritz and I arrive. The little Pug is already ahead 2-0 in the poo sweepstakes before we reach the green. I let Fritz roam at this point and he heads almost immediately for the caff, where he selects a convenient trash barrel for the bestowal of his first contribution. Thereafter he heads east, trotting down the Randolph roadway, making many a stop for a sniff, and getting almost to the exit before I can coax him to return to the green with a few well-placed tosses of the red rubber ball.

Once arrived among the dogs ranging around the cricket crease, he has time to remember that yesterday Charlie's mom had a squeaky toy with her—he stops climbing her leg when there is no evidence of its presence today. Then my dog addresses himself to breaking up the spirited play of Roxy and Ziggy, which he considers misplaced in *his* space. Having completed his job as park policeman he heads for the Grantully gate and then does a slow half circle—checking out all the other canines, including the little Korean dog, Gumchee. He seems to tolerate my dogging his steps in all these wanderings, and consents, at last, to be collared as we head in for coffee.

The café still has one of its windows in mourning. Hanna has noted, however, that they kept all their lights on last night, a security suggestion that does not sit well with the stern Finn—"Don't they care about global warming?" Outside, congratulations are in order as Janet is taking delivery today on a new Fiat Panda. Fritz wishes her well by standing in her lap throughout the morning session. Dan says he has planted wisteria outside his kitchen door. Liz says she has been invited to a book launch but she can't remember which book. Ofra's phone rings and it is Dorothy, who has messages for three of us. Liz has to check in on theatre dates, Dan has to stand by to help with the purchase of any needed tickets, and I have to get home because the plumber is on his way. By this time Winnie has bitten both Janet and Kate in the course of her feeding frenzy.

Thursday, September 14:

Fritz and I enter the park after a very stormy night in Maida Vale. Lightning and thunder began almost a four hour assault around nine, letting up just long enough for us to get simply soaked during our late night walk. But as the intensity of this assault increased poor Fritz began to suffer markedly. He started to hunt for hiding places, pawed the carpet in some sort of strange obsessive ritual, and panted uncontrollably. I couldn't sleep, naturally—not only because I had a dog panting in my ear but because we had to close the window against the rain and it was unpleasantly stuffy. Then I remembered that Hanna recommends a dose of Rescue Remedy on such occasions and so I put a drop or two on the dog's tongue, and this seemed to work—or perhaps the thunder just died out.

Today I am keeping a close eye on Fritz, but he seems to be okay. I am about to let him off lead as we approach the green when I decide that there is no point—the park's motorised madness (the tractor picking up trash bags, the leaf blower in front of the club house, and the lawnboy circling the green) having convinced me that it is safer to keep my dog close at hand. We head for the doggy area near the Grantully gate and here, loose at last, he has a good leisurely sniff before we begin a circle of the green ourselves, though at a safe distance. The same can not be said of Charlie the little black Poodle or Roxy the Beagle—both of whom chase the lawnmower down several times. The other dog owners have been driven to a more central position by this encirclement—like sheep in a pen—but at last they break free and head in for coffee.

At the next table Tanya the dog warden is sitting with Chelsea's mom and Franca—the fourth chair being occupied again by the chilly Frank, who has been buried in a coat with a fur collar. Kate is in a bit of a shock after enduring another assault on her personal property by Skye—who has been in her purse and chewed her shoes. Feeling that we may have dodged a bullet this time she turns over to me the mud-splattered petition which has survived the attack on her purse. The dogs, small in number today, have a toast feast and then Dorothy and I get up to head for home. Just as we are about to reach the back passage Georgie reminds us that they have closed this off again—and so we head for the Morshead gate. Overtaking us is a hurrying Peter, commanding the attention of a wandering Hector with the voice of Stentor.

Friday, September 15:

There has been a little light rain this morning and I am wearing my rain jacket as Fritz and I reach the park on a grey Friday. Koko and

Sparkie are arriving just ahead of us—with Janet this time. Fritz, still on lead, is approached by his cousin, Gus, but this is not a welcome visit and a fearsome growl sends the younger Schnauzer packing. On two other occasions Gus makes a similar overture, each time registering his rejection with a look of disappointed bafflement. When we reach the green we can see that Georgie, entering from the Randolph Avenue side, is calling her dog—with Sparkie rushing across the grass for a joyous reunion.

Janet has brought with her a green ball with red spots. It evidently had a much more profound squeak than it now possesses but Fritz is charmed by the object nevertheless and soon makes off with it. As usual, he suspects that I will try to take it off him and he heads for the margins with the prize in his mouth. Gradually he relaxes and we are able to return to the centre of green. Michaela is here with Skye the Cairn and it is gratifying to see that she is just as likely to kick the tennis ball into the flanks of her pet as the rest of us. Meanwhile Sparkie has made off with the green ball, much to Fritz's distress. The mischievous little Yorkie runs in circles, Fritz in lumbering pursuit. When my dog gives up, Sparkie runs by him tauntingly, squeaking the toy as he draws near.

At 9:30 we head in for coffee, joined by Kate, Dorothy, Ofra and Davide. The latter is complaining about the cold, since he has arrived in shorts. His legs are covered in scratch marks applied by the insistent Winnie—who always behaves as though she has never been fed. Davide eats a piece of the dog's toast and takes a call from Dan, who can't find the M1 as he and a friend head for Stanstead and a campground holiday in Sardinia. Hanna arrives after Janet has gone off to work and attaches her dogs to the legs of the vacated chair. Spadge starts to bark hysterically when she goes in to make her order and every time he does this he backs up half a step, pulling the chair with him. Georgie tries to hold on to the chair but gradually it leaves the orbit of her arm. George's lead is taut by this time and he has to get up to follow the chair as well. We are all laughing at this tableau but Hanna doesn't seem so amused when she at last returns. We have been comparing notes on how we survived the thunderstorm of the night before last. Hanna says that she revelled in the heavenly fireworks and—as for her dogs—they were unperturbed. They are, of course, mostly deaf.

Saturday, September 16:

Under grey skies Fritz and I penetrate the park scene, lively with a large Saturday turnout. On our left I can easily tell—from the high-pitched screaming—that the American School hockeyettes are hosting a home game. Charging toward us is Natasha, jogging along with a dancing Leila at her feet. I can see that some of the park regulars are already heading hopefully toward the café, though the clock on the clubhouse cupola, repaired at last, suggests that they may still have a ten-minute wait.

Still in play is Fritz II, whom we often see only on the weekends now since his parents have gone back to work. Richard gives Fritz a squeaky toy—with the understanding that it will be returned later to the large puppy, five months old today. The toy, a round version of a Christmas pudding, takes up temporary residence in my dog's mouth, where it seems to resemble a pair of false teeth. I *do* succeed in extracting it a few minutes later, returning it to Richard covered in slobber. He and Christine head in for coffee but I persist in giving my dog some real exercise, aided not only by his own red rubber ball, but by a beautiful yellow football, a real one undamaged by any doggy teeth marks, that someone has abandoned on the green. I kick this around a number of times, Fritz in pursuit, and, while he is chasing the ball down, I also keep Skye the Cairn's tennis ball in action with my spare foot.

Dorothy arrives and after a brief conference with Kate on the final episode of *Sleeper Cell*, which my wife has failed to record, we head in for coffee. The others are already discussing the news story of the hour—Islam's violent response to a speech by the Pope in which he has quoted an anti-Moslem Byzantine emperor (if only to dispute his assertions thereafter, a nicety lost on the protestors). I suggest that better than burning the Pope in effigy the injured parties should vent their anger on the true source of this outrage—with another attack on Byzantium. While these weighty issues are under discussion the dogs get through a mountain of toast—and then we head off for our exit gates.

Sunday, September 17:

It's a pleasant, sunny Sunday morning and I am back to wearing just a short-sleeved shirt. As Fritz and I enter the park we encounter the little Dachshund, Gigi, and Snowdon, the white Alsatian. Gigi wants to ingratiate herself with Fritz, who, for once, tolerates this attention without growling—though he does just miss the little dog with a stream of pee. Snowdon's owners want to know how the petition campaign is going and so I give them an update. By this time we have reached the green and I unhook my dog to begin his adventures.

There is a dog owners' coven seated on the grass on one side of the cricket crease while a father and son are tossing a Frisbee around on the other. (Nemo, the black Labrador, makes off with this object once, but he is made to yield the prize.) Fritz doesn't seem to be interested in any of this activity and heads off for Mt. Bannister, where he follows a Briard and two Dachshunds uphill. Eventually I get him to chase his red ball but he seems disinterested in this sport and by the time I give up I can see that the other owners have departed for the café, so I follow suit.

The dogs are playing musical laps and Janet notes that, from their perspective, collectively, we humans all belong to *them*. They are scarfing down another super-sized helping of toast as Faz reports on a number of incidents from the crime blotter. A flat was turned over in his building but, since there was no forced entry, the crime was traced back to the cleaners, who had copied the keys of their client. Arrests followed. Faz himself has to report for work at 2:00 this afternoon, but it will be a day behind a desk as he has to get ready for a day in court tomorrow—and he needs to study his notes. It turns out that the suspects have been in custody for nine months, awaiting trial. This seems like a long time without bail but Faz explains that one of the miscreants had only been a day out of jail before re-offending and that the other had 46 arrests on his record. Dorothy, bothered by the sun in her eyes, borrows my dark glasses as we hook up our dog and head for home.

Monday, September 18:

Fritz and I make our way into the park on a cool grey morning. Fritz has a slow smellathon as we approach the green deliberately, and by the time he is unhooked there is not much activity in the centre. This doesn't mean that there aren't other dogs about, just that they are in twos and threes scattered throughout the vast empty space. I try to interest Fritz in his ball but he is not amused today and when we encounter Hanna, making an even slower progress from the Grantully gate to the café, we head for the latter in her company.

We are discussing the brazen fox population that makes its own secret life among our own. Indeed, Fritz spotted something that excited him in the alleyway behind Hanna's flat last night (she heard him barking, but thought it was Yoyo). When we get to the café Fritz doesn't head into the forecourt but disappears out the other side and I have to follow him, catching up just as he is squatting with his second poo over an abandoned black refuse sack in the Carlton roadway. When we sit there is more data in the annals of unsuitable poos. Davide says that Winnie deposited one in a scratchy bush and that he picked up a thorn in his hand as he retrieved it—while Hanna says that last night George snuck into her flatmate's room and left an uninvited offering. "What have you been feeding him?" I ask. "Last night he had a lamb chop, and peas and potatoes," she replies. "He ate better than I did," I conclude.

Fritz now insists on getting his nose into an orange plastic sack containing some of Sparkie's toys. "There are no squeaky toys," Georgie assures him, but he does manage to winkle out a little rubber ball, one that he promptly crushes the life out of with his teeth. Davide then gets a phone call from Dan, just an hour or so before the latter is set to return from his camping holiday in Sardinia. In this fashion we learn that Dan and his pals (whom Davide won't travel with because they get so drunk) have gotten into a fight with some line dancers. Davide is appalled, but you can't tell which bothers him more—that Dan's friends have lead his partner into trouble again or that line dancing has made its way to Sardinia.

Tuesday, September 19:

A brisk, sunny morning greets us as we begin our slow walk toward the green. Fritz pauses to poo next to a trash bin and, as sometimes happens, one offending blob continues to adhere to his backside when this process is complete. All of our Schnauzers, it seems, have usually chosen to freeze at such moments—refusing to press on until the offending object is somehow removed. It is removed, in almost all cases, through the good offices of the dog's master, and so it is today. I take a small stick and have a go—but the blob is so liquid that it simply drips down Fritz's backside, and there is no way to complete the clean-up process. This means that my dog will not be sitting in any laps this morning, especially not mine.

Again I have great difficulty in interesting Fritz in any exercise. I follow him all over the place as he visits small knots of dog owners, spread all over the green. He checks out Tara the Kerry Blue and Yankee the Labrador and then I see him heading for the clubhouse. There is a vehicle about to cross his path but, for once, I don't worry about this intersection since the vehicle is being driven by the always cautious Tanya, the dog warden. After she passes by Fritz heads along the walkway that leads to the clubhouse offices and then into a surviving corner of our old private picnic grounds. Here I run him down him in a fenced corner and we emerge outside the pavilion entrance, where they are just setting off their own burglar alarm in a controlled experiment.

We walk over to the café next and, after leaving Fritz with Ronnie, I go in to order my coffee. Here I learn that thugs have again conducted an assault on the premises, cracking but not breaking the same window that was shattered last week. Hanna says that she heard them hammering on this thick sheet of glass last night at 10:30. I was walking down Grantully about 45 minutes later and did observe the well-lit café and one of the new recycling bins on its side at the Grantully gate, where it had already demonstrated its usefulness as an instrument of escape. Over coffee, where a tanned Dan ends up with both Winnie and Bailey in his lap at the same time, we continue to discuss crime. Our own resident thug, Winnie, attacks both Bailey and Koko, and Ronnie, who used to own jewellery stores, adds another chapter in the poetic justice department. "They broke one of *my* plate glass windows once," he says, "they succeeded in shattering the glass but when the police examined the debris they did find two fingers."

Wednesday, September 20:

Fritz and I are a bit late as we make our way into the park this morning but we approach the green rapidly and soon we are among the regulars milling about in a bright, brisk sunshine. Almost as soon as we arrive, however, I can see the other dog owners heading for the café and so I try to keep Fritz moving as we visit the margins of the green. He shows no interest in chasing his red ball for quite a while but eventually I manage to get his attention and he charges down the hill in pursuit.

When it is time to join the others I tie Fritz to a busy table in the forecourt and disappear for a few minutes, a man on a mission. This requires me to march over to the clubhouse for a little venting. I get the attention of a Courtney's official—once he has dealt with the problem of tennis courts locked in the face of eager QK students (probably a good idea)—and have a go. "Did you know that there was a football game, with all the floodlights glaring, until 10:30 last night?" The chap *does* seem to know and indicates that they've been expecting protests (the park officially closes an hour earlier) but that they had double booked and it was a cup final (aren't they all?) and that Westminster said it was okay. I point out that when floodlights were first installed years ago there was neighbourly consultation, and that we were promised that the park would close at 9:00. This is news to the current park management, which has gradually extended (business) hours. I am assured that last night's episode was a one-off and that my concerns will be passed on to the park manager.

I return to the café and get in line for my small black decaf. The Slavic waitress has so little English that she thinks the "milky tea" ordered by my predecessor in the queue means "tea with no milk"—so there is some delay. At our table Janet (and her friend, also Janet) are getting ready for their motor trip to Cornwall. They are passing around photos of their former selves, vacationing on Sark. The subject of plastic surgery comes up (Dorothy and Liz having sighted Sharon Osbourne at a charity gala performance of *Wicked*). Dan does a wonderful impression of a trout-pouting bimbo. Skye the Alsatian is barking in my ear, a piercing sound indicative of her desire to have a bit more exercise. Kate gets up to honour this demand and I use this opportunity to make my exit as well.

Friday, September 22:

An all-night rain has just stopped as Fritz and I head for the park. I have missed a day in Paddington Rec, having spent a very warm and sunny Thursday hiking in Hertfordshire. No one would call today warm or sunny, but there is a knot of loyal dog owners standing in the centre of the green and here we head. Or here I head, I should say, for Fritz isn't interested in any of this—taking off immediately in pursuit of Ellen and following Jack and Sandy as they head for the Randolph Avenue gate. This means that I have to follow as well. I spend a great deal of energy trying to interest my dog in the delights of his own red rubber ball, but it does take me a while to get him turned around. Even then he seems more interested in ranging along the margins of our great public space and at 9:30, when the others head for the café, we follow suit.

There is only a small group of dog owners at table this morning—Kate is off to view another house and doesn't have her usual weak tea, and Hanna is slow to arrive with Spadge and George. This means that only Georgie, Dan and Faz are seated when I return from ordering my coffee. There is a rainy puddle at our feet and doggy paw prints have soon decorated my tan trousers in brown. Sparkie is operating at his mischievous best. He jumps into my lap, gives me a big kiss, and then starts barking at Fritz, trying to wind my dog up. Somehow the topic turns to dangerous animals. Faz tells the story of the tour guide who told his charges that it was okay to swim in this lake, only to have two of them eaten by crocodiles. Dan says that he wouldn't go into any body of water in Australia—since the entire continent is full of animal peril. "I was once at Manly Beach," he explains—only to be interrupted by Faz, "*You* were at Manly Beach?" Dan accepts the goodnatured insult as I tell Faz, "Just because he hands you a straight line doesn't mean you have to use it." Faz returns to more survivals from the dinosaur era—"to survive all you needed was large teeth and a small brain." "Then Jasmine must have a great chance of survival," Dan retorts, getting his revenge at last.

We all head off at the same time for the Morshead gate. Fritz, having had so little exercise, is eager to show off, dancing ahead with his lead in his mouth. Jasmine, off lead, begins to tease him by charging in and out until he chases her away. Dan, meanwhile, has just stepped in a pile of puppy poo—with Faz suggesting that this is just retribution for the earlier insult about Jasmine's tiny brain. As we near the gate five or six black girls are heading into the park with their notebooks and mobile phones—one of which is chipping in with a tune from *Carmen*. They are discussing their urgent need for spending money and this reminds Faz that while he was at boarding school he earned £20 with a weekend job and used the money, to the delight of all, to buy fish and chips for all his mates. "But you see," I conclude, "you made an early connection between effort and reward. We have lots of guys in our society who have yet to make this connection."

Saturday, September 23:

Today Dorothy departs for a three day junket to Brussels (in order to visit her sister and her niece) and we have arranged for her to make her departure just *after* Fritz and I have left for the park—so as to save the dog from the unnecessary anxiety of this separation. We have a lovely, warm and sunny early autumn day for our outing. The ASL hockey team is warming up in the first field, their sticks rattling together in some obscure sporting ritual. Dan is just leaving with Winnie as we at last reach the green, a space lively with dogs and their owners—including Roland's Saturday morning obedience class.

We usually see Fritz II on Saturday mornings and I am anxious to see if he has arrived today. I think I see him mixed up with the other pupils but when I approach I discover that there is a *second* Standard Schnauzer in our midst, a year-old grey bruiser with a jewelled blue collar named Casper. I have to encourage Fritz to move away from the easily distracted scholars, and he is soon pursuing Jasmine and Sparkie as Georgie and Faz head for the Randolph gate. At one point my dog finds a narrow space behind the newly refurbished tennis courts but I am able to call him back with the prospect of some puppy kibble treats. Faz and Georgie are over at this end of the park because a dog, with Sparkie's ball in his mouth, has run away in this direction. We don't find the ball and shortly before 9:30 we head in for coffee—just us three.

The café staff have already started on the orders for the other two, soon brought out to us by Elian, who also takes my order. This is service—since they haven't even gotten any money from any of us yet. Faz is basking in the warm sunshine as he and Georgie both celebrate another day without smoking. Georgie is on her way to the hospital to visit the old age pensioner Tom, whom she keeps an eye on and who is now dying of cancer. Ronnie and Hanna come in just as the rest of us are about to leave and Richard and Christine walk by with Fritz II. I tell them about Casper and they head out to the green where an aggressive little black dog has just been dumped on by the rest of the pack. Jeremy is also here with her Cressida; she spills her coffee when she trips over the curved bottom of the gate pillar. I excuse myself at this point—as Fritz and I head for our exit.

Sunday, September 24:

A brief rainy spell has just cleared as Fritz and I head for the park on a pleasant Sunday morning. There is not much action on the green itself—just Georgie throwing a new ball to Sparkie. I bring out the red rubber ball and Fritz has a go at this, but before long we hear the seductive sound of a squeaky toy somewhere else on the green. I can see my dog streaking toward Charlie the Cocker and then heading away in triumph, a yellow ball his prize. Unfortunately this turns out to be Charlie's favourite toy and the Asian man who has brought him today is quite anxious to have it back. I promise to return it eventually but I have to stalk my dog for about five minutes before retrieving it. This is really embarrassing.

In the meantime Georgie has been joined by Dan, Davide and Faz. They head in for coffee soon thereafter but just then Fritz II appears with Richard and Christine. The large puppy is full of beans this morning and keeps trying to get Skye the Alsatian to play with him. He makes great loping charges at Skye's head but she is only interested in chasing her ball. He has no better luck with my Fritz, who chases him away from Richard's knee since the latter is petting my dog and Fritz doesn't want any distractions.

I tie my dog to a leg of a table, where Hanna, Kate and Ofra have now joined the others, and head in to order my coffee. Kate tells us that she has bought a house in West Kilburn, indeed she bought a house last week as well but her engineer said it needed so much work that she'd be in negative equity before she moved in. I tell her that I have to repeat what I said to Dan when he finally secured his new flat near the Harrow Road—"There goes the neighbourhood." Dan and Davide have by now had time to identify their problem neighbours, some of whom require regular police attention when they descend to domestic abuse. Hanna asks me if I have ever thrown anything in anger (I can't recall having done so) and adds that it is quite therapeutic. Dan says that he and a boyfriend once had a slagging match that ended when Dan destroyed every one of his friend's Peter Pan figurines, starting with Tinkerbelle. The image of fractured ceramic reminds me that I have to get home for the tiler—and so Fritz and I make an early departure.

Monday, September 25:

There is an early sign of park life at 9:00 this morning when, while shaving, I can already hear Dan's voice out on the street calling for Winnie. When Fritz and I emerge a few minutes later I am surprised to see a wet pavement—it is spitting just a bit and I have nothing more useful as protection than the bill of my cap. Nevertheless we persevere, making our slow progress out to the green—where Fritz rushes forward to see all his pals, standing at the far end.

Indeed there is a second set of owners back near the cricket crease and this gives Dan a chance to pretend that here we have the Jets and the Sharks about to have a rumble in Paddington Rec. Janet is back from her Cornish holiday and so is Koko. Sparkie has a new green ball. Skye the Alsatian is chasing tennis balls and Fritz is chasing Gus away from our group in the latest version of his patented "I'm the only Schnauzer in this park" routine. Thereafter he begins a wandering circuit, me in pursuit, and by the time I have gotten him turned around with his red ball the others have headed for the comforts of one of Metty's outdoor awnings.

Sparkie immediately makes himself at home in my lap, where his wet paws have a chance to dry out. Georgie has noticed that there is a sign attached to the Morshead gate seeking help in locating a missing toy Yorkie. The photo shows a dog who even looks like her long-disappeared pet, Pebbles, and there is a lump in her throat. She has broken down and bought ten cigarettes on the way to the park but Faz, who arrives late, says that he is now in his fourth no smoking day—though yesterday he felt so ratty he wanted to shoot someone. "In the line of duty," I add. "No," he corrects me, "I just wanted to shoot somebody." Skye is nagging Kate with her piercing whine, which I can even begin to understand, "Wee wee now!" Kate gets up to head for the green, where it turns out that Skye just wants to play, but I follow this pair out and head for home in the drizzle.

Tuesday, September 26:

It's bright outside (I am wearing my dark glasses) but there is still a bit of a chill in the air as Fritz and I make our way onto the green. Again there are two groups of dog owners. One, stationed in the metal gazebo at the foot of Mt. Bannister, is presided over by the pregnant Franca, who is discussing childbirth options. Not far away we have Dan, Liz, Davide and a woman named Trudy—who has brought with her the rangy sheepdog Phoenix and a noisy Dachshund named Freddy. The latter is trying to get a rise out of Winnie, barking at the Pug until she emerges from beneath the legs of an owner to chase her tormentor away.

Fritz, for his part, is having no part in this, and travels widely around the eastern margins of the park, emerging from his reverie only when he spots Yoyo, who is accompanied today by both Tim and Lizzie. I get an update on the world of wallpaper. The pair have just completed another trade show and they are also working on a project at the Winn Hotel in Las Vegas. Lizzie offers Fritz a piece of sugar-free flapjack. He eats it anyway. She says that Fritz is the only dog tolerated by Yoyo, who disappears every few minutes to chase her blue Frisbee. I have to excuse myself after a few minutes since I can see that my dog has already gone in for coffee.

I arrive just in time to foil Roxy's attempts at pinching a cheese croissant from Trudy's plate. I then find out how Trudy knows Dan. They have met while walking their dogs at Lincoln's Inn, where Dan takes Winnie when she has accompanied him to work. He tells me that there is a dog society there too, and that they even have their own web site. More intriguingly, one of the leading figures is this society is John, the son of one of the former stalwarts of Paddington Rec, the late Doreen Lehar. We met Doreen when we had our first Schnauzer, Bertie, over twenty years ago. Her ball-obsessed Jack Russell, Harvey, was a part of Bertie's pack and little Ben, a second Jack Russell whom Doreen acquired when Harvey died, was a part of our Toby's circle. When Doreen herself died we were obviously concerned about the fate of Ben—but we heard that John had adopted him and that he had moved to Covent Garden. Dan says that Ben, whom he often saw at Lincoln's Inn, died last winter. Rarely are we able to follow the exploits of former Paddington dogs as in this case—so it is nice to have a chapter closed at last. At the end of our session Roxy jumps up and steals the remaining half of Trudy's croissant.

Wednesday, September 27:

Fritz and I head for the green under grey skies and here we discover an instant replay of yesterday's dog scene. Freddy (of Freddy and Phoenix fame) is once again barking hysterically, his teeth bared, at

Winnie, and Winnie, after enduring this insulting behaviour for several seconds, charges out and chases him away. The only variation today is that Freddy actually manages to bite his adversary on the bum. This unusual behaviour is explained by the fact that, as a puppy, the little Dachshund was attacked by a Pug—and ever since then he has borne a special antipathy to all representatives of the breed.

While we are standing in our little circle Liz wanders onto the green—accompanied by the rotund Roxy. "I'm in despair," she says, "I don't know what to do with her—last night my dog ate two pizzas!" At first we think that Roxy has somehow managed to purloin two *slices* of pizza but, no, we heard right—the greedy beast waited until the babysitter had laid out the recent delivery on the diningroom table—and then pounced, while no one was looking. A second order had to be phoned in and Liz, when she got home, decided that her pet was sure to explode. "I gave her Perrier instead of regular water to ease her digestion," she says. Roxy, however, shows no signs of distress and is soon mixing it up with the exuberant Ziggy.

Fritz manages to stay fairly close to the pack and when he wanders off I keep him interested in chasing his own ball. Early on in the proceedings Dorothy arrives with a box of biscuits from Brussels and we go in for coffee. The dogs get through a mountain of toast while their owners keep a wary eye on their own croissants whenever a Beagle's nose appears above the lip of the table. Georgie spends the session with a plastic cigarette substitute in her mouth but Faz says he is now on his sixth no smoking day and Dianah on her fourth. We make our way toward the Morshead gate where, often these days, Davide or Dan gives Ronnie and Rosie a ride home in the car.

Friday, September 29:

I have missed another Paddington day with my second Thursday walking expedition in a row. After thirteen strenuous miles on a bum left leg I am not in the best of moods, and it certainly doesn't help when Fritz pulls on his lead in the early stages. I let him loose after he has done his poo (not the solid consistency one would hope for) and he makes his way onto the green—where there is a large turnout of dog owners under threatening grey skies.

When Fritz starts to wander around the periphery of the green I have to follow him wearily, making slow progress as we pause at one sniffing patch after the other. We spend some time in the company of Scamp and Oscar the Schnauzer; Sabina is keeping Oscar on lead because she has endured two recent unpleasant incidents—first Oscar was attacked by Paddy, though the latter's muzzle prevented major damage. Then a jogging black man threatened to have Oscar put down if he didn't keep his distance. By this time we have done practically a full circle and Fritz is ready to return to the mid-crease ruck, where a yellow hedgehog belonging to Ziggy proves to be a major attraction. So also does David the dogsitter, who is keeping an eye on Skye the Alsatian today. Ziggy's mom (Celine) says she would never bring a ball if it had a squeak because she knows Fritz's ways, but there is a reasonable chance he will release the hedgehog—and so he does. Dan makes arrangements for Rhianne, who is clutching Otw, to take some professional photos of Winnie.

We go in for coffee so that Dorothy and Liz can relive the highlights of last night's caper as book launch party crashers. Their "victim" had been Martin Amis (who has played tennis in our park in the past) and Liz (who had actually forged a set of invitations) introduced the puzzled author to an Asian couple whom she called Mr. Barnes and Mrs. Noble. Behind us there is a crash. A black-faced fuzzy puppy of some size has been tied to a chair; when it tips over he becomes frightened and dashes off, the chair in pursuit. Now terrified, the pup dashes all over the place—with several people, including the very pregnant Franca, in pursuit. Quiet has just been restored when it begins to rain and everyone scatters. There is still some protection under the cover of the trees and we are only slightly sodden when we at last make it home.

Saturday, September 30:

More rain has slashed its way through the park overnight; indeed the skies have only just cleared when Fritz and I make our way through the gates. For Fritz the storm has been most unsettling and the thunderclaps that followed each lightning bolt (just three and a half hours earlier) have brought on another panic attack, with panting and rug pawing as the chief attributes. I had to get up to keep him company, dosing him again with a few drops of Rescue Remedy. He seems okay now and makes his usual slow progress out to the green, where we have the Saturday obedience class on the left and the rest of the dog owners on the right.

Things start off in a lively enough fashion when my dog is blindsided by his pal Pepper. Linda sees that the latter is beginning to interfere with the concentration of the obedience pupils, including the Standard Schnauzer Casper, and she takes her dog off. Fritz steals a little boy's ball and after this is retrieved he is again content to steal Ziggy's yellow hedgehog. (It's all right—Ziggy is happy to make off with Sparkie's decayed tennis ball.) I get a chance to congratulate Georgie on her winning over £1000 in the national lottery—there is universal agreement that she is not to let him indoors drink up her winnings but Georgie says that she may just use it to hire a hit man instead. David again has Skye and there is real jealousy from the large white dog when Fritz arrives for an obligatory cuddle. When it is time to go in for coffee we invite Celine, Ziggy's mom, and, though she has brought no money with her, she agrees to accept our hospitality.

Dorothy has just arrived with Liz, but there are fumes rising from the latter's ears—after a domestic barney involving a forgotten ticket to Bermuda and a Blackberry that has not survived its visit to the nearest wall. Winnie is sitting in Dan's lap (snapping at the other dogs), Bailey is getting a grooming in Ofra's lap (with clouds of hair blowing in our faces) and even Ziggy still thinks he's a lap dog. After several weeks' absence Albert returns, this time with both of the Yorkies—Saffy, whom we have met before, and Tinkerbelle. Lots of other dogs are running around our table, inciting in Fritz a proprietary growl. First we have Rebel, then Max the Boxer, who seems capable of pulling down the entire fence he is tethered to, then Frank in his Superdog costume. We have a jolly time and then Dorothy and I have to get ready for an expedition to Sainsbury's.

October, 2006

Sunday, October 1:

Another rainstorm had lashed its way through London during the night, but now the sun is fighting it out with the clouds as Fritz and I make our way into the park for the first session of a new month. While Georgie keeps Sparkie busy chasing his ball, the other dog owners are gathered in a knot around Dan, who has arrived with Davide. Davide has just returned from a trip to Hong Kong and Dan has just returned from a night on the tiles. The latter occasion was an annual reunion with pals whom he met years ago when they were all working as ushers for the Drury Lane theatre. Dan had gotten so drunk (and perhaps he still is) that he had fallen onto his face on the Strand (where there are often quite a few prone people) and hurt his ankle—which is swelling up as we speak. On the bus home he met a couple; he somehow remembers that the girl sat on his lap but he can't quite recall how the guy managed to tattoo his arm with the legend "George Loves U."

Ziggy arrives and soon begins to mix it up with Humpty. There is a size mismatch in this pair but Ziggy can run faster than the Basset Hound and he does manage to chew on Humpty's ears. We also have three Shih-tzus present since Jasmine has just come in with Faz and Janet has both Koko and Jonesie. Fritz, as usual, has little interest in this melee. He begins a single-minded trot along the Grantully hedges and only looks up occasionally to see if I am still trailing. I get him to chase the red ball a few times but just as we all seem to be heading in for coffee he spots two unknown dogs heading for the Randolph gate and he has to join their pack—with me in slow pursuit well behind. Fortunately he turns back by the time I get over to the Randolph walkway and we are soon headed for the café.

We have a good turnout at table—including Dorothy, Dan and Davide, Ofra, Janet, Celine, Jo Lynn, and, eventually, Ronnie and Hanna. Dan has the full English while Dorothy distributes toast. The skies are again beginning to darken and we add a large purple umbrella to our table. Sure enough it begins to drizzle but we persevere long enough to sing a medley of songs from the *Sound of Music* before heading for home. Just as we are nearing our steps the heavens open up again and we begin another day of showers and thunder that soon enough has poor frightened Fritz pawing the turf.

Monday, October 2:

There is a touch of cool autumn in the air this morning, but there is a bit of sun as well. We meet Hanna at the Morshead gate and my first impulse is to say, "Haven't you forgotten something?" since she is, for once, unaccompanied by any dog. She tells me that she has been out with the dogs a bit earlier and is now just coming back for coffee. We soon meet up with the trio of Michaela, Liz and Suzanne. The latter draws me aside to ask about the dogless Hanna. I suppose there is always a fear that when you seen the owner of dogs as elderly as Spadge and George now walking without either animal that perhaps some tragedy has ensued.

Out on the green Ziggy is chasing around with a young Lab named Rufus. The latter is covered in muddy paw prints. David is out here with Skye again and he and I discuss the intricacies of American football. Fritz begins his daily ramble, crossing the green to visit with Oscar and Scamp. When we return to the cricket crease Dan is just arriving with Winnie. She has a pee and Fritz immediately sticks his nose into the wet grass. "I'm not kissing you this morning," Dan says to my dog, "I know where your face has just been."

As we begin our march to the café Dan suddenly comes to a realization—he was supposed to pick up Koko at Janet's house before coming to the park this morning! Davide is dispatched by mobile phone to complete this errand and Dan turns to his coffeemates in order to make sure that no one lets Janet know about this little gaffe. I suggest that no one will say anything now, but at some time, perhaps three or four years from now, Janet will read this account of Monday, October 2, 2006—and the secret will be out. At this point Dan forestalls all such difficulties by phoning Janet at work and, on speakerphone setting, confessing all. Janet laughs and this part of the crisis is over. Fritz now jumps into Dan's lap, sticks his suspect face into Dan's latte, gives his whiskers a shake, and sprinkles foam all over my eyeglasses.

The other part of the day's crisis involves Davide, who is more than cross. He calls from Janet's house to report that Koko is growling at him and refusing to go on lead. "Bribe her with some food," Dan says. Then he explains to the rest of us that at 5:00 this morning Winnie had started to throw up on Davide's sleeping face and that he had caught the offending matter in his own hands instead. Unfortunately he lost all the gratitude that this gesture deserved when, climbing back into bed after washing his hands, he inadvertently struck Davide in the face with his elbow. The victim now arrives with Koko, who looks like a thundercloud. Dan tries to cheer his partner up but Davide continues with a catalogue of grievances—it seems that drunken Dan made several unremembered phone calls on his way home from his adventures on the Strand. Skies are darkening now and, fearing a repetition of yesterday's tempest, we all scatter.

Tuesday, October 3:

There is definitely a touch of autumn in the air this morning; a real chill presides over the darker corners of Paddington Rec and I am looking forward to standing in the sunshine of the brightly sunny green. Unfortunately my wishes have nothing to do with the pace of my dog, who continues to be as slow as molasses. We work our way past the prams and a leaf blower in our path and finally get the first order of business out of the way in front of the clubhouse.

Fritz is then freed to seek out David the dogsitter, still accompanying the ball hawking Skye. The Mastiff Rambo is in evidence today (David warns Fritz not to mix it up with the bruiser) and so is Rya, the delightful Westie puppy. Dan, on his way to work, gives way to Davide, and Georgie and Ofra arrive as well. I don't have an opportunity for much chat because I have to follow Fritz in his perambulations. These include a long stop at the loos, where Peter (of Peter and Holly) has just gone into the men's room to fill up a water trough for the dogs. The red rubber ball comes into play and I manage to get Fritz to return to the green in time for the place to lose all its resident population to the café.

Dorothy arrives and there is a long conversation with Ofra on the subject of shoe sizes and the wonders of the Top Shop. Liz says that her husband has at last discovered the SIM card belonging to the shattered Blackberry. Davide gets a call from his missing builders, who have lost their keys and need him to come home to let them in. He tells them he'll be there in ten minutes but says to us that this will be just a pit stop for him. He's heading for Janet's quiet flat with Koko—and as long as the builders are in-house he plans to stay there.

Wednesday, October 4:

Another crisp sunny morning sees us enter the park just as Kate is departing with Skye, and Dan, leaving Winnie with Davide, is heading for work. The little Pug is continuing to show signs of stomach distress, munching on the grass at her feet in a gesture we often see when dogs feel the need to adjust the balance of their digestive tract. Fritz visits the four corners of the green without quite disappearing and so I am able to stay in conversation with Davide and Liz. I am in a good mood, having solved Dorothy's computer problems the night before. Scamp and Oscar the Schnauzer come out to greet us and Fritz doesn't chase them away for once. I can see my dog's white tail bobbing around outside the café fence and so I follow the others in at coffee time. By this time, of course, I discover that Fritz has only played through and is nosing around on the Carlton roadway.

For some reason two tables have been pulled together in the centre of the café forecourt, though today, with only Georgie, Hanna, Ronnie, Davide, Liz and Dorothy present, we could easily have done with one. Ronnie, with his 60th birthday fast approaching, is making plans to get his bus pass—though he never uses public transportation. Behind us the ticking Spadge gradually retreats from his anchored lead, the one attached to Hannah's chair, and backs up into a chair containing only a tennis racket. The chair collapses on the poor confused animal but the tennis bimbo, considering herself sorely put upon, won't even acknowledge Hanna's apology.

There is a good deal of doggy activity going on all around us. Roxy, having made off with only one bite of Hanna's croissant and half a napkin, has climbed atop an empty table in the corner and then stationed herself at Franca's feet. Frank, in his Superdog cape, is sitting on his own chair—which Franca moves into the sun for the always frigid dog. He snatches Bianca's toy out of her mouth and, from his lofty position, teases her with it. Meanwhile, Hector is sitting in a tree well, trying to bury his biscuit and all his toys in the earth. We get up to leave but now new dogs are coming into the park for the first time—as we pass Giant, Leila and Ziggy on the way to our gate.

Thursday, October 5:

I am keeping a close eye on Fritz as we enter the park on a cool, grey Thursday morning. This is because yesterday afternoon, as we were completing our afternoon walk, there was an incident. Peter was walking his Hector and Jody, both on lead, as we rounded the corner near the school. As usual, Fritz attempted his tough man growl at this pair, but this time Jody snapped back, quite surprising our dog, who seemed to be in shock for much of the rest of the evening. He wouldn't eat his dinner, for instance, and seemed quite subdued. This morning he trots along with his usual insouciance, so I guess he is okay.

There is a spirited dog scene near the cricket crease, with Rufus and Sasha rolling one another over in the mud. The Alsatian Ryah is also here and Ziggy is mixing it up with Roxy. Fritz doesn't seem to be very interested in any of this. Soon he wanders over to the Grantully gate and seeks admission to the doggy area nearby. There is no one else present, unless you count a flock of pigeons, soon sent skyward. After we return to the green Fritz heads over to see what Jack and Sandy are up to and soon thereafter he follows them into the café and I follow all of them.

Everyone is complaining about the return of cold weather and the little dogs are seeking out laps where they can keep warm. Sparkie sits in Suzanne's lap, Winnie in Davide's, and Bailey moves from my lap to Ronnie's. At the next table Frank, always susceptible to cold, is wearing a t-shirt and a camouflage suit. He is soon joined by the giant Doberman, Blake—and by Tanya the dog warden. I ask her if there has ever been any definitive pronouncement on Blake's illness. Tanya now says that it *wasn't* poison—after all the paranoid mutterings. I comment, "I hate to say it, but this is good news"—and Tanya agrees. No one wants to linger for long in the chilly air and so we make for the gates—Suzanne and I having a long parley on the way there on the subject of our computers.

Friday, October 6:

A fine mist is still evident as Fritz and I head in to the park—following Kate and Skye the Alsatian. Skye heads immediately for the green and

Kate lingers behind, hoping that her dog will notice that she is all alone out here and trot back. Meanwhile David the dogsitter is heading our way with the black Poppy in tow. Fritz is advised that his pal is present, but it takes a while for him to zero in on his target and rush forward for a tummy rub. David gets nervous at such moments because today's client often resents the intrusion of yesterday's. Today the matter is made worse by the return of Skye, who also wants to dance around David, making huge leaps as though she would like to kiss him on the cheek.

We make it out to the green just as Dan and Winnie are departing. Ziggy is again mixing it up with Rufus and Martha—always eager for a wrestle with dogs who obviously outweigh him. Fritz wanders over to the Grantully gate, with me in pursuit, but he manages to stay within the park—and then I get him to chase his ball back toward the cricket crease. Nearer the café there is a chap exercising his little curly-haired dog with a squeaky ball. Fritz becomes fascinated by this toy, and the guy is content to toss it to him several times. Eventually my dog settles down to crush it in his jaws and I am able to extract it and return it to its proper owner.

When we go in for coffee there is only the smallest of turnouts—just me and three Scottish ladies. Georgie passes around a birthday card for Ronnie, who will celebrate his 60th next Tuesday. It has pictures, prepared by Janet, of all the dogs. We have selected a table out on the café forecourt but the rain intensifies and begins to blow in on us from all angles. When there is a brief lull I collect Fritz and head for home. Naturally my dog accomplishes this task at a snail's pace.

Saturday, October 7:

We enter the park under sunny skies but there are also chilly winds and I long to reach the green—where it might be a little warmer than under the shadow of the entrance trees. Instead Fritz makes his usual slow progress, pausing to discourage the attentions of any other dog until he is blindsided by his pal Pepper—who manages to kiss him and gangtackle him at the same time. I have to let my dog off lead at this point and after a few more rounds with Pepper we continue into the sun in front of the clubhouse. Here there is a brief face-off between Ilan, a black Lab with a red collar and his chunky chocolate cousin, Charlie.

There is a large turnout on the green—I count twenty humans at one point—since we have a lot of the regulars and the Saturday morning obedience class all attempting to enjoy a fine autumnal day at the same time. The green itself is lush, such a contrast with its shape only a few months ago, but it is almost too wet to cut. I spot two new characters today. The first is a fifteen week-old adorable Bernese Mountain Dog puppy named Benjy. His owner says that they actually live in Kensington and that Benjy has never been off lead. This soon changes as Benjy is allowed a romp with all the others, including a lovely white and tan Labradoodle named Jesse. Humpty is also in evidence, baying as though he were pursuing racoons rather than mere canines. Fritz manages to stay pretty close to the action but, as everyone continues to enjoy the sunshine, he heads restively toward the café—where he finds Peter and Ellen waiting for their sausage order. He realizes that this is the place that he ought to be and he jumps up on the bench next to Jack to wait his turn for a handout—Jack is not all pleased.

When our lot finally does begin to filter in we make up a dozen dog owners crowded around a single table. Liz has brought her husband, Tom, and her younger son Jack. Many of those present have been on a group expedition to a little theatre in Islington the night before and they are eager to compare notes. Fritz jumps from lap to lap, especially enjoying an extended cuddle from his Uncle Dan. Jasmine, Ziggy and Sparkie also get in a lot of lap time—perhaps they are being used as tummy warmers on a brisk day. There is a lot of food consumed by man and beast. At the next table Suzanne is beginning another backgammon marathon with Ray Blanch, who, it turns out, is the current math teacher of Liz's Ryan—I think we are about to have a parent-teacher conference over muffins and croissants. I don't have a dog in my lap and, chilled, I decide to leave at last, making my excuses and exiting past the table where Frank is dressed in his frog costume and Blake is hovering pantingly over a plate of chips.

Sunday, October 8:

It isn't quite as chilly or as intensely bright as it was yesterday and Fritz, for once, makes a fairly brisk entry into the Paddington scene. Yesterday we had some twenty souls in action out on the wet green; today I can see only Ivana with the honey-coloured Rufus. Heading toward the foot of Mt. Bannister, however, I can see Janet, Faz, Georgie and Dan. Here we head as well, since I have to give Georgie my contribution toward Ronnie's 60th birthday present. Thereafter Fritz gives in to wanderlust and I have to follow. At one point he wanders through the little garden area adjacent to the Randolph walkway and here I discover six rather unwholesome youths puffing away on their fags. On the other side we follow walkways back to the green and here Fritz discovers David the dogsitter perched on a bench. Of course my dog insists on jumping into David's lap.

I can see the others heading in for coffee so I cross the green one last time, my shoes sending up a squirt of moisture with every step. While I am in the queue I overhear Bouzha complaining to Janet about Peter and Hector. The large free-range Cocker has been bothering other diners and Peter has not exactly been cooperative when reminded of the café's dogs-on-lead rule. Then we join the others outside and the question is raised—should someone speak to Peter? I suggest that it should be someone with a warrant card. Faz says he's off-duty.

Again we end up with a dozen or so dog owners sitting at two adjacent tables. There is so much chatter and so many dogs barking that it is hard to hear our own voices. Ziggy, all legs, settles into Celine's lap, basking in the sun. Tilly reports for dog treats, which I have brought in a yellow Selfridge's bag. Suzanne has brought not only Sunny but Suki, whom she is dogsitting these days. The most unusual occurrence comes when Ronnie, attempting to loft a tennis ball over the head of those seated opposite, plunks Hanna with the ball instead. She is not amused and as we get up to leave I can hear her scolding her attacker sternly.

Monday, October 9:

We again encounter David the dogsitter as we are penetrating the park on a grey Monday morning. He has just watched every episode of the last series of *Six Feet Under*—and he feels desolated that there are no more. The green too is desolate, not a single member of the regular pack anywhere in evidence. Fritz makes for the Randolph Avenue exit, out of boredom, and I have to put him back on lead in order to turn him around in the right direction. This means that twice we have to pass the bushes at the bottom on the tarmac path down Mt. Bannister, plants stripped completely bare after some park keeper brainstorm.

By this time some of our gang are beginning to appear—Jasmine, Ziggy, and Winnie in the middle of the green, Skye the Cairn and Hercules on the edges. Dan is in a state over the shoddy treatment he received yesterday afternoon when he called his vet's emergency number after Winnie had begun vomiting and fitting. It took them five minutes to pick up the phone and then they only offered to make an appointment for the next day. When Dan protested the receptionist put the phone down on him. He is still fighting mad, though Winnie seems to have recovered and, indeed, she *will* see the vet today. We have three Westies at our feet by now, Scamp, Elvis and a new pristine white fellow named Elgin. "They named their dog after the street?" I ask but Sabina agrees that the owners *do* live on Elgin Avenue.

At breakfast we have Georgie, Faz, Albert, Ronnie, Liz, and Trudy. Trudy is with her Freddy and also Phoenix, who has a bloody leg wrapped in plaster—the result of a torn scab. To add insult to injury he is then attacked by Rebel—who has to be pulled off. I give him some biscuits to cheer him up—and Fritz some as well. For some strange reason no one has ordered any toast this morning—a first. Liz says that she had eight fourteen year-olds sleeping at her house last night and that she now has to go home and fix them breakfast. "I think they got up to mischief last night," she says, "I discovered two empty egg cartons in my trash." "In that case," I add, getting up to make my return journey, "tell them that they must already be full—after eating all those omelettes."

Tuesday, October 10:

It has rained just a bit and I am wearing my rain jacket as I enter the park on a dreary Tuesday morning. We find David the dogsitter standing on the grass next to the Morshead roadway. He has both Poppy and Skye the Alsatian in his care today, and he is talking to Finn's mom, Maggie, who also has the care of Hootch. I don't recognize the latter since he has no thunderball with him. He seems to be at a loss without a ball and Maggie suggests that she must get his favourite toy from Guy. "In the interests of our ankles," I suggest, "perhaps you should not."

There isn't much activity on the green, though Janet has arrived with Koko and Georgie with Sparkie. Dan dashes past bearing a birthday cake for Ronnie, whose 60th we will be celebrating later. I get out the red jingle ball and keep it in action while Freddy dances in hysterical circles around Winnie—who emerges periodically from her spot at Dan's feet to chase her tormentor away. Fritz begins another of his thrusting forays in the direction of Randolph Avenue. This time I get him turned around by rolling his ball down the walkway toward the café. By this time the others are heading in for breakfast.

Ronnie has started a tab for everyone's drinks and there are lovely treats at two adjacent tables, one of which is surmounted by an awning from which a helium balloon with a dog motif hovers. Dan has made a wonderful chocolate cake—following one of Nigella's recipes. Candles are lit and we sing "Happy Birthday." Ellen, Peter, Barbara, Trudy, David, Ofra, Dorothy, Georgie, Liz, and Linda are all present. Fritz and Pepper have an extended face fight under the table and then Janet gets Koko to sing by intoning "woo woo" in her pet's ear. This prompt works but, to everyone's surprise, first Pepper then Fritz join in this howling chorus as well. It is suggested that there should be an excursion to see *The Devil Wears Prada*—since everyone will want to see it. I add, "Everyone will want to see it as long as they are not a guy." Dan says, "*I* want to see it." I say, "I rest my case." Dan retorts, "Bitch!"

There are a lot of goodies left over when we get up to leave and these are bundled up for the café staff, who have been very helpful in today's festivities. Dorothy and I walk with Fritz toward the Morshead gate; over on our right a runner has hopped the track fence in order to pee against an innocent chestnut tree.

Thursday, October 12:

It would appear, from the date of this entry, that I have missed a day in the park. This is not entirely true for I was here briefly yesterday—but Dorothy wanted our dog home sharpish so that she could give him a bath, and I didn't have time to sit down for coffee or to talk to any of our pals. Today, as I enter, I can see Hercules, Roxy and Jonesie (and their owners) attempting a walkway circle outside the running track. (The back route is again blocked.) Jonesie has claimed a tennis ball—which a number of the Asian lads, on their way to Westminster College, also have an interest in. That is they have an interest in it until it has gone into Jonesie's mouth—whereupon they renounce any claim to the object as though it were the carrier of plague, and making it a birthday gift to the little Shih-Tzu. (Today, in fact, *Fritz* is three and a half.)

The grass has at last been cut but the job has obviously been completed while the green stuff was still wet and there are tire marks everywhere. It is soaking underfoot, which may explain why there is little activity here. I try his ball out on my animal but he isn't much interested, mesmerized instead by the appearance of what seems to be a war dog on the rampage. This is Lancer the Lab, who is wearing a giant Elizabethan collar in transparent blue plastic—in order, I discover, to keep him from licking his toes—since he has some sort of foot fungus. He is having trouble adjusting to his new reality and manages to knock the water trough over as he tries for a drink outside the ladies loo.

I sit down at the same pulled-together tables that hosted Ronnie's birthday party, though today there is hardly any need, since we have just Ronnie, Ofra, Georgie and Liz. The conversation returns to Islamic hostility toward dogs and everyone, offended, adds a new instance from personal experience. On my way home I am snagged by Suzanne, who wants to borrow some computer start-up disks from me. She and Sunny follow us home and I am surprised that Fritz tolerates Sunny's darting presence in his home with such alacrity—only a couple of perfunctory growls when she gets into his personal space.

Saturday, October 21:

Over a week has passed before my usual park routine can resume. During this period Dorothy and I have been on the Amalfi Coast and Fritz, who has made several afternoon appearances in the park, has been staying with the Taggarts—a very successful visit, I understand. (Wouldn't you know that just as my dog returned to the sanctity of his own home some cretin in the street began a fusillade of pre-Fawkes rockets—and so I had to administer a dose of Rescue Remedy as the newly returned Fritz cowered in the bathroom.)

Today we make our slow progress toward the green where Kate is slinging the ball to her Skye. I ask her if she has made any progress with her latest copy of the famous petition, since I want to wrap this project up as soon as possible. She says she has a dozen or so signatures and will turn these over to me soon. At the foot of Mt. Bannister Roland has brought in a half dozen dogs (no owners in sight) and tied most of them to the metal gazebo. The inevitable result is that a chorus of disapproval is rising from the frustrated canines. Finally a chap goes over to make representations on the subject of this doggy delinquency and quiet resumes. Fritz begins his wanderlust roamings and I follow, coming to a rest only when I see that he has stationed himself at the feet of Peter and Ellen, who are waiting for a plate of sausages to cool off.

I sit down with Ronnie at a table in the prow of the forecourt but it takes quite a while for the others to come in from the green and when they (and Dorothy) do, it begins to drizzle and so we all move to two adjacent tables beneath the café's overhang. Here there is a big turnout and we see just how much Fritz II has grown in the last few weeks. Ziggy has grown some too but Celine is still able to get him into her lap. Janet has a friend who does greeting cards with your dog pictured thereon, and she passes samples around in case anyone wants to order. Dorothy and I begin our walk home, with Fritz pausing to sniff every blade of grass on the way.

Sunday, October 22:

It's another grey day but today there is far less activity in the park than yesterday. Only Celine is on the green with Ziggy, but soon Rufus the Lab makes an appearance and these two dogs have a romp. Fritz wanders around the periphery and finally returns to the centre, where, by this time, we also have Skye the Alsatian, Jasmine, Tilly and Koko. It is obvious that a number of dog owners are the worse for wear after a riotous weekend featuring a UNICEF Ball presided over by Kate.

I notice that Fritz is wandering off again and I follow him, encountering Ellen with Sandy and Jack at the foot of Mt. Bannister. Ellen is carrying a bouquet of flowers. These are obviously for Peter's wife, who is in the Royal Free Hospital—after suffering a stroke a few weeks ago. Peter eventually shuffles up with his Holly—he looks stricken with worry. While I am chatting with them I see that our group is heading in for coffee and so I start to follow. I ask someone why Georgie hasn't been seen these last two days and the answer is that she is visiting her sister Jean in Glasgow. It is obvious that Sparkie must have made this trip too.

At coffee I present some lemon cookies that we have brought back from Italy. The dogs are munching on carrots, biscuits and toast, though Fritz would just as soon have a lemon cookie. Ofra arrives with Bailey and the latter jumps into my lap, the better to launch an assault on the tabletop. He succeeds in toppling his mistress's coffee cup in his predations. Ronnie, at his mischievous best, suggests that we could overcome Muslim objections to our dogs by dressing the latter in veils—an amusing image, but calculated to cause offence. Once again it begins to drizzle and I decide to make a break for it before it starts to rain in earnest.

Monday, October 23:

The rainy day doldrums continue and I am back in my rain jacket as Fritz and I head for the park. I keep him on lead as we approach the green—where a large party of dog owners is having a circular walkround. I attempt to catch up with them but this takes a long time as Fritz is slow to produce his gift and then he takes his sweet time getting into stride, distracted by Tara the Kerry Blue and several other dogs. We don't catch up until the others have reached the Randolph walkway—where I can at last unhook my dog.

Jean-Baptiste is just describing a recent trip to Montreal and Toronto, where he was spooked, on a day off, by a sign in the woods warning of the presence of bears. We have nothing as serious to contend with here, just Hercules barking, Skye the Cairn pestering everyone so that they will kick his ball, and Winnie running furiously after some guy who has said a cross word to her in passing. I pass on to Liz an article about James Joyce for her Tom, who belongs to a Joycean society—though he doesn't much care for the writing.

At breakfast there is a poignant reunion as Fritz jumps into the lap of his surrogate Mom, Linda, while Pepper dances in jealousy at her feet. The conversation turns to teenage misbehaviour after Kate comes in to report that some yobs threw a firework at Skye last night—the big dog escaping by jumping into the canal. On the subject of misbehaviour I report that I have recently witnessed a judge on *Strictly Come Dancing* round on a fellow jurist with the retort, "The hills are alive with the sounds of bullshit!" and that just yesterday, also during the early evening hours, on a live feed from the Formula One broadcast in Brazil, I heard Kimi Raikkonen, responding to a question on why he hadn't attended a nearby ceremony in honour of Michael Schumacher, reply, "I was taking a shit." Hanna says she sees nothing wrong in this Finnish frankness, but then she is known as a straight talker herself.

Tuesday, October 24:

Under leaden skies Fritz and I pick our way through the puddles on our way to the green. We are soon overtaken by a portly female Schnauzer, Poppy, who is eighteen months old. She seems quite interested in Fritz and then, as we reach our destination, in every other dog as well—barking at them in a high-pitched yelp when they don't pay her instant attention. Just at this point we encounter Spadge and the almost shaved-naked Yoyo, so it is Schnauzer Central (Oscar and Pepper make it an even half a dozen a few minutes later). I notice that there is no one on the green and the reason is easy to divine—a lone black lad in cleats has occupied the cricket crease and is having a battle keeping his ball away from Martha the Boxer. He has left a pile of equipment at one end of this space and dog owners instinctively know that their animals are sure to pee on this if given half a chance.

Fritz is kept occupied with his ball and then we join the others at an outside table in the café's forecourt. The chief topic of conversation is the storm that ripped through our world last night. Another very uncomfortable night for Fritz began when we were out on our walk—and a loud firework exploded nearby. Tucked in bed, lightning and thunder soon followed, and I had to get up to administer a dose of Rescue Remedy to my panting dog. Linda says that Pepper was also cowering and she had to carry him downstairs and out to his favourite tree. Hanna seems to have revelled in the heavenly outburst, a Valhalla maiden in her element. But Ronnie and Susie experienced a really bad leak in their conservatory.

While we are discussing last night's storm we get this morning's. It starts with a driving drizzle that soon soaks the backs of Ofra, Liz and Dorothy. As we all get up to leave, the rain straightens out its direction, falling on my head as I wait for Fritz to find the right spot (a completely exposed one) for his final poo poo. We then run to catch up with the others, who have reached some shelter under the trees that line the Morshead roadway. Suzanne now notices another Springer Spaniel, Rex, a dog whose brown and white are the reverse of Sunny's pattern, mostly white where Sunny is mostly brown. It doesn't matter a great deal because by now all anyone can think of is getting home and into some dry clothes.

Wednesday, October 25:

The weather has definitely embraced an autumnal chill as Fritz and I head for the Morshead gate, and I am wearing my leather jacket and scarf against the cold grey skies. Dan is heading our way with a charging Winnie and the two dogs head toward the green side by side. Here Dan peels off to walk with Jean-Baptiste and Hercules while I head across the wet grass, passing Ziggy, who is rolling two Jack Russells into little balls. It starts to rain and I stand under the metal gazebo while Fritz has a good sniff round. Then we head for the café, where our gang is forming at two adjacent tables under the roof of the coffee house.

Ronnie hands me a letter he has just received from our Maida Vale councillor, Jan Prendergast. She says that she will be presenting our petition to Westminster Council on November 8th. She wants to know what the petition should be entitled; her own suggestion—"That dogs continue to be allowed to exercise off the lead in Paddington Recreation Ground"—seems satisfactory to me. She also asks if there are any more signatures and there are, which I will send along as soon I get one more copy from Kate—who has lost it somewhere within her own house.

The good news is that her cleaning lady is coming tomorrow and *she* might uncover it. More good news comes Dorothy's way when Kate remembers that she has discovered re-runs of *Sleeper Cell* on FX, one of those myriad cable channels that we can now get on Sky. Dorothy is delighted, since she missed the last episode. The women continue with chatter about shoes, teeth veneers and facial scrubs while Dan, perhaps driven to desperation, tries to get Koko to sing. As yesterday, it begins to rain and so we troop off in the wet. Liz announces that she has a parent-teacher conference with her youngest son's teachers today—"I shall bask in the glow of his achievements and deny all knowledge of his misdeeds."

Thursday, October 26:

As Fritz and I enter the park we again have cool, grey weather—though bright patches in the sky promise a morning without rain. As we near the green we encounter Tanya with Pasha and baby Isabella and Michaela with Skye the Cairn. The latter, of course, wants me to kick his ball. Tanya says that the baby, sitting in her stroller, will be a year old next week—hard to believe. On the grass we edge closer to our group, which is standing near the cricket crease. Dan is holding forth on the subject of Winnie's pee—since the little madam is seen squatting repeatedly. Dan says that Winnie doesn't seem to know whether to expect a pee or a poo when she squats—and he demonstrates this action himself to general merriment. "Wait a minute," I add, "I get confused sometimes too. Can you do that again?"

The others gradually slope off into the café while I try to keep Fritz moving with his red rubber jingle ball. However on one relatively short toss this ball goes missing. There is no other dog about and Fritz hasn't made off with it in his mouth, but repeated crisscrossing of the relevant patch of wet grass produces nothing. There are a lot of large leaves about but, after turning each over, I have to give up. This is another great loss—for Fritz really enjoyed this ball, and it had provided a lot of pleasure in its all too brief a life.

I join the others, after a long wait in the coffee line. Several of us have seen this morning's feature on the effects of fireworks on dogs—broadcast on GMTV. This is a particularly relevant story since Fritz is now afraid to go out at night—the once fearless animal reduced to jelly by the nightly fusillade that precedes bonfire night by a month—and succeeds it as well. I begin a rant, wondering why our government, which is considering a complex system of taxing cars on the basis of their gas consumption, which wants to regulate every item of refuse so that we recycle properly, can't regulate the obviously public nuisance represented by this autumnal spectacle. "Oh well," I conclude, "they can't end the explosions in Basra—why do we expect them to do a better job in Maida Vale?"

Friday, October 27:

There is actually some sunlight penetrating the heavens as Fritz and I make our way into the park. I have brought a small, lightweight blue ball, hoping that it might make some sort of substitute for the lost jingle ball. Unfortunately it has so little substance that it is hard to throw and it won't bounce and Fritz soon tires of chasing it. We do work our way across the wet grass in this fashion and I am able to catch up with Rizzo and Denise—she is collecting for a card and gift for June, Peter's ailing wife.

There is only a small turnout at coffee—just Hanna, Kate, Davide and Dorothy, who buys the dogs some toast. Kate says that Skye disappeared last night in pursuit of a fox—which appeared at the end of her mews. Fortunately the Alsatian returned a few minutes later, looking very pleased with herself. Davide says that Winnie's peeing seems under control but that she wants to go into the garden for a poo every morning at 5:00 am. Hanna has left her dogs tied to the legs of her empty chair but Spadge begins his bark and back-up routine, and I have to sit in this chair before Spadge drags it (and George) over to the next table.

All this time I am staring at an unclaimed cheese croissant (which is soon shared out among the dogs). Enquiries reveal that Davide has ordered it (and an equally lonely latte) for a missing Georgie. After a while her whereabouts become the sole topic of conversation since no one knows where she is, she isn't answering any of her phones, Janet and Koko have not been heard from as well, and Kate now sets off to knock on Georgie's door. Davide says that there is a worker at his house who is a mate of Georgie's husband and he will see if he can use this contact to let us know about our missing friend. By the time we get home there is a phone call from Dan—everyone has forgotten that Georgie is taking a course in "Disability Awareness" this morning.

Saturday, October 28:

There are a few bright patches in the sky as Fritz trots briskly toward the park; this pace is such a contrast to his late night performance these days—during which I have to drag him from tree to tree as he trembles in fear over the prospect of the next bomb attack. He squats for the first of three poos, a surprising productivity these days since he often doesn't eat his dinner when it is noisy outside—a circumstance avoided last night as he had to keep up with his cousin Pepper, who spent the day with us on a playdate.

When we reach the green there is a lively Saturday morning scene and the first thing I notice is that Dan is wearing a reindeer tiara. This object, and several others soon on display, are the latest evidence of Internet shopping gone awry. Kate is demonstrating the effects of another—a foundation garment that has arrived apparently several times too small. It is supposed to stretch and there is much encouragement for her to try it on, but she isn't having anything to do with such a process. Also in evidence is a set of four pink leg warmers that have been purchased for Winnie. These are tried on the Pug, but they fall off almost immediately, and thereafter several other dogs are thrust into them—but no one seems to warm to them and the last I see of this item is that Bray, a black Lab sort of dog, has one in his mouth and is playing keep-away. Poppy and Archie, Basset Hounds, join the mix, though they miss contact with Humpty, who comes in later. The card for Peter's wife is passed around on the cricket crease and signed by many of the dog owners. A lot of useful exercise is undertaken, even by Fritz, who chases one of Skye the Alsatian's balls, and at about 10:00 a migration to the café begins—Winnie leading the way with the antler tiara on her back.

We are fourteen at breakfast, with two large tables pulled together—with Hanna, at one end with her own little table, and Albert serving as an outrider at the other end. He has brought the delightful Yorkies, Tinkerbelle and Saffy. Also present underfoot is a second dog brought in by the dogsitting Celine, another mostly black Lab called Kiro—evidently "black" in Japanese. Kiro goes for a piece of toast intended for Fritz and gets growled at. The mood is light-hearted and we sit for quite a while, but the dogs are getting bored (Skye jumps on Georgie's back in frustration) and so we head off at about 10:45.

Sunday, October 29:

Fritz and I enter the park after another desperate night. Once again I have had to drag my dog from tree to tree on a very abbreviated late night walk, one that followed our return from an evening out with visiting cousins from California. Instead of his usual panting and pawing he then began, with every breath, to make little clicking noises in his throat, a particularly unnerving sound for those of us whose pillows surround his sleeping place. This morning he seems quite lethargic—showing no interest in his usual breakfast treats. He trots along quite smartly (it is bright and sunny) and shows no obvious signs of distress—but I am keeping an eye on him at all times.

His poo seems fine and he even gets up once to lope after one of Skye the Alsatian's balls, but most of the time he is content to sit on the cricket crease with the other small dogs (Janet has both Koko and Winnie—since both Dan and Davide are off to South Africa this morning). When Dorothy arrives on the green I let Fritz know this fact and he does head off in her direction but she is distressed that he does so with none of his usual urgency or joy. Since I know they have an hour open for emergencies—even on a Sunday—we have loaded the number of the Hamilton Vet Clinic into Dorothy's mobile phone. By the time we have gone in for coffee Fritz has an eleven o'clock appointment.

Our dog shows no interest in any of the usual titbits, content to gnaw on a purple rubber ball belonging to Frank and Bianca. Above his head, the conversation turns to local restaurants—since Celine and her husband are great connoisseurs and food is a natural topic today when there are rumours (later confirmed in a copy of the *Wood & Vale*) that Gordon Ramsey may be extending his empire to these here parts. And it is also true that Liz and Tom are about to take over the management of an Italian restaurant on Kensington Church Street. Fritz has a big drink of water from one of the grey troughs and at 10:30 or so we set off for Boundary Road—the dog again bouncing along in his normal animated fashion.

At the clinic it is a mad scene since, along with the other emergencies, some people have come in just for pills or dog food (including little Lisa and her mom in the latter category) or regular jabs—and the place is only open for an hour. One woman comes in with a Miniature Pinscher whose limp miraculously clears up before it is time to see the doc. The latter is Rachael today and she listens patiently to our recital of symptoms, which include not only the recent breathing problems and this morning's lethargy, but the sad history of fireworks neuroses. She takes Fritz's temperature and listens intently with her stethoscope and agrees that he seems very subdued and that he may be having some respiratory problems. Her decision is to keep him overnight and to take x-rays and blood tests, transferring him to the Finchley Road branch of the Hamilton Kingdom—where she can keep a better eye on him. The receptionist works on an estimate of likely charges (astronomical but not to be queried under such circumstances—and we have insurance) and we turn the dog over to his caregivers, leaving the place at a despondent pace. By 1:00 Rachael has already called, reporting that blood tests and x-rays are normal and that the little fellow seems much perkier. A course of antibiotics is begun and we are to call tomorrow morning. Somewhat reassured, we resume life in a very empty house.

November, 2006

Friday, November 3:

Five days have passed since I last reported on park activity but today is the first day that Fritz seems well enough to resume his normal routine—allowing me to catch up on the life of the park, canine and human, at last. This is not to say that we haven't been in the park itself—we have been here almost every day, but only for very short stretches so as not to overtire the dog, who returned to us after spending only one night in the care of his physicians. Indeed we travelled through the park with him on our way to and from his check-up on Wednesday—when he was examined by Frank Seddon himself (without much progress on a definitive diagnosis). Still on a heavy course of antibiotics, he seems a bit livelier today and it is a lovely day in the park—still chilly in the shade (it has been very cold these last few days) but warm enough in the sun. Fritz continues to have the greatest problems with night time walks, now very much abbreviated affairs due to the nightly blitz in the run-up to bonfire night—with me carrying him a suitable distance from home before putting him down on the pavement for a quick scramble home. Even last night, when we returned for the second time this week to find him hiding under our bed, a fusillade coming from Paddington Rec itself sent him scurrying back up the stairs. Furious, Dorothy called the police. Today, at the little triangle just before the green, there is a box of sixty-four expended rockets among other debris left by the night visitors.

Fritz, let loose at last, gets a warm greeting from the other dog owners—with cuddles from Dan, Janet and David the dogsitter. Winnie is wearing a green coat and I remind Dan that they are accepting candidates for the next series of *Brat Camp*. Joining us on the green for the first time is the cuddly black Newfoundland, Suki, and it is hard to picture what a giant she will grow to be. Also on the green are Mozart and Billy, for Jean is once again visiting from Glasgow. Fritz travels from group to group, seemingly enjoying himself and behaving in his usual self-assured way. When we go in for coffee we notice that poor Bianca the Boxer has a tender paw encased in a bandage—after a recent mishap.

At coffee Fritz sits in Liz's lap and then in mine. I am happy to see him scarf down his allotted portion of buttered toast. Janet is snapping away with her camera, getting ready for next year's calendar. There's a debate over whether Mozart and Billy belong in the calendar this year—but it is decided that they are still honorary members of the Paddington pack. Dan is organizing a night out at a Greek restaurant on Marylands Road but Dorothy and I have decided not to abandon Fritz again so soon. At a more exalted culinary level there is much excitement over Gordon Ramsey's purchase of the Warrington Hotel, only a few short minutes walk from the park. Dan is worried that the old pub clientele will be driven away but Kate says that this is her pickup pub—and she wouldn't mind an upgrade in the ranks of the customers. We sit for a long time in the sun and then Fritz and I make our way slowly home, the dog stopping to sniff every blade of grass in his accustomed manner.

Saturday, November 4:

I have to nudge my dog awake as I get ready for a Saturday morning in the park. He has slept deeply after spending most of the evening in his mommy's lap—as the weekend bombardment got under way. For the first time in his life there was no late night walk at all. Now he seems brighter, playing with his toys in the hall, having a long drink of water, eating some of his largely ignored dinner. In the park, where he deposits a quick poo, he is also far more alert. He trots around the green, visiting the smells of yesterday in a leisurely inspection before returning to the centre, where the other dogs are having a spirited romp while their owners, most of whom have been out partying the night before, try to remember how the night came to an end.

There is a large turnout at breakfast and Dorothy, who has ordered some recuperative sausages as well as the usual buttered toast, soon has a furry contingent at her knees. Those living close to the park compare stories of the recent loss of water in their flats—the consequence of several burst pipes beneath Elgin Avenue. We have had water since Thursday afternoon but my upstairs neighbours, the ones from Uzbekistan, still hadn't received their first drop when they came knocking on our door last night (welcome to the Third World). I pass around an article from the *Ham & High* reporting that Paddington Rec has received a million dollar grant for a pre-Olympics upgrade to its sports facilities. No one seems interested—but they will be when we have yet more interruptions to our normal routine to accommodate more jock culture.

Exercise is not completed for the day since Fritz and Pepper, in our attempt to tire them out before civic celebrations add their voice to the private noisemaking tonight, are taken by Rob and me to Regents Park. Here we meet Karen the dog groomer amid Schanuzers and Westies. We take a giant circle around the central grassy core, with Rob slinging the tennis ball to Pepper every now and then and both dogs having a mad chase in pursuit. I must say that it is gratifying to see the fellows having such a grand time—neither showing any signs of recent illness (tummy problems in Pepper's case). It is almost dark by the time we have completed our walk and Pepper joins us for the evening while Rob and Linda go to a bonfire at the sailing club at Welsh Harp. Almost my first act, as the first shells fall, is to dose both dogs with a squirt of Rescue Remedy.

Sunday, November 5:

Fritz and I enter the park after another distressing night. Even a second dose of Rescue Remedy failed to forestall hours of hysteria (Pepper did much better)—with our dog disappearing beneath the bed for sustained periods of panting, drooling and pawing the carpet. At one point Dorothy convinced herself that Fritz had managed to get himself stuck at the far end of his escape tunnel, and we had to pull a drawer out in order to extract him. When we put him between us after midnight he continued to pant in our ears and Dorothy had to get up as sleep proved impossible. Sometime after 1:00 am the bombardment slackened and so did the dog's heavy breathing. Nevertheless he had crawled for succour beneath my pillow and I had him on my chest for several hours of uncomfortable rest as well.

This morning there is little sign of last night's problems—give or take a beard that is still frozen with drool. We follow yesterday's routine, which seems to include a minute inspection of every bush and patch of grass. I keep Fritz on lead during this process and we circle the green at some distance from the others—who are basking in the bright sunshine in the centre. Quite a few people, having heard of his recent visits to the vet, pause to ask how he is doing. More and more I am convinced that his condition was not organic, just hysterical.

We begin the breakfast conversation with some post-fireworks analysis. Hanna is outraged because, for the first time in years, neighbours have set off their own display in a nearby garden. Even George, who is deaf, was so distressed that he ran to hide in Spadge's bed. Rosie, according to Ronnie, wanted to attack the noisemakers, particularly when rockets began to bounce off the glass ceiling of the conservatory. Winnie was evidently in attack mode as well; today Ronnie produces a puppy t-shirt for the little Pug bearing the letters A.S.B.O. (anti-social behaviour order, for those of you reading this outside the UK). Fritz, the ninny, climbs into my lap, then Dan's, then Faz's, then Ronnie's, then mine again. The conversation shifts to the universally loathed bendy-buses, one of which almost decapitated Ofra while a second was the cause of a serious accident outside Dan's theatre yesterday. It is pleasant sitting in the sun (I usually take the seat facing the sun since I bring my dark glasses with me) but eventually we have to enter the chilly shadows at the beginning of another day of publicly scheduled shock and awe.

Monday, November 6:

Fritz has spent a much more comfortable night, though the bombardment began as soon as night fell—and he did spend a panting half hour under the bed. He was roused from his lair by Linda, who had arrived to borrow some more Rescue Remedy for a distraught Pepper and, after receiving his own dose, Fritz settled down on his back between us in the TV room and slept pretty comfortably throughout the rest of the evening.

Today he seems fine and I head off for the park at our usual time and follow him around his investigatory circuit. For the second time in a week we are overtaken by the pounding feet of Marty Cornelius, a student of mine (twenty years ago) who lives on one side of the park and serves on a ward committee (with Jan Prendergast)—where he has a special responsibility for overseeing park matters. He tells me that he is worried about the misbehaviour of local youth and that their numbers may be augmented in the park by students from the new nearby city academy. He is also concerned about the congestion charge, which, though not covering our area in its new February 1 boundaries, is likely to bring more traffic to our local streets from people trying to avoid the fee. I always chuckle at the reincarnation of this once wild youth as a pillar of civic responsibility. I remember him as an eighth-grader whom I had to march into the principal's office because he was running down the stairs with a jack knife in his hand.

I don't stop for coffee this morning because Fritz has a check-up on Boundary Road at 10:00 and here we report on the dot. Dr. Seddon listens carefully to heart and lungs and says he can't hear any problems anymore—so Fritz is discharged. I can tell he is feeling better for when he is not endlessly prolonging the adventure by sniffing every lamppost and curbstone he is grabbing his lead in his mouth and dancing off with it. As soon as I get home with the good news, Dorothy calls St. John's Pets to reschedule the much needed the haircut that was cancelled due to his indisposition.

Tuesday, November 7:

Another night of the ninny, one in which Fritz disdained further progress on the pavement as soon as he heard a distant pow (and then tried his heavy panting routine until I put him off the bed). We now head for the park on a foggy grey morning. Fritz makes slow work along the walkways and by the time he has finally found a squatting spot it is time to head in for coffee.

There is a sizeable turnout and two tables are drawn together. Ofra has brought some goodies back from Barcelona and these are shared out over the coffee cups. For that matter, coffee is the chief topic of conversation since Ofra has fallen in love with a brewing system made by Krups. Ronnie says that this is still the same company that manufactured gas chamber doors during the war (I am not so sure) and he would certainly not drink their coffee. The coffee-making palaver has grown so protracted that Kate begins to protest that here is certainly an entry in the most boring conversation department. She puts a definitive end to it when she rises to continue Skye's exercise—"You could invite people you don't like over to the house for a coffee and then gas them at the same time."

When everyone gets up to leave, Hector, who has been staring intently into Ofra's eyes, follows her and Bailey as they head off to the parking lot, collectively parting an incoming file of screaming teenaged girls. Only at this point does Peter notice that his off-lead pet is missing. When he is notified that his dog has done a runner he explodes in expletives, mostly directed at Ofra for not stopping. Liz, whose Roxy ran away in terror when a firework was exploded in the park recently, heads off in the direction of the lot herself—we have appointed her referee. Most of the rest of us (with nine dogs in all) head for the Morshead gate—quite a procession of pooches.

Wednesday, November 8:

It is very dark outside and there is a hint of moisture in the air. After our usual stops we proceed to the green just as Ofra is arriving. She is quizzed on yesterday's incident but she says she would have been unaware of Peter's meltdown (though she did see an enraged face as she drove from the parking lot)—had Liz not called her with the details. Today it is Ofra who is the injured party, just spoiling for a fight, though Hanna is anxious to remind her that Peter was just acting out of panic over his missing pet and that, reprimanded for his rudeness, he has admitted his fault.

Our two tables are still pulled together and we manage to fill most of the seats, making us the only café customers on a day in which every now and then we feel a touch of mist. Ofra has brought printed evidence for her new passion, an Argos catalogue featuring the famous Krups coffee system. Ronnie isn't here today but there is growing doubt that there is any relationship between the Krups company, though German in origin, and the Krupp steel company (Hitler's armourer)—whose brand name caused Ronnie to explode yesterday.

Dorothy returns from making her order at the counter to report that Ché has jumped on Vicky while she was delivering orders and that John has said he knows nothing of the dogs-on-lead-at-the café rule. Dorothy tries to pass this intelligence on to the others, though John is sitting at the opposite end of our table arrangement. "Who's John?" Dan asks, adding to the embarrassment of the moment. The dogs eat a mountain of toast, Fritz growling at Sunny when she lunges for a piece he considers his own. Today we are the first to leave but Fritz is so slow on his exit lap that I can see most of the others coming up behind us.

Friday, November 10:

On a chilly grey Friday Fritz and I enter the park, having missed a day because our dog had a 9:00 appointment with Karen at St. John's Pets. As usual she has done a terrific job with our overgrown boy, who missed his regular slot due to his recent indisposition. He has also recovered much of his aplomb and he scoots over the green, checking out everyone else and returning when I call him for some treats from my yellow Selfridges bag.

I have also brought with me a new tennis ball, also purchased at the pet store, one that squeaks and makes an agreeable pock when chewed by Schnauzer jaws. Unfortunately there are a lot of ball-loving dogs encircling us and so I have to put the ball away. Billy is one of these rivals and so is Skye—who has one ball that has gone dead after repeated chomping. (However Skye has finally lost the white blip in the middle of her tongue, where it has been growing for months). Kate says that yesterday she ran into Councillor Prendergast, who asked her if she was a regular user of the park. Kate used the occasion to apologise for the sorry state of the last petition, which bore the mud splatters indicative of its passage through the park. Not at all, Jan evidently replied, it lent authenticity to the proceedings when the document was presented (successfully, so we are told) to the City Council on Wednesday night.

We go in for coffee, with Sparkie jumping into my lap on four occasions and all the little dogs rushing to the fences to bark furiously at all the larger dogs whose owners happen to be passing by on the outside. (Sunny is put on lead several times for excessive woofing.) I tell the others that I read in the *Times* yesterday that China was adding to its one-child-only policy an addendum: one dog only. The Chinese are also adding a size limitation— "That means no one like Skye," Kate adds. She also tells us that she is going to the races at Cheltenham tomorrow with a pal and that, because she will be leaving Skye at this chap's Oxfordshire farm while they are away at the races, she will be bringing David the dogsitter along as well!

Saturday, November 11:

Rain, which has dominated the scene for many hours, gives way to bright skies and milder than expected temperatures, and Fritz and I make a lively entry into the Paddington scene on a sunny Saturday morning. Many of the dogs are dashing about in mad circles, chasing balls and one another—Billy, Mozart, Sparkie and a mud-soaked Ziggy among them. Only Koko looks eternally out of sorts—she would just as soon head straight for the café—where she could sit in a warm lap instead of having to endure all these canine hi-jinks with a bum nestling in the wet grass. Fritz wanders off once (just to take a second poo) but he is happy to be with the rest of us most of the time and even gets interested in an orange plastic ball that has been abandoned on the green. What he would really like is that squeaky grey squirrel that one of the dog owners in the obedience class has brought with him as a teaching aid.

We go in for coffee, the others twitting Faz on the arrest of several North London cops on money laundering charges. Faz looks fagged out, not from catching criminals, but from studying for his next exam. He reports that he and Dianah had an awful meal at the Savoy and the conversation again turns to the plans that celebrity chef Gordon Ramsey may have in store for our own locality. Again there are mutterings about the change in clientele at the Warrington pub that may follow its rebirth as part of the Ramsey chain, but Dan says that there are already lots of media types there on a Saturday night. I point out that there is a huge, provocative figure of Gordon staring out at passengers leaving the Maida Vale tube stop from the window of Threshers—just to remind us that Gordon rules. Everyone agrees that he can't keep up the quality in his evergrowing realm now that he has become just another franchise dealer in the food world

The dogs eat a lot of toast, though many—like Koko—are seeking any warm lap they can reach. Koko's mommy is in New York; last night she texted Dan to ask for the name of a recommended restaurant on 36th Street and Dan had to call Dorothy to get the exact reference. Meanwhile that world traveller, Davide, has just returned from a run to Newark—just as his parents arrive for a visit from Sardinia. As we leave café staff are sweeping up a huge leaf fall from the precincts of their catery.

Sunday, November 12:

Fritz begins to agitate to go out, whining piteously in the precincts of our front door—about an hour before we are, in fact, scheduled to depart. I am dressed so I take him outside for a brief wee wee run, but he continues to whine even when we return. This pattern may be the consequence of his outrageous nightly behaviour when, during our late night walks, he wants to turn around and go home as soon as he hears a distant boom. Last night there had been quite a fireworks barrage (it never ceases) north of us and I had to drag him from tree to tree just to get out three little pees. When we finally do reach the park today, a bright and brisk Sunday morning, he does a lot of pooing—so perhaps some of this should have been deposited last night by the ninny.

We pass Tinkerbelle and Saffy, both in plastic collars after having been spayed. Out on the green there is a lively scene with a furious barking circle made up of Sparkie and his two northern cousins, Mozart and Billy. Ownership of a yellow ball on a string is fiercely contested by these three, with Koko outside the circle in a disapproving mood and Fritz wandering off to the four corners in order to investigate all the other dogs. Jo comes in with Tilly and makes a big fuss over the recently manicured Fritz—who allows himself to be cuddled in the grass.

When we go in for coffee we have Lynn (Georgie's daughter), Jean, Georgie herself, Hanna, Ronnie, Dan and Ofra with her son Guy. The latter eats three croissants, one with cheese, two with chocolate. Both Dan and Ofra have received calls on their mobiles ordering me to call Liz for further instructions on the upcoming quiz night at ASL. Dorothy arrives and goes inside to make our order but after ten minutes she gives up because the queue is long and the staff are very slow. Then she is off to buy her Sunday papers and I sit coffeeless until it is time to go. Hanna tells me that the back passage is open again and so Fritz and I try it out. There is a macadam path now that runs between the old picnic ground and the new playground, thus actually shortening the route somewhat. On our right there is still a bombsite encompassing the spaces left by the destroyed cricket nets, the lawn in front of these, the five-aside courts and the little green field at the end. "Every time you look around," Hanna says, "there is less park."

Monday, November 13:

Under bright skies Fritz and I enter the park at a lively pace. We have experienced no sequel to yesterday's false start—in part because we had a near normal night time walk last night. (Although there had been some fireworks soon after nightfall, the heavens remained silent during our late night excursion and Fritz trotted along without objection for once.) The green seems empty this morning but I spot a knot of dog owners over on the walkway near the metal gazebo and so Fritz and I head for this spot.

Dan is just about to leave for work but Davide remains behind with Winnie. He tells us that his parents have arrived from Sardinia with a suitcase full of food—including half a piglet. He is carrying a shopping bag full of these delicacies for Hanna now. Liz is present with Roxy and we spend some time comparing notes on our experience at parents' quiz night at the American School. We didn't win but we did well enough—since our table was undermanned (well, I was the only man) and during the first round we had only half a squad. Best of all, we managed to get nine out of ten sports questions right—quite unexpected.

Dorothy arrives for coffee and actually manages to wait out the line and come away with some refreshments this time. There is quite a turnout this morning; we rarely have a dozen owners on a weekday morning. Today is the last day for Jean, who returns with Billy and Mozart to Glasgow this afternoon. Mozart has to be separated from Ché, whom he dislikes. This makes sense to me since Mozart, a creature of the European aristocracy, would naturally recoil from a Red. There is a mountain of toast for the dogs to get through and they do. Albert arrives with Tinkerbelle and Saffy—they don't have to wear their collars any longer. As we get up to leave Linda arrives with Pepper. She and I use the back passage while Dorothy heads out the Morshead gate on the way to her gym. It is starting to drizzle.

Tuesday, November 14:

After another very successful night walk Fritz enters the park on a grey Tuesday morning. Ofra and Bailey are at our heels and together we make our way toward the green. One group of dog owners is stationed here and first Ofra, then I have to locate Sparkie's yellow ball on a rope—which has gotten lost in the leaves and with which he travels to the park every morning. Janet arrives back from New York for a reunion with Koko. At the road junction at the corner of the café fence a second group of owners is having a huddle—Jean-Baptise, Dan, and Michaela. I join them for a while and then I have to depart in order to keep an eye on

Fritz. He runs into the forecourt where a lonely Ronnie has staked out a place at two conjoined tables.

I ask him if he has received a copy of the letter I got today from Charlotte Dale, Senior Committee and Scrutiny Officer of the Cabinet, Committee and Scrutiny Secretariat of the City of Westminster. The matter at hand is, our course, our famous petition. "The petition has been passed to David Kerrigan, Head of Parks and Leisure, who has been asked to prepare a report on the issue for the attention of Councillor Daniel Astaire, Cabinet Member for Customer and Community Services, detailing either the action taken or seeking instruction as to the action to be taken." It would be hard to keep a straight face in all this bureaucratic fog were it not for the importance of the outcome for the dog gang of Paddington Rec.

When the others have taken their seats for coffee Liz passes out the cartoon catchphrase quiz—which she, Dorothy and I took at quiz night on Sunday. She has brought as a prize a bottle of wine from a French vineyard in which her Tom holds a 1/50th share—and a large supply of pens and pencils. It doesn't take too long for those assembled to complete their papers—though Georgie blurts out one answer before being shushed by the quizmaster. Kate is the victor, with seven out of ten captions correctly pencilled in. Skye, meanwhile, has a red squeaky ball in her mouth and this causes Fritz to fall into a jealous rage. He refuses to take any further sustenance until he gets the prize, but I make sure Kate has it back before we head for home.

Wednesday, November 15:

It is a pleasant, sunny morning as Fritz and I make our way into the park. Our new night-time routine seems to have taken hold (last night we walked with Natasha and little Leila) and there is less desperation prior to our departure for the park, which takes place at 9:15. Almost immediately we run into Linda, who is waiting for us with Pepper—who will be Fritz's play date. Today is her father's birthday and Linda wants to take him for lunch at Fortnum's and so after we have walked close to the Randolph exit she hands Pepper's blue lead over to me and I have two Schnauzers in tow (Fritz is off lead) as we all head in for the café—where I can anchor the fellows to the feet of my chair.

Dorothy arrives as well and we sit in the sun while Ofra continues her obsession over coffee making (now it is the coffee itself that she is preoccupied with). Dan announces that Helen is returning for her graduation and will be visiting us in the park on December 16th. Ofra says someone will have to remind her—but then, when her Guy was born and they asked her for the date of her marriage, she had to phone her mother for the answer as she had forgotten that too. Meanwhile her Bailey seems to be an object of desire both for Hector, who keeps wandering off before being collared (quite literally) by Peter—and Ché, who keeps poking his nose under our table—a matter of extreme outrage to Fritz—who spends much of the session in Ofra's lap. No one can figure out why Bailey should serve as such a siren to the other male dogs, though Dan has always had his doubts about the King Charles' sexuality. Liz brings some doggy biscuits that she picked up in a bakery in New York during the summer and these are shared out to the assembled pooches. Noticing Fritz in Ofra's lap, she says, "Of all the dogs here Fritz is the one who most resembles a real person."

When we leave I show Dorothy the new back passage. Both Fritz, who does an endless circle dance before depositing his plop, and Pepper, who usually does his right on the pavement, move along in a fairly brisk fashion—while hockeyettes are banging the ball in the fenced field on our left. Once returned, the two dogs have the first of several extended wrestling matches, parting at last to enjoy a rest period—Fritz preferring the sofa in the TV room, Pepper nestling down next to me on my blue sofa and finishing up with a snooze on his favourite perch, the brown sofa in the sitting room.

Thursday, November 16:

A light rain is falling on a dark, grey morning. Fritz doesn't seem too discomfited by moisture like this and so we head for the park at about 9:15. In the doggy playpen on Morshead Road I can see David with two Staffies, Stella and Pudding—earlier at 7:00 I could hear him in the same space with Pasha the Weimaraner. When Fritz and I reach the green I can see none of our usual group, though there are a few dog owners making a stroll along the walkways. This is not too surprising, since wet weather often reduces our numbers considerably.

I can see Ronnie emerging from the café with his espresso and Ofra arrives with Bailey—so I take Fritz under the protective covering of the café's eaves. Rosie is dressed in a raincoat that is the same colour as Ronnie's Barbour jacket. Bailey is still attracting the attention of other males—this time it is Phoenix who has to be chased off. Hanna arrives with Spadge and George, both sodden, but they join the queue for handouts of puppy kibble from my yellow Selfridges bag. Ofra spends most of the session on her mobile phone. Vicky pokes her head out of the door to greet the loyal doggy faithful—who now include Tanya the dog warden and the heavily pregnant Franca. I have been carrying two items in my leather jacket pocket, an article about *Lost* for David and the recent letter from the Council for Tanya. Naturally, on a day in which I see both, I am wearing my rain jacket not my leather one.

Conversation topics include mobile phones and genetics. Ofra, who has been getting text messages from 118 118, shows us that she can also get texts in Hebrew. Hanna has seen a program in which it was proved that all those who claim to be 100% English are no such thing. I add that Americans have always known that they are a mixed up lot. Hanna says that all humankind is descended from just twelve individuals—but about this I have my doubts.

Friday, November 17:

Just as we are leaving the house the drizzle, which has been dripping since dawn, intensifies, and I am regretting the fact that I am not wearing my rain jacket today. Fritz makes quick work of his first poo however, and we cross the wet green, where only Kate stands, bravely slinging the ball Skyeward. I can see two shapes huddling in the bushes at a corner of the café and these prove to be the moms of Rizzo (Denise) on the one hand and of Oscar and Scamp (Sabina) on the other. They are hiding from the rain and I join them for a few minutes before rounding the corner to join Liz in front of the café. These ladies have told me that Peter's wife June has died—and that the funeral is today.

We are joined by Kate, who leaves rather quickly, and by Dan and a dogless Hanna—the turnout is almost as poor today as it was yesterday. At an adjacent table we have Tanya the dog warden (whom I give the Council letter to read) and Franca, now only a week away from her due date and complaining about water retention and high blood pressure. I don't see Frank but Bianca comes over to our table for some toast—as does Hootch, who comes in with Finn and his mom (Maggie). I don't recognize him at first—he has lost a lot of weight—but I must say that he has a wonderful collar, with turquoise beadwork prominent: Navajo dog.

Dan is planning an outing with his old school friend Bryan (they have known each other since they were eleven—when they were famous enemies). Hanna suggests that the two always get up to mischief and, indeed, Dan regales us with a long account of arriving drunk at posh Rosmarino in St. John's Wood, an evening punctuated by his knocking their table over as he sat down and Brian ordering a cheap bottle of plonk and then telling the waiter, "You order the food for us; you know what goes best with this wine, my good man." Fortunately, Dan adds, the restaurant was almost empty while these shenanigans were ongoing—the only other table being occupied by J.K. of Jamiroquai. A lot of toast is handed out to the few dogs at our feet and then a shivering Fritz jumps into Hanna's lap and we soon head off with Dan for the gates. It rains all day long.

Saturday, November 18:

It is chilly but very sunny this morning and this makes quite a change from the weather as we have known it for the last few days. Even before we have reached our gate we encounter Dan with Winnie, who releases a veritable lake as she squats for her first pee. Out on the green we meet David the dogsitter with the Staffie, Stella. He is afraid to let her off the lead—not only because she is a bit rough with the other dogs but because she never comes back when called. I have brought an article about the resumption of *Lost* this weekend, but he is outraged that this program has gone from Channel 4 to Sky 1.

Pretty soon our group heads in for coffee (the Saturday morning dog training class is slow to form up). We now see several faces missing during the recent period of inclemency—including Georgie, who says that every time she started out with Sparkie and Koko she was driven back by lashings of rain. Janet has some Hershey's cookies to share out—they taste very much like the mint chocolate delicacies peddled by the Girl Scouts. John sits down with Hanna at the next table, which means that Ché sticks his head into our proceedings on a number of occasions—and whenever he does so Fritz, sitting in my lap, lets out a roar of disapproval;

as far as he is concerned Ché is not a member of his group, at least not as far as sharing in the *table d'hote*—and he needs to know this.

Today is Rosie's sixth birthday, but there is only one problem. Neither she nor Ronnie, who has invited us to the celebration, is present. After a while we get worried and Dan calls Ronnie on his mobile phone—he has been delayed by the window cleaner but he will be here soon. In the meantime we address ourselves to the usual variety of topics: exchanging Winnie's ASBO t-shirt for a larger size, Janet's trip to a Harlem gospel service, Liz's search for prints appropriate for the walls of Romano's restaurant, Sparkie's punkish hair-do, Jasmine's underbite, Dan's forthcoming trip to Blenheim Palace. Ronnie arrives at last but we are almost all ready to leave by this time.

Sunday, November 19:

Today is a repetition of yesterday, weatherwise—that is very sunny and quite chilly at the same time—I am glad that, for the second day in a row, I have worn my long underwear. I have also brought with me a new tennis ball, grey with pink dots, that I have purchased at St. John's Pets. It doesn't have much life to it but Fritz is eager to give it a chase in the wet grass and, for once, he manages to get in some good exercise in its pursuit. This means that we don't get to spend too much time with the others, huddling around the cricket crease, though I do notice that Miss Koko is refusing to get down and dirty (that is cold and wet) with the rest of them today. She is wearing a quilted coat and Janet has added her own scarf to the protective layers as the senior Shih-Tzu is carried about in a disapproving heap. Only when we go in for coffee do I see that Koko has had a short haircut—and she's making a meal of it.

That I can get Fritz to make mad dashes after his new ball is all the more remarkable since last night we again had to deal with a sustained bombardment. The timing could not have been worse since loud fireworks went off somewhere to the east almost as soon as we stepped from the front door. Fritz, of course, wanted to head back up the stairs almost immediately, without lifting his leg once, but I persisted in dragging him around the corner so that we could head west along Essendine, that is away from the noise. He managed to trot along in a lively fashion as far as Shirland Road but getting him turned around for the trip home was a sore trial—even though by now the firing had stopped. Of course he started to pant as soon as we went to bed and I had to get up and go into another room until, calmed a bit by a dose of Rescue Remedy, he returned to a calmer state. Both Janet and Georgie say that they heard the bombardment as well—our government can tell us that you can't advertise Sugar Smacks during a kiddie's TV program because there might be a weak-willed mum who wouldn't know how to say no, but our society can't find a way of keeping our neighbourhood from sounding like the Israeli-Lebanese border.

Ronnie has laid on the refreshments in honour of Rosie's missed birthday yesterday and we have a jolly time—though our twin tables look a bit unbalanced since I am the only one with dark glasses and everyone else has taken a chair on the opposite side so they won't have to look into the sun. Dan reports that he and his friend Bryan had a good day out and didn't get into any mischief unless you count the game they made of seeing how many little old ladies they could squeeze into each shot. The dogs are playing musical laps. At one point Fritz is sitting in Ofra's lap while, across the table, Bailey is sitting in Dorothy's. I have Sparkie, Bailey and Fritz in my lap, and Dorothy is visited by Albert's Tinkerbelle—who gives her a big kiss on the nose. A great deal of toast is delivered to our table and even two extra coffees by mistake. Fritz, meanwhile, has to be unhooked so that he can visit Ellen's table for his sausage fix. Winnie has a brainstorm and attacks the dozy (and innocent) Roxy.

Monday, November 20:

Another night of wind and rain has given way to clearer skies; leaves have fallen in great numbers and it seems that Fritz wants to check out each one as we make slow progress toward the green. Peter has returned to the park with his Holly and I pause to offer my condolences. He seems to be bearing up well and has posted a very nice thank you note on park trees to all of his well-wishers.

I take out the tennis ball and Fritz has some more good exercise but the ball also proves of great fascination to the other dogs. Oscar has it for a while, using it as bait to get four other pooches to chase him. Then Charlie the Spaniel makes off with it and I have to bribe him with a treat before he will let go. Fritz is not in a mood to contest matters for long and soon trots off to see what Saffy and Tinkerbelle are doing over near the bandstand. As we head in for coffee we encounter a twelve week-old

Boxer puppy named Chica. She is also an object of fascination to two senior cousins, Bianca and Max, who come tearing over to check her out.

We have a rather small group at coffee—since Kate and Liz depart before refreshments. Today only Ronnie, Georgie, Dan and Peter (of Peter and Hector) are present. Georgie has the care of Koko, who still looks miserable and won't indulge us when we ask her to sing. Winnie has a newer, looser-fitting version of her A.S.B.O. t-shirt and some time is spent trying to come up with alternate versions of this legend—I suggest, "Always Serene, Bark Off!" Dan says that in the doggy department of Debenhams he has spotted a Vicky Pollard costume (in pink, with the *Little Britain* catchphrase, "Yeh, But No, But Yeh" on it)—so I guess we know what Winnie is getting for Christmas.

Peter eats a plate of beans on toast and the dogs have their usual snacks before the group makes an early departure. As we head for the exit gates three Thai nannies form a phalanx with their pushchairs. They are chattering away in their native tongue and Dan says, "Won't the parents be surprised when baby's first words are "Bingau, Binga, Bado?" As Fritz and I walk along the doggy pen fence a wind-disturbed limb comes crashing down right behind us. We are uninjured but I'm not so sure about the roof of that black Volkswagen.

Tuesday, November 21:

It is quite cold, though bright, as Fritz and I make our way past the ubiquitous leaf blower. It takes forever for my dog to part with his gift; he circles some newly planted bushes outside the kiddie playground and I consider it rather unseemly for him to fertilize the foliage in this fashion—so I pull him free just as he lets loose. Surprisingly, there is not a soul out on the green, though I can see some of the owners, in small groups, walking on the roadways and around the perimeter. Inside the café forecourt I can see Ronnie sitting by himself with Rosie and so, without Fritz having had any real exercise, we go in to join him.

The other owners trail in but we are still a small group, again oddly positioned—with Ofra, Liz, Dan, Georgie and Ronnie sitting with their backs to the sun and me on the opposite side, staring into the fiery orb with my dark glasses on. Liz is planning a busy few weeks, with a Thanksgiving trip to Ireland this Thursday, house moving on Monday, a trip to Bermuda to surprise a friend on her 50th birthday, and kids at home for a two-week Christmas holiday. Ofra is on the phone, trying to get the builders to get a move on—as she and her family, in alternate accommodation for a month or so, are planning to move back home this weekend. There is another discussion on which actor might serve as the *alter ego* of some of our dogs. Brad Pitt gets to play Sparkie and Rupert Everett takes the role of Bailey. There is a debate over Winnie's casting. I suggest Margaret Rutherford but Dan seems to favour Boris Karloff.

Ancient Doofie comes in and his mom asks me what ever happened to Michael and his Charlie. Meanwhile, Doofie's alternative guardian, Michael the Pirate, wheels his bike in. I haven't seen him in some time but he tells me that he has been more unwell than usual these days. Indeed, to prove his point, he produces a piece of orange note paper on which he has listed his weight (down to eight and a half stones) and some twenty symptoms—hoping that the clinician he is planning to visit might actually say he qualifies for disability payments. As we make our way toward the Morshead gate, Georgie, to continue this medical theme, says that her doctors would like to install an arterial stent at St. Mary's. She is hanging back now because Koko has turned off to walk onto the running track next to an open gate. She is not contemplating a few laps (Koko doesn't think much of running these days) but because she has spotted a puddle where she can get a long drink.

Wednesday, November 22:

Fritz and I are about ten minutes earlier than usual today but I can't say that there is much change in the Paddington scene. The thumping sounds of construction continue to thunder in the background. Middle Eastern moms are walking back through the park after dropping their kids off at the Essendine school. Chica is trying to greet all the dogs, a gesture discouraged by a snarly Fritz. And Rizzo makes a dashing entry in the basket of his mommy's bicycle.

I have brought the tennis ball with me and I am soon following my dog around the green in a vain attempt to get him to *drop* the toy before he takes it into the bushes or loses it in the leaves. We do manage to get in a lot of exercise, particularly on the dryer surface of the Randolph walkway. A little girl asks if she can pet Fritz and he does a good job of coming when I call him and of sitting patiently while he is touched by the little blondie. Then we go over to see Ziggy at tug of war with Chilli—the prize being a tree limb. Outside the café Peter is standing with Holly, explaining in patient detail how he is getting through all the tasks that have followed on the death of his wife.

At 9:30 I join the others at coffee. Liz is having a meltdown over the price quoted by Banham for safety and alarm installations at her new house. They want £4,000 and she says she had an entire house wired in the States for $800. Ronnie says that as a jeweller he has had a lot of experience with alarms—and he calls a friend on his mobile and sets up another visit for Liz from a firm he recommends. Liz then explains that last night she attended a group Thanksgiving fete with other ASL parents. Each guest was supposed to bring something that represented a "family tradition." ("And in your family, take out is the tradition, right?" I ask). Stumped, Liz went to Ambra on Abbey Road and tried to buy something that *looked* homemade. She ended up with an apple pie—but Ryan, her son, dropped it on its side and then presented it to their hostess before Liz had a chance to take it out of its box. Meanwhile, at my feet, our two dogs, Fritz and Roxy, are having a furious barking match over possession of a piece of buttered toast. Perhaps it is just as well that I have to leave early because of my haircutting appointment on Boundary Road.

Thursday, November 23:

Even though a brief shower has washed over the park only an hour or so before we arrive, it is now bright and sunny as Fritz and I enter the park on a chilly Thursday morning. A mother is heading our way with a little toddler and I can hear that they are chattering away in French. I can never understand how a baby can speak French—and I can't! But then I have known some awfully dense people who can play the piano beautifully.

I take out the grey tennis ball with the pink dots and Fritz and I begin our usual toss, recover, gobble, abscond, drop and abandon. I manage to keep track of the ball for quite a while, even pursuing my dog into the still closed café, but, when he runs off with the ball in his mouth and decides to visit a nice black dog in front of the clubhouse, the ball goes missing in the leaves and this time I can't find it. That's the bad news. The good news is that I find an abandoned pink throwing ring and Fritz soon switches his attention to this plastic toy—which, unlike the tennis ball, proves to be very airworthy. For some strange reason a little black Scottie (seemingly ownerless) is part of the mix today and this means that Fritz, the boss of the green, has to put the newcomer in his place—in this case on his back. Jean-Baptise complements me on my new green and white scarf—which is, in fact, an ancient garment knitted by my sister-in-law so that I could wear it to Michigan State University football games. I appreciate the complement but I too have suffered a loss—my old brown cashmere scarf has gone missing while Dorothy and I were out with Ronnie and Susie at the ballet last night.

Fritz is sitting on the bench next to Peter and Ellen when we go in for coffee. The dogs all have wet feet and there is some reluctance on the part of the owners when it comes to admitting these soaking feet to dry laps. I get Bailey in my lap, Hanna has to fight off Winnie, and Dan, after shielding his trousers with Koko's coat, allows the Shih-Tzu a perch on his lap. I tell Hanna, who accompanies me as we take the back passage home, that I want to take a picture of George with his muzzle on—the Hannibal Lecter of Paddington Rec. She says she has to give him a bath first—and, indeed, the little white dog is the worse for wear—having sat down in a puddle on the one hand and scraped his back on a tailpipe on the other.

Friday, November 24:

Fritz and I meet Janet, just as we enter the park; she is accompanied by the heavily quilted Miss Koko—who looks very cross as she puts her paws down on the wet ground. I am carrying the pink throwing ring inside my jacket and when Fritz has accomplished the first order of his business I pull it out and get it into play. It can really travel a great distance and Fritz can't really catch up with it if I give it all my strength. At any rate he isn't used to looking up to see where his quarry is heading and often charges off in the wrong direction. It is also very muddy underfoot and every time I pick the toy off the grass my hand is encrusted. When it is time for coffee I have to leave Fritz with the others and go in to wash my hands—never a pleasant experience in a loo whose drying machines never work.

Although there are two tables still drawn together at one end of the café forecourt we only need to use one—since only Davide, Georgie and Janet are present. Koko is by this time swaddled not only in her own coat but in Janet's black scarf. Both Bailey and Sparkie manage to saturate my trousers with their wet paws. There isn't much toast but I supplement these provisions with some kibble from my yellow Selfridges sack. Jo comes by with Tilly and the little dog comes over for a handout as well. Much of the morning's conversation is devoted to the first evictions on *I'm A Celebrity, Get Me Out of Here!*—the consensus seems to be that the voting of viewers in these matters is an extension of the bullying instincts that flavour this whole production.

We decide to have a traditional back passage walkround. There is much heavy construction on our right as we wend our way in a narrow fenced passage between the playing fields and the building site. As we walk along the cedars at the back I note that Sparkie likes to wind up the dogs located in the back yards of the Kilburn Park Road houses over the fence. His provocative barking in their direction is such a poignant reminder of Michael's Charlie—who used to like to do the same thing. We make slow progress toward the gates—but at least it hasn't started to rain on us.

Saturday, November 25:

Rain has been falling on a brisk and fresh Saturday morning as Fritz and I dodge the puddles in order to make our entrance into the park. Dan, in an orange rain jacket, is just ahead of us with Winnie. Out on the green I can see that we have the usual Saturday morning division, with Roland and the obedience students nearer the café and an independent group of dog owners nearer the cricket crease. When Fritz finally does his poo poo I unhook him and we head for the latter group.

I can see one new member, a Golden Retriever with a filthy sodden coat. His name is Buddy or, as his mom Saskia adds, Muddy Buddy. She says that the former rescue dog loves mud and seeks it out in order to have a good roll. "I hope you live near a large body of water," I say. Buddy spots Skye and these two are soon at raucous play. Thereafter Skye begins to leap up against her favourite, David the dogsitter (here with Molly the Cocker) and Fritz, who believes that David is *his*, objects vociferously to this behaviour. Fritz is also very interested in the obedience class and spends a good deal of time on its periphery. Once I whistle for him and to my amazement (and, I hope, that of the canine scholars) he responds immediately. Dorothy arrives and we head in for coffee. Behind us the pupil from Staffordshire is attacking one of the other students.

We have a large group at breakfast, with most of us seated at the two adjacent tables and others arriving as outriders. These include Hanna, at her own table, Jo, standing up, and Albert who sits as a satellite with Saffy and Tinkerbelle—dressed in identical pink raincoats. Conversation again returns to *I'm A Celebrity, Get Me Out of Here!* and Jo says, "It's everything good and everything awful about television. But you just *have* to watch it." Fritz is looking for a lap to jump into but Dorothy is reluctant to admit him, since he is standing in a puddle and from this position he manages to spray both Faz and me with his wet paws. I have to use my handkerchief on my glasses and while I am thus distracted Fritz jumps into *my* lap. I get up to leave and Hanna hands me a roll of wrapping paper that she has purchased at Ikea for Linda. Hanna has been joined at her little table by Peter—who has been telling people that some woman is getting up a petition to have him (or Hector or Jodie) banned from the park.

Sunday, November 26:

The skies are very unusual this morning—much sun penetrating thick cloud and producing pink and yellow touches in the grey. Long before we have to make our way into the park the heavens open and, unusually for this early hour, we have the first low rumblings of thunder. Fritz doesn't seem too bothered by this noise but I begin to wonder what it will be like if he and I have to walk in this deluge. In the meantime not one but two wonderful rainbows arch across the northern skies. Dorothy gets drenched as she makes a run for her Sunday newspapers and in the quiet zone that follows Fritz and I at last make a break for it.

It is fairly bright outside and the rain is just dripping now. We make a lively entrance into the park—which is virtually empty. Eventually we cross paths with Barbara and her Hendrix, heading for home, and reach the deserted green. Fritz manages to part with his gift in a pile of leaves and we continue in a grand circle around the green, meeting only a chap under an umbrella who is walking two Labs. I keep my dog on lead, not knowing what the consequences might be if a lightning bolt were to land near us. By the time we have rounded the far corner it begins to rain again in earnest and we take refuge in the metal gazebo where Peter and Ellen have sheltered with their dogs. Fritz manages to get his wet paws on Ellen's slacks. Another rainbow covers the northern horizon, embracing every corner of the park.

There is no one at the café and, at any rate, I want to get Fritz home before we get the next peal of thunder. As we reach the clubhouse I can see Georgie, Janet and Kate hiding in the alcove with their dogs. I explain that I am not stopping for coffee and we continue to make progress toward the gates. By now the heavens have really opened up and it is really throwing it down. The stormy weather persists until the early afternoon and more than once we can see only the bum of our frightened dog—the rest of him having disappeared under the covers of our bed.

Monday, November 27:

I am still wearing my rain jacket when Fritz and I return to the park—but there is only a little moisture in the air and the temperatures are mild enough. Out on the muddy green Oscar the Schnauzer is visiting with Rufus and Charlie the Cocker. Fritz, however, shows no interest in this scene and heads for the foothills of Mt. Bannister, where, to my horror, I see him squeeze under the fencing in order to penetrate the building site behind the café, future home of the newest version of the displaced cricket nets (—as if anyone plays cricket around here anymore). To get him to retreat I begin to run in the opposite direction, a spectacle that does rivet his attention—soon he is at my feet as we approach the paved walkway up the mount itself. Hanna is struggling up this path with George and Spadge—so we continue to the top. Here we encounter a continuation of the fencing that Fritz knows how to squeeze beneath—and he does so here as well, disappearing down the hill toward the Carlton roadway. I have to drop down to the parking lot on this side and make my way forward to the tarmac and here I can see Fritz emerging from the building site after a close inspection. It is time to retreat to the café itself.

There are no large tables under the eaves and so we make do with two little ones, Georgie, Ofra and Kate at one, Ronnie and Hanna joining me at a second. Ronnie and I discuss the *Sunday Times* review of the ballet performance we went to on Thursday and then he has to go off to the Randolph surgery to have his sinuses checked out. I ask him to drop my prescription renewal request off for me. Hanna and I feed toast to our dogs but they soon grow bored and we throw the leftover pieces of bread to the pigeon with one leg.

Hanna accompanies me on a back passage walkround. On our right, trapped behind fencing, is a lonely red poo poo bin at the head of what will eventually become a third football pitch. Hanna is still bewailing the loss of green space that the construction of this facility necessitates. When we reach the back of the running track Fritz is blindsided by a bouncing Leila and we are passed by the 118 chap who is pushing a bike and wearing a red knapsack. Hanna speculates that his little black dog, Jasper, goes in the bag when David is riding his bike. I say I like it when dogs settle down in the front baskets of their owner's bike. We also pass a huge Rottweiler named Bobo and his owner confirms that Franca has given birth to a baby girl in St. Mary's a few days ago. I ask if the baby has a name and she thinks she's called Valentina. I say goodbye to Hanna at the Essendine gate and then both of us have a giggle for, in the wake of our earlier conversation, we spot Rizzo, his big ears flapping, as he sits in his bike basket for the ride home.

Tuesday, November 28:

Not surprisingly, it is spitting outside and so I put my rain jacket on and Fritz and I enter the park on a very grey morning. There aren't many people around, also not a surprise, and so I keep Fritz on lead as we head around the green in a grand circle. Only when we near the café do we encounter someone we know, Georgie, who this morning has both Sparkie and Bailey. It is only about 9:20 but even so the café seems to be open—so Georgie and I sit down at a table under the overhang and wait the arrival of the rest of the regulars.

These include Hanna, Dan and Faz. Dan wants to make sure that I notice that he is wearing Wellington boots and that this therefore symbolizes his official recognition of winter. Faz, who has earlier reported by phone that he and Di have been unsuccessful in attaching Koko's harness because she growled at them (she was at their house on a sleepover last night), now arrives with Jasmine and Koko, though the harness experts are convinced that he's put this object on wrongly. Faz is taking the second half of his sergeant's exam today but he has to endure some ribbing—what kind of a tough cop is afraid of an elderly Shih-tzu?

Georgie is obviously upset because her downstairs neighbour has again passed a note through her box (he has *said* nothing, though they have met several times in the street) complaining that Sparkie has been whining and barking for the last three weeks when left alone in the morning. Adding to her consternation is the fact that she can remember only two days when Sparkie has been left alone in recent days. Her attempt to call on the snarlyboodle to discuss these matters was met by silence—though he was obviously at home. Recognizing that someone facing heart surgery doesn't need this kind of anxiety, Dan reminds Georgie that others would gladly have Sparkie in the mornings.

Toast is administered to our dogs while quite a few casual visitors float by our table. One of these is the ancient Doofie, another is the muddy Buddy (though surprisingly clean this morning) and we even have an appearance by the bigheaded Scottie, Raffy, whom I have not seen since January—2005! Fritz isn't charmed by the appearance of this stranger in our midst and he makes the usual protests. Hanna passes around a flyer announcing a Doggy Christmas Party, sponsored by the dog training class and others, here in the park on December 9. In the meantime I am getting mightily cold and when the others at last head for the green for some post-coffee exercise I take the opportunity to head for home.

Wednesday, November 29:

Bright sunshine presides over a chilly park this morning and Fritz and I are not alone, for once, as we make our way toward the green. The owners of some of the smaller dogs say that their animals have just had a bust-up with a Labrador. They are keeping cautiously to the walkways, their dogs on lead, and undertaking a shady stroll near the Grantully gate. I put Fritz on lead as well but there doesn't seem to be any menace coming from any direction and before long we have completed our circle and entered the café.

Fritz camps out at the feet of Peter and Ellen but they have to tell him that the sausages have not yet arrived. At our collection of tables we have Georgie (still fretting over her tetchy neighbour), Dan, Ronnie, Ofra, Hanna, Celine and Dorothy. Ronnie tells us that Susie lost her bracelet after attending an engagement party at the Royal Hospital in Chelsea last night and found it again in the gutter next to her car this morning. Dan says that Davide, exulting in the strength of the pound *vis-a-vis* the dollar has called him from Macy's in New York to ask him if he wanted anything. (Dan says he was so excited that he couldn't think of a thing.) Ofra tells us that three youths robbed her son Guy and two of his friends at knifepoint yesterday. It was the first day that Guy had been allowed to walk home from school—and now he'll have to be driven again.

For the first time in a number of weeks we have one of those long, collective walkrounds—eight owners and their dogs (including Kate, who has joined us with Skye). Especially when we reach the narrowed walkway opposite the recently rubberized playing pitch we tend to be squeezed into a long queue—while an Australian games mistress is lecturing her maroon-clad hockeyettes in the art of lunging. Koko does a poo poo in the middle of this perambulation, which ends when Dorothy and I peel off at our gate in order to get ready for the next assault on Sainsbury's.

Thursday, November 30:

The sun is again shining as Fritz and I travel along the pavement, heading for the Morshead gate. From the opposite direction I can see Martha the Boxer and Ziggy, both still on lead, walking towards the same gate with their owners. Fritz is the first to reach the gate and, after a quick pee, he decides to protect the park against all comers by growling in his usual bullying fashion at the young dogs who have now reached the gate as well. On this occasion, however, he meets his well-deserved comeuppance when Martha, showing that she is a true Boxer, reaches out with a left hook and bops Fritz on the nose. My dog is quite surprised by this gesture and, his dignity restored, continues along toward the green.

We see Fritz II. Yesterday a woman I have never seen before had charge of the fellow. Today it is Oscar and Scamp's owner, Sabina. Fritz II is quite shy and it is a struggle getting close enough to give him a pet. Fritz the First and I continue round the green, encountering only Georgie with Koko and Sparkie—who is barking away at everyone. Georgie tells me that she encountered our Michael on the Harrow Road recently and that he complained of depression. While I am digesting this information we encounter Dan and Davide near the café. With reference to the recent spy poisoning murder (in which a radioactive substance was used) I suggest that I can now tell these two apart by seeing which one of them glows in the dark. Davide's BA loyalties are tested by this joke about radioactivity aboard the Moscow flights—he insists that it is *not* funny.

At breakfast Ofra tells us another tale in her desperate campaign to become the poster princess for forgetfulness. This time, she tells us, she had just driven away from a petrol station on the Finchley Road when she remembered that she had left her mobile phone of the car's roof. She and her daughter walked along the pavement for several blocks attempting to find the phone in the gutter—but they didn't have Susie's luck. In the meantime Ofra spent the next hour trying to dial her own number—but no one was answering. Finally a Scotsman, who says that he was just walking down the Finchley Road when a mobile phone landed at his feet, answered the ring. He said he would return the phone to Ofra's house as soon as his car was fixed. Later in the afternoon he duly arrived, though by this time Ofra, fearing the worst, had surrounded herself with all the rest of her family, including husband Ricky. The Scotsman turned out to be a teacher—who said he had always been fascinated by Jewish people. He chattered on for two hours and by this time Ofra had gone to bed. This story takes a long time to tell and by now we are ready to begin a back passage walkround (more hockeyettes under instruction, though these are smaller than yesterday's group and clad in green, not maroon).

Bailey at breakfast

Buddy takes his place on the green

Koko and Jasmine wait for their treats

Skye the Alsatian has a moment of relaxation

Davide with Winnie at the Park Café

A breakfast scene: (from left) Ofra, Georgie, Hanna, Janet

Albert with Saffy and Tinkerbelle

Young Liam on the green with Pepper (l) and Fritz

December, 2006

Friday, December 1:

Rain has just ended as Fritz and I make our way into a grey park on the first day of December. Not surprisingly, there is no one about—not on the green, not at the caff.

I keep Fritz on lead as we stroll along the Carlton roadway and then penetrate the parking lot, finally climbing the hill—the steepest and shortest route to the top of Mt. Bannister. A fine prospect opens up with each new step, though the trees have lost most of their autumn foliage by now.

We begin our descent to the green and I can at last see Georgie, Dan and Janet making their way in our direction. By the time our paths intersect Dan is deep into a scene-by-scene rendition of *Borat* the movie while Winnie is almost bringing a jogger down at our feet. We decide that a safer place might be inside the fence of the café and here, somewhat earlier than usual, we repair—joining an already seated Hanna, who is soon protesting over the presence of Winnie's wet paws on her trousers. Dan tells us that he has purchased an Advent calendar with chocolate doggy treats for his pet and that each day she gets to put her paws on a new window—preparatory to receiving her treat. "I can get one for you too," he tells me. "Fritz is Jewish," I respond defensively, putting an end to this theme in our conversation.

Dan now tells us that an Elvis impersonator has been haunting the booking office of his theatre—encouraged by the staff, who are easily bored. I mention that earlier this week Dorothy and I witnessed another West End incident when an hysterical woman, having just sat down for a viewing of *The Devil Wears Prada* at the Trocadero, discovered that a mouse had jumped into her lap! Kate comes by at this point with Skye—who has been poorly of late. Her symptoms began with an itchy ear but, perhaps after an adverse reaction to the medicine, she began to have a kind of fit, and the vet discovered a much slower than average heartbeat. The huge dog seems fine to us now but the mere recital of this saga has brought the tears to Kate's eyes and, no longer in the mood for additional merriment, Hanna says, "Is anyone walking round?"—a cue for all of us to begin the march home.

Saturday, December 2:

The sun is trying to break through a thick grey sky as we make our way into the park. When we reach the green we encounter Janet and Georgie, who are searching the leaves for Sparkie's lost ball-on-a-rope. I find this end of the green to be a black hole for doggy toys—but I spend a good deal of fruitless energy searching for this object as well. Fritz is let loose to pursue his wanderings and I follow at a great distance—with my attention soon drawn to Fritz II, who enters with his own parents this time. He has grown into a beautiful, sturdy boy—at least twice the size of his namesake. Both Fritzes take some time off to integrate the dog training class. We receive handouts of the flyer advertising the doggy Christmas Party next Saturday—"mince pies and Bailey's for owners."

At breakfast we are joined by Hanna, Dan, Ronnie, Dorothy, and John—whose Ché completes his patented patio poo. John shows us a long plastic sleeve—which should have been *two* of Tanya's green poo poo bags, but here they are strangely fused (pity that Liam is not collecting such objects any more—this would be the inverted biplane postage stamp of poo poo bags). Janet is collecting doggy birthday information for her annual calendar and asks for photo contributions as well. The sun at last comes out and for those of us facing it there is a lot of squinting required. Fritz jumps on my lap and tries to knock my cap of with his nose. Then he jumps in Dan's lap.

A back passage walkround begins as we pass Angie, looking well on her wheelie zimmer frame. A leathery games mistress arrives to inspect the pitch before committing her lasses to this morning's competition. As we near the Essendine gate there is an odd instance of global warming. The fragrant yellow mahonia is beginning to bloom; this *is* a winter flower—what is unusual is to see three bumblebees (in December) inspecting the blossoms. I have been in the park for an hour and a half and, thoroughly chilled, I am glad to get back inside.

Sunday, December 3:

It is still raining lightly, after an extremely stormy night, when Fritz and I emerge from our dwelling place and crunch over all the fallen twigs that have settled on the pavement leading to Paddington Rec. I keep my dog on lead and this makes for a difficult moment when he decides to squat over some flowerbeds near the bandstand and I have to deal with a low chain fence to reach the prize. I continue to keep him on lead, as I have no desire to go chasing after him on such an unwelcoming day.

After a grand circle I approach the café, where only Richard and Christina are seated with Fritz II. I try to continue yesterday's lesson in kibble catching but the dear boy is rubbish at this sport and one piece after another lands on his eyebrows or his nose. When Janet (carrying Koko again) arrives with Georgie there is a debate over whether we can comfortably sit down in the patio or not. By this time the rain seems to have stopped but it is still breezy and cold (I am wearing my rain jacket *over* my leather jacket and my gloves as well). Eventually we decide to brave it out, and we are soon joined by Dan, Ofra and Faz.

Janet says that Koko is very cross with her—since she would have preferred a warm bed to nature in the raw. She tries to bribe her pet with a small piece of cheese but Koko will take this morsel only when it is offered to her by Georgie. The latter and Faz relive an incident that occurred yesterday afternoon when two young hoodies questioned them closely on the monetary value of their dogs. I would have expected Faz to produce his warrant card at this point (along with a stern warning about dog theft) but he says he only kept close to Georgie for protection.

There are two other echoes of yesterday's events. Dan suddenly remembers that he has a packet of sausage slices in his pocket, leftovers from the largesse of Metty's kitchen yesterday afternoon. And I learn that John, in addition to being a builder, landscape gardener, antique dealer, motorcycle mechanic and shaman, is the rightful heir to the throne of England. So he has told others, even, evidently, producing books of genealogy to illustrate which illegitimate royal bastard he descends from. Janet has told him that there are too many royal bastards already.

I spot Pepper heading our way and before long he and Fritz are giving one another their usual raucous greetings under the table—with Sparkie jumping in my lap to referee. Rob and Linda come up and I turn over Fritz's lead, for he is having a playdate at his pal's house today—while

Dorothy and I attend a funeral. Rob and Linda depart with both dogs and I have to make my way home with no company at all, a most unusual feeling. At least the skies have turned blue and the sun is now out.

Monday, December 4:

It's sunny outside this morning but quite cold and I am wearing my wool hat instead of my usual baseball cap. Just in front of us we see Dan—trying to recover a wayward Winnie from the forbidden rose garden. He kneels to give Fritz a customary cuddle and it is nice to see that Winnie doesn't seem to get jealous at such moments. We walk out onto the muddy green and, when I mention that we have not seen Liz is some ten days, he pulls out his mobile phone and gives her a call. I know she moved houses a week ago and that she is probably preoccupied with these matters but Dan echoes my fear that we don't want to see her sloping off to Regents Park with Roxy—now that she has moved closer to that inviting green space. Liz says she will be back in Paddington Rec tomorrow.

The café, which we reach after a few minutes on the green, will be closing from December 22 to January 3—which, at least, is a shorter period than in previous years. Dan says that he and Davide will be away for much of this period anyway—as they will be flying down to Rio. Hanna asks us if anybody knows how to get the scent of dog urine out of the carpet—as Spadge has had a mortifying accident ten days ago, and every substance she has tried has been defeated by the stench. Ronnie says that shortly after preparing the lunch he planned to bring to his 95 year-old mother in her sheltered accommodation yesterday, she called him to say that she was lost—in her own flat. Kate reports that Skye continues to improve after her recent mysterious illness. She has brought a bag of doggie treats and Fritz, sitting in Dan's lap, is well positioned to command some of these and toast as well.

I suddenly remember to ask if Good Neighbours Day was held in the Rec this year, and Hanna says it was not—in spite of a petition asking for the reinstatement of a true local tradition. GND is used by many of the local entrepreneurs and those raising funds for charities and its loss is keenly felt by them. We ask Hanna what reason was given by the park management for cancelling the event—and she says that the only answer she received was "Well, there's one in Queen's Park."

We rise from our perch in the bright sun (I am wearing dark glasses) to begin a walk round the back. I ask Georgie how I am supposed to spend the rest of a day that now lies blasted in ruins after she has handed me a newspaper with the dire news that Thierry Henry is suffering from sciatica. We walk past the kiddie playground where moms are pushing delighted tots on the new swings. Ronnie notes that you couldn't get a wheelchair along the narrow confines between the fences that now surround us. I am pretty chilled, in spite of all the sun, by the time we have reached home.

Tuesday, December 5:

After a night of gale-force winds there is still a stiff breeze with occasional lashings of rain this morning, and I am wearing not only my leather jacket but my rain jacket stretched tautly over this—I feel like the Michelin Man. The green, not surprisingly, is devoid of customers with the sole exception of Sabina, who has brought Scamp and Oscar out into the middle. We chat for a bit and then she receives a call from Denise, Rizzo's mom, and they agree on a rendezvous point for their traditional walkround. I continue on with Fritz, off lead. He visits a number of distant corners and then I decide to have a peek into the café, even though I have seen none of the gang out in the wild.

In fact there is a pretty good turnout here as we have Dan, Georgie, Ronnie, Ofra, Liz, and Dan's mom Christine seated around a large table in front of the café door. Over coffee Liz begins a detailed recital of the great move, which took place last Monday. The moving people showed up only a few hours late and efficiently transported all the goods and chattels of the family. The latter continued to sleep at their old address for the next few days, with day two devoted to the arrival and set up of lots of expensive electronic equipment, including computers and TVs in the new house. Next day was going to be devoted to the installation of alarms and new locks and Liz was just beginning to congratulate herself on a move well done when she arrived to find that every piece of electronic equipment had been purloined. The police, insisting it was an inside job (movers and other installers at the head of the list) have been first rate, according to Liz, but this is small consolation—it is uncertain whether some of this brand new stuff is even insured. Then hubby, who had hardly been having a hands-on experience in this project so far, pronounced this the worst managed move he had ever heard of. After the explosion that followed, Liz—downing tools—disappeared from the radar for a day, going to four movies and not answering her cell. There will be a cooling off period, fortunately, since she flies to Bermuda for a few days tomorrow.

While we are hearing this woeful tale toast is being distributed to the dogs—who are seeking comfort from the wet floor in any convenient lap. But the moisture continues to seek us out—the rain driving horizontally at us so that pretty soon everyone has squeezed into a semi-circle, with backs to the café door, and even this is ineffective. We are all getting drenched, even though we are under cover. For a while everyone stands up with backs to the windows but when there is a brief lull we make a beeline for the nearest exit—no leisurely walkround along the back passage for us today.

Wednesday, December 6:

Skies have cleared and the sun is bright this morning, but it is also quite breezy and chilly. Fritz seems invigorated by this weather and dashes about with great purpose. Dan tries to interest him in a hard round ball belonging to Winnie; it has a squeaky noise when shaken or rolled but because it is impervious to Schnauzer teeth Fritz soon loses interest in the object and lets some of the other dogs have a go. One of these is Jasper. It is confirmed that he *does* ride in the backpack when his master gets on the bike. More surprising is that the little black chap is not a mongrel, as even his owner once supposed, but something called a Patterdale Terrier—or at least that is the vet's opinion.

While I am learning all these details Fritz wanders off. I see him following Oscar and Scamp and so I head toward the Grantully gate, which is where I last saw him. By the time I have crossed the marshy hillside I note that *my* dog is actually on the opposite side of the green, checking out some of the other dogs. One complication in keeping up with Fritz these days is that, more and more, he has a twin in Oscar, particularly at a distance. Sabina has the same problem. Entering the precincts of the café the other day she thought she saw *her* dog in my lap—but this was Fritz.

When we are reunited I head in for coffee, joining Dan, Ofra, and Georgie. Ronnie comes too but he has had to wait in to have his carpet measured as part of his insurance claim after water poured in from his conservatory roof some weeks ago. Dan is complaining that Davide is behaving like an Xmas Grinch—threatening to burn the Christmas tree that Dan now wants to decorate. Kate tells us that she has had to take Skye outside for plenty of very early morning poos after her pet has devoured a whole bag of Winalot. Sparkie jumps in everyone's lap in turn, kissing us on the nose and settling down for a nice snooze. The dog owners are still stunned by the damage to Liz's property, as reported yesterday, and to her self-esteem.

Thursday, December 7:

The rain has again cleared on a blustery wintry morning, and there is bright sun shining down on the antics of Fritz and his friends as we enter the park today. As we near the green I see a ghost, a toy Yorkie who is the spitting image of the long missing Pebbles. Of course it isn't Georgie's lost pet—for this darting presence is a much younger animal and a male to boot. His name is Jack and he is running about in delight, greeting everyone with great good humour.

Fritz starts off in pursuit of this fellow and soon finds that he is part of a long march around the green in a group that includes Holly, Scamp and Oscar. Fritz has never warmed to the latter, even though they share much in their general appearance—though he doesn't mind running side by side with the younger animal, growling as he goes if Oscar gets too personal. For his part, Oscar is indefatigable in his efforts to win the favour of the senior Schnauzer, and he never gets too discouraged when Fritz chases him off. By the time we have reached the entrance to the café there is quite a collection of dogs at play—these include the puppy Chica and her adolescent cousin, Martha. Dan has again brought Winnie's hard plastic ball, the one that squeaks when shaken or rolled—but Fritz can't be drawn into any long-lasting affection for the toy since he can't make it squeak with his teeth.

I go inside to order my coffee—though if Bouzha spots me on my way in she has often already begun work on my small black decaf. (I suppose that pub regulars get the same smiling service.) Dan invites us to a Christmas party at his place on the 17th. I ask him if there will be a Christmas tree and he says yes, having triumphed over the bah humbug objections of his partner. The tree is half decorated now but I suspect more progress might have been made if Winnie hadn't eaten some pine needles and started foaming at the mouth. We begin a back passage walkround but one chap, coming our way, bristles when Spadge barks at him. (Spadge can't see whom he is barking at, in fact—he just barks.)

Friday, December 8:

There is a light drizzle falling when Fritz and I head into the park on a grey Friday morning. Walking toward us is an ambulatory group of dog owners, also including David the dogsitter, who is minding muddy Buddy today. I turn around, hoping to join this parade and then we can see, coming up behind us, Celine with Ziggy. The latter is wearing a raincoat and looking a bit miz—after fishing a terrine of dodgy paté out of a bin. Fritz isn't having anything to do with this grouping, and we are soon turned around again anyway to head in for coffee.

The rain seems to have stopped but we are still squeezed round a table with Georgie, Janet, Davide, Celine, Kate and Nicholas—whose Monty manages to sneak into the café itself before being ejected. Georgie has been out onto the green to check out the tiny Yorkie, Jack. Skye's face is freckled with mud after pursuit of the ball has lead her through many a puddle. Kate says she went to three Christmas parties yesterday—"Lucky the second was so boring—otherwise I would never have made it to the third." Nicholas quizzes Davide on the kind of flight discounts a long-serving air steward can get. I ask about the kitchen business and Nicholas, who is suing a client for non-payment, sighs, "Funny how stress can completely eliminate any interest in sex." Celine then adds that if she sued every client who owed her money she'd soon be out of business. The rest of our conversation is devoted to the local tornado—which ripped through a portion of nearby Kensal Rise yesterday. The violence of the storm that brought this unusual phenomenon to our midst also seems to have unsettled Fritz—who shivered much of the rest of the afternoon.

The morning session ends somewhat chaotically. Rex, the Springer Spaniel, is penned into the café forecourt, where no one has ventured because of the moisture. This is so that his mistress, accompanied by a giant baby buggy and a dismounted toddler, can make her order inside the caff. Rex reacts with a bout of hysterical barking and Winnie and Jasmine respond by barking back—from the safety of the fence. Meanwhile some dog (not Fritz, who is on my lap) lets off two pungent farts. Rex finally figures out a way to hop the brick wall and soon thereafter we discover two dog turds behind our table. Georgie gets up to clean this mess out of the goodness of her heart and we decide to head out. Koko, as usual, trails far behind and the consequence is that Janet is out of earshot when the Shih-Tzu lays down *her* gift on the walkway between the playground and the picnic area. Celine picks *this* up—talk about responsible dog owners. It is starting to rain again.

Saturday, December 9:

It is very sunny this morning but also very cold. When we at last reach the green there is a lively collection, including several animals not seen out here before. First there is a King Charles puppy named Sam; I tell his mistress that we have other members of this breed in our midst, but she says, "So they tell me, but I've never seen them." A teenaged girl has two Pomeranians in tow; these we have seen in the park before but not this close up—their names, Buddy and Sparkie, are an odd echo of other members of our group—since Georgie is here with her Sparkie and David the dogsitter has young Buddy the Golden Retriever in his charge.

At breakfast we have Celine, Georgie, Kate, Dan, Albert, and Janet. Ronnie arrives late for this ceremony, having had to deal with another crisis in his 95 year-old mother's dotage. This time she has fallen in the night and, bruised and with a sprained wrist, she has spent the last few days in hospital. Meanwhile Rosie has had another of her convulsions. Somewhat rattled by these events Ronnie can't settle, moving his coat three times. At the second location he manages to knock his espresso over; the liquid pours over the side of the table and saturates our Fritz's bum. The latter doesn't seem to mind and certainly this must have improved the fragrance of this part of his body—earlier he had backed up to the outside fence and deposited a wet poo poo that stuck to the fence post about a foot above the ground. Everyone now has a good chuckle over his present discomfiture; Fritz manages to dry off in Dan's lap, where he climbs for a riotous cuddle. Kate tells us that last night she cooked some liver in a pan for her dog but when she returned from taking a phone call she discovered that Skye had jumped up on the cooker, eaten all the goodies, and replaced the pan lid!

Out on the green preparations are just getting underway for the dog school's Christmas party. We are all invited to partake of the goodies and Roland tries to organize the first game. Someone brings out some water bowls and Nemo falls on the first of these. I don't linger for long as I am thoroughly chilled and I still have a hike to Sainsbury's ahead of me. I accompany David to the gates—by this time Buddy looks like he has been swimming in a swamp.

Sunday, December 10:

It is again very cold outside, with frost on the grass and bright sun blinding those who are facing into the wrong direction. We are followed onto the green by Georgie and Sparkie. The latter drops his omnipresent ball-on-a-rope in order to bark hysterically at one of the park keepers, a chap who is raking fallen leaves into a huge sack. Georgie explains that Sparkie resents any attempt at restoring order, and that he barks at street sweepers too. I say that this is because Sparkie is only happy amid chaos.

Out on the green people are trying to move about in the sun while their dogs get in some exercise. Koko, the diva, won't participate, and Hercules just wants to bark as well. Rufus would like to engage the Cocker's attention, but this doesn't seem to be working. Kate is slinging the tennis ball to the indefatigable Skye while Fritz and Sparkie have sloped off together to check out the bushes near the playground. I try to get my dog to enter the precincts of the café, but the usual cue ("Coffee!") doesn't seem to work after yesterday's drenching in this stuff.

We are ten at two conjoined tables, the only café customers who are brave enough to sit outside. I have remembered to bring my dark glasses so I sit squinting into the sun while Janet, Faz, Ofra, Georgie, Dan, Ronnie, Hanna, Albert and John try their best to avoid it. Ché poos in a tree well and everyone offers John a bag; this time he has one of his own. Ofra says she has broken down and bought a Christmas tree. Janet reminds us that this year's Paddington dog calendar is almost ready. A lot of dogs are sitting in laps today. At one point I have both Fritz and Sparkie in mine. "When you can fit two dogs into your lap at once," Kate says, "perhaps it's time to open up that can of Slimfast." Sparkie returns to Georgie's lap—which means that he has Winnie as his nextdoor neighbour. The Pug lashes out at him with considerable fury but two minutes later they are licking one another's faces. Janet says that in profile Winnie looks like Pacman on speed.

Monday, December 11:

High winds have abated somewhat but it is still raining as I make my preparations for another morning in the park. Once again I have to pull my rain jacket on over my leather jacket before facing the elements. By the time Fritz and I have reached the top of the running track we encounter Kate and Jean-Baptiste. Fritz receives some well-deserved complements from this pair for he, too, and for the first time, is wearing a raincoat, a handsome black affair with an edging stripe in old gold. He doesn't seem too bothered by this impediment to his usual freedom, and we fall in line behind the others for a circuit of the mucky green.

Progress is slow and we soon lose contact with Skye and Hercules. By the time we get around to the café Jean-Baptiste has gone home and Kate is the only occupant of the greensward—bravely propelling two tennis balls to her dog in the teeth of renewed winds flying in our faces. I have had a peek into the café to see if anyone else is about but none of the other dog owners has made it yet. None of our lot *ever* do today, but some of the other folk eventually brave the rain and I can see them making a circuit of the walkways as Kate and I settle down at a table in front of the café's doors.

Coffee for two must be the lowest turnout in our breakfast history; had I been the only one present, I would just have headed for home. Kate shows me pictures of the holiday accommodation she has rented in St. Veep in Cornwall. We discuss some tax matters—she says that everyone has tax problems and that she is always being drawn aside at parties for free advice. The rain is being driven into our faces by the wind and once we get up to move our table even closer to the doors. When this doesn't work we give up and head for home, hoping for better weather and a better turnout tomorrow.

Tuesday, December 12:

Well the weather has certainly improved with the return of a bright sunlight—which presides over a sparkling cold day in Paddington Rec. As Fritz and I make our way toward the green I can see Sabina, struggling to put her Oscar on lead. She explains that Yoyo is in season and that Oscar won't leave her alone. A minute later Lizzie, back from four weeks in China, marches through with the aforementioned seductress. When I mention Oscar's intentions she says, "Oh he's like that all the time—and Yoyo considers him to be absolutely impossible."

Over on the grass near the loos I can see some of our lot—so Fritz and I make our way gingerly across the mucky grass in that direction. Dan is still trying to interest Fritz in the hard plastic ball that emits squeaks when shaken or rolled. Fritz is entranced by the sound and, indeed, warns off all the other dogs when they take an interest in this object—but when he can't elicit a sound from the toy himself he soon loses interest. I tell Dan that this reminds me of that old Virgil Partch cartoon in which the barfly enters the saloon and is mesmerized by the silky blonde hair of a woman seated with her back to him. When he tries to light her cigarette, however, he illuminates the face of an old hag, and drops the lighter in horror. So Fritz and the plastic ball: it seduces until he possesses it—and then he is deeply disappointed.

At coffee Kate and I chide the others for their non-appearance yesterday. We hear a variety of excuses—I was here but I turned around when it started to rain, etc. I tease the Israeli Ofra over her purchase of a family Christmas tree. Hanna loans a frigid Ronnie a pair of stretchable mittens. Dan lets Koko sit in his lap—since she has a visit to the vet scheduled for later in the day. Beneath our feet Fritz is whining because he senses that there are sausages at Ellen and Peter's table—and Bailey is doing a dance, his paws on the tabletop, as he spies some puppy kibble he fancies.

On the walkround there is a real bottleneck as joggers try to overtake us on the narrow passage between fences. One woman has been jogging while conversing breathlessly on the mobile phone for the last half hour. I tell Ronnie that I am worried that so many of our fellow citizens seem to be incapable of enduring even a moment with their *own* thoughts—using the telephone instead as a desperate means of keeping in contact with the only reality that validates their existence. He is somehow reminded of the woman who applied for a job at one of his jewellery stores. He asked her why she hadn't been working before this and she said that, although her condition was controlled by medication, she was, in fact, a schizophrenic. Ronnie says that he then told her, "Well, actually, we're looking for two workers. You can be both of them."

Wednesday, December 13:

It's a grey and chilly morning as Fritz and I follow Dan and Winnie into the park. The green is soggy with moisture and it is impossible to walk for long on its surface without carrying along acres of mud on the bottoms of our shoes. Nevertheless there are a few brave soles/souls in evidence, with Dan trying to keep Winnie amused with the plastic ball and Yorkie Jack and a little black dog named Zack joining in the chase. Even Fritz is cajoled into chasing this object again, but—after driving Winnie away from her own toy—he settles for haunting the precincts of the café in search of handouts. Koko arrives, having been to the vet (throat infection, tooth that must come out).

I have a blood test later in the morning so I am fasting and forego refreshment this morning. This leaves me somewhat shamefaced when Mrs. Metty (i.e. Vicky) arrives with Christmas cards and chocolates for the regulars. Dan is telling us that Davide has again suffered the loss of his luggage on a flight to Sardinia—a suitcase that included the Christmas presents for his parents. Kate tells us that she has lost her mobile phone—blaming this loss on the fact that she was wearing a high-necked dress and therefore couldn't store this object in her bra, as usual. Ronnie, attempting to land me in it, says, "Anthony here thinks we should nevertheless undertake a mission of discovery to see if it's still in there." Kate calls her own number, as Ofra did when she lost *her* phone, but reports not even a tingle in her bra.

Ofra, for her part, seems to have the loudspeaker function turned on when she takes a call. Dan says that she is risking an A.S.B.O. for such anti-social behaviour. We start off for home, a matter of some confusion for Bailey—since Ofra heads for the parking lot as we turn left. Hanna is completing a long account of the gradual restoration of her flat after damp was discovered in her bedroom two years ago—she has been sleeping in the sitting room ever since. That a tenant should require the intervention of Environmental Health and the threat of legal action to accomplish such a necessary repair is a scandal. By this time we are stretched out in a long line heading for the exits—only Spadge and George behind a dilatory Fritz.

Thursday, December 14:

It is grey and rather unfriendly this morning and there is even a hint of moisture in the air. On the way in we encounter David the dogsitter with Skye. He has spent the night at Kate's so as to be ready for a lengthy assignment—which began today when he also picked up Campbell, a West Highland Terrier. There are lots of dogs on the walkway outside the café, concentrated here perhaps because the green itself is so mucky. I keep Fritz on lead for most of the session and manage to pick up two poos while we are walking about.

Near the café I pause for a chat with Maggie, who is here with her own Finn and with Hootch. The latter seems incomplete without his thunderball but, evidently, it is locked up in Guy's car and could not be secured for this journey to the park today. I ask Maggie whatever happened to the mostly Staffordshire pup called Monkey—whom we have not seen is some time. She says that she had undertaken to get him re-housed (after his original owner went to prison) but that she fell in love with the fellow and thought about keeping him herself. However there were so many dog-hating people in the park last summer that life with the rambunctious pup was a nightmare. One picnicker, in the middle of the green, threatened not only to cut the dog's throat but also Maggie's as well. So, reluctantly, it was back to Plan A; today Monkey lives in the New Forest with an owner who works outdoors much of the time—a happy ending.

I have coffee with Ronnie, Ofra and Georgie. Fritz manages to arrive in time for some sausages at Peter and Ellen's table and thereafter whines until I produce my goody bag—a gesture that interests all of the other dogs except for the ancient Doofie. Georgie tells us that, out of loyalty, she has stayed on for years at the Windsor Castle pub on the Harrow Road,—but if the ancient manager retires, as he might do in the New Year, she will hand in her notice. She is perturbed that no one told her that there was a horse named I am Spartacus running yesterday (it won). She and I walk together toward the Morshead Gate—trying to get home before the weather worsens.

Friday, December 15:

Michaela, whom we meet at the entrance gate, is complaining about how warm it is today but after a few minutes in the grey and damp morning I find no warmth at all on a chilly Friday morning. Fritz and I pass by the roiling mass of dogs outside the café entrance and pursue our solitary pathways in the direction of the Randolph gate. Above the tennis courts Fritz thinks there is something worth chasing up a tree, and after this exercise we turn around and head back for the café ourselves. Fritz sprints ahead, having just remembered that they might be serving sausages in there.

I sit with Ronnie, Georgie, Dan and, back from Bermuda, Liz. Dan says that Davide has finally received his luggage—just in time for his return flight from Sardinia. Ronnie reports that his mother, still on antibiotics, remains in the hospital. Georgie says that she has to leave early so that she can admit a carpenter to Janet's house. Doofie is at the next table but it turns out that Guinness doesn't have a category for the world's oldest dog—and there is some sentiment that they need to start this category with Doofie in the holder's chair. Little Jack, the tiny Yorkie, comes by for a visit, and we learn that he knows how to shake hands before receiving his treat.

Liz settles down to continue the saga of her recent move within St. Johns Wood—in the wake of the moving day burglary. The alarm company recommended by Ronnie never called her back. The Sky Television installer has stood her up twice and she has been reduced to whining about her poor kids not being able to watch any Christmas TV. A workman, following a liquid lunch, has drilled through her gas line—requiring the evacuation of the house and a phone call to the National Grid. The latter capped the leak but Liz had to call her own plumber to get other things fixed. Finally the telephone installer refused to install more than one jack on his official visit—implying (with a wink) that he could come back and finish the job as an independent contractor. So Liz has had to give in to this blackmail too. Is it any wonder that migrating Americans sometimes feel they have just come to live in a third world country?

Saturday, December 16:

A light rain has fallen during the night but skies are clearing as Fritz and I begin our Saturday stroll in the park. There are lots of dogs about, including a contingent of training school cadets, but Fritz, as usual, has other fish to fry. He has a peek into the café and then ascends Mt. Bannister—with me in slow pursuit. *I* am trying to get him to follow my lead while, at the same time, I can hear *Sabina* calling her distant Oscar: it is an exercise in wilful Schnauzer behaviour. After a while Fritz heads out along the Randolph walkway but I am at last able to get him turned around for a direct assault on the café itself.

A large group, including Peter and Ellen, are seated at a table outside the café doors. I am still working on Bouzha to keep the café open during the Christmas break—but my suggestion falls flat. Janet says that she is waiting for an estimate on the dental work needed by her Koko—that sounds ominous. Dan reports that Winnie, who is often taken on walks into Covent Garden, has become so mesmerized by the delicious cheesy odours arising from the Neal's Yard dairy that she now does a little dance when she nears this establishment. Bailey is trying to hump some of the other small dogs, including Jasmine—though Ofra is relieved that, for once, her dog is not the humpee. Faz reports that a pair of expensive leather gloves has gone missing from his desk—in the police station! We are all waiting for the return of Helen, who is back in town for her graduation ceremonies. When she doesn't arrive we head for our various exits but our group is lucky enough to encounter her at the Morshead gate—where it is agreed that all the dog people will reconvene at the café at 3:30.

Thus, unusually, Fritz and I make a return visit to the park in the late afternoon—when the skies become clearer and the air is even colder. In addition to our visitor from Washington we have David the dogsitter (here with his new charge, the Westie Campbell—and Kathy's Paddy), Ofra, Janet, Georgie, Hanna, Dan and Davide. We get an update on the development of the little Pug Cleo (now considered a bad influence in the District of Columbia) and Helen's own work with special needs children. Two plates of chips arrive and Fritz has some of these and the foam out of my cappuccino cup as well. Winnie patrols the pavement; she would really like to snatch that chip out of Koko's mouth and she does mug Bailey. The latter is seen as a totally unprovoked attack but I say that we don't know what Bailey has said to her first—"Hey Winnie, you are soooo fat." The public address system is advising park users to make their way toward the exits and our party comes to an end as we head for home in darkness.

Sunday, December 17:

Under clear sunny skies Fritz and I enter a frigid park on a quiet Sunday. There aren't many people about, just some joggers on the running track and half a dozen dog owners clustered on the cricket crease of the green. Fritz rushes over to receive a tummy-rubbing greeting from David the dog-sitter, here accompanying Campbell the Westie again. For once my dog seems content to remain with the group, rushing about to check out the scene and never straying very far from the action. When the others head in for coffee he follows them—and I follow him.

Again there is not much sign of life at the café. It will be closing at the end of the week for its Christmas hiatus and a number of the dog owners will be leaving the city as well—so we have even farther to go in levels of desertion. One Peter is sitting at a separate table with Hector and a second Peter (and Ellen) are around to the side with their dogs. In the centre, at our twin tables, we have chairs for Ronnie, Dan, Georgie, Kate, Janet, Ofra, Faz, and Albert—who arrives with the Yorkies Saffy and Tinkebelle—now wearing lurid orange and yellow coats against the cold. Fritz begins to agitate when the sausages are delivered to Peter and Ellen and I have to let him off lead. Sparkie, who is always free, jumps twice with his wet paws into my lap, and then climbs to the top of the brick fence so that he too can survey the sausage dispersal at the neighbouring table.

Janet distributes the 2007 Paddington Rec dog calendar (the first of these was presented to Helen yesterday) and I end up with three, one for us, one for our friend Janet (who arrives in ten days) and one for our helpful councillor, Jan Prendergast. Faz reports that he went ice skating on Hampstead Heath yesterday and he is much teased after he admits that he had to push away a little boy who was about to take him down at full speed. Dan gives directions to his house, where we will all be part of a Christmas party later this afternoon. Winnie, who twice attacked Helen last night, polishes her skills as hostess by biting Kate on the finger.

Monday, December 18:

The rain has thinned to a fine mist as Fritz and I penetrate a gloomy Paddington Rec on a grey Monday morning. As we reach the green I can see Hanna, approaching slowly with George and Spadge. She tells me that her bedroom has been re-carpeted two and a half years after damp was first discovered here, and that she enjoys lying in the empty space, making imaginary angels in the luxurious void. Behind her the giant curly black Poodle, Charlie, is coming up—he is not to be confused with the tiny black Poodle, also named Charlie. I see that Tanya the animal warden is back at her usual post outside the loos and so I am able to repair my desperate deficiency in the poo poo bag department (down to three used fruit and veg bags).

Kate announces that she won't be coming in to coffee this morning because she has to have her nails done. This means that we are a much-reduced assemblage featuring Dan, Davide and Georgie seated at a large table outside the café's doors. Dan has brought with him a sack of goodies left over from the Christmas party that he and Davide hosted the previous afternoon—Dianah's birthday cake, mince pies, chocolate muffins. I note that in thirty hours this weekend I have attended no fewer than five social occasions: Helen's tea party here in the park Saturday afternoon, dinner with Linda and Rob soon thereafter (Fritz and Pepper at home), a Christmas party at Michaela's following this dinner (Skye as host), Dan and Davide's party yesterday afternoon (Winnie as hostess), followed by dinner with Liz and Tom at Romano's, the Italian restaurant they are now managing in Kensington Church Street. I am particularly struck by the fact that every one of these occasions is the result of friendships struck up at the end of a dog leash in Paddington Rec.

Just as the others are getting ready for a walk along the back passage Dorothy emerges from the mist and together we head for Boundary Road in St. John's Wood, where Fritz has a 10:30 appointment with Dr. Frank Seddon. No crisis today, just an annual kennel cough booster—though our dog does get his anal glands cleansed before receiving two complimentary Schmackos.

Tuesday, December 19:

Such conditions do not prevail that often these day, but this morning a thick *fog* hangs over Paddington Rec. Dorothy insists that Fritz wear his new coat—though he has taken against the ripping sound of the Velcro fasteners and it takes a while to pin him down. I don't dare let him off lead in the freezing fog—giving his wandering ways I would never be able to pick him out in the mist. Instead we wander around the green, encountering well-remembered poochy pusses and, as the sun at last makes an effort to break through the murky atmosphere, we even venture over the frosty grass out in the direction of the cricket crease.

At breakfast I suggest that it is hard to imagine why someone would choose to lie on the Copacabana beach in Rio when they could be enjoying this invigorating London climate instead. The remark is meant to tease Dan, now arrived with Winnie, who will be undertaking the former activity a week from now. Angie comes by on her wheel-enhanced Zimmer frame and distributes Christmas cards; she is wearing one of her famous holiday tiaras and some Xmas earrings. Kate also distributes cards (I have been doing so in the park for a week) since she is about to take off on her holidays—which include house rental plans in Cornwall. She wants Dorothy and her friend Janet to consider the film potential in an Irving Welsh script that she will be sending along via e-mail. I tell her that, as a screen story analyst at MGM, this task was the essence of my father's profession. Ofra arrives with Bailey, who manages to climb into Dan's lap in order to be closer to Kate—who is in charge of food disbursement. Unfortunately Koko is already in Dan's lap and she is mortified to be in such close proximity to another dog's bum—climbing up onto Dan's shoulder in protest. In the meantime the others are attempting to fill Georgie in on the final stages of Sunday night's party—since she has no memory of it or how she got home.

Near the end of our session Linda arrives (with Pepper) and she accompanies us on our return journey. Once again they have closed off the back passage so everyone inches toward the Morshead gate. I can see that Skye is munching on a branch of twigs, as though this was so much Christmas candy. But when Pepper and Sparkie begin to share another branch Winnie intervenes in their fun with such passion that the contestants have to be separated. I think we will not see Skye anymore this year—every day there will be another canine subtraction as holiday travel gets under way.

Wednesday, December 20:

It is again very foggy in the park this morning. There is also a deep, penetrating cold and I am soon regretting that I am not wearing my long underwear. There is a knot of dog owners at the western end of the green and we go among them, Fritz again on lead. Rufus and Buddy are chasing a football that a boy on a bicycle is kicking to them. Winnie waddles in, her collar pushing a roll of fat over her brow—"She looks like she is growing her own hoody," I tell Dan. He and then David the dog-sitter kneel to give Fritz a cuddle; he growls in delight, warning all competitors that he is not going to share these moments with any other canine.

At a table in front of the café there is a hardy group of dog owners toughing it out: Ronnie, Ofra, Georgie, Albert and Dan. Bailey keeps jumping into the chair that I intend to sit in, then he climbs into my lap, then he picks my pocket and comes away with the bag containing the puppy kibble. When I dispense some of these goodies I leave the bag on the tabletop and this means that Bailey does a tiptoe dance on his back feet, his front ones tattooing the table as he reaches for more treats. No one wants to linger for long in these frigid temperatures and there are frequent suggestions that we get moving.

The fencing that yesterday prevented access to the back passage has been removed so, minus Ofra and Bailey, we head west. Saffy and Tinkerbelle, back in their pink coats, make a big fuss of Fritz but the latter is very slow off the mark, pausing twice for poos before we get fairly started. It thus takes us a long time to catch up with the others—which we do just as we reach our gate. The others ask about Dorothy as we part, but she is at the doc getting more antibiotics for no fewer than three infections.

Thursday, December 21:

Fog persists as we make our way into the park on another frigid weekday morning. Fritz and I turn right when we reach the green and edge our way around the grand circle—once again I am reluctant to let him off the lead since there are many parts of our great space than cannot be seen. It is surprising that, in spite of the terrible temperatures and the murky gloom, there are still lots of dog owners exercising their pets. I count fifteen canines milling about in a line that runs roughly from the clubhouse to the loos. The most recent arrival to this scene is Winnie, dressed in a lime green coat, an appearance that reminds Hanna of a lettuce slug.

It is the last opening for the caff for some days now—and I spend some time chatting with Bouzha in the warmth of its interior. A lot of last minute Christmas cards are exchanged over coffee and toast. Fritz, back in his own coat, is unhooked so that he can get his share of sausages from Peter and Ellen, but someone has ordered these delicacies for our table as well. Bob the sheepdog arrives to mount Bailey, and Franca arrives (still without baby Valentina) to regale us, from the next table, with every graphic and painful detail of the birthing process. The baby's feeding schedule is to blame for her non-appearance in our midst so far but, since Franca is breast-feeding, it is suggested that she complete this process at the café. But perhaps they have a policy against eating your own food here, I joke.

I fall behind the others on the back passage walkround—while Hanna comes up with a list of remedies Dorothy must now undertake to counter her many infections. Yoghurt is one of these and indeed, some tzatziki is later selected at Sainsbury's, where the shelf stockers have outdone themselves by running out of the store's own brand of dog biscuit. While packing the fridge with frozen specimens an hour later a few of Fritz's hidden squeaky balls are uncovered—and Dorothy relents long enough to let the dog have a green one with red spots. When I take him downstairs for his afternoon walk I discover that he still has this beloved object in his mouth. Around the corner a car stops and from it there emerges a veteran Paddington Rec character, Henry, who has walked many a park mile over several decades with King Charles Spaniels like Lucky and Polo and Jasper the Staffie. Henry and Sheila, whom we also encountered on a return visit to her dentist a few weeks ago, moved away a few years ago. Jasper, a dog who could get three tennis balls into his huge mouth at once, died recently at age twelve.

Friday, December 22:

Another morning of fog (and misery for stranded passengers at Heathrow Airport). And again there is more life in the quiet park than one might expect from an initial examination. I do not mean the leaf-blowers or the digging machines clanking over the pavements or even the clean-up work going on in the padlocked café. No, there are still plenty of dogs being walked around the green and in the middle, all by herself, Georgie is trying to keep a manic Sparkie amused with his ball on a rope.

I begin another leisurely circuit of the green, noticing, as I pass the Grantully gate, that I cannot see the top of the steeple of St. Augustine's—which usually dominates our views to the north. Near the bottom of the walkway up Mt. Bannister I see a large group of dog owners dropping down from the heights—a clear sign that this route, fenced off at the top of the hill for some time, is available again. The group includes David with Campbell and Skye the Cairn, Natasha with Leila and a visiting Shih-tzu named Smudge, and Celine with Ziggy.

I decide to turn around and follow them, Fritz off lead, and so begins a very pleasant ramble on a circuit and a half of the entire park. Smudge, an elderly chap, doesn't like it when the other dogs sniff his bum—but he has to endure this repeatedly not only from our lot but from other dogs we meet on the way. Fritz seems to enjoy being part of a pack and doesn't stray too far away. David and Natasha peel off as we near the Morshead gate but Celine and I complete another circle. We meet Sabina with Oscar and Scamp and she wants to know where Fritz got his handsome coat. Outside the café Ziggy encounters Rufus and begins a mismatched wrestling competition that succeeds in knocking a trash bin off its perch. Buddy soon joins in this competition and Fritz, fearing for Ziggy's safety (the latter is still only nine and half months old) intervenes on behalf of his young pal's safety. After we have climbed the hill, the first time in months from this side, we spot still more dogs below us. We are soon making our way through them and past the empty café (Fritz is most puzzled) and so out of the park at last. We have survived the shortest day of the year.

Saturday, December 23:

The fog has at last lifted this morning, but we are still surrounded by grey gloom. Just behind us, as we enter the park, I can see Ofra accompanied by Bailey. The latter is wearing a red coat and, as so often happens these days, he proves irresistible to a Westie heading in the opposite direction. Ofra tries to discourage these unwanted and misdirected attentions by marching as quickly as possible toward the green—but the owner of the Westie asks her to *stop* so he can catch up with his errant dog. This is always a moment of strain among dog owners—you want to get away as quickly as possible but the source of the irritation can't even be impeded in his quest until there is a halt to the proceedings. Thus the Westie can at last be attached to his lead. Ofra is fuming, especially when she is asked by the Westie's owner, "Is she in season?"

Fritz and I begin a leisurely circuit of the green, catching up at last with Ofra and then with Georgie, Janet, Celine and Dan. We pass Hanna, who is distributing Christmas cards. Georgie tells us that she has been feeling a bit rough for the last few days; this makes the others especially protective when the naughty Sparkie won't stop hectoring his mistress, barking madly and tugging at her cuffs. Perhaps Sparkie is another of the dogs discomfited by the closure of the café. Hanna says that her George is very perplexed and keeps putting on the brakes in the vicinity of its shuttered presence.

Our group passes Roland, whose very small turnout for Saturday morning obedience class is one Giant Schnauzer. The others continue on toward the Morshead gate, very slowly, with first Koko and then Fritz having a stroll along the running track because someone has left a gate open. Then Fritz switches sides for a forbidden run in the rose garden. The others, desperate for their morning coffee, are heading down to Porridge on Lauderdale Parade—but I have errands to run and so Fritz and I head for home. Rocca, an Alsatian cross with the head of a wolf, is trying to mount Bailey.

Sunday, December 24:

Gray skies continue for another day as Fritz and I encounter a Lab puppy on our entrance into the park. His owner says that the youngster is heading for a bath—since he is streaked in mud. I keep Fritz on lead as we make a leisurely circle around the green but when we catch up with the other dog owners, near the loos, I let him off and he dashes about sniffing his pals. Hanna is here with Spadge, Georgie with Sparkie, Janet with Koko, Celine with Ziggy, Ronnie with Rosie, Peter with Hector, and Faz with Jasmine. Faz tells us that on his way into the park a few weeks back he ran into the actress Keira Knightley, who paused to ask questions about his pet. He then says that the same thing happened when Jasmine put her paws on the red coat of TV presenter Vanessa Feltz in Marylebone. Neither of these ladies suggested that the Shih-Tzu's face reminded them on an Ewok, but this is the consensus among the other dog people.

We join a procession making its slow way toward the Morshead gates and another rendezvous with the Porridge café on Lauderdale Parade. As yesterday, I have trouble reconnecting with my wilful dog, who this time makes a break for it with Sparkie as they dash into the open gate of the forbidden children's playground and then into the equally taboo rose garden as well. When I finally succeed in reeling in the Fritz he follows Janet to her car on Morshead Road and tries to jump in while she is depositing a package. I tell him he has to walk to Porridge and he excitedly joins a group that now includes Bailey, Rosie, Jasmine, Sparkie and Koko. Hanna, having deposited Spadge at home, arrives with George, and Dan and Davide pull up in their car soon thereafter—Winnie has already begun her week as an Essex girl with Dan's dad.

The staff at Porridge seem quite laid back about this invasion of the dog people—not that there would be too many other customers willing to sit at outside tables in temperatures as frigid as these. Hot chocolates and cappuccinos follow while Ronnie has a croissant (and a cigar) and Georgie and Janet have paninis. Ronnie says that his mother is still in hospital. Ofra says that has she lost track of her mobile phone again—Ronnie says she'll probably find it under her car. Faz says that his father once arrived at Heathrow and got on the train to Bedford—only to discover himself by the sea: he was in Bournemouth—and a taxi had to take him to his true destination. This recital of the vicissitudes of the wandering mind concluded, we say goodbye to Dan and Davide, off to Brazil tonight, and to Janet, who will be visiting her mom in Kenilworth. Fritz has been keeping a sharp eye on all the passers-by on Lauderdale Parade but it is almost 11:00 now and he is profoundly bored.

Monday, December 25:

Fritz and I head for a quiet park on a grey Christmas morning. Georgie is exercising Sparkie out on the green but she is already able to report that Porridge is closed until Wednesday. Last year, faced with this problem, we found Starbucks open even on the holidays, but Ronnie, who soon arrives with Rosie, says that they are closed as well. Starbucks has been in this country too long: Britain has managed to subvert even this go-getting enterprise.

Fritz and I follow the curve of the green on dry land and, released, my dog climbs Mt. Bannister. I can see Ronnie, Georgie and Hanna in conference below us and so we retreat to participate in this parley. Georgie, who is not feeling well, wants to see if there is a market open on Maida Vale Parade and so I accompany her, Fritz again on lead, as I am looking for a pint of milk which Dorothy needs to make a Christmas Yorkshire pudding. We find two markets open and I hang on to Sparkie's lead while Georgie makes our purchases. Then she goes home and I return to the park.

A security guard wishes me a Merry Christmas (often they do not speak to us at all) and I find Hanna and Ronnie just as the latter is heading for a bench—since he needs a sit-down. Hanna promises to walk him to his street on her return and she and I complete a very slow back passage walkround. She says that she got confused yesterday and fed her dogs three times instead of two. It is time to go home and see what treats are hidden in Fritz's Christmas stocking.

Tuesday, December 26:

Not a sign of sunshine in days, but at least the temperatures are fairly mild this morning. Fritz has to be dragged out of the bushes, where he is interested in some surviving dry leaves. When we reach the green we fall in line behind Jean-Baptiste and Georgie, and Fritz is freed to pursue his own interests as we attempt to catch up. Jean-Baptiste is just describing last night's Christmas Beef Wellington and Faz, newly arrived, says that Jasmine was delighted by her first experience with cranberry sauce.

Fritz has run off to follow Ellen and Barbara—if he thinks this strategy is going to result in a plate of sausages, he is in for a real disappointment. We continue our walkround as far as the caff and here Jean-Baptiste peels off—on his way to buy shoes at the post-Christmas sales. The rest of us decide to continue along the back passage, though it takes some time to recover Fritz, who is at the head of the Carlton roadway, exploring. On this stretch, during which we are joined by Celine and Ziggy, Faz tells us that the purloined pair of gloves—the ones that went missing in the police station—have been returned to his in-tray, though stuffed with the clippings from the hole-punching machine.

We discuss the Pound-Dollar ratio and Celine says that the Americans just didn't show up at the Asian art exposition this year. Sparkie races ahead and then makes a lot of noise when he is at last collared at the end of his morning in the park. Georgie says she will take him to work today—that is he will be stationed behind the counter at the Windsor Castle (where he barks at any customers who dare to speak to him). The good news is that Porridge will be open for business tomorrow morning.

Wednesday, December 27:

The park still seems largely deserted as Fritz and I make our entrance on a cold, grey December morning. Near the clubhouse we encounter Ofra with Bailey and Georgie with Sparkie. The latter rushes up to Fritz and kisses him on the head but the more passionate encounter is taking place behind us as Charlie, the little black Poodle, tries to mount the ever-enticing Bailey. Fritz senses that this is an attack on one of his group and rushes forward with some vigour, driving the interloper off. The women are heading for the Morshead gate and, I assume, coffee at Porridge—but as we have just come in I continue toward the café. I can see David the dogsitter with Campbell and Skye the Cairn, but they have disappeared over the brow of Mt. Bannister by the time we reach the foot of this eminence.

Assuming they will come down onto the Carlton roadway I cut through the forecourt of the abandoned caff, Fritz still on lead, only to see no sign at all of the rangy dog walker. Heading toward me from the playing fields is Celine with Ziggy and we join this pair—Fritz off lead at last—for a leisurely grand circle and a half. First we climb Mt. Bannister ourselves, Ziggy dashing down its slopes at great speed because he can see some dogs at the loos. As we near the Grantully exit Fritz actually wanders out of the park for a moment but he does answer my imperative requests for his quick return. Then both of the dogs disappear into the bushes adjacent to the rose garden, emerging at last in order to invest the bandstand—where three Middle Eastern workmen (some from the park, some from the street) are enjoying a snack. They do not seem too perturbed at the presence of our grey petitioners and we are soon moving around the running track.

Fritz seems to enjoy the exercise, the freedom to explore rarely visited areas of the park, and he seems quite content to lead Ziggy into mischief whenever possible. He heads left when we want to go right at the café corner—but I am able to extract his attention only when I offer my goody bag to Ziggy—this produces a furious charge back in our direction. Still, my dog is not going to let me off too easily for the next thing that happens is that he turns right at the clubhouse and pokes his nose onto the running track—Ziggy just behind him. Again I have to distract these dogs with my kibble sack but this time, after thirty minutes on the trot, I re-hook my dog so that we can make our exit at last.

Thursday, December 28:

Fritz has just thrown up in the kitchen as we make our way into the park on a mild Thursday morning. His poo isn't that great either—I blame the street food he has gobbled down yesterday. He is such a scavenger—it almost seems that he is not truly happy with an afternoon's walk (yesterday it was with his Aunt Janet from Michigan) unless he can crunch a discarded chicken bone—or worse. In front of the clubhouse Sparkie is barking furiously at a leaf-blowing gardener, who is shattering the morning peace with his noisy (and unnecessary) machine. Georgio is embarrassed by this behaviour—but Sparkie is only doing what we'd all like to do, if we could bark.

There is a substantial contingent of doggy people standing in front of the abandoned café including Jean-Baptiste (with his own coffee thermos), Celine, Hanna, and David the dogsitter—who is keeping an eye on both Skye the Cairn and Campbell again. He has taken the latter home for Christmas—and a good time was had by all. There is some concern that the little Westie may just have rolled in dog poo (one of his specialities), but maybe it is just mud.

Fritz, off lead, follows others on a walkround along the back passage. We are overtaken by a jogging Lizzie and a severely shorn Yoyo. Ziggy tries to keep pace with her but he is soon distracted by the giant Ruby, whom he likes to lead on a merry chase through and around the bushes. When we reach the Morshead gate we encounter Georgie, Ofra and Faz. They invite me to join them for coffee at Porridge but I have an appointment at the haircutters in St. John's Wood and have to decline.

Friday, December 29:

It is a bit colder today and still grey. I walk with Fritz around the green, but it soon seems obvious that he is not going to do any poo today (having been starved yesterday) and so I let him off his lead. We encounter Georgie, sitting on a bench at the east end of the green—Sparkie sitting there as well. He jumps off to give Fritz a greeting but I continue along to the junction of the Randolph roadway, where dogs and owners are abundantly gathered.

Kathy Andon is here with Paddy, Nix is here with Billy and, back for another visit, Bunny is here with the besweatered Whippets, Biscuit and Milly. David the dogsitter is also here with Campbell and Skye the Cairn, and Celine arrives with Ziggy—we soon join these dogs for a back passage walkround. I ask David if he has made any use of YouTube. He has, and we discuss the vices and virtues of egalitarian access to every form of media these days. I say that it certainly sounds like a democratic process but the fracturing of the audience means that no one can address the nation as a whole anymore. It meant a lot to Americans, as a people, when Walter Cronkite announced that he felt our presence in Viet Nam was a mistake but today there is no one who could command such a share of the audience for any similar statement.

We continue on for another go round and when we reach the green David's dogs both canter toward the centre—where both Campbell and Ziggy like to mix it up with Rufus. Fritz is uncertain—fearing that Rufus may be hurting his young pals—and he drives Rufus off with an intemperate growl. Thereafter, police work over for the day, my dog takes to the running track where, twice, a jogging and stretching Lizzie manages to trot him out of there. Tim is out on the green with Yoyo and I join him in tossing the Frisbee to her. It is beginning to look like rain, however, and I decide it is time to beat a hasty retreat.

Saturday, December 30:

A tempest has lashed its way through the night skies but this morning all is sunny and calm. Fritz, ever sensitive to changes is atmospheric pressure, has spent a restless night, snapping at his mistress and panting repeatedly as the storm increased in intensity. There is no sign of this distress in his demeanour today and we make rapid progress toward the green.

We begin a slow walkround here, soon encountering Janet with Koko, Georgie with Sparkie, and Faz with Jasmine. The latter, so it is reported, has sulked over her desertion last night—and deposited a vengeance poo poo next to the sofa on which Faz normally lies. Fritz, I tell them, also objected to being abandoned when Dorothy, Janet and I went shopping yesterday, though in his case all we got was one of his patented deep throaty protest howls. The others are turning around to head off for Porridge and so I use Dorothy's mobile phone to pass on this intelligence. We think that both Sparkie and Fritz have used this moment to disappear into the rose garden but after the Yorkie emerges someone says, "Isn't that Fritz on the running track?" Sure enough, there is my dog, doing a lap with Lizzie again. It isn't clear how he got there, since the gate is closed today (Yoyo waiting patiently on the other side), but he quickly finds his way back to us when we call him.

On the way to Porridge the subject of the Post-Christmas sales comes up. Some of the others are considering braving the crowds and so I tell them that I too had a choice yesterday—"I could either go clothes shopping with two women or cover my head with honey and thrust it into a nest of fire ants." Nevertheless it was a successful outing (I was the only one to buy any clothes)—if you don't count the fifteen minutes we wasted waiting for the only working lift at Marks and Spencers. Dorothy, still operating on only half of her vocal cords and Janet, still recovering from a tummy bug, soon arrive to join us at our outdoor tables on Lauderdale Parade. We have a good time, though nothing is ordered for the dogs here and they seem to be a bit cross.

Sunday, December 31:

Rain persists this morning (Fritz and I were drenched on yesterday afternoon's walk). Somewhere within the park I can hear Sparkie barking at someone and Georgie apologizing, "He duz na bite." I keep my dog on lead as we near the green and scoop up his first poo nearby. Thereafter, Fritz, still on lead, tugs me toward the café, perhaps because he can see Peter and Ellen heading that way as well. They are just checking out the sign on the front door so that they can see when Metty plans to reopen (January 4)—so if Fritz thinks that he has just gotten into the sausage parade he is *again* mistaken.

Janet and Georgie are making their way toward Porridge but I disdain this enticement today, heading instead across the green toward David the dogsitter. On the way we encounter a chap in an ancient Rothmans Racing jacket; he has a thick Irish brogue and he is using a hurling bat to loft a ball for his mutt—but when I enquire about this weapon he says that it is part of the arsenal of ancient Celtic sports and adds, gratuitously, "Too bad we couldn't teach the rest of you how to play cricket. And we couldn't do that successfully because of the superiority of English ignorance." When I reach David, he too complains of having gotten an earful from this embittered visitor.

Linda arrives next with Pepper and, after hiding a while in the alcove of the club house, we decide to undertake a circumnavigation of the green. Another dog walker, intent on her conversation, fails to note that Andrew the Akita, trailing behind her, has just done a poo—this enrages Linda. After we have completed our circle Fritz, who is dashing about madly in great delight, penetrates the empty children's playground and we have to go in there to retrieve him. David takes advantage of this foray to try out one of the new pieces of equipment. He is explaining that he has two invitations to New Year's Eve parties but that only one includes an invitation for Campbell and, since this is the one he really wants to go to anyway, his choice is made for him.

Leaving the park is fraught with incident. Skye the Cairn is insistent that we kick the tennis ball so he can chase it. Then Fritz tries to follow Linda and Pepper toward the Grantully gate. Then he goes jogging on the running track again. Then he disappears into the rose garden. I follow him but I can't find him anywhere. I walk back to the green but by this time David has found him emerging from the rose garden near the Morshead gate. He is soaking wet but happy and in this mood we head for home.

January, 2007

Monday, January 1:

We begin a new year under bright and sunny skies—quite a contrast to the weather of the previous evening when the sounds of fireworks alternated with those supplied by lashing wind and rain. I had taken Fritz out at about 10:30 but there was already enough noise to cause the usual distress. I persevered for several blocks and he managed to hoist a brave leg against a series of standing objects—but when we returned I had to get out the bottle of Rescue Remedy. This elixir seemed to work its magic and he had a much more comfortable night thereafter.

As we enter the park today I can see that we have just been preceded by a sleepy David the dogsitter—who has both Skye the Cairn and Campbell the Westie on lead. He tells me that no sooner had Campbell accompanied him to the aforementioned New Year's Eve party then he ran into the back garden and first rolled in and then ingested a fair quantity of fox poo. Thereafter the little dog, hurriedly bathed, tried vainly to go to sleep on the sofa—as the humans at this party fought over the PlayStation karaoke microphone

I fall in line in a slow moving trek around the green and onto the back passage. As Fritz and I draw even with the cypress trees I can hear a cry of despair as the holiday morning football players manage to kick their ball over the fencing and into the trees. One of them asks for my assistance and I penetrate the foliage to recover the prize—watched by a curious dog, who wants to know where I came up with another football. The ball safely tossed back over the fence, I receive a sincere round of applause from the lads and we complete our fairly brief walk at the next gate. The walk is over but not the exercise because a few hours later Pepper accompanies Linda and Rob when they arrive for brunch—and the two dogs have a wonderful play period in the house.

Tuesday, January 2:

It is bright and sunny as Fritz and I enter the park—with the caff still closed and a number of dog owners still away, it seems as though we are still in a holiday atmosphere. While Fritz is sniffing a tree, young Leila, wearing a skull and crossbones on her coat, dashes up and, surprisingly, lifts *her* leg too. "Your dog has gender problems," I tell Natasha, but the latter insists that Leila is so dominant a personality that she even likes to piss on the heads of male dogs.

Fritz has escaped this treatment and we soon join up with David and Celine and their dogs for a long walkround. When we reach the café we turn for a stroll along the back passage. Sabina is heading our way with Oscar and Scamp and this causes a bit of confusion—as she has one Schnauzer and one Westie in her group and we have the same combination in ours. Skye the Cairn is relentless in his efforts to get someone to kick his tennis ball for him and I do oblige on a number of occasions. Campbell chases after this object too, but never succeeds.

For once Fritz penetrates neither playground, running track nor rose garden, but this does not mean he earns good marks for doggy obedience. As we are midway through a second grand circle he decides to trot *out* the Grantully gate and I have to chase after him. To make matters worse, he has also seduced his pal Ziggy into equally bad behaviour and at one point I have to grab both of them by the collar before they can be bustled back into the park. As we reach our front door we encounter a disappointed Aunt Janet, on her way to meet all the park canines—only to be told that, by this time, they have all scattered.

Wednesday, January 3:

It is spitting a little bit as Fritz and I penetrate the park on a grey Wednesday morning. I can see David the dogsitter walking in a small doggy party that includes Campbell, Skye the Cairn, Jonesie and Hercules. They are heading toward the Essendine entrance on a reverse back passage walkround and so we head in this direction—rather than toward the green. Fritz is freed even before his first poo poo—I despair of ever seeing the latter since Fritz refused to eat his dinner last night, perhaps in protest over our abandoning him to see *Spamalot* in the West End.

As we near the café (where a car parked out in front promises a resumption of services tomorrow) I get a phone call on Dorothy's mobile phone. This is a prearranged conference so that I can advise our Janet on where to head for a morning rendezvous. The other dogs have by this time wandered out onto the muddy green and this and the light rain predispose me to suggest a meeting under the awnings at Porridge. I retrieve Fritz with the bribe of some kibble (Ziggy sticking his nose into this process) and soon we are marching down the street in pursuit of a Porridge-bound party that includes Georgie, Janet, and Ofra.

The latter spends the entire morning session chattering away in Hebrew on her mobile phone at an adjacent table. "Some date she turns out to be," I suggest. Ofra is not the only source of noise pollution, however, since the clamper truck is moving cars away from the curb—where some builders want to work. The car alarms on these vehicles work well and we have horns bleating for most of breakfast. Ronnie arrives with Rosie and she and Fritz have an ill-tempered food fight over some titbit. Our Janet orders a panini and much of this ends up in canine mouths as well. Once a piece is proffered to Koko and Bailey, making a magnificent leap, snatches it out of the air on the fly. The rain has stopped for a while so it's time to make a move—Ofra, afraid that her meter will run out, has dashed off without ever rejoining the party.

Thursday, January 4:

The sun is again dominant this morning but it is also quite chilly. Ahead of us I can see Dan with Koko and Winnie. Dan has a Copacabana tan and Winnie, after a week as a butcher's dog in Essex, has another roll of fat around her neck. Dan says that *he* has Koko because Georgie has not been heard from this morning, and this is worrying. He uses his phone to call the missing person but her phone is not answering. There is a huge reunion in front of the clubhouse since Michaela is also back after a week "skiing" in France—where there has been precious little snow.

I walk with Fritz around one side of the green, soon encountering Hanna with Spadge and George. While we are talking I see that Fritz has broken into a headlong dash for the café, which must be serving its first customers at about this point. I follow him, having to dodge a giant cement lorry in reverse—arriving to discover that Peter and Ellen have just taken delivery on the first sausage order of the new year. More of these comestibles are ordered for our table, where we soon have our Janet, Dan, Ofra, Celine, Hanna, and, at last, Georgie. The latter looks very much the worse for wear, after having gone to bed only at 4:00am following a night of partying with visiting relatives.

Janet and I accompany Hanna as we complete a back passage walkround. Hanna is still complaining about the sterile narrow fenced passageway that has been left for pedestrians between the oldest and the youngest of the playing fields. The newest pitch contributes to the concentration camp atmosphere—with padlocks on every gate. Hanna speculates that here we will have holding pens for dog owners—"if they don't pick up after their dogs," I add. We round the corner and here Hanna notes that they have blown all the Leylandii cones off the walkway—and she can't find any to add to her collection. We pass quite a few unknown pooches, walking in the opposite direction—it is nice to see park life returning to normal.

Friday, January 5:

Somewhat groggily I take Fritz to the park on a mild but grey morning—after seeing Janet off in her airport-bound cab at 5:30. There seem to be more new dogs having their walkies as we circle the green, heading for the foot of Mt. Bannister. Here I can see Celine, surmounting the precipice, and calling her dog. I promise Fritz that his pal Ziggy will shortly make his long-legged descent—but I am wrong. Celine is spitting feathers because her dog hasn't even made the journey up the hill, having stationed himself at a table in front of the café instead. And she has lost one of her gloves.

We decide to bite the bullet and head for the famous eatery ourselves, joining Ronnie, Hanna, and Georgie. Ronnie is usually not seen at this time of the week but with his mother still in hospital he can make a rare Friday appearance. Hanna hands me a Polish stamp, one affixed to a Christmas card from Angelina, one of the first baristas to serve our lot from Metty's counter. Most of the dogs desert us when Peter and Ellen receive a sausage delivery at their table. Another table is occupied by Nicholas with Monty and Natasha with Leila. These dogs come prospecting at our table while our dogs are visiting Peter and Ellen's. While we are drinking our coffee Celine finds the missing glove in an inside pocket.

It starts to drizzle and we decide to make a move—only Hanna and I making use of the back passage walkround. Some workmen are standing on the tarmac of the newest playing field and she asks them if this is the final surface. They say no, but they don't know what comes next. She tells them that she feels imprisoned in the narrow walkway between the fences and they evince not a shred of interest. We make very slow progress toward the gate, but at least it has stopped raining.

Saturday, January 6:

Skies remain grey and lowering as Fritz and I enter the park today. I can see quite a few dogs on the periphery but only Saskia with Buddy and David the dogsitter with Campbell are out on the green. We join them for a moment but as soon as my back is turned my dog turns tail and heads immediately for the Grantully gate. I have to give pursuit, not knowing if he has again left the premises, but by the time I get close he is dashing back toward me and my sack of puppy kibble. Buddy gets in line for a treat as well and thereafter presents me with his purple Frisbee—which he won't let go of when I try to give it a toss. Campbell has his foot in plastic, having had a sliver of glass removed at the vet's two days ago. Kate returns to the scene with Skye the Alsatian. "I must give you a New Year's kiss," she says. "In that case you can give me a birthday kiss as well," I respond.

At breakfast I show the others, especially Janet, the author of the famous project, a very nice note I have received from Jan Prendergast—to whom I sent one of the famous Paddington Rec calendars last month. Celine says that she has never seen one of these objects and Janet promises to bring one in for her. We are seated at an outdoor table, under an awning, and this is just as well because it soon starts to rain. Fortunately there is no wind—so it is only our backs that are getting soaked. This is too much for Hanna, who takes one look at us and goes to sit under the overhang. Here I present to her my supply of recently received Christmas cards, which she plans to turn over to a friend for recycling. Soon joining us, however, is Leslie, the mom of Maddy, a King Charles puppy, here on only her second visit to the park. Everyone soon has a wet lap after giving refuge to his or her pet.

Kate fills us in on her long stay in Cornwall, where she went on a seven-hour walk (well she did get lost on the way). Celine attempts to make a break for home but Ziggy, back in his raincoat, keeps returning to our table. He begins to make the homeward journey only when the rest of us get up to leave—and then I can't see his mistress anymore. I am getting a bit worried but just then we discover Celine and Saskia hiding from the rain in the alcove of the clubhouse. Even after this reunion Ziggy makes only painful progress toward the exit. He usually resists any attempt to leave the park, where he has so much fun, but he also dislikes the rain. So he compromises by inching along at my side, brightening up only when Skye and Buddy begin a muddy play period on the roadway. Ziggy now has a mission, as barking referee, and Fritz, as boss of it all, has a mission in getting all these underlings to break it up.

Sunday, January 7:

There is still a hint of moisture in the air as we enter the park on another grey Sunday in Paddington Rec. Fritz and I make our way around the green and I am careful to make sure that we have passed the forbidden Grantully gate before I let my dog off the lead. He does manage to disappear a few times, as we near the Randolph roadway, but his naughtiness gives him only a poor second place finish today. This prize goes to the mischievous Ziggy. At one point I can see Celine heading toward me at a jog, hoping to entice her boy into some strenuous exercise, while, behind her back, I see Ziggy responding with a furious lope of his own—in the opposite direction.

The attraction, of course, is the café, and when she, Fritz and I reach this sacred spot ourselves Celine has to beg all concerned not to feed Ziggy unless she is present to approve such disbursements. She coaxes her pet out of the place but on at least three occasions he returns in hope—only to be spirited away again each time. Ronnie now joins our table beneath the overhang—where we already have Georgie, Janet, Dan, and Ofra (again on the telephone in Hebrew). Under discussion is the Neald pub, which evidently enjoys a mistaken pronunciation in local lore—as the Needle. Dan also tells us that he is worried that the fold of skin on Winnie's brow is interfering with her breathing—and we all laughed when a local vet suggested that he could give her a facelift. Now Dan can't figure out whether the fold of fur is because she is too fat—it is a critical judgement because if she loses weight the skin might hang even more loosely over her nose. It is not easy being a Pug.

We get up to begin a back passage walkround, leaving a late-arriving Hanna at a small table next to the café's front door. She has taken Spadge to Karen at St. John's Pets and is delighted with the result (Fritz has a similar appointment next Friday). As we are walking between the tall wire fences Winnie admits herself into the new huge playing field, and then can't figure out how to get out. The rest of us are unkind enough to make jokes about her discomfiture as she stares balefully at us from behind bars—Winnie, who has earlier snapped at Ofra's finger, may be a bad girl—but she doesn't deserve to be put in a concentration camp.

Monday, January 8:

Skies are actually clear as Fritz and I head for the park this morning. I can see Michaela, Jean-Baptise and Dan just leaving the park with their dogs—and then turning around to re-enter the Morshead gate. This mystery is solved in the next moment when I discover that Dan has just reported the loss of his car keys, and the others have agreed to help him hunt for them. Only a few steps are taken before Michaela suggests that perhaps Dan has put the key in his own backpack. This, indeed, turns out to be the case and order is thus restored.

Near the bandstand a group of workers is raking leaves from the hedgerows and mocking the voices of dog owners with their own falsetto version of dog names, "Buster, Oooo," "OooOscar." I can see Linda out on the green and soon there is a roar of recognition as Pepper and Fritz collide. Inside the house Fritz remains fascinated by Pepper's every move but outside he soon loses interest and I have to follow him along the Randolph walkway—where he pursues his lonely quest. Emerging at last from the bushes above the tennis courts, he then crosses the green, Pepper in pursuit, and enters the café. Linda, having given up the quest for her dog's lost ball-on-a-rope, joins us briefly at an outdoor table in order to record the latest outrage of Tony Blair.

Our table also includes Hanna, Georgie, Ofra and Ronnie. Ronnie is a bit knackered, having forgotten that the Randolph Avenue gate is closed for the next three days—requiring a long hike around to the Grantully gate. "You've been sitting next to Ofra too long," I say to him—whereupon Ofra says that Ricky is buying her a game that is supposed to improve the memory. There is an awful lot of noise this morning, with Spadge going off every few seconds and the other dogs frequently joining in. Koko is insulted by this behaviour and goes into the forecourt and turns her back on the rest of us. In this fashion she misses another outrage—Jasper the Springer Spaniel jumping up on an abandoned table and knocking over a coffee cup. For days Dorothy and I have been waiting for better weather in order to walk to Sainsbury's. Today is supposed to be the day—but as Fritz and I complete our back passage walkround with Hanna I am beginning to realize that we will probably have rain again today as well.

Tuesday, January 9:

The wind is whistling as we head for the park today, and we get no further than the doggy pen fence facing the Morshead pavement when there is an incident. A small terrier, spotting Fritz from the confines of this space, rushes over to investigate and the two dogs, nose to nose, begin a noisy colloquy on the subject of who's tougher—with the fence itself preventing any chance of our actually finding out. Do good fences make good neighbours? This morning they lead only to superfluous discord.

We make it as far as the green, where there is a lively scene. Kate is slinging the ball to her Skye and Winnie is chasing a ball too. Fritz doesn't spend much time with this lot, making an early exit for the café scene. I follow him as well but the Schnauzer at the feet of our group is Oscar, not Fritz. The latter has marched straight through and out to the Carlton roadway—where I can see a crisis in the making. Some people with a French Bulldog and a chocolate Lab are urging the latter to pick up his toy, a yellow rubber ball that has rolled to the feet of my dog. This is another version of the exact same ball that Fritz received as part of his Christmas stocking treats and I am worried that he will think this toy belongs to him too. Fortunately he decides just at this moment that he has to see whether the sausages have arrived at Peter and Ellen's table—and so there is no need for a second confrontation.

I have to remove Bailey from my chair when it is time for me to sit down with my cappuccino. Both Jaspers, Patterdale Terrier and Springer Spaniel, are lurking nearby and we have one disappointed visit from Ziggy, who is being frogmarched around the park by Celine as she tries to break him of his lust for handouts. We discuss the antics of Rory, the Shetland pony, who has been much featured by the media since bonding with the dogs at a rescue centre in Essex. Then we discuss the price of automobile insurance, or the others do—I zone out, glad at last when we begin a back passage walkround.

Wednesday, January 10:

I take Fritz to the park about half an hour earlier than usual this grey morning—knowing that I have to take off for an appointment at about the time we usually settle in for our morning coffee. Rain, which has been lashing our window much of the night, has at last cleared, and we have a dry but chilly day for it. I see a number of dogs whom I don't usually see—just an adjustment of a few minutes can change the canine line-up considerably. The park workers, who have been scrubbing the leaves out of the hedgerows, have uncovered about ten lost balls in the process and these are piled up at the Morshead entrance on a first-come, first-served basis. I select a newish yellow tennis ball for Fritz and we continue our walk.

Fritz must be bursting, or so I assume, since last night our walk had hardly begun before an unscheduled fireworks bombardment brought a rapid end to our adventures. When we reach the green I can see the intemperate Irishman with the hurling bat over to my right, so we head left and begin a grand circle. Half way round we encounter Jean-Baptiste and Hercules. We discuss Paris and, knowing of our planned trip to Egypt, he asks me how my course in hieroglyphics reading is going. Knowing I have to leave early I keep Fritz on lead, not wanting to have to spend any time hunting him up when the time comes.

I can see Ronnie making his slow way toward the café with Rosie. By the time I reach this spot he has taken a seat in front of the doors of the eatery, some fifteen minutes before it is scheduled to open. Fritz has time for a slice of carrot and then, checking in briefly with Kate and Skye on the grass, we return to our gate. I can see that just about all of the balls have been claimed by the dogs, save for one lonely cricket ball. However, when we get home, there is a surprise. Fritz has claimed another hard rubber ball—which he has managed to carry home in his jaws, depositing it in the hall as we reach our front door.

Thursday, January 11:

Night-time weather rarely persists into the day here in northwest London—but today is an exception. Gale force winds have been rattling the windows for hours and there is no letup as Fritz and I prepare to leave the house. There is also some evidence of rain against the bedroom window and so Dorothy fastens his raincoat over Fritz's body before we brave the tempest. Georgie and Janet are just ahead of us, Koko trailing her mistress in disapproval, and Sparkie barking hysterically at his. I cross the green to a grouping of large dogs at play and Fritz inserts himself into the wild tumult, growling furiously whenever one of these dogs gets too close.

Hanna is walking with George near the metal gazebo; she tells me that her building is without water today—as the long overdue replacement by the water companies of our Victorian-era pipes engulfs our neighbourhood. I follow Fritz around the green and then attempt a direct crossing of this sodden surface, mud oozing with every footfall. By this time we have reached the big boys again, though I notice that Ziggy has inserted himself in the melee; he and Buddy seem to be dragging one another around by the cheeks. On the walkway a yellow tractor is speeding along with a load of earth in its maw; we wait for this danger to rattle by and follow the others into the café.

Our table includes Ronnie, Ofra, Georgie, Janet and Hanna. The wind continues to whistle but this doesn't deter the dogs in their insistent search for sustenance. I have to let Fritz off lead so he can make his way over to Peter and Ellen's table at sausage time. Bailey jumps into my lap in order to get his nose into my kibble bag. Then Hanna feeds a returned Fritz with pieces of egg on toast. At one point her gloves go airborne and I have to retrieve them. Then the paper that Georgie usually brings unwraps itself and one by one each page has lift-off. Hanna gets up to retrieve each sheet and in her absence her gloves take off again. We begin a back passage walkround and soon we are able to leave the howling behind.

Friday, January 12:

Winds have abated somewhat as Fritz and I enter the park on a grey Friday morning, a hint of moisture in the air and a new black Lab to growl at arriving just as we reach the green. I am not wearing my park shoes today and so I eschew the turf, completing a circle on the walkways with Fritz still on lead. We pass Sabina and Denise and their dogs but here I have to do a real double take. "Is that Rizzo?" I have to ask—for the mostly Yorkie with a head as big as the rest of his body (that's all you can see anyway as he sits perched in his bike basket) has been shorn. This is presumably more comfortable for the little fellow, who still looks cute, though he fails to resemble his former self in most respects.

The others are making an assault on the café as Fritz and I near this sacred spot and so we take our place at table—though again I skip the coffee since I know I will be having one at a Starbucks on Oxford Street shortly. Rhianne is here with Otw and while we are at table a chap with the leaf blower stops by to tell us that he has a pile of recovered balls for Tanya the animal warden. Fritz is unleashed once—when there are sausages at Peter and Ellen's table—and he manages to get loose a second time when I am too busy with my kibble bag to keep an eye on him. Tim, who has just arrived with Yoyo, manages to snag him for me, and all the dogs have a treat from my goody bag. Ofra tells us that she has forgotten to bring her Christmas cards in to Hanna and that her daughter, following in mom's footsteps, has forgotten to tell her father that she has GCSEs in the middle of a week during which he has booked a ski holiday for her. Dan tells us, somewhat sheepishly, that he has bought a £300 pound pink corduroy *chaise longue* as a dog bed for Winnie at Heals—though reduced to a mere £50. Ronnie arrives just as I am getting ready to leave for St. John's Wood—where Fritz has a haircut scheduled for 10:30.

Fortunately the Randolph Avenue gate has reopened—I have no intention of crossing the muddy green to reach the Grantully gate. Our walk is a halting affair, with Fritz unused to the discipline of marching to someone else's drum—but after about ten minutes of stop, go, and yank he falls into the rhythm of the enterprise and we amble along without further problems. When I pick him up two hours later I can see that Karen has worked her magic and he does look a treat. Also he is back in a useful walk rhythm sooner this time and the return trip is more pleasant than the outward-bound journey. It is still spitting a bit as we leave the Wood but there are bright patches by the time we have made it back to Maida Vale.

Saturday, January 13:

The smartly-trimmed Schnauzer receives the first of many complements on his spiffy appearance from Peter and Ellen as we enter the park on a grey and unfriendly Saturday morning. The green scene is divided, as it often is on Saturday mornings, into two groups—dog training in one corner and the rest of us in another. Humpty, whom we have not seen in some time, comes out to join the second group, which also includes Koko, Sparkie, Winnie and, recovering from a stomach bug, Jasmine. No one feels like lingering for long on the muddy cricket crease and soon there is a migration in the direction of the café.

Here we are joined by Celine and Ziggy. The latter has a chunk of fur missing from one shoulder—the result of some rather vigorous play with his pal Rufus. Jasmine is not allowed any treats, though Janet does let the Shih-tzu lick her fingers—only to have Winnie bite these same digits when it is discovered they contain no food. Sparkie jumps into my lap and Fritz makes himself at home—first in Faz's lap and then in Dorothy's. My wife is making a rather rare appearance these days and Fritz is thrilled; he gets to drink cappuccino foam from both of our coffee cups. Leslie brings her Maddy over for a visit; today the little King Charles has brought her brother with her—Louie is almost twice her size. Ronnie now appears with Rosie as well.

We celebrate Faz's recent success on the sergeant's exam—he evidently had the fourth highest score in the nation—so now he is DS Faz. He tells us he plans to take the inspectors exam in November and, I add, "then he gets his own TV show." These promotions carry a lot more responsibility and require much more paper work and you can tell that Faz misses the intimate interaction with the crime scene. He reminds us of the day he investigated six unrelated murders in Wembley but when he gets to the part about the head blown off by a shotgun I have to remind him that Celine is a vegetarian. It is beginning to mist up by now and so we begin a prompt walk toward the Morshead gate. For such a lousy day there are lots of people in the park.

Sunday. January 14:

Sunshine returns to the park today—I should have brought my dark glasses, though it has been so long since they were needed I'm not quite certain where they are. It is also quite chilly and it helps to stand in the direct sunlight rather than in the shadows of the muddy green. Out here there is a collection of dog owners stamping their feet on the cricket crease. Saska is a bit worried about muddy Buddy, whose poo shows some signs of blood. Fritz soon takes off for the foothills of Mt. Bannister and I follow him around the margins of the green until it is time to head into the café.

A table in the sunny forecourt is selected and we soon have Faz, Hanna, Janet, Georgie, Dan, Davide and Ofra seated around it. Ofra has been having lower back problems and there is a lot of advice on where she should go for assistance. Georgie has a coughing fit but the offer of mouth-to-mouth resuscitation from several of the gents soon puts a stop to her spasms. The dogs are a riot of activity. First they make their presence felt at Peter and Ellen's table—because there is an early delivery of sausages. Then, after wolfing down a large amount of toast, they begin a game of musical laps. I have Sparkie, Bailey and Fritz in my lap (the latter enjoying the last of my cappuccino foam), then Fritz moves on first to Ofra and then to Dan. Koko, sitting on Janet's lap, is not at all happy to have Fritz as her neighbour, and barks furiously in his face for several minutes. Meanwhile Winnie and Sparkie, on adjacent laps, are licking one another's tongues furiously. "How cute it that," I say, "even though it is disgusting as well."

Davide is complaining about a parking ticket he received after missing a well-hidden street sign. Janet says she received a similar ticket at 3:00 in the morning (as well as one for speeding). Updates are offered on *Soap Star, Superstar* and *Celebrity Big Brother*. Faz says that he and Dianah spent a lot of time yesterday in a curtain shop in Fulham. He complains of the extreme cold and Janet loans him a pair of gloves. "Are these chenille?" he asks. "Faz," I interrupt, "you've been spending too much time in the curtain shop!" We begin a back passage walkround, jostled about a bit by charging joggers coming up behind us.

Monday, January 15:

Skies are beginning to brighten as Fritz and I enter the park on another chilly morning in Paddington Rec. I can see over on our left that there is one parade, including Rufus and Ziggy, heading round the running track, while ahead of us there is a group of small dogs including

Charlie, the small black Poodle, Oscar and Scamp and, soon arriving in his bicycle basket, Rizzo. Fritz joins the latter group once he is freed to choose his own path and he seems, again, to enjoy moving forward as part of a pack. I have to ask where the real Rizzo is because this shorn version appears to be an impostor. Denise tells me that her pet was named after a character in *Grease*, not after Ratso Rizzo in *Midnight Cowboy*.

We make a slow circuit of the green and I can see, heading in for coffee, that we have an augmented Scottish contingent this morning—since Jean has arrived with both Billy and Mozart. Jean looks well, through her hair is quite long and greyer than we remember it; she tells us that she has not smoked in five weeks and that she plans to get her sister to join her in this category. At our table in front of the café doors we have Dan, Georgie, Jean, Nicholas, and Ronnie. Hanna thinks about sitting down but Spadge is having one of his hysterical barking fits and she thinks better of it.

Dan shares a phone photo of Winnie lying in her new pink bed and then accepts Fritz for an extended cuddle in his lap. There are lots of complaints about the loss of needed parking spaces—since our entire neighbourhood seems to have fallen prey to the water main revival. Before we begin our walkround a bit of sad news is circulated—Doofie, the park's oldest canine citizen at age 21—has died. Hanna says they buried him in the back yard. He was an inspiration to all of us. Especially us geriatrics.

Tuesday, January 16:

A light mist has just lifted as Fritz and I enter the park on a gloomy grey Tuesday. For once it has *not* been twenty-four hours since last we gazed upon this scene for yesterday *afternoon*, as the sun was setting, we attended Faz's birthday party at the café. There were eleven of us present—including Faz, of course, Dianah (who brought a gorgeous chocolate cake), Hanna, Jean, Georgie, Dan, Davide, Jo Lynn, and Janet. At one point I counted seven small dogs in laps; no wonder that a group of little girls passing through this space began to squeal, "Oooh, it's a puppy party!" Had they known that little Tilly has by now killed *three* squirrels they might have been less charmed.

It was also interesting to see how calmly Bouzha dealt with the cheeky soccer kids who often finish up a game by ordering something entirely unsuitable from the kitchen. One lad, dressed in a kit much too large for his skinny frame, kept changing his mind and he never quite grasped what she meant when Bouzha repeatedly asked, "Is that to eat here or take away?" "Huh?" On the whole, though, I didn't care to be walking around in the darkness as we at last headed for our gate.

Today there is a much smaller turnout, though Fritz comes to a halt as soon as we are inside the gate because he has heard the voices of the Scottish ladies behind us. Lines of dog owners are streaking over distant hills and there are lots of complaints about the grim weather. I let Fritz off the hook and we squelch out to the centre of the green, where Kate, in a black hood, is heaving the ball skyward for Skye. Winnie is bustling about and so is the irrepressible Chica. Dan makes an early departure for the café and we follow him.

No sooner have we found places for ourselves in front of the café doors then the moisture begins again and our end of the table takes the worst of it. Janet is organizing a trip to a dinner theatre in Islington for the weekend. Fritz makes his way to the sausage queue at Peter and Ellen's table and then returns to go from lap to lap, first mine, then Dan's, then Ofra's. He slips off once and when he is rescued he earns the disdain of the diva in the next lap, Koko, who sets up a litany of protest over his presence. Back at her empty space is Liz, who has just reclaimed her dog after six weeks of house moving and travel. As might be expected after leaving a dog in the care of Italian chefs, Roxy is as fat as a cigar. "Look," Dan says unkindly, "she even has a roll of fat on her head."

Wednesday, January 17:

The clouds are opening as I make my preparations for our morning sojourn in the park, but we have only a light rain to contend with when, at last, we venture forth on a nasty winter's morning. I am lofting my large umbrella, the one I have been known to leave behind at the café, but at least the winds have dropped a bit and I am able to keep it in a more or less vertical position. I keep Fritz on lead as we head past the clubhouse, but he can hardly get into any trouble this morning as, for once, there is no one on the running track, not a soul on the green, only Ellen sitting with Jack and Sandy in front of the café.

In front of us I can see Liz with Roxy and when we meet up I reverse directions and we walk with them around the green in a grand circle. A man has now appeared with a ball, a branch for hitting it, and a Staffie named Buster. This is a matter of some concern for the owner of Charlie, the small black Poodle—who wants to make friends with the bruiser. In fact Buster seems to be innocent of any evil intent and Charlie is soon collared. Liz and I discuss faculty matters at the American School and when we have done a complete circle we enter the precincts of the café—just as Dan and the Scottish ladies are arriving as well. We also have Ofra and Hanna at a table that I insist on moving closer to the front door—as the rain is blowing in under the overhang.

I take the most exposed seat and I can still feel the rain sprinkling my back and kissing my neck. The dogs are out of sorts with the wet weather, especially Koko, and they begin to bark hysterically whenever a workman in a lime slicker approaches. "They really don't like that colour," Dan says—a remark we all accept at face value until we notice that he is adjusting the hood of a lime green outfit over Winnie's furry head. The topic of the morning is racism, particularly the accusations levelled against *Big Brother* contestants whose mistreatment of a Bollywood superstar has caused a national outcry. The conclusion: it's not racism when it comes to Jade Goody and her mother—it's just ignorance and bullying.

To lighten the mood Dan falls into a reverie on the subject of Miss Vanessa Feltz. There are lots of opinions on her social life—though why this should be a matter of public record is beyond me. But Dan tells us that, in another one of his high-spirited moments, he and a friend crashed a theatrical revue during Gay Pride Week, directed all the celebrities as to when they should go on next—and that Dan himself, finding Miss Feltz in a low-cut ball gown, buried his head in her bosom.

David now arrives with Otw in tow (notice the anagram) and she is not at all happy with the wet weather either. These two (continuing the anagram) accompany Hanna and me as we complete a back passage. Ofra is heading for the parking lot—after a park employee has had to rush up to remind her that she still has a takeout order at the caff. Fritz is, of course, soaked, but his Auntie Cathy is waiting with his purple towel as we reach home.

Thursday, January 18:

We enter the park under gale force conditions again, and there is even a little moisture in the whistling wind that rakes over all the empty spaces of Paddington Rec. Georgie is standing in front of us, waiting impatiently for that little madam, Koko, to get a move on. Koko is sitting in the roadway disconsolately, presumably waiting for weather conditions to improve. We pass them by (and Mozart and Billy as well) and head for the green while the Scottish ladies make a beeline for the café.

I am determined to give my dog some exercise today and so I squelch out to the centre of the grass where Chica is playing with Charlie the Cocker and Sasha is waiting anxiously for the first attack from her cousin Buddy. Fritz heads for the bandstand and I follow him along the perimeter of the green. There is quite a queue of animals heading our way but at the last moment Fritz has to explore behind the tennis courts and we have to veer off. There is a building site, with lots of temporary fences, as we near the Randolph walkway and here we encounter a confused Albert, trying to figure out how to get to his favourite bench. Fritz is finally ready to head for the café, though he has missed his turn in the sausage line at Peter and Ellen's table.

Today we have Hanna, Georgie, Jean, Liz, Dan and Ofra braving it out at a windswept table in front of the café doors: every piece of paper on our table, paper plates, napkins, etc., is soon airborne. Dan wants to know if Hanna would give a reflexology treatment to a visiting friend's toes. Hanna says she will—but she doesn't charge for such services. Georgie begins to choke on a piece of toast (she is trying to give up smoking again) and Jean thumps her twice on the back. "Great," I say, "she's stopped coughing but now she has two broken ribs." You can tell that Georgie is unnerved by the gale and wants to start for home soon, so, with Fritz having finished the last of my cappuccino foam, we can make our move.

Friday, January 19:

The weather has improved immeasurably as bright sunshine, with only the occasional breeze, now presides over a park that bore the full brunt of the dangerous high winds that raked much of England yesterday. Indeed, the park locked its gates hours before closing time yesterday—the management wisely seeing that there could be no guarantees for the health and safety of visitors in an environment where branches and other loose objects were cascading across the open spaces. Even this morning one cannot walk (or run on the track) without a crunching sound provided by all the fallen twigs.

We meet Janet, just arrived by car, and Fritz and Koko enter the park together. When we reach the green we encounter Liz with Roxy and we join her on a walkround—with Janet hanging back at one point to wait for Georgie and Jean. There seem to be three or four groups like this, all enjoying the relative dryness of the perimeter walkways in preference to the soft centre that is the greensward these days. Fritz seems to enjoy moving in a pack and he manages to stay in close formation until we have reached the café. Here there are a lot of dogs milling about and when Liz pauses to chat with some of the other owners Fritz grows bored, visits Hanna—already seated outside the café—and then trots alone up the Carlton roadway, where I spot him nosing around the traffic circle just as a school bus is arriving!

I get him on lead and join a table where the Scottish ladies, Hanna, Janet, Albert, Ronnie and Liz are soon stationed. I have to let Fritz go when Peter and Ellen get their sausage delivery; then Peter wanders over to our table to get some advice from Janet on how to install his first Internet connection. Georgie is having a series of vivid dreams—which she associates with the nicotine patch she has been wearing during her recent struggles against cigarettes. Ronnie is enjoying the sunshine (I am wearing my dark glasses) and the milder temperatures, and he agrees to join us on our back passage walkround. We have quite a turnout, ten dogs in all; unusually, three of our number—Hanna, Albert and Jean—are each accompanied by two animals.

Saturday, January 20:

Early morning rain has just cleared as Fritz and I enter the park on a brisk Saturday morning. Rounding the corner near the bandstand we discover quite a collection of canines—including Skye with Kate and Buddy with Saskia. I can see that it would take a soil scientist to determine which of these two ladies has more mud on her costume. Other dogs are being lead around the green and it is my hope that Fritz will join one of these parades—but in this wish I am to be bitterly disappointed.

My dog starts off in the right direction but he disappears into some hedges beyond the bandstand and then there is no sign of him for about five minutes. I anxiously backtrack, have a look into the rose garden, walk forward to the doggy playpen near the Grantully entrance, call, whistle and clap my hands—all to no avail. This must be a strange vision for passers-by, but I doubt that the young woman, pushing a pram and clutching at her mobile phone, is paying any attention—"I would think that putting us together at family occasions would be even more awkward, as neither of us is speaking to the other."

Finally I spot my dog back at the trees at the head of the Morshead walkway and I try to attract his attention one more time. He agrees to be hailed in this fashion and my heart relaxes as he dashes across the green, his white ears flapping, but when he reaches me he keeps on trucking, ignoring my admonitions, and escaping the park altogether to trot down the Grantully pavement! Here, worse luck, he spots a squirrel and this requires him to give chase. It takes me a while to catch up with him and get him collared at last. Hanna is just leaving the park with Spadge and George and she says that Fritz is just showing his complete comfort with the park as his spiritual home.

We make our way around the green and join the coffee crowd at an outdoor table: Faz, Georgie, Jean, Janet, Ronnie, and Albert. Koko again takes exception to Fritz's presence on an adjacent lap and Winnie, out of sorts, even refuses some opportunities to stuff down more foodstuffs. Jean explains that Billy is having a sleepover at his Auntie Gerda's house and this will explain why she has only Mozart in tow. Hanna returns for her breakfast, with both of her dogs now at home. She is the only source of cigarettes when Ronnie has a craving—since Faz and Jean have both given up and Georgie is a work in progress. We have what I hope will be a final conversation on the subject of racism and bullying on *Big Brother*—now that Jade Goody has been voted off. Most of those present continue to feel that Jade's behaviour was loutish but not racist. Our resident policeman says that the law, in its politically correct manifestation, would disagree.

We head for the Morshead gate, somewhat chilled as the skies have now cleared, and, at home, Fritz continues to assert his Alpha-dog position—tossing pillows about, chewing forbidden objects, running off with my socks. His health is the subject of a most welcome inquiry a few hours later, however, when Dorothy and I bump into Michael and Frances at Sainsbury's! Michael seems a lot better than the last few times I have seen him—no longer breathless and with clear skin and good colour. There has been some talk of the dog people getting together with him for coffee while Jean is in town and he seems most receptive to this idea.

Naturally I have to tell him all about Fritz—but it does my heart good to see how the king of the park takes it all in.

Sunday, January 21:

Torrential winds have again raked Maida Vale in the early hours of the morning and somewhat groggily I prepare to depart for the park this morning—not forgetting my long underwear. Fritz is wearing his coat this morning and, though he doesn't like it, I keep him on lead throughout our walk—not wishing a repeat of yesterday's shenanigans. We fall in line behind Mozart, Koko and Sparkie as we conclude a circuit around the green. As the sound of the cock crowing is the first utterance of a morning in the countryside so the sound of Sparkie barking in the park is often the first sound I hear when I open my front door.

The wind is still active this morning and it brings truly chilly temperatures. Jean, Georgie and Janet settle down at a table in front of the café doors and we are eventually joined by Dan, Ofra, Hanna and Albert. Many of those present were part of the dinner theatre party in Islington last night (*The Musical of Musicals—the Musical*) and they seem to have had a grand time; some don't even have their hangovers any more. Dan is getting ready for a second Latin American holiday as he and Davide fly off to Acapulco this week. I say that it would be poetic justice if BA went on strike and they couldn't go. Someone else adds that it would be even better if BA went on strike *after* they had reached Mexico and they couldn't come back.

The dogs are in a noisy and lively mood. Skye the Alsatian has somehow ended up with a dollop of cappuccino foam on her nose. Koko is barking hysterically at Saffy and Tinkerbelle, though Janet does get her to sing a bit by intoning "Woo woo" into her dog's ear. Buddy, mud-covered as usual, stops by for a snack and Kate *does* give him some toast—now he'll come every day. Fritz is allowed to charge Peter and Ellen's table in order to get a few slices of sausage—then I can tell him that we have sausages at our table too. When he is finished snacking he jumps into Dan's lap and settles down; to my surprise Winnie retaliates by jumping into my lap—here she sits contentedly in the sun until it is time for us to begin a breezy back passage walkround.

Monday, January 22:

A light rain is just lifting as Fritz and I head for the park on a sodden Monday morning. We get as far as the green when the rain starts pounding down again. Liz passes us with Roxy and a few minutes later we attempt to follow these two on a walk round the perimeter—but Fritz is less bothered by the cold, the wind and the rain than I am and we manage to complete this journey at a painfully slow pace. I am aiming for the shelter of the café overhang and here I stand like a dummy, waiting for others to arrive and the café doors to open.

I can see the Scottish ladies heading our way and I spend some time pulling a round table closer to the doors so that we can all sit down without getting drenched. Sabina comes searching for Oscar, who is also being wilful this morning—and, after he has refused to answer her call on a number of occasions, she puts him back on lead. Liz arrives with Roxy also collared—the nervous Beagle has just run out of the park, spooked by some distant sound—and almost gotten herself run over in the street. I hold Roxy's lead while Liz goes in to get our coffees. The Scottish ladies arrive and Sparkie throws up three or four times in a grand circle surrounding my chair.

We discuss Dan and Davide's forthcoming trip to Acapulco (Davide's parents are coming too) and Hanna, who now arrives with Spadge and George, says that the Mexican city is currently occupied by tanks after the country's president got fed up with the drug wars there. Liz tells us that she has taken her kids to see *Rocky Balboa* and that, surprisingly, she enjoyed it. She had also ordered two and a half seasons worth of *The Sopranos* but, having just missed the Parcel Force van, she had to run after the chap at a street corner nearby. He was reluctant to let her have her package because she had left the delivery card at home—but, when she produced an ID and reminded him that her husband was just coming home from hospital, he parked his vehicle, got out, gave her the DVDs—and a hug as well. By the end of this tale I am thoroughly chilled, especially my hands and feet, and glad to accompany Hanna on a back passage walkround in the direction of some central heating.

Tuesday, January 23:

Frigid temperatures continue to prevail as Fritz and I make our way into a bright and sunny Paddington Rec. Shortly after reaching the green we encounter Hanna, walking with just George at this point, and we stroll together in a counter-clockwise fashion along the pavement. There is a lot of activity at a spot on the slope closest to the Grantully doggy area; first some park workers are fertilizing a young tree and then, a few minutes later, they are joined by other park staff in what is clearly a solemn moment. Hanna says that this must be the memorial service for Reg, a clubhouse worker who died recently.

After we have completed most of a circuit we head into the café—where Fritz has to growl at young Chica, who has committed the serious breach of kissing him on the head. Georgie, Jean, Dan, Albert, and Liz are already sitting in a table bathed in sunlight; this *sounds* warming but there is no heat whatsoever on this iceberg of a day. Fritz jumps into Liz's lap, which is my signal to brave the queue inside the café. Metty has some new additions to his chalkboard menu, including several pasta dishes, but it is too early to think of anything other than coffee and toast. The little dogs enter a manic barking phase when an orange-clad park worker, the one with the leaf blower on his back, drops his weapon at the café door. "Careful," Albert says to them, "he's got a gun."

Today is Dan's last morning for a while—since tomorrow the Acapulco trip gets underway. There is an even greater milestone in Georgie's life tomorrow—as she has her last day behind the bar at the Windsor Castle on the Harrow Road. The elderly publican is at last packing it in and perhaps there will be a period of refurbishment in the offing. This will present a dilemma for the "care in the community" crowd—for whom the pub *is* the community; some even come inside to ask for a glass of water so they can take their medication. Georgie has been working behind the bar in a number of local establishments for the better part of a decade and she looks forward to packing it in.

Nicholas arrives with Monty and accompanies us on a back passage walkround. He says that one of his clients has a child named Monty but he hasn't told her about his dog—it's an awkward situation in a world in which dogs and children often end up with the same names. A jogger jostles us in the narrow defile between the playing field fences, a place made all the more uncomfortable today by the Siberian winds at our side.

Wednesday, January 24:

The scene is different in more ways than one as I open the blinds on the park scene this chilly January morning. Snow covers every surface and Fritz, sitting on the arm of a sofa in my study, does a double take as the curtains are parted. We make certain to tie on his coat before our departure a few minutes later and we enter a park raucous with the shouts of larking school children and barking dogs. There are more of the latter than usual as every owner in the neighbourhood wants to see how his or her pet will react to the white stuff. The flash of more than one camera lights up a corner of the green as Fritz and I begin a slow walkround on the melting pavement.

In this hive of activity, however, someone is missing: little Koko has died. Only eight, the Shih-Tzu had been poorly of late, growling at the other dogs and refusing even the most tempting titbit. An exploratory surgery revealed the recurrence of cancer and Janet has made the brave decision not to bring her dog back from her deep sleep. Dan called with the news last night and now it is shared out with others as Fritz and I make our way round.

I tell the news to Celine, who is off to the Continent with Ziggy today—because of the timing of his rabies shots they will not be able to return to England until March. I tell Sabina and Denise as we climb Mt. Bannister. They are upset but at our feet is a new distraction—a tiny Beagle puppy named Baija (after a Polish fairy tale). The pup stands on Fritz's head but he is pretty cool about this. Her owner, an American with a camera, also has in tow an unrelated male Beagle named Charlie. I tell him that there are half a dozen Charlies these days. Sabina says that her Scamp was almost a Charlie too.

After we have descended to the Carlton walkway I turn off to join my pals at coffee. To my surprise a tearful Janet is sitting with her friends here and there is much talk of the departed one, who was sitting here in her magenta cardigan only a few days ago. Fritz, offering his own form of therapy, jumps into Janet's lap and gets a nice cuddle. Georgie tells us that her hubby has suggested, now that she has reached the last day of her work at the pub, that she might as well get a paper round—so she can deliver papers while she is out walking the dog. This gives us all a good chuckle, when we are not too close to tears, and then we scatter—Fritz and I making our way over to the Randolph Surgery, where I have to leave off a prescription renewal request.

Thursday, January 25:

Shortly after entering the park we meet up with Liz and her Roxy: "Yesterday, when there was snow on the ground I was surprised that it wasn't colder. Today, when it is clear, I can't believe how cold it is." With these sentiments I agree—it is truly frigid as we attempt to keep some warmth in our limbs while walking along the margins of the mushy green. Fritz take a long time to find a suitable spot for a poo—I think he is not entirely comfortable with his coat perched on top of his tail.

We are half way round when Liz spots the Beagle pair of puppy Baija and the slim-line Charlie. "No way I'm going anywhere near them with my dog in this shape," she says. I think she is kidding but the prospect of having the podgy Roxy standing next to these newcomers is so daunting that she reverses direction on us. A few minutes later, when I am talking to Albert, she notes that the new Beagles are heading in this direction too. This time there is no escape and soon she is comparing notes with the American chap who introduced us to his dogs only yesterday. "I've faced my fears," Liz says proudly, encouraged by the news that Charlie is almost anorexic and that Baija is already a very greedy little girl.

We now head for the café, where we sit at a table outside the front door with Ofra, Hanna, Kate, Jean, and a euphoric Georgie—celebrating her first pub-free day. Hanna has picked up two newspapers inside and these give us a series of topics to start with: a new species of prehistoric shark found in the ocean depths, a fox who has wandered into a Notting Hill shoe shop—Hanna is delighted by all these stories until, disapprovingly, she discovers one that lists Gordon Brown among the hundred handsomest men. Someone asks how Janet is doing and Georgie says that she sounds exhausted after a day of tears. Somewhat sobered by this intelligence, we undertake a back passage walkround.

Friday, January 26:

A brief snow flurry has just ended as Fritz and I head for the park under grey skies. When we reach the green I can see a bunch of Charlies and a gaggle of tussling blondes. Today we have Charlie the Beagle (accompanied by his Hush Puppy sidekick, Baija), Charlie the Cocker, and Charlie the little black Poodle. The blondes are represented by the Labrador Rufus and the Golden Retrievers Sasha and Buddy. Fritz gives a wide berth to all of this activity and we complete a capacious circle that even takes us over the top of Mt. Bannister before we join others in front of the café.

Hanna, Jean, Georgie, and Liz are present—with Albert sitting as an outrider. Jean is planning an early visit to the Glasgow vet since Billy's bad breath may be the sign of some rotting teeth. Georgie is still happily adjusting her schedule to a life without pulling pints. Liz tells us that she has again been a crime target since—as she was about to drive off from a parking space in front of the Odeon Swiss Cottage yesterday, a chap with blonde-dyed Rasta braids tried to break into her back seat—fortunately the door he tried to use is permanently jammed. Her little boy was, of course, traumatized. Liz says that New York is beginning to look like a safe haven.

We begin a back passage walkround during which Hanna retells the long history of her own battle with muggers—one of whom felt the lash of her Bruno's dog chain. Behind us come Buddy and Rufus, but no one would call them blondes now; this morning's wrestling match on the green has turned both of them into muddy messes—you could grow pot plants from the residue that must now be removed from their coats. As we clear the cypress trees we can see two of the newly installed poo poo bins. They look like bits of bright red Samsonite but they have nice maws and, for those of us who often have to wander quite a bit with a sack of warm poo in our hands, they will be quite welcome.

Saturday, January 27:

Temperatures have moderated and the sun is dominant in the skies and, though I am still wearing my thermals, Fritz is allowed to exit the premises wearing only his own fur. When we reach the green I can see Georgie, Jean and Faz in front of the bandstand and we join their procession around the perimeter. Fritz is allowed to ramble off lead and he does a good job of remaining in sight—even though he often races ahead a bit while the others seem rooted to the spot. This is because the Scottish ladies are trying to teach Faz the rules of Kalooki, a card game which resulted in the transfer of £21 from one sister's pocket to the other's last night. Jasmine follows Fritz into the bushes and I can see that she is just as puzzled as I am when she can't find him where he was last seen. He has somehow gotten ahead again and rushed up to give a still teary Janet a warm greeting. When Jasmine does re-emerge she has a spit of dog slobber on her nose and this requires an instant tissue. "That'll teach you to kiss on the first date," I say.

At coffee we sit at the only two tables, a large pair yoked together, still resident in the café forecourt. Peter and Ellen are dispensing sausages at one end and I take a seat next to Ellen because I have remembered to bring my dark glasses and the sun is now streaming into our eyes and even providing a little warmth. Ronnie joins us after the absence of several days—as both he and Susie have been suffering from a tummy bug. For some reason Faz wants to learn some Hebrew and so Ofra obliges with an impromptu lesson; soon she is in a deep reverie about growing up in Jerusalem. Meanwhile her Bailey hops from lap to lap, misbehaving himself. I mention that Dorothy and I will be in Cairo in two weeks. Faz says it is a very dusty city and Albert says that when he was there the locals stepped into the street in order to let him pass on the pavement—a remark utterly baffling until I remember that the veteran is talking about his service in World War II.

We have a group of nine dog owners making the back passage walkround—including Ofra, Ronnie and Albert, whose Saffy and Tinkerbelle are wearing new terry-cloth body suits—Saffy in bright yellow, appropriately, and Tinkerbelle in leopard prints against a pink background. Billy and Mozart are making their last appearance in the procession for a while, as Jean returns to Glasgow this afternoon. Such a large and slow-moving assemblage is not easy for the joggers to dodge, especially in the narrow defile that is left between the playing field fences. Janet has walked to the park and so she can leave at the Essendine exit. As if her week isn't bad enough the docs have told her that she has high blood pressure, high cholesterol and that she needs to lose weight. "I'll see you tomorrow morning," she says, "unless it rains—I don't have to go the park when it does that now."

Sunday, January 28:

Long before we make our entrance into the park Fritz is sizing up the action from the vantage point of my lap—as he stares out the window over my desk. Truth to tell, there is not much going on in the park on a grey Sunday morning. We pass a toddler who starts to cry when it appears that my dog is intent on his wanderings—and is not going to stay to be played with. Faz and Georgie are alone in the middle of the green—which is where we head next. David soon arrives with black Poppy and Skye the Alsatian. He too bewails the lack of action, though things are surely picking up on the periphery, and Fritz II, now a handsome and graceful fellow at ten months, joins us with Richard and Christina.

Fritz soon discovers a clear rubber ball that issues an unearthly scream every time it is bounced, and this manages to keep him preoccupied as he chews away at its surface while Skye chases her ball and Poppy tries to get me to throw her stick. I succeed in doing this a few times and even find her a better stick, but my hands are now well muddied. I place Fritz's new toy in a plastic bag and follow my dog into the precincts of the café, but I have to turn my pet over to Ronnie in order to head for the men's room for some soap and water. This is always a desperate process, particularly so on a frigid day like today. The water is icy and no method exists for drying the hands—perhaps we could use some of the netting that lies unused in the brand new cricket nets behind the café—a facility that seems to be totally superfluous.

Faz is also suffering from cold hands; he has to borrow a pair of mittens from Janet but she is only able to offer one blue and one black specimen. At the next table Franca holds up her mobile phone and asks us to provide a round of applause. This we do, and then she tells us that the accolade has been bestowed on a vet friend of hers who yesterday saved a dog whose earlier hip transplant had gone septic. Franca also has a plate of sausages cooling in front of her and this has attracted quite a canine contingent—including her own Bianca and Frank, Blake the Doberman (who is muzzled because he has been scavenging again), plus Rosie and Fritz from our table. The feeding process is protracted—first because of the telephone call, then because Blake takes off after a cursing jogger, and finally because giant Ruby arrives, unsettling the doggy balance—which now erupts into a snarling pack (Fritz excluded). In fact the sausages are still undistributed when Faz announces that he is cold and wants to begin a back passage walkround. At home I wash the new screaming ball but Fritz soon begins to take large bites out of it and we have to throw it away.

Monday, January 29:

Temperatures are mild enough as Fritz and I head for the park under grey skies. A naughty Jack Russell is penetrating the forbidden rose garden but then so is Sparkie—who gets muzzled after a prolonged period of barking when Georgie can at last extract him. Lizzie and Tim pause to admire Fritz's beard and moustache. "In Iraq," Tim says, "they would say he has a moustache big enough for an eagle to land on." Out on the green Fritz suddenly becomes interested in a tennis ball which little Jack the Yorkie and Chica the Boxer are playing with. This actually leads to some exercise—even some for me since I have to follow my dog to the spot where he has gone with the object before we can start all over again. Fritz, who actually pisses on George at one point, seems determined to have a sniff into every corner of the green but at last, ball still in his mouth, he undertakes a graceful curve around some pipe-laying workmen on the Randolph walkway and, without pause, admits himself to the café's forecourt.

I get in line at the counter but Fritz twice decides to follow me through the open door and, long before I can order my cappuccino, I have had to usher him out and then follow him along the Carlton roadway until he stops a nose length away from Tara the Kerry Blue's bum—just as that lady is engaging in what should be some very private behaviour. I have to put Fritz on lead and pass him on to Ronnie before rejoining the queue—though later I do get a chance to eject Roxy from the café on my way out. At breakfast we have Peter, Ellen, Ronnie, Georgie, Liz, Hanna and Albert. For a while we have both Jacks—as the Yorkie keeps escaping his master in order to see if there is still any food going at our table. When it is time to go only Hanna and Albert are prepared to use the back passage.

This route always brings us close to the proposed wildlife and nature study site—which is the topic of public meetings next week and the subject of an article in this week's *Westminster Reporter*. From the latter some interesting facts are adduced. The Rec has over a million visitors a year, including "an army of dog walkers." The Ecology Centre, which will have ponds, wetlands and various types of woodland (mostly on parts of the 27-acre site previously inaccessible to the public), is part of a £3.5 million makeover for a site that has been a public treasure for 120 years. I suppose that the only fly in this ointment is the phrase "subject to external funding." Does this mean public money or private? I can see it now—"This tree is brought to you by your local friendly Tesco."

Tuesday, January 30:

Grey skies predominate this morning but temperatures are comfortable enough. Fritz and I begin a counter-clockwise circuit of the green but a small Alsatianate dog runs up to give my dog a sniff and I can spot a potential difficulty. The dog is carrying a miniature soccer ball in his teeth and Fritz is eyeing it covetously. Sure enough, a minute later, the ball is in Fritz's mouth and I can tell that the other dog's owner wants to leave. Fortunately there is a dented green plastic ball on the grass as well and I am able to get my dog to drop ball one in favour of ball two. The soccer ball returned to its proper owner, we continue on our journey—the plastic ball rattling on the pavement as I kick it along. A chap wearing a Rizla Suzuki hoody is sitting on a bench, his dozy Staffy in tow, broadcasting the scene on his mobile phone: "She has a cute bum and she's wearing a red hat. She should be here any minute." I can see the jogger being described in this conversation but she sits down on a bench before pulling even with the voyeur. Fritz and I continue up Mt. Bannister, where one of the lady dog walkers has four or five beasts exercising themselves. Also present is a small black dog wearing a camouflage harness. Fritz chases him and then we go over the hill and down to the Carlton roadway.

There is already a breakfast set sitting at a table outside the caff doors and our group eventually swells to ten, with Peter, Ellen, Ofra, Ronnie, Georgie, Kate, Albert, Liz and Hanna making up the numbers. Rizla Suzuki comes in and sits down at an adjacent table with Vlad, the chap who always accompanies the red bandana-wearing Rhodesian Ridgeback, Tara. The latter now tries, unsuccessfully, to climb into her master's lap. Michael the Pirate is here as well—the first time I have seen him since the passing of Doofie. I pass around the article from the *Westminster Reporter*. A late delivery of sausages arrives and these items are quickly distributed by Ellen. The little black dog appears and he gets into a scrap with Sparkie—I can see shards of carrot flying during the contretemps.

Pretty soon someone notices that Bailey has thrown up, and a flurry of activity begins as the ladies attempt to clean up the mess—Ofra even goes inside to get some water. There is a lot of speculation that the sausages, which Bailey doesn't stomach well at the best of times, were just too hot this morning. One can certainly see rings of the forbidden food, which have been swallowed whole, in the mess at our feet. Fritz, also a participant in this morning's banquet, has been sitting in my lap after finishing off my cappuccino foam. All of a sudden Hanna notices that he too is beginning to heave. I get him down in time for a protracted period of purging, another mess which Hanna and Georgie very kindly clean up. We begin to walk toward the Morshead gate, encountering Monty the Schnauzer on the way, but a few minutes after our return Fritz begins to vomit again. I am able to slip some newsprint under his chin just in time to save our carpets—though it does mean that I have to sacrifice two unread editions of the *New York Review of Books*.

Wednesday, January 31:

There is bright sunlight this morning and this imparts a cheerier note than that struck on all the grey days we have had recently. It takes forever for Fritz to part with his first gift and this means that the others have all taken their seats in front of the café by the time we arrive. I start to hand my lead to Ronnie but Hanna reaches for it; both Spadge and George have already had their outings in the park and are at home now. This means that I am now free to enter the café where Metty is presiding over a trio of Balkan baristas, one of whom always says, on hearing of my medium cappuccino, "I bring."

Georgie is now entering her third week as a non-smoker and there are congratulations all round, even from Ronnie—who is smoking a cigar. Ofra is telling us that she now uses her toothbrush on her lips as well as her teeth—Ronnie rolls his eyes. No one has any sausages, except for Hanna, who produces a clipping from yesterday's *Evening Standard* on the subject of park keepers. It seems that Westminster Council is to reintroduce this ancient profession in 54 open spaces, including Paddington Rec. The keepers will have the power to enforce council bylaws, though the article seems to suggest that sleeping rough, drunken behaviour and littering are the chief offences. (No mention of any night-time wardens, though there were young people in the park again last night.) The new wardens are to carry out their duties in distinctive blue uniforms and on bicycles—this will make enforcement of the no cycling rule in Paddington Rec a challenge indeed. "The move is part of an £18million contract with Continental Landscapes Ltd for 109 parks over eight years," according to the *Standard*, which also editorialized that the scheme will make park users feel much safer and that the scheme should be applied throughout the metropolis.

Feeling safer already, some of us begin a back passage walkround. I manage to step in some other dog's poo (where is a warden when you need him?) and Hanna very kindly uses a tissue to mop up a string of the same substance hanging from my dog's bum. Near the exit we encounter Jennifer with Giant; she tells us she is moving from Kilburn to Primrose Hill. Also blocking our way is a tiny Papillion named Pippa—all of our dogs have to undertake a detailed sniff before we can reach the exit.

February, 2007

Thursday, February 1:

Soon after entering the park we meet up with Liz and Roxy and, in turn, we are soon overtaken by Jean-Baptiste with Hercules and Michaela with Skye the Cairn; only Linda, soon arriving with Pepper, is needed to turn this into a famous fivesome. Together we begin a grand circle of the park. Pepper broadsides Fritz on a number of occasions but most of the time he is fending off the lustful attacks of a confused Hercules. Jean-Baptiste, just back from celebrating his father's seventieth birthday in France, must continually pause to say, "Hercules, today zere is no boom-boom." Skye is carrying a tennis ball and, even as we scale Mt. Bannister, he keeps trying to insinuate it between my shoe and my next step—in the hopes that I will give it a good kick.

It is still too early for coffee so, once we have reached the Carlton roadway, we persevere, beginning what would normally be a back passage walkround. Albert, just heading into the park with Saffy and Tinkerbelle (who are getting too plump for any of their outfits) is quite confused by this gesture, but I assure him that we are not leaving. Michaela and Jean-Baptiste peel off as we complete a circuit near the Morshead gate—another moment of confusion since Skye wants to stay with the rest of us and Fritz would just as soon head out.

This time we report for coffee, with Georgie and Ofra already in position. Ofra has brought a section of last weekend's *Sunday Times* showing interior pictures of the house that her Ricky has converted on Hall Road in St. John's Wood. We are joined by Tanya who has with her both baby Isabella in a pushchair and Pasha the Weimaraner. She tells us that there is already some problem with the entry of the former into a local nursery school since most mothers register their offspring from the moment of conception. Pasha delicately attempts to pry one of Metty's coffee biscuits from the fingers of her brown-eyed human sister—but in this she is unsuccessful. I leave the women chattering and take a seat at

Michael the Pirate's table—it is the first time I have been able to talk to him since Doofie's death. Michael says he is looking for Angie—since he intends to use his mechanical skills on the wheels of her Zimmer frame. Today we head for the Morshead gate, but it is first necessary for Fritz to run off the ever-hopeful Gus. I can see that the latter doesn't have blue fur this time—but a few curls on his forehead have been dyed orange.

Friday, February 2:

The thunder of the waterworks machinery in front of our house sends Fritz skittering off to the left as we cross the street this morning, and so we enter the park from the Essendine gate for once and, then, having started off on the route actually favoured for park entries (until the recent park refurbishment got under way) we continue to the left and undertake a back passage walkround in reverse. Fritz is able to go off lead from the outset here. We pass Albert, sitting in the bright sun with his Yorkies at his feet, and soon reach the café—where I can see an early group including Peter, Ellen and Ronnie—waiting for the doors of this establishment to open. Here we begin to circumnavigate the green, following a group including Charlie the Poodle and Rizzo—but Fritz decides to admit himself to the doggy area near the Grantully gate and so I follow him inside.

I can see Georgie and Janet on the walkway outside and I can hear Sparkie barking hysterically as usual, but all eyes seem riveted by the approach of Faz and Jasmine and it is necessary for me to extract Fritz as quickly as possible from his wanderings because Faz is obviously carrying some very precious object in his arms and one that requires close and immediate attention—Faz and Dianah have a new Shih-Tzu puppy! Findlay, who has brown fur punctuating his black and white coat, is an adorable thirteen week-old nephew of Jasmine, arrived only on Wednesday. He's had all his shots and can mix with the other dogs already but Faz lets him do his own walking only occasionally. Pictures are taken and much is made of the little fellow but Fritz grows bored and I see him heading for the Grantully gate—where he even takes a few forbidden steps on the pavement before being bribed to return with a handout of puppy kibble. Thereafter we make a more protracted visit to the doggy area, finally crossing the muddy green to join the others at coffee.

Here Peter tells me that his Holly and several other participants in the last sausage feast were also ill—there seems to be no doubt about the origins of this mysterious illness. Kate distributes some treats, including a lot of toast, and Findlay, a rubber band creating a topknot on his head, is passed around for everyone to cuddle. Janet is very strongly affected by the little fellow, who does resemble dear Koko in a number of ways, and there are tears. Hanna asks her if she is tempted—"Yes," is the reply, "but not yet." Others suggest that the silky-haired youngster reminds them of a guinea pig. "I feel like getting him an egg.com credit card," I add. The presence of the newcomer delays our departure for the gates but eventually there is a large contingent at work on the back passage. This time little Findlay is allowed to do some of his own waddling.

Saturday, February 3:

I give Fritz his choice of directions this morning and he chooses to reprise yesterday's back passage route. This is a very slow progress indeed, since he pauses for a long period of grazing on the grass shoots at the head of the running track. His appetite at last satisfied, we continue forward on tarmac, threading our way past dozens of young five-a-side scholars who are being told what to do at every moment of the game by assertive coaches and anxious dads.

When we at last reach the green the sun is shining brightly again and I have to squint to see who, among all the dogs out here today, we actually know. The answer is precious few—for most of the canines in action here are part of Roland's Saturday morning training classes—and they too are under instruction. Fritz checks in for a minute or two and then follows me across the green to a spot where Kate is exercising Skye and Georgie Sparkie. Fritz would like to check out the doggy play area on the Grantully side again but I notice that someone has just dumped cubes of bread for the birds here, and I know that Fritz will make a meal of them if allowed. Instead, back on lead, we make our way around the green and along the pitted Randolph walkway in the direction of the café.

For such a lovely morning we have only a small turnout—just Georgie, Ofra, Albert and Kate—though, sensing that there may be food present, a number of other dogs pause for a brief visit at our table. Hector soon has his paws on my knee, Buddy presents his big head (Kate is searching for the one spot that will not impart a layer of mud, if petted), and even

Ché puts in an appearance today (managing two messy poos, as usual, which John now cleans up). Ofra is trying to decide whether to have Guy's bar mitzvah in London or Jerusalem, Georgie is still struggling against the urge to smoke, and all the women have a debate on whether they'd rather have Leonardo DiCaprio or Brad Pitt as a bed partner. There is even some warmth in the sun this morning and we linger for quite a while before beginning a back passage walkround (during which Fritz manages to snag his lead on the cypress trees). By this time the park is a hive of activity: water fountains are preparing the hockey arena's playing surface, joggers are circling the running track, the Saturday exercise club is doing jumping jacks, and sullen soccer players, looking for a field, are scowling at all the rest of us.

Sunday, February 4:

Fog is thickening as Fritz and I make our way toward the park on a cold and damp Sunday morning. I don't dare let my dog off lead, given his wandering propensities, for fear of losing track of him altogether. Instead we make our way slowly around the margins of the green until Fritz is willing to add a poo to a pile of dirt that workmen have left behind near the metal gazebo. Peter is trying to get Hector to get off the same pile—which has a muddy potential that all dog owners must fear.

I can see some familiar faces newly returned for Dan and Davide are here with Essex girl Winnie; the lads are returned from ten days in Mexico, both very tan, and Winnie is back from a session with Dan's dad, having made herself the queen of the house—even cowing the two resident Pointers in the process. The proud parents, Faz and Dianah, are both here with puppy Findlay. The little fellow is passed around among the other dog owners like a furry parcel, with much cooing and cuddling. Kate and Georgie are here, trying to exercise their dogs, but Fritz has to content himself with rushing forward to challenge any strange dogs who manage to come too close to his group. Anxious to see the newcomer, Jo Lynn arrives with Tilly. Seeing the latter, I say, "Lock up your squirrels!"

At coffee only dog owners are brave enough to sit outside; at our two conjoined tables we have all of the aforementioned plus Albert, Ofra, and Hanna. Spadge, his lead attached to a chair leg, begins his patented barking retreat while Hanna is inside making her order, and soon the ancient Schnauzer has dragged the chair (and George, attached to the other leg) half way across the forecourt. Findlay continues to make his way from lap to lap, ending up inside his dad's zippered jacket. The Scottish ladies are bewailing England's victory over Scotland in the first of this year's matches in the Six Nations rugby tournament. Faz says, "Scotland had a great team in 1983." I say, "You might as well say Carthage had a great team in the Second Century BC." Then, just as Ché arrives to launch another attack on the forecourt foliage, we begin a back passage walkround—quite a contingent with eight owners and our dogs shuffling toward the exits. On the way we encounter little Lisa, with Zara, Dash and braces on her teeth—we haven't seen her in the park for some time now. The first of the daffodils are in bloom at the head of the running track.

Monday, February 5:

Grey skies and cool temperatures preside as Fritz and I pick our way through the bombsite that is Morshead Road and into the building site that is Paddington Rec. There seem to be plenty of dogs about but none of them belong to our breakfast circle and, under any circumstances, Fritz has not expressed any interest in park dogs since Charlie departed over a year ago. (He does enjoy a romp with Pepper, who came for a play date yesterday, but in the park he plays hard to get even when this pal is around.)

In consequence we just wander around, Fritz off lead, as a sniffathon begins. At one point Fritz follows some other dogs along the Carlton roadway but he soon grows bored with this and heads back to the green where I find a tennis ball worth kicking a few times. Kate is out here with Skye and Davide with Winnie but even such a stalwart as Georgie is absent—something about waiting in for the gasman. After this boring bit on the grass it is a relief to head in for coffee. Fritz, back on lead, jumps through the fence so as to get closer to Peter and Ellen, and I have to find some way of rejoining him. He's out of luck anyway, since these two seem to be foregoing their usual sausage order after last week's debacle.

Only Davide and Kate are present for coffee this morning ("It's quality not quantity that counts," I tell her). Eventually Albert pulls over a chair and Nicholas arrives with Monty. Nicholas is trying to pick Davide's brain as he formulates plans for a September honeymoon. Fritz helps by jumping into Nicholas' lap—where he growls whenever Monty tries to get close to his own master. We discuss Cairo, on the eve of our departure for this Middle Eastern metropolis, the parlous state of Italian football, and Kate's move to West Kilburn. We are about to leave when she passes on some news that brings a sudden damper to further conversation: on Friday, Ronnie's ailing and ancient mother has died in hospital.

Tuesday, February 6:

Again Fritz chooses to head for the Essendine rather than the Morshead Gate as we pull up opposite the park, and I am just as happy to comply—it means that I can let him off lead all the earlier. It is a lovely day; there is still frost on the grass but a bright sunshine is rapidly adding a sense of cheer to the surroundings. A couple of small dogs (including the one who penetrated the rose garden the other day) are coming up behind us with their own Thai nanny. I can see now why these dogs wander—their mistress is wedded to her mobile phone, though at the volume she manages one can wonder if she really needs *any* instrument. Fritz now races ahead but, to my astonishment, he actually waits for me at the curve in the bend of the tarmac path. In this fashion we reach the green, where half a dozen dogs are at play. Four park workers are supervising the extraction of a sack of dog poo from one of the new Samsonite bins.

When I enter the café I notice that there are two long tables with place settings—each marked with a bottle of Evian. Bouzha tells me that there will be a meeting of Westminster Council here and, indeed, the place is soon full of people dressed far better than our usual lot. I tell the others that they need to be on their best behaviour but there isn't much action, truth to tell—just the usual raucous call for Hector and one penetration of the café interior by Monty. Nicholas has another fine cuddle with Fritz, even offering him some cappuccino foam at the end of a finger. Peter (of Peter and Holly) tells me that old Hendrix, suffering from a tumour, has had to be put down. This makes a trio of canine deaths all in the last few weeks—with those of Doofie and Koko already noted—and puts a damper on proceedings indeed.

When we get up to leave both Ofra and Dan agree to walk the back passage with Georgie and me. Dan is out of sorts—I tell him it is because he has actually had to do a day's work after all of his holiday-making but he claims it is just jetlag. As we pass the five-a-sides courts we can see workers beginning to carpet the ugly tarmac with Astroturf of some sort. This will make our walk between the fences slightly less oppressive—as long as those Westminster dudes don't decide to Astroturf the entire park. Sparkie barks at one of the workmen (he's barked at everything else today) but I say he's just giving off a warning. "Yes," Dan adds, "he's warning the workman that a Pug is coming." There is no relief from all this activity as we exit the park—tarmac is now going down on Morshead Road.

Wednesday, February 7:

Dog-haters, one of whom catches a high heel in a pavement crack, are heading toward the Essendine gate this morning—so Fritz and I head for an alternative point of entry. It is very cold this morning, though the sun is again shining brightly. I begin a walk around the green but after a while we head over the grass in the direction of Kate, who is slinging the ball toward Skye. It is almost a pleasure to walk on the pitch today for it is well-frozen and, for once, the shoes manage to stay mud-free. I follow Fritz for several minutes, though he is halted by fencing from penetrating the Randolph exit—which is closed these days—and we have to turn to the right, where we encounter Hanna out with the slow-moving George. She tells me that, bothered by a parked car which belched smoke from its running engine for close to two hours in front of her house last night, she approached the passengers (who were fiddling with a computer) with a simple question—"Hey, is this your new office?" and they soon drove off.

At the café Ronnie is present, the first time since his mother has died. He tells us about the funeral and the melancholy task of cleaning out her flat, and distributes carrots and biscuits to the dogs. Georgie, following an ancient ritual, then folds the green poo-poo bags in which these goodies have arrived, and then returns them to Ronnie for re-use. Ofra tells us that she has booked a synagogue in Jerusalem for her Guy's bar mitzvah. Dan tells us that he is still bothered by jetlag and that his disposition has not been helped by Winnie's conspicuous naughtiness. It seems that she has learned that if she barks at cats in the back yard then Davide will get her to quiet down by bribing her with a piece of cheese, and so she therefore just barks now whenever admitted to this space—just for the cheese at the end of the process. Yesterday Dan chased her all over the house before being able to make her sit out her penance on the new doggy bed.

Twice an impatient Skye jumps with her paws onto Kate's shoulders, a symbol of her irritation that mommy is still drinking tea and not going out on the green to sling the ball again. A woman comes by hunting for her two dogs, a Cocker named Kiva and a Yorkie named Bubbles. The latter won't emerge from beneath our table because he is getting some toast and even when the woman accepts her own order of sausages he stubbornly remains hidden by our knees. Later, when she offers the rest of this treat to us, Dan has to explain that one theory is that sausages are too rich a diet for canine pancreases (this was certainly what the vet said of Koko, whose grieving mom is present today)—and there are only a few takers for this substance this morning. I have errands to run so Fritz and I are the first to depart, dodging a truck that is actually *speaking* its warning about backing up instead of offering the usual beeping. On the green Leila has come to a standstill, crouching low as she prepares to jump on Fritz—who is also creeping forward in a similar stealthy fashion as the menace is sighted.

Thursday, February 8:

They have been promising it for days but it is finally here—snow covers everything as we open the curtains this morning and the large, wet flakes are still falling. It takes a long time to get ready to go out—as both long underwear and hiking boots must be donned by me, and then there is Fritz's coat. We descend the slippery steps, make our way to the Essendine gate and soon after our entry into the white wilderness I let Fritz go. He bustles along happily, though I have to pause twice to retie my boots, impossible to do with my gloves on. I suppose he does a poo while my back is turned—I never see him perform this essential part of the morning ritual.

Little black Jasper comes up behind us by the time we have entered the new fenced chasm and Fritz offers an admonitory growl—and then chases after his friend as we approach the café. Out on the green there are lots of people and lots of dogs chasing about and there are some truly serious attempts at snowman building; one dad is even carrying sticks with him so that he can fashion arms for his creation. An hour later and all these efforts have left us with a little snow circle, an icy Avebury. Fritz gallops over the white surface as though he were really enjoying himself but he is not slow in accepting my offer of a retreat to the café when the time comes.

There is a very poor turnout at the one table that has been set out in front of the doors of our morning eatery—and we have only Peter and Ellen and Hanna present, though the second Peter, his chest having borne the brunt of a snowball fight, sits down after the other Peter, full of complaints about today's wintry imposition, has departed. We don't linger for long over our drinks and then Hanna and I undertake a back passage walkround. Fritz is truly into this snow thing by now, cantering merrily—his nose close to the surface, pausing for the occasional pee or a delicious mouthful as he goes.

Tuesday, February 20:

It is my first day back in the park after eleven days in Egypt—and I feel pretty much like a zombie after a bad night. Not only do I have a monstrous head cold (nothing that a head transplant wouldn't fix) but I am also walking under the burden of another bit of awful news in the annals on our Paddington Rec dogs: Peter's Hector has been killed under the wheels of a speeding van. David has told us of this quite recent development after yielding our Fritz to us after a long period of dog-sitting; Fritz, whom we have missed very much, is just fine—though after an initial wild greeting he keeps looking at us as though he can't quite remember why we figure so significantly in his life.

I am stunned with the tragedy of young Hector—whom we have all known since he was a little puppy and whose emergence, into a very large and handsome specimen of the Cocker breed, we have all delighted in. Fritz and I make our way along the back passage, encountering Suzanne and Sunny for the first time in weeks, and then, as we approach the coffee crowd, I can already see a stricken Peter hunched over at our table. He looks like he has been through a battle but he accepts my condolences and goes looking either for some Rizla papers or a cigarette he can buy off someone. Some lads, making their way from the park after practice, tell him they don't smoke—"What's the matter with the youth of today?" I ask. At least Peter has the company of Jody, whom he also looks after these days. He is astonished when she refuses a handful of kibble.

Also seated are Liz, Ofra and Georgie. Ofra is complaining about the costs of a London root canal. Georgie, whose wet Sparkie sits miserably in her lap, says that she won't walk past the Windsor Castle for fear they'll rush out and ask her to return behind the bar—as they have ever since she packed it in. I have to begin all over with a recital of our adventures in Egypt ("glad we went," "wouldn't go on a tour again," "too many pre-dawn wake-up calls") every time someone new sits down. (I do not mention that our enjoyment of this trip was undermined for us by the presence of Dorothy's persistent cough.) Kate now sits down; she says that she has at last gotten rid of the tenants who were still ensconced in her new house—and that she plans to start moving in a few days. She accompanies Georgie and me as we complete a back passage walkround. I notice that one corner of the new five-a-side pitch will lie just outside the environs of the new woodland ecology lab: I can just see the toddlers intently poised at the margins of the pond while their elders are turning the air blue with the obligatory sports obscenities behind them.

Wednesday, February 21:

Skies are just clearing and we have a springlike sunny morning for our entry into Paddington Rec—some of the trees on the Morshead Road side of this great public space are already beginning to flower. Albert is sitting on a bench in the sun, Tinkerbelle and Saffy craning their necks to see what Fritz is up to. He is not up to much, sniffing each blade of grass, eating one or two, and making very slow progress behind the playing fields. When we reach the café they are just setting out the tables and so we continue on a leisurely circuit of the green—by which time the others have taken up places in the forecourt.

I hand Fritz over to Ofra and wait out the queue in pursuit of my mid-sized cappuccino. There is only one barista today and I have to hold the door open for her as she heads outside with a tray full of coffees for the earlycomers. Then Monty trots in and I have to leave my place in the queue in order to usher him out. Then Dan comes in looking for some sugar and I have to keep the door open for him too. I haven't lost my place, but progress remains painful.

In addition to Ofra we have Georgie, Kate, Nicholas and Dan this morning. Dan has swollen glands and a sore head and is taking a day off work. Nicholas is arguing that he would rather see thugs with Staffies than with knives—though neither seems to be a desirable prospect. Bailey is at his annoying best, repeatedly jumping into my lap in order to get closer to my kibble bag. Not only are his feet wet, but he can't settle—and manages to lash the foam off my coffee with his tail. Eventually I put Fritz on my lap as a form of protection. Skye is carrying on her usual noisy colloquy on the subject of ball, boredom, and mommy. To distract her, Nicholas chases her around the table three times, and this seems to work. Soon we are moving toward the exits, with Skye proudly carrying a tree limb in her teeth in case we run into any thugs with Staffies.

Thursday, February 22:

It is a grey morning and the skies are spitting a bit as Fritz and I enter the Essendine gate and begin a back passage walkround. Before we can make much progress I see Liz approaching with Roxy and we turn around to accompany her on a grand circle. Fritz seems happy enough to have a chubby companion, though the Beagle does surprise us once by jumping up on an empty bench. Out on the green, where Kate is slinging the ball to Skye, we can see that Sparkie has gotten into an ill-tempered clash with another small terrier over possession of his own ball. Ofra and Bailey join us as we reach the top of Mt. Bannister and by this time the café is open and a queue is forming at the counter.

Progress is very slow again, since Bouzha has to start off with a huge take-out order for the park staff (who really ought to come last in this line-up). Matters are made worse by the nasty habit of queue jumping—which I have often disparaged—with one after another member of the dog-walking fraternity shouting in their orders to Georgie, who is at the head of the queue (while the rest of us wait patiently for our turn). I give up and return to an exposed spot at a little table to the left of the door, where Dan, still complaining of a sore throat, is handing out a special non-allergenic kibble to Winnie and the other dogs—since Winnie is under treatment for a series of rashes. At one point the Pug wanders near a woman in a headscarf who has just approached with a buggy and two little kids. The youngest of these begins to shriek hysterically and there are a few uncomfortable moments during which the woman casts baleful glances at the rest of us—though why you would bring canine-phobic kids into an environment where ten dogs are dancing about is a mystery. Twice, first on pushing her way into the café and then, five minutes later, as she exits, she hits Winnie with the buggy and Dan, springing to his feet, is very upset—there are words.

There is more upset as we settle down at our little table again. I learn that Kate has had an operation for breast cancer and must begin chemotherapy on Friday. And that Faz and Dianah, overfaced by the presence of a new puppy, have decided to return Findlay to the kennel. Some of this intelligence is digested as Georgie, Dan and I begin a back passage walkround—the skies are still gloomy and wet.

Friday, February 23:

A night of rain has come to an end as Fritz and I enter the park on a cloudy Friday morning. Almost immediately we are surrounded by dogs—since Denise and Sabina are heading our way with Rizzo, Oscar and Scamp, and they are accompanied this time by a dog walker who has a number of animals in her care—including the Weimaraner Pasha—while behind us Albert is entering the park with Saffy and Tinkerbelle. Fritz manages to greet this menagerie without a single admonitory growl and we are soon alone as we pass the cedar trees. Here Fritz races ahead—no waiting for me at the right-hand bend this time—and I don't see him again until I have reached the green.

Here we begin a walk along the Randolph roadway and then turn right to begin a circuit of the muddy green. Near the hill atop the tennis courts we encounter Sabina and Denise a second time (I can just hear the former saying, "In your own time, Oscar!"). When we reach the Morshead roadway we also meet our own gang, undertaking a rare circuit themselves. So we reverse directions and follow Dan, Georgie, Ofra, and Kate (plus dogs)—with Fritz content to charge in and out of this melee happily. Tim enters with Yoyo and Fritz follows his old friend out to the centre of the green, where she squats for a poo. "Leave her alone," I shout to my inquisitive animal, "she needs a little privacy, please!" When we at last reach the café we take places around a table in the forecourt for the morning's coffee klatch.

Hanna reports that her wrist has given way and that she has spilled her first cup of coffee at the counter—Georgie brings her a replacement. Ofra reports that she has left some cash in her car—and the others are horrified. Dan says that he still has a very sore throat but that his g.p. hasn't given him anything for it—another dismissal of the sufferings of those with "man flu." Georgie receives a phone call from Jean; the sisters are trying to figure out the source of a song used in a current TV commercial, but none of us can help. I tell Kate that she probably shouldn't be flinging the ball to Skye in her condition, but she says, "It was my left breast. I throw with my right arm."

Skye, meanwhile, has an undercoating of mud. Sparkie is also encrusted; he looks miserable, shivering in Georgie's lap until she wraps him up in one of her own scarves. Saffy and Tinkerbelle are charmed by the noisy Skye, who continues to nag Kate for some action—the little Yorkies actually like to put their heads in the Alsatian's mouth—but they manage to escape without injury. Kate finds a tennis ball and throws it to Skye—who returns from the bushes with a rusty football. This prize is carried in her mouth on the return journey, where, twice, I have to go behind the cedars in order to retrieve it for her. I pass Fritz's lead off to Hanna on these occasions but when I throw the ball to Skye my dog takes off after it as well—almost pulling Hanna's arm out its socket.

Saturday, February 24:

Rains have again cleared only a short time before Fritz and I make our appearance in the Rec. We now choose the back passage most mornings—I can let Fritz off the lead much earlier and still keep track of him in the narrower confines of this route, and he does seem to enjoy a thorough sniff-a-thon back here. Ahead of us today I can see an impediment: dozens of kids are choking the narrow fenced corridor between playing surfaces as they get ready for the first day of play on the new five-a-side courts. Already I can see that Hanna, making slow progress with George and Spadge, has reached this impasse and that she is not happy. Sure enough, she tells me soon enough, she has received only cheek from the coach in charge of this lot—even though she has only asked him to make sure that his charges have left space for other park users. As I pull up to the spot, Fritz back on lead, I can see part of the problem. They haven't unlocked all the necessary gates in a timely fashion, they have set their registration desks up in the crowded defile, and they have brought with them a generation of youngsters who aren't used to sharing space.

Fritz and I pick our way gingerly through this resentful mass (as we have to do most afternoons if we are walking along the public pavement in front of the Paddington College—where the older brothers and sisters of this lot congregate) and make our way out to the green. I let my dog off the lead again and he follows Georgie and Sparkie along the Randolph roadway. Soon it is evident that Georgie is on an errand to the shops and that I need to re-hook my dog once again or he will follow her out of the gate. We begin a circle around the green instead and by the time we have completed this the troops are beginning to foregather in the forecourt of the caff.

By the time we are all seated I can count ten of us, a traditional Saturday morning festivity, with Albert, Janet, Dan, Davide, Georgie, Ofra, Hanna, Kate, even Dorothy joining in. My wife sits down next to Saffy and Tinkerbelle and before long they are both in her lap, giving her an unending series of delighted kisses. Dan still hasn't discovered a food that doesn't hurt his throat, though he manages to struggle on with a toasted cheese and tomato sandwich. Kate admits she may be a bit overfaced by the arrival, at her new house on Friday, of three containers that have been in storage. She is a bit subdued this morning, having weathered her first bout of chemotherapy yesterday, but she joins us for a back passage walkround. It's still not easy running the gauntlet outside the five-a-side courts, where baleful glances are a most unpleasant addition, but we are soon on to the cedars. Skye has again appropriated a fallen limb, sweeping all before her. Perhaps we should have given it to her a hundred yards sooner.

Sunday, February 25:

It looks like we are certain to get rained on during our morning excursion in the park, but the usual pattern reasserts itself just as Fritz and I hit the street, and, again, we have dry weather—though very wet underfoot—as we enter the Rec. There is a mini-replay of yesterday's bottleneck outside the five-a-side courts: kids milling about, gates to the courts locked, a puzzled dog who pauses to stare up at all these strangers quizzically. I put him on lead in order to guide him through this chicane—just as well because a Westminster sports bus is disgorging yet more youngsters as we reach the Carlton roadway.

I can see Georgie and Dan having a walk round the green and I set out to catch up with them, but Fritz, with his sniffing, smelling and pooing, has other ideas. As I am backtracking to pick up his mess I give up all hope of drawing level with my friends and we continue a slow progress round the green on our own. There are lots of dogs around—it is as if the neighbourhood dog owners, having waited out the weather, are now arriving in large numbers with their pets. On the track yet more youngsters are being marshalled by adults wearing Westminster Mile regalia. For a moment I am afraid that Fritz will find the open track gate too inviting but we manage to get past this obstacle and make it to the café in one piece.

Weather has reduced our numbers and we have only Hanna, Georgie, Janet, Ofra and Dan today, though Kate appears several times with an increasingly mud-coloured Skye. Winnie, unable to share in the toast bounty because of her non-allergenic diet, is cross beyond all measure. She snatches at the pieces being offered to the other animals and even manages to sink her teeth into Janet's thumb. Dan, mortified, makes his pet sit all by herself in the empty forecourt. Then, when the Pug is restored to the company Dan stands up in order to toss pieces of her diet kibble to each of the dogs. Fritz is the only one to shine in this activity, the others having to retrieve their treats on the bounce, and the blind Spadge missing contact with his altogether. Just before we get up to begin a back passage walkround Ofra discovers that the cup indentation of her coffee saucer is not in the centre of the little plate, but off to one side. I tell her that she is entitled to a second cup of coffee. Still without a word from Ronnie in some time, Dan now says he is going round to see if Ronnie is okay—as soon as we leave the park.

Monday, February 26:

The sun has returned, though temperatures are chilly enough as Fritz and I make our way toward the cedars on a bright Monday morning. Soon enough we encounter Tim, walking with Yoyo—these two were also present during last night's late walk when Fritz, who often explodes with surprise when someone emerges suddenly from an apartment building as he is trotting down the pavement, let out a roar of disapproval when this happened with Tim and Yoyo last night. Tim reports that the park is almost empty but by the time we have made our way onto the green the action is picking up.

Suki, the half-grown Newfoundland puppy, is withstanding the playful assaults of Chica the Boxer and Flash the Border Terrier. Skye is chasing down her tennis ball and Winnie is bustling about at Dan's feet. The latter confirms one of our worst fears—Ronnie really has been ill. It seems that while taking a bath last Tuesday he was unable to get back to his feet and had to lie in the water for four hours—at last able to crawl to a spot where he could alert his neighbour, Tanis. She helped him to bed but when Susie got home she could see that he needed additional care and an ambulance was phoned. Since then he has been in hospital with pneumonia, though Dan reports that he has talked to Ronnie, who now seems chipper enough, and that he may be able to come home tomorrow. This sobering story is repeated a number of times as we join others at a table outside the café's front door.

There is only a small turnout this morning, just Peter and Ellen, Kate, Dan, Georgie and Albert. Neither Georgie nor Peter are feeling that well, Dan is still recovering from his sore throat and Kate, of course, has been poorly too. This places the persistent cough that *I* have had ever since a day at Abu Simbel in its proper context at last. The dogs eat toast and squabble whenever there is an intruder. Rex the Springer Spaniel gets into a scrap with Oscar the Schnauzer, much to the distress of Sabina, and, as we are concluding our walkround, old Poppy attacks Skye as well. There is something in the air today.

Tuesday, February 27:

A light rain is falling as Fritz and I, both in our rain jackets, make our way into the sodden park on a gloomy grey Tuesday. We fall in line behind Hanna and her two dogs and Tim with Yoyo—and head for the green in a counter-clockwise direction. Tim says that he plans to sharpen his culinary skills while Lizzie spends two weeks in China—and that last night he got the project off to a good start by ordering takeout from Deliverance. He has Yoyo's blue Frisbee with him and, opposite the Grantully gate, he sends a long low liner into the centre of the grass and, in spite of this difficult trajectory, the little black Schnauzer manages to snag it in her teeth by the time it has reached the cricket crease.

Tim and Hanna exit and Fritz and I continue around the green (three poos!). We are overtaken by Georgie with a muzzled Sparkie (this tactic reduces the mindless barking considerably) but I have to tell him that the part of the Hannibal Lecter of Paddington Rec has already been cast. Ofra, who is complaining on her mobile to her marble supplier about slow progress in her new kitchen, is waiting for us at the entrance to the café and so is Dan. To our chagrin our usual rainy day table outside the front doors is occupied by five puffing Polish ladies, each looking tougher than the next. We have to settle down at two small tables to the right of the door.

I tell Kate that in order to be especially conscientious I went home yesterday and put the card of the handyman service I recommend into my jacket pocket so that I would be all ready to give it to her today—and then I put on a different jacket this morning. Dan, who is collecting money for a card and a present for a convalescent Ronnie, tells us that yesterday he and a friend were followed by a young weirdo as they left the Prince Alfred pub and that when this chap threatened Winnie he ended up in the gutter for his pains. Little Jack rushes in to see if there is any food going (I give him two tiny pieces of kibble) and then, after being retrieved by his owner, he rushes back four more times. He is probably still doing it but we have left by now, Georgie offering one last complaint about the weather—"I'm fed up to the back teeth with it." Like a little kid in Wellington boots, Sparkie manages to wade into every available puddle as we exit.

Wednesday, February 28:

The weather is extremely volatile this morning, with sun alternating with lashings of a rain that has rattled against our windows all night long. Fortunately we are going through a calm period when it is time for us to enter the park. There is no one on the back passage at all (well, two joggers perhaps) and we make speedy progress toward the green. Here we meet a new Labrador puppy named Jess; she is an adorable little Andrex clone, very interested in all the other dogs, and already well-splattered with mud. For some reason Chica the juvenile boxer acts a bit too rambunctiously with the pup, who squeals in fear—but the crisis is over soon. Fritz is a model of decorum and manages to keep in touch with a very large turnout of dogs and their owners outside the café fences.

Jasper's owner David, down to his skimpy running shorts, is running around the green—looking more and more like the original 118 character than ever. Jasper has a go at keeping up with him every now and then and Winnie takes a turn trying to nip his heels. Out on the green Kate is trying to keep Skye occupied and I am trying to make sure she has as much assistance as possible for her forthcoming move—having now supplied her with the number of a handyman and of our cleaner. The woman from Queens Park is here with her amber-coloured Cocker Kiva (my version of a long Irish name that begins with a C) and, again to our surprise, Skye twice jumps on the visitor—who also squeals in terror. This seems like very uncharacteristic behaviour for Skye and then we realize that she has confused Kiva with two of her play pals, Hercules and the late Hector.

Joining us at breakfast this morning is the mom of Rya, the Westie. She says that she wants to breed the pretty white fluffball and I mention that we have heard this from many an owner—but that no one has actually done this yet. The others (Dan, Hanna, Georgie, Ofra) chime in with tales of just how much hard work breeding your female entails and this seems to drive Rya's mom from the table in defensive confusion. The dogs are feasting on sausage and toast—except for poor Winnie, who gets only her non-allergenic kibble. On our back passage walkround Dan urges us to back him up in his dietary quest—which has certainly helped produce a slim-line Winnie—because, so he tells us, Davide is already weakening and starting to add titbits to her dinner bowl.

March, 2007

Thursday, March 1:

It is a bright and chilly morning and Fritz and I have most of the back passage to ourselves today—if you don't count the veteran Tibetan Terrier, Cosmo, who gets only an obligatory growl of recognition from my dog. Out on the green I can see quite a few dogs at play and, at a spot along the Randolph walkway, Dan is having people sign a get-well card for Ronnie. Half of them haven't heard that Ronnie is ill and this requires Dan to start at the beginning more than once. Fritz runs to the top of Mt. Bannister while all these sedentary humans are shuffling about, but he does a good job of recall when the time comes and he gets a reward biscuit in the bargain. Peter comes up and asks me if I have taken any pictures of his Hector—since he has only puppy pics of the poor fellow.

There is a little warmth in the sun and I choose a table out in the forecourt, but every time a cloud comes over we can feel that there is also a chill breeze blowing from the north. Hanna blames Scotland; I blame Finland. Also present are Kate, Dan, Davide, Liz, Nicholas and Ofra—Georgie has another workman arriving at home. Nicholas begins a searching inquiry into the Italian restaurant business with Liz, Kate describes her recent experience in the suntan spray room, and Liz says she has to go to New York so that she can apply for a new British visa from abroad. Guy walks by with Finn in tow—at first it looks like his Hootch has shrunk, but Hootch is also present; Finn and Jody are now look-alikes.

The others are still chatting away so I accompany Kate on a back passage walkround—this will be her fastest way home when she completes her move next week. Skye wants to get every other dog to play with her, regardless of size, and she initiates the dialogue by mugging the next candidate. The tiny Jack Russell Tay, he with the half black, half white face, is so chosen—but there is a display of angry teeth in response. Next it is the turn of Rex the Springer Spaniel—he is more of a match but there is still quite a size disparity and so Skye can only grab a branch in her teeth and march off to inspect her new quarters.

Friday, March 2:

It is again a bright and sunny morning, even warmer than yesterday, and as we begin our walk toward the cypress trees we walk among daffodils and other wildflowers in bloom. Liz is heading our way with Roxy and I would have been willing to reverse directions to accompany them but Fritz is well ahead of me here and I can't get his attention redirected to this end. Also heading our way is a chap with young Ryah, a kind of diminutive Alsatian who manages to snag a forgotten cricket ball that Fritz has missed altogether. Nearer the café we meet Kate, on her way to deliver the keys to the painters at her new house.

Skye the Alsatian has thus been left in the care of David the dogsitter and we find the latter out on the green—where there is a rapturous reunion when Fritz at last detects the presence of his old pal. Ryah has by now completed a park circuit and she keeps dropping the cricket ball at my feet so that I can give it a good kick. I manage to do this without breaking my toes and then I follow a mob into the forecourt of the café, where we are soon eight seated at a table in the sun. Faz and Janet are sharing custody of Jo Lynn's Tilly today and after we are seated Michaela comes by with Skye the Cairn and Hanna takes up her own little table with Spadge and George. Fritz spends most of the session in Janet's lap. She offers him some cappuccino foam at the end of her finger and he likes it so much that soon he has his nose buried in my cup—but well before I was through drinking from it.

Teasingly, Faz says that he has recommended that Hanna publish her own book of opinions; I suggest *Home Truths from Finland* as a working title. Ironically, Dorothy has sent me into the park to sound out Hanna's thoughts on allergies as a possible source for her persistent coughing. Janet explains her plans for a forthcoming two-week holiday in Goa. Liz says that the Irish consulate has informed her that *something* is in the post. If it is her Irish passport she may not have to go to New York after all. A large party sets off on a back passage walkround with Albert, Georgie and Davide joining the procession.

Saturday, March 3:

A light rain has just lifted as Fritz and I head for the park. I am planning to avoid the back passage, fearing another crowd scene outside the five-a-side courts, but I can see that there isn't a soul in this narrow passage this morning, and so we begin our march toward the cypress trees. Heading toward us is Andrew the Akita. He is wearing a red coat and lumbering along on his tiptoes. Andy is nine now, a gentle giant who pauses for a pat on the head before we continue toward the café.

Outside its fences I discover Janet with Tilly and Georgie with Sparkie and Rosie. She has picked the latter up from Ronnie's house just a few minutes earlier and she reports that she found Ronnie, still convalescing, chopping carrots for the dogs. We follow Janet and Georgie as they circle around the café and head up the slopes of Mt. Bannister. The sun is making an appearance and all the little purple bulb plants are crowning the hilltop with glory. At the bottom we encounter Daisy, a Westie, and a woman with a black Lab. She says that her usually docile pet is bewitched by a female cousin—who seems to be coming into season out on the green. We pass the Saturday morning training class and take our positions at a table in the centre of the forecourt. Here we are joined by Dan, Ofra and Albert.

I am sitting with my feet in a puddle and this gives first Bailey and then Fritz a chance to dip their paws in water before jumping into my lap. Dan gets up to have a conversation with Tanya, who is outside the fence with baby Isabella and Pasha the Weimaraner. He reports, on his return, that Tanya is again expecting, and this is greeted as happy news by all. Then he tells Janet the tale of his Prince Alfred adventures last Monday night. This time he says that on the next day he passed by the site of the final scuffle and was alarmed to see a crew of men in shiny green coats—but they turned out to be water workers, not scene of crime officers. He volunteers to take Rosie home and this leaves the rest of us to complete a back passage walkround without him. I have seen cleaner bottoms than that sported by my pet.

Sunday, March 4:

Grey skies predominate as Fritz and I head for the park on a quiet Sunday morning. We pass Saffy and Tinkerbelle on our outlap, but we get no further than the grassy field at the corner beyond the cypress trees. Here Fritz feels he has to sample a number of grass shoots and there is no budging him for quite a while. I try Michael's old trick—announcing that I'm leaving, but it works as well for me as it did for Michael. Eventually Fritz does start moving forward again, indeed he outraces me to the green, where he discovers David the dogsitter with another of his canine charges, and there is a joyous reunion.

The others have all gone in for coffee and Fritz is still strolling about, managing to squat for the second time this morning on a poor innocent daffodil. Dan hangs on to him while I order my cappuccino; Dan has been to see Ronnie and to deliver the candy, flowers and card that we have all contributed to. He says that Ronnie appears to be in good spirits, though still quite weak. (Georgie has again brought Rosie, while Janet still has Tilly.) Winnie snaps at Janet's already sore thumb and she is made to sit on the naughty step for several minutes. Tanya comes into the forecourt for a chat and I am afraid that Fritz is about to pinch one of the felt toys belonging to baby Isabella. Pasha is still a lively presence (the baby calls her "Car," one of two words she knows so far). Tanya tells a long tale about her return to work this last summer, one month doing public relations for a restaurant—that she now has to sue because they haven't paid her. Ché rushes in and we fear the worst—but other than licking up some other dog's pee, nothing dire happens here.

I feel a few drops and this is a signal for us to get moving. Faz says he will take Rosie home today but he now joins us for our back passage walk with Jasmine. Sparkie begins to bark as soon as we start our walk and then he disappears altogether into Fritz's grassy field. I can hear Georgie calling for him, though I have now seen him dashing by the rest of us in an attempt to get to the front of the queue. Even after I have left the park I note that his naughtiness persists. A young black woman is stretching out with the assistance of some exercise bars and Sparkie begins to bark at her too. Fortunately she takes this assault in good humour and the parade moves on.

Monday, March 5:

The sun is shining brightly as Fritz and I make our entrance into the park on a chilly Monday morning. We are prevented by a "Footpath Closed" sign from making our usual left turn and, still on lead, I coax my dog toward our green—utilising the opposite direction. We soon encounter Jean-Baptiste and Suzanne but they know about the path closure—they are marching back and forth with Hercules and Sunny, prevented like the rest of us from the satisfaction of completing a grand circle. I walk with them around the green and over the top of Mt. Bannister.

There is a lot of activity on the green and the adjacent walkways and we can observe one dog fight, with the contestants quickly separated, in front of the loo. The focus of this discontent is a newcomer, a small dog named Tas, who is being walked by a chap for the real owner. Matters are not helped when a plush toy belonging to the newcomer falls from this chap's pocket—and Hercules claims it. Fritz is falling behind as we make our way over the hilltop, pausing repeatedly to have a sniff at every other dog. On the other side I head for the café just as Ofra steams through; she is not feeling well and is on her way home without a pit stop at the café at all today.

I take a table in the sun, sharing it initially with Hanna alone. She has Spadge only, George having already had his morning exercise. Soon, however, we are joined by Georgie, who has Rosie and Sparkie, and Janet who has Tilly and Winnie. Kate also arrives and so does Nicholas. Skye stations herself at Bekki's feet at a nearby table, hoping for a treat. This is curious only because Bekki's Chica is stationed at Kate's feet, hoping for a handout. Kate has brought some cheese in her purse and all the dogs seem to like this, though Winnie is frustrated in her hunger for the food because of her diet. Fritz jumps into Nicholas' lap for a cuddle. Someone spots a ten pound note on the pavement—the consensus is that it belongs to Kate and that it has fallen out of her pocket. Kate turns over to me a screenplay that she wants Dorothy to evaluate for her. Skye now begins an agitation on the subject of Mommy, Ball and Now and this leads to an end of the morning's session. Janet and Georgie head off to Ronnie's to return Rosie, Kate continues to fling the ball, no one can walk the back passage, and so Fritz and I head for the Morshead gate.

Tuesday, March 6:

A night of high winds and torrential rains has left us with mixed skies—and the prospect of still more volatile weather to come. The back passage is still fenced off, so we use the Essendine gate and then turn right, soon encountering Pasha out with her dad. (Dan reports that Pasha went missing the other day and was discovered with what appeared to be a ghastly head wound—she had been foraging in the café bins and was covered in tomato sauce.) Next we encounter Jean-Baptiste, Liz and Michaela and I attempt to follow them on a stroll around the muddy green. I don't do a very good job because Fritz is making progress at his dilatory best and I fall well behind my friends—until he overtakes me and heads into the café—following Liz.

Hanna, Georgie and Dan are already seated at a table in front of the doors, but the latter are still not open. Ofra is absent today but I have to tell the others, who expected her to head for her bed yesterday, that she was spotted by Dorothy and Linda three hours later on a street corner in Hampstead, talking on her mobile phone (London is such a small town). Liz is still planning her brief trip to New York (though she has now been *promised* her Irish passport) and she tells us that, in spite of her best efforts, Roxy doesn't seem to be losing any weight. She and Dan indulge in a fantasy in which he "turns" and they spend a wild weekend together (well, how wild could it be with breakfast at Simpson's in the Strand as part of the scenario?).

There are lots of dogs underfoot today, including a number not usually seen here, and our dogs take exception to this and there is a great deal of raucous barking. Then a brief shower begins just as we are heading for the exits and we have to take refuge from it (and a giant Aggregates lorry) in the vestibule of the pavilion. Here Hanna admits that she is actually wearing her pyjamas (the knees now bearing Winnie's pawprints) as she hasn't had time to have her morning shower yet. Exiting the park is a bit of a challenge. They have reopened the Morshead gate (closed because they have been trimming the trees on the street outside) but the woodworkers are still grinding away, the water people are putting up fencing on the opposite side of the street, tarmac is being rolled into position on some of the park's interior walkways and the street is covered in twig litter. We are home at last.

Wednesday, March 7:

We have a lovely sunny morning for our session in the park today. I guide Fritz away from the Essendine entrance, not just because the back passage has been closed of late, but also because the tree trimmers are grinding away down there as well. Instead we enter via the Morshead gate and soon enough we are on the green, where I return to Kate a script she had asked Dorothy to read. Then we continue on toward the Randolph Gate with Sabina and her Oscar and Scamp but when we meet Suzanne and Sunny we reverse directions and climb over Mt. Bannister. On the other side I discover that the back passage has reopened—but by now it is time to check out the café scene.

Today we have Dan, Hanna, Albert, Kate and Nicholas, whom I have to stake to a cup of coffee. Kate receives a number of calls on her mobile phone but the first few go unanswered since she can't find this object. Dan says that he has seen Georgie and Sparkie on the street but he doesn't know where they are now. The topic of anti-tail docking legislation comes up—but there is little sympathy for this latest intervention by the nanny state. The debate seems to deal only with alleged cruelty, without any consideration of aesthetics—I point out that the Old English Sheepdog is nicknamed "the Bobtail," but I suppose we won't be allowed to have any more of these at all. The conversation inspires Nicholas to propose that we have our own Paddington Rec version of Crufts. Dan wants a "most aggressive" category so that Winnie will have a chance of winning something. Most of those at the breakfast table shrink from the work that would be involved in organizing such an event (and the fee that Paddington Rec would want to collect) and quite a few of us think that the whole affair could easily turn nasty.

When we get up to leave we are able to use the back passage again and so we do. Hanna holds Fritz while I clean up his third poo—her own dogs have already been walked. As we near the Essendine exit we encounter Peter. His long blue coat streaked in mud, he not only has Jody in his charge but he has a second, Alsatianate dog on lead as well. This is "Steve," a rescue dog from the Mayhew Home, one whom Peter is thinking of adopting. Hanna says that Steve has a nice temperament but that he needs to be kept on lead for a while since he is, in origin, a Romanian street dog. I see that Britian, having opened its doors to migrants from all over the world, is now admitting the world's dogs as well.

Friday, March 9:

I have missed a day in the park, though I got plenty of exercise on the next-to-last section of the London Outer Orbital Path where, at the end of eleven miles of mud, I reached a true milestone, 4000 miles on

British footpaths. I don't know how much exercise Fritz got, though Dorothy reports that he resented my desertion mightily and misbehaved in consequence—running out of the Grantully gate for instance. On extremely stiff legs I am able to resume my duties on a bright and sunny Friday morning as we head for the park at our usual time.

We take the back passage and I note that the gardeners have been active in the patch that fills the corner between the original football pitch and the new children's playground. Hanna has been lecturing them on the unsuitability of the original planting in such poorly drained soil here, and they seem to have listened because there is a far greater variety of plants, including some bamboo now. Fritz is trotting along with Frank and Bianca as Franca quizzes me on the opening hours of the café (answer: not yet). In front of the loos I meet up with Georgie, Dan, and Liz and Dan wants a brisk walk around the green—since he has driven to the park today. This we set out to do, Fritz managing to keep up for once, though Dan himself falls into conversation with David the dogsitter at the little hill above the tennis courts and we lose track of him. There are a lot of dog owners congregated here—perhaps this slope is less muddy—and I can see Chica mixing it up with Humpty. The rumour is that this energetic Basset Hound is moving to Brighton.

When we have circled the green Georgie, Liz and I take our seats in the forecourt of the café and eventually Dan manages to join us as well. He has been suffering from a rash—which some associate with the sore throat that he experienced last week. At any rate he is off for four days in Cape Town tomorrow (nice to have a partner who is a member of the cabin crew) and Winnie will be in the care first of Janet, then Georgie. Winnie is in a pissy mood and attacks Sparkie for no discernable reason, whereupon Fritz, who is observing this scene from Dan's lap, jumps into the fray and the little Pug changes her mind quickly enough.

Liz commands our attention for much of the session, telling us the tale of her brief trip to New York, which ended in disaster. She had let her visa lapse because she expected an Irish passport, but when this failed to materialize she needed to return to a non-EEC country to get a new one. All went well at the British embassy in New York until they discovered that she had no more pages in her U.S. passport on which a visa could be attached. The U.S. passport people needed extra time to sort this out and she needed to return to the UK quickly because she had her husband's passport with her and he was due to travel soon. So she flew back to Heathrow, mission unaccomplished, but they didn't want to let her into the country and it took a tearful hour and a half before they reluctantly agreed to give her a six-month extension (on the back cover of her passport)—which, of course, had been her goal in all this travel in the first place. At least the trip to New York hadn't been a complete bust, for one piece of business had actually been completed—she *had* picked up my copy of the magazine previewing the 2007 baseball season!

Saturday, March 10:

As Fritz and I enter the park on a sunny Saturday morning I see something I have never seen before. A red Virgin rescue helicopter is slowly descending to a spot on the Grantully side of the village green of Paddington Recreation Ground! I get Fritz to move directly toward the green, instead of our usual back passage entry, and by the time I get there the helicopter has landed safely and crowds of the curious are gathering. Dan has preceded us with Winnie and Liz has arrived with Roxy and we agree to do a circuit of the green together but before long we reverse directions to accompany Georgie with Sparkie and Faz with Jasmine. Faz says that there has been a bad motorcycle accident on Elgin Avenue, with the unconscious rider ending up a long way from his bike—and this will explain the presence of an air ambulance.

We are the first customers at the café and Liz has brought a special treat for us, a box of Krispy Kreme doughnuts from Harrods. These are shared out and it is Dorothy's first taste of this confection—but it may be her last as well as the food police are gunning for trans-fats, with New York about to ban their use altogether. For that matter, so Janet tells us, this distrust of moderation in all things has had another local instance in the attempt, if the nannies who want to control every aspect of our private lives have their way—to require that all dogs to be kept on lead—at least in Camden. And this comes in a week when global warming enthusiasts want to introduce any number of measures to restrict the freedom of movement of their fellow citizens by air—while despoiling the countryside with unproductive wind farms at the same time. Global warming, I can see, comes as manna from heaven for the puritans of our society, the fundamentalists of energy conservation. There are already faculty at the American School, so I am told, who don't bathe every day in an attempt to conserve precious water resources. I say, give soap a chance.

Dan and Davide receive the best wishes of the rest of us as they get ready for their trip to Cape Town this afternoon. Georgie says that she has seen Ronnie and that he seems unsteady on his feet and still quite tired. Winnie, in Davide's lap, begins to snap at Sparkie again, then she rushes off to scold a barking Alsatian who is conveniently tied to a fence post. We use the back passage to make our return journey. Kids are having their Saturday morning football games on the central pitch, soccer moms and dads lining the sidelines to cheer their youngsters on or to deplore the sloppy tackles of the other side. The helicopter is taking to the skies again, but we cannot see if it has taken on any stricken cyclists.

Sunday, March 11:

Another beautiful early spring morning beckons us to the park today. Fritz makes slow progress along the back passage, sniffing and sampling the foliage, then he falls in line behind a chubby exerciser and trots purposefully forward toward the café. There is already an early turnout of patrons, but the café is yet to open its doors and so we continue forward—where a lively scene is taking place among larger dogs on the green. I am basking in the warm sunshine and I lose track of my dog for several minutes. I am looking for him next to the tennis courts when he has rushed back to the green. Next he seems to be headed for the café again so I follow, noticing that the new cricket nets are being utilized for the first time—by some American kids who are tossing a baseball around.

There are six of us at table in the bright sun as we join Hanna, her nose buried in *The News of The World*, Janet with Winnie, Georgie with Sparkie and Rosie, Faz with Jasmine, and Liz with Roxy. Near the end of our session Ofra arrives with Bailey as well. I tell Janet that the *Ham and High* reports a protest demo on behalf of dog owners threatened with the latest threat to doggy freedom in Camden. There is disapproving gossip after "News of the Screws" reports that Heather Mills McCartney is willing to give up custody of her daughter in return for a nice chunk of change. It is also reported that Winnie snores in her sleep and that her first act, upon being delivered to Janet's house yesterday, was to rush into the kitchen to see if there was any food in Koko's bowl. Today there is a constant struggle to keep forbidden treats out of her mouth—or Roxy's too for that matter.

The weather is so nice that I take off my wool cap. Faz says he would like to do the same but he is having a bad hair day. We get up at last to attempt a back passage walkround. I can see that Ofra is wearing her green sweatpants with the legend "Adored and Loved by Everyone" on the bum. The football players are even tinier today than yesterday; soon we will have infant soccer. Liz reports that the teenage chums of her sons, also into sports, stink up the house with their sweat—so perhaps this "no bath" thing is catching on. More candidates for Give Soap a Chance.

Monday, March 12:

If anything, it is even warmer today than yesterday and almost from the outset I am able to store my wool cap in the pocket of my leather jacket. Fritz continues to make slow progress along the back passage, having to break off at one point to see why it is that Peter has three dogs today, Jack and Sandy as well as his own Holly. There is a lively scene on the green, though among the contestants I note only one newcomer, a Chow named Pippin. Fritz wanders around checking out all of the other dogs but when I see him disappear into the café I realize it is time for me to join the others at breakfast.

Today we have Janet, still with Winnie, Georgie with Sparkie, Faz with Jasmine, Ofra with Bailey, Kate with Skye, Liz with Roxy and a dogless Hanna. Fritz seems genuinely jealous when Bailey climbs into Janet's lap and before long he is there himself—and enjoying the occasional finger dipped into cappuccino foam for his delectation. Faz is able to join me today in going capless and Kate is even wearing flip-flops. At one point she gets up to give Skye a vigorous grooming with a brush; Hanna advises her to leave the hair on the spot since it is a favourite nest building material for all the birds. Metty has a new waitress—who is *also* afraid of dogs.

It takes a long time for us to get moving this morning—since it is so pleasant in the sunlight. The kiddies playground is also crowded with moms and toddlers enjoying the spring-like weather. Sparkie is as hard to keep moving as Fritz and Charlie once were. Georgie is remembering his infancy—when she went into a shop on the Queensway to buy a basket in which she could sneak the infant into Whiteleys—only to be given not only a basket but a pashmina to line it with by a puppy-struck shop assistant. Skye and Farrah's Poppy have a barking match as we near the Essendine exit; somehow poor Corky, on his way into the park, gets rounded on as well.

I soon have positive proof that it is spring, however, for looking through the blossoming leaves of the tree that overhangs the pavement here (a spot currently favoured by a tribe of greenfinches) I can see Frank, the Chinese Crested Dog. For once he is wearing neither costume nor coat; he is absolutely naked.

Tuesday, March 13:

The sun is not quite as intense this morning, but high clouds mean that we again have a lovely day for a stroll in the park. A gaggle of American moms is just passing our gate as we enter this morning and, for a while, Fritz keeps pace with Flash the Border Terrier, Abby the Lab and a winded Kelly, the Wheaten Terrier. Out on the green there is also a very lively scene, with blonde dogs predominating—Sasha, Buddy, Rufus and Skye, the latter in the care of David the dogsitter. Another blonde bundle is a twelve week-old Golden Retriever pup named Sunny. He is in the temporary care of Peter, the Peter whom last we saw when he had Henry the Pug in his care. Sunny is a delightful and brave puppy with very sharp teeth. (Henry himself has moved to Greenwich—meaning that Winnie, who soon arrives with Georgie—really is the only Pug in this village.)

Also present is Fritz II, having a rare weekday outing with Christine, who is suffering from a bad head cold. She leaves the handsome beast in my care when she goes in for coffee—these days this can mean a fifteen-minute wait as the (understaffed) staff cope with the crowds. Fritz II is a bit nervous about this desertion and almost jerks my arm off at one point, so I attach him to my chair. His presence doesn't seem to bother our own Fritz—though the latter does come crashing down when he tries to jump into Liz's lap with too little slack in his lead.

The dogs share out lots of toast (not you, Winnie), though Georgie says that Sparkie will only take a piece of toast if it is not too large, has plenty of butter on it, and contains no crust. She has had three visits from an electrician recently; like the rest of us she can have all her power go off when just a single light bulb burns out—so delicate are our fuse boxes these days—another instance of something that seems like a step backward but which the nannies know is actually for our *own good*. Liz is about to make the rounds of the embassies again since the Irish have given her son the wrong birth date on *his* passport and the Americans have to add pages to *hers* so that she can get a visa to India. As we get up to begin our errands I note an unfamiliar face climbing out of the animal control van; this discourages me from getting in another queue—one for poo poo bags.

Wednesday, March 14:

The beautiful spring weather persists and I find myself removing my hat almost as soon as Fritz and I get underway. Nearing the café I miss my shot into a nearby trash can (the missile in this case consisting of a bag of poo) and, while I am going back for it, Fritz joins a caravan of dog owners as they stroll along the Carlton walkway and begin to climb Mt. Bannister. I soon catch up with this group, Ofra, Faz, Georgie, Liz, Janet and Dan—just as the latter, returned this morning from Cape Town, is enjoying his reunion with Winnie. The latter accepts this moment with great nonchalance and we are soon heading downhill. We can see, at a great distance, a lively scene on the green—here is Hootch pursuing his indestructible thunderball and Chica having her early morning wrestling match with her cousin, the Boxer Sid.

Just as we are entering the precincts of the café we see Tanya driving in. I tell her we haven't seen her in a long time and she reports that she has been ill and that, no, she is all out of poo poo bags. Our group finds a comfortable posture around an outdoor table and the dogs begin circling—expect for Bailey, who is into lap hopping in a big way. Dan tells us of his encounters with a tribe of baboons, Janet passes around a card for Kate with pictures of our dogs on it (Koko with wings), and Faz tells us that he is thinking of letting Jasmine's hair grow. Maggie comes by to say hello and tells us an interesting tale: just as she was leaving the house with Finn and her mother's Jack Russell, the latter charged out furiously and bit a man, standing next to a car, in the ankle. Maggie says she was mortified and full of apologies until the man ran off—leaving his crowbar behind!

As we are getting up to leave Peter is arriving with Jody and the former Steve, the rescue dog he has renamed Gypsy—after his Romanian origins. Christine is still bothered by her cold and Fritz II is having a barking anxiety attack while she is in the café. For some reason no one wants to use the back passage today and so we follow along in pursuit of those heading for the Morshead gate. A little toddler, seeing us coming, runs to his mother for comfort. She tries to interest him in the doggies: "Look, there's a little Pug dog and, and some others . . . ."

Thursday. March 15:

I have to take my hat off immediately—for warm sunshine presides over the park scene yet again. Fritz and I use the back passage to reach the café and then we join a lively collection on the green. David is slinging the ball to Skye but he has to stop in order to give Fritz the cuddle my dog demands as his due. For the second time in the last few minutes Fritz gets snarled at by a dog who is not happy with his olfactory intentions. First it is Poppy near the cypresses, now it is a little Westie (one of a pair) who resents the intrusion of my dog's nose.

Peter has Gypsy on a long, loose ribbon lead and once or twice other dog owners get tied up in this. Lancer, the low-slung chocolate Lab, is here today, and Chica and Rufus are gamboling about. Ofra is quite upset with the latter, however, because—like many a male dog—he is attracted to the odours wafting from her Bailey and more than once she has to use physical force to remove the larger dog's tongue from her fellow's willy. Today's contretemps is not witnessed by Oxana, fortunately, but in the past there have been words: Ofra furious over a line of spittle on her dog's stomach, Oxana perturbed by another owner's foot on her dog's head. Dan tries to calm Ofra down as we head in at last for coffee.

We crowd around a table in the sunny forecourt—though there is no agreement that our coffee specifications have been met correctly at delivery time. Hanna is worried that her mobile phone won't accept a battery charge anymore, though it *is* six years old. Liz has been to the Irish embassy where they have promised to update her son's birth date within a week (within two *days*, they said on the telephone). Suzanne is thinking of modernizing her kitchen and this leads to a long conversation with Nicholas, the kitchen maven. Sunny has joined the barking chorus, perturbed, evidently, by the presence of shadows—which spook her. Perhaps we can have a return to gloom tomorrow—then at least one of us will be happy.

Friday, March 16:

I have switched to a baseball cap for this morning's outing in the lovely springtime sunshine of Paddington Rec. Fritz and I make our way slowly along the back passage and I am struck by how blissfully quiet it is today. For once the saws of the woodchoppers on Grantully Road are silent and there is not a sound coming from the water workers on Morshead. Nor are we assailed by the sounds of any sportsmen—the closest we have to any of these are a contingent of the burkha squad, sedately strolling around the running track, as they do most mornings these days. The peace is shattered only when we see David the dogsitter heading toward us near the children's playground with Skye. Fritz expects immediate attention, climbing one of his pal's tall legs, and soon he is chortling in delight over the attention he receives; to others it must sound like torture.

We continue forward along our narrow paved walkway and here, just on the opposite side of the playground fence, a French mom is pointing out the strolling doggies to an infant who grasps the bars as though he were in the zoo, an ecstatic grin of delight on his face. Fritz sidles through the café's precincts and out onto the green—where there is surprisingly little activity. I follow him on a start-and-stop perambulation of this surface, presided over by the distant calls of "Os-cah!" As we near the doggy area on Grantully I hear *my* name from within—Hanna is sitting on a bench here with George and Spadge. I cross the green to a spot outside the café entrance, where Davide and Liz are in earnest conversation and then I select a table in the sunshine for this morning's session.

We have only a small turnout—as no one has seen Georgie—and Hanna, Faz and Nicholas are late to arrive. Davide is complaining that he is on a very strict stand-by regime, one that requires him to spend eight hours at a time in a Heathrow hotel. Dan calls him from work to report that his rash is back and that he is not feeling at all well. Liz is bombarded with advice when she asks whom to see about having some curtains made, a task made all the more urgent since her new home in St. John's Wood comes equipped with a neighbourhood flasher. Hanna, who has only returned to her bedroom for the first time in almost two years, complains that her new mattress is making her black and blue and that the cat wants the bed all to herself. Hanna has let Spadge wander in the forecourt but, to everyone's amusement, he does much of this on his bum, backwards. I have to undertake an expedition to Sainsbury's soon so I am on my own in making an early exit today. Fritz and I use the Morshead gate—where the noise has returned in force.

Saturday, March 17:

Temperatures have begun to dip and skies are predominantly grey as Fritz and I make our way into the park this morning. Two elderly Bulldogs are pulled over to the side by an owner who is not certain what kind of interaction might result in nose-to-nose contact—but Fritz marches past as though such a confrontation would be beneath him. As usual he takes a long time to complete his progress along the walkways, past the cypresses (where he disappears on some interior mission), past the hectoring soccer dads and out to the precincts of the café.

For a weekend there is a surprisingly small turnout on the green, though the obedience class is forming ranks and David the dogsitter has just arrived with Skye. Also present is Georgie with Rosie and Sparkie. It soon becomes obvious why we did not see her yesterday—as she appears with a new, much shorter and quite handsome haircut. We meet for the first time a magnificent specimen named Digby. He looks like a water spaniel on steroids but is, in fact, an Italian Spinone—though surely that's a dessert. Dan now arrives with Winnie and we head for the café ourselves, but not before I have to return to the centre of the green in order to put my dog on lead. This is because Peter is using a squeaky toy to summon Gypsy and Fritz is immediately entranced by this sound.

There is already a very long queue at the counter of the café and Dan waits a while before joining it, long enough for him to share with us his continuing adventures. It seems that yesterday he was nearing his West End offices aboard his bicycle, a common means of transportation for him. A black Range Rover was causing him a lot of problems, its driver stopping suddenly, cutting him off and, finally, opening a door in his pathway. Screeching on his brakes Dan now decided to address the driver—in order to express his outrage over this treatment. The driver had quickly shut the door and was making fulsome signs of apology as Dan wound up his diatribe: "This is no way for anyone to behave, especially *you*." This unexpected end to the conversation had resulted from the fact that, while he was reaching the peak of his outrage, he had actually recognized the driver: Sir Paul McCartney.

Dan tells us that he once gave a similar dressing down to Denis Waterman, years ago, and then he continues with the saga of his recurrent rash, one that has caused him to see his GP twice, though neither visit has resulted in either pill, unguent or even diagnosis. In this he shares a fate with Dorothy, who now joins us for coffee, coughing away as she has done for almost four months—during which time the medical profession continues to insist that she is not ill.

There is a lively doggy scene taking place at the café this morning, with several new puppies off in the distance, Frank (back in sweatshirt) cadging for biscuits at our table, and Blake fishing food wrappers out of the bin. There isn't the same impulse to linger over our coffee on this cool morning and we soon head off in opposite directions, Dorothy heading for the halal butcher at Solomans in Maida Vale Parade for some chicken—and the rest of us making our way toward the Morshead gate.

Sunday, March 18:

After a stormy night we have brightness, sun presiding over the scouring winds that rake the park. Fritz begins his day by growling at a young black and white dog named Mungo. Then we continue along the back passage until we encounter Sunny with Suzanne. The latter asks me if I got my copy of the *Standard*. She is referring not to the *Evening Standard* but the *ASL Standard*. I have to admit that I have not seen this school publication (once so central to my teaching duties) in years—but she insists she left me a copy yesterday on the planter just inside our entrance gate. I wonder why I missed it.

I discover our gang sheltering from the winds in the alcove of the pavilion. They are about ready to head for the café, so we join them: Georgie and her daughter Lynn, Janet, Ofra (again wearing her "Adored and Loved by Everyone" track bottoms) and Dan. There seems to be no shelter from the chilling breezes so we select a table in the sun and wait for our coffee to arrive. Winnie is waiting outside the café doors for Dan but she can hear Janet unwrap some dog treats and returns like a shot. Later she snaps at Dan himself in a vain attempt at securing a piece of toast—and she is made to sit in the naughty corner for some time. Hanna, at a nearby table, insists that Spadge has always skated backwards whenever he is upset by the presence of other dogs, but others feel he is just losing control over his back legs. Fritz sets up a howl of protest when Ché arrives but he is okay with the arrival at our table of Gypsy—though the later does growl at the restored Winnie.

Most of the dog people pride themselves on their willingness to walk to and from the park with their charges but Dan now asks if Janet has room for him in her car—since he is chilled to the bone. Pretty soon Georgie and Lynn, who has Rosie in tow, want a ride also. I suggest that we are about to find out just how many people (and dogs) you can squeeze into a Fiat Panda. At any rate, and far earlier than usual, we head for the Morshead gate. Fritz just has time to end where he began, that is by growling at another dog—in this case his own cousin Gus.

Monday, March 19:

As Fritz and I enter the park on a frigid Monday morning we seem to be swimming upstream against a great canine current heading in our direction. First we encounter Rizzo, Scamp and Oscar, who have foregathered at the feet of Albert. The latter, another drop of snot hanging from his nose, is tethered to the busy Yorkies, Tinkerbelle and Saffy. Then we meet Holly, Sandy and Jack, a famous threesome, with Holly always off lead, Sandy always on, and Jack somewhere between these extremes—he is attached to a lead but drags it along the ground himself. Then, as we near the right hand turn we meet up with Denim and Suede, the Whippets in coats, and, finally, with Andrew the Akita—eleven dogs before we have even reached the green.

Shivering near the cricket crease are David the dogsitter, Davide, and Liz—who has just lost a filling (things happen to Liz) and is on her way to a dentist on Wigmore Street. Fritz doesn't linger for long out here and soon I can see him checking out some of the aforementioned dogs near the Grantully entrance. Next he attaches himself to Peter and Holly, a kind of outrider, and I lose track of him until he emerges from the bushes in time to chase Gus out of the way. Standing in front of his van is our old friend, Lee, the animal warden. He is substituting for Tanya as he is on "light duties" after falling through an attic floor while on a pest control assignment and injuring his leg.

Liz holds on to Fritz while I order my coffee from Metty, then I take a seat at a small table where only Georgie, Davide and Nicholas are also present. Davide, as always, has the latest in airline gossip for us—including the story of the first class passenger on a flight from

Delhi who wants compensation after discovering that the cabin crew has propped up a recently expired economy passenger in a seat near his own. Faz arrives with Jasmine and the latter is turned over to Georgie who will look after the Shih-Tzu while Faz and Di are in Manchester for her dad's back operation. Faz has only finished work at 7:00—after a night devoted to investigating the shooting of a drug dealer. Chilled by this tale and the weather itself we make an early departure.

Wednesday, March 21:

Although I was briefly in the park yesterday, our visit was short (no café time) because I wanted to accompany Dorothy on a visit to her GP at 9:40. It was interesting to note that just a small adjustment in our arrival time, say half an hour earlier than usual, presented an entirely new line-up of canine personnel in the park; the only dogs I recognized were Suzanne's Sunny and the little "Korean" Gumchee, whom Fritz and I often encounter on our nightly walkies.

By the end of the afternoon it was Fritz himself who needed medical intervention as we had, first, a yellowish throw-up (neatly captured on next week's *Radio Times*) and, next, a less neat house poo poo—fortunately deposited on the kitchen floor rather than the carpets. I had to take the poor fellow out immediately but he hadn't had his dinner yet—and we could therefore begin a day's starvation immediately. If I had to find the origins of this tummy trouble I would trace it back to all those chicken bones that our dog has been gobbling down as he follows in the footsteps of our local youth—down Essendine and in front of the college on Elgin Avenue.

This morning he seems to be in a happier frame of mind and we follow Jasmine and Sparkie (barking through his muzzle) out to the green. It is sunny on this first day of spring but not in any sense warm; indeed, a freezing wind is whistling across the grass and there is an early exodus for the café. Here one of the park workmen is hammering pickets into the empty spaces in the café's low fence—an activity which the baying Roxy clearly disapproves of. Liz, who is on her way to get her shots for her forthcoming trip to India, says that her attempts to curb the Beagle's food intake are leading to an obsessive quest for purloined comestibles, one that lead yesterday to an attack on the garbage that also resulted in considerable damage to Liz's new carpets. We get up to begin a back passage walkround, again driven forward by the chill winds. While we have been sipping our coffee the hammering workman has also fixed the latches on the fence doors. Hanna says that there were a lot of important looking chaps in suits here yesterday—so perhaps this belated round of fix-up is an outcome.

Thursday, March 22:

Snow flurries are just ending but I'm glad I am wearing my long underwear as Fritz and I enter a park under low grey skies. We make our usual slow progress toward the café, where we find Metty and Vicky rushing to get the café opened before there are too many cold noses pressed up against the door glass. Our lot are stamping their feet on the walkway outside the loos and I stroll along a bit with Hanna and Spadge, waiting for Fritz to deposit his first recuperation poo—not bad, but needs improvement. Fritz then insists on a cuddle from David the dogsitter and then rushes to the top of Mt. Bannister—from which I coax him to head in for coffee only with the brandishing of my biscuit sack.

At about this time Wendy, under an umbrella, comes strolling through looking for her missing Corky. The small, grizzled black dog is hard to spot at the best of times since he prefers the cover of bushes but today he has gone missing altogether. We see Wendy marching back and forth while we are at coffee but after twenty minutes or so we can see that she has collared the rascal at last. She says that Corky was discovered in the old and abandoned children's playground and, as if we needed any evidence of his progress, there is a long twig sticking to his backside.

There is only a small turnout at coffee: Hanna, Nicholas, Dan, Liz, and Georgie—with Albert as outrider. Georgie is already fretting over losing an hour's sleep when we go on to summer time this weekend while Dan announces that he has been ordered into a medicinal sunbed at St. Mary's for his rash. Liz is facing a day of parent-teacher conferences at ASL while getting one son ready for an international orchestra conclave on Malta. Nicholas sulks when his sausage arrives with untoasted bread and his explanation—"I thought all bread was toasted"—is not accepted by the others. Hanna is now complaining about Spadge's barking *and* the cold weather—and so we make an early exit for the gates.

Friday, March 23:

As usual, as Fritz and I head for the park this morning, we have to weave our way through the fences and potholes associated with Morshead Road waterworks. (Signs constantly refer to the need to replace Victorian water pipes; if we had the Victorian work ethic this job would have been wound up weeks ago). It's a grey, damp day though there is no actual moisture falling, and Fritz and I make our way along the chilly walkways between the oldest of the playing fields and the line of cypress trees. Here I find a beautiful new blue and white football, a round object that must have cleared the fence after a really disastrous miss-kick—and I throw it back into the field before some large dog gets his teeth into it.

Out on the green David the dogsitter presides over a small group of exercising dogs. These days he is usually with Skye the Alsatian but he always has to stop his ball slinging when he finds an insistent Fritz climbing his leg in pursuit of a cuddle. Meanwhile a mobile-phone mom is pushing a pram through a knot of dogs and I can hear her chatting a bit about the behaviour of her loose Staffie, Lola—without actually doing anything about it.

We continue our walk around the green and Hanna introduces me to an ASL mom who owns the giant Poodle, Charlie. Hanna explains that Susan's flat is next door to that of the late Sue Wilkinson and that, though she has heard a lot about George, this is the first time that she has met the Hannibal Lecter of Paddington Rec. Charlie tries to get Fritz into a chase but my dog is more interested in seeing what Peter and Holly are up to near the Grantully gate. Rizzo, Scamp and Oscar approach this spot as well and for a while I think I am watching Fritz when it is Oscar I am in visual contact with. I decide to collar my dog, and it is on lead that we complete our circle and head in for coffee.

Again there is only a small turnout—just me, Liz, Georgie, Hanna and Nicholas. Today we discuss property prices in Maida Vale, a topic only marginally more interesting that Liz's curtains. Spadge is having one of his manic barking days and even after Hanna and I begin a back passage walkround he persists. At one point George actually turns around and lashes out at the ancient Schnauzer in protest. Again I recommend the removal of Spadgie's vocal cords—and I am only half kidding.

Saturday, March 24:

They have been promising warmer weather for the better part of a week but the temperatures under which Fritz and I make our way into the park demonstrate, once again, that someone is a lying bastard. I would be in better shape if Fritz were actually on the move but these days he seems to make progress only inch by inch. Still it is pretty quiet back here; we meet no other dogs, only the occasional jogger plods by, and the only noise is raised by the Saturday morning football kids. Fritz manages to make it as far as the old red poo poo bin, suddenly accessible again (though jam packed), before parting with his own gift.

Out on the green I see members of the obedience class getting ready for their paces and a small group of dog people on the cricket crease. One of these is Kate, who had a last dose of chemotherapy only yesterday. Another is Rowena, who has not only Toby with her, in his tight purple sweater, but a new dog as well, a rescue dog she has adopted from the Mayhew Home. This is Timmy, a lively low slung little dog with a silky black back, who seems to be a mixture of Norfolk Terrier and Dachshund. Soon appearing is Fritz II, gambolling across the green and helping to test the obedience of the pupils in Roland's class. My Fritz insists on a cuddle from Richard and then warns his big cousin to stay away from his own master while he is enjoying this experience. On the walkway near the Grantully exit I see David the dogsitter with Billy the Bearded Collie, so we have to head over here for a second cuddle. Here also we encounter the Whippet pair of Denim and Suede. The latter is on lead because, released in Hyde Park recently, she ran and ran with such urgency that she did herself an injury. (And many people think all dogs need to be on lead at all times.)

We are a bit late getting into coffee and here we discover only a small group made up of Georgie, Hanna, Faz and Kate. The latter is feeling a bit unwell and leaves before she can get down any of her tea. Dorothy arrives and she too has to endure an inquisition as she tries to explain why the London medical profession, after four months of coughing and choking, still can't tell her what her problem is. The dogs eat some toast and rush up to the fences to protest the presence of any other animals and even of some people. I can see that Barbara, who lost her Hendrix recently, has returned to the park as a member of the Saturday morning exercise club. Faz says he had such a great sleep and feels so relaxed—that he drove to the park today. He tells us that yesterday he put two thirteen year-old boys—who had held up a pregnant woman at knife point—into cells for six hours. They cried.

Sunday, March 25:

On a static Sunday morning in the park I have plenty of time to complete my minute observations of nature while waiting for my dog to show any signs of interest in completing an orderly progress toward the green. Fritz sniffs and grazes with great intensity while I see that the sun is at last trying to penetrate the clouds and that a fat magpie, weighted down by a huge nest-building twig, rests on top of a flagpole before floating into the cypress trees. Above all, it is very quiet—it is almost as if half the world has forgotten that the clocks went forward last night and that we are now on summer time. They will not get any help in this matter from the clubhouse clock—which is stalled at 2:00 again.

When we at last reach the café Hanna is already assuming her role as first customer and she takes my cappuccino money in with her. We sit down almost immediately, therefore, with Georgie, Ofra, Hanna and Dan. Dan has had the early shift this week and we haven't seen him for a while. He is still trying to persevere in feeding Winnie only non-allergenic pellets, a strategy that often fails here at breakfast—when the dog owners forget and slip her some toast or a bit of croissant, on the one hand, or Winnie, on the other, darts at the last minute into the path of some titbit aimed at another dog's mouth, and scarfs the lot.

Ofra is beside herself because Israel has held a hapless English footie squad to a no-score draw in Tel Aviv. Georgie says that she has gotten a text from Janet, who loves her hotel in Goa and has even made friends with some of the local dogs. Rowena comes by, manic with pleasure over the arrival, two and a half days ago, of the lively Timmy. She tries to get Ofra interested in fostering a dog and recommends use of Mayhew's web site. (Earlier Rowena had served as a volunteer at this splendid institution.) We get up to begin a back passage walkround: the door latch, mended with such care only a few days ago, is again hanging by a thread.

Monday, March 26:

The beautiful spring weather, which we all remember with affection from two weeks or so ago, suddenly makes a return visit this morning. It is in radiant sunshine that Fritz and I make our way past the pink armchair that guards the Essendine entrance to our park and thus begin another slow progress toward the green. Nearing us are Sabina and Denise and Fritz utters a fearsome growl as Oscar approaches. "Fritz, you're a grumpy old man," one of these ladies says. I reply that this is true—even though my dog won't be four for another two weeks or so.

Dogs can be seen jumping about in the centre of the green and there is also a formidable collection of dog owners who are marshalling outside the café entrance. Here I find Suzanne with Sunny and we accompany them over the summit of Mt. Bannister, where Peter's Holly, remembering that Suzanne keeps treats in her pocket, sits down in her path, awaiting a reward. We pause to let a troupe of yellow-clad youngsters enter via the Carlton roadway and then we report to the café, where the early comers have already staked out a place in the sun. Here also a little girl in school uniform is eating an ice cream bar.

Workmen are just in the process of making repairs to the coffee machine so there is about a ten minute wait for our drinks to arrive—the dogs get their toast far more speedily. Today we have Dan and his mother, Christine, Nicholas, Liz, Hanna and Georgie. Georgie is contemplating a trip to Glasgow over Easter, even though she would have to take both Sparkie and Bailey with her—the latter will soon be in her charge while Ofra makes a two-week trip to Israel. Nicholas is keen to display Monty's new red velvet collar—though Liz says this is a girl's collar and that it would look much better on Roxy. She says she has to make some changes at her Italian restaurant today—and that she is putting off the awful moment as long as possible. Suzanne and I discuss the Thames Path and I promise to turn my notes over to her. She accompanies us part of the way toward the Randolph surgery, where Fritz and I have to drop off a prescription renewal request.

Tuesday, March 27:

It's a beautiful, even warm spring morning and I am only hoping that no dog places a wet paw on my tan cord trousers, a substitution for my usual dark brown anti-mud cords—since I have errands to run after morning coffee. Behind us I can hear Tim on the mobile phone and by the time we are nearing the café Yoyo has overtaken us and she and Fritz are dancing about in the bushes happily. It all turns to tears a moment later when Tim kneels to give Fritz a cuddle and the little madam is so mad with jealousy that she twice attacks my lad; then, when Oscar rounds the corner to see what all the fuss is about, she attacks him for good measure.

There must be something about this junction because I can hear two of the park keepers getting ready to plant some young trees in some freshly prepared earth next to the narrow walkway outside the children's play area—and one of them is complaining that yesterday a dog and some kids got into mischief somewhere near here. Just as we sit down for coffee, however, there is a noisy fight here between Tay (here with the Lab Monty) and Chelsea, terriers who share the same street and a deep antipathy for one another. Owners have to intervene in this scrap, which succeeds in scattering fresh earth all over the walkway.

At our table we have Liz, Georgie, Suzanne, Ofra, Hanna and Davide. Ofra is here to turn Bailey over to his Auntie Georgie. Liz explains that Nicholas is coming by to measure her curtains this morning. Davide says that he has to fly to Zimbabwe, of all places. I turn Fritz over to Suzanne so that I can use the loos (canine cries of distress), part of my preparations for the first errand of the day, a walk with my dog to St. John's Wood and his appointment at the beauty parlour. We depart at 10:00 and make good progress through the streets, arriving at the appointed spot just as Fritz, remembering where he is, loses all the life in his four feet.

Wednesday, March 28:

It's another lovely morning as Fritz and I penetrate the park on a quiet Thursday morning. Two park keepers are encountered as they stare up at the overhanging leylandia behind the oldest of the artificial pitches. One of them is complaining about this canopy, which is even stretching over the perimeter fence now—"I don't know why they let this grow so long without trimming it." Dog owners would have quite a different view—as this sheltered spot is a haven on rainy days.

There is lively scene on the walkways outside the café, where I find half a dozen dog owners—including Georgie, Liz, Dan and Franca advising the Italian chap who owns the lively young Boxer, Sid. He wants to know if he should have his dog castrated. The unanimous decision: yes. Sid is soon hectoring little George and Hanna is protesting. This scene takes place out on the green where Fritz has spotted David the dogsitter. I too venture this far because I have spotted Suzanne and I want to turn over to her my printed account of walking the Thames Path. Then it is time to head in for coffee, but in my case I just sit for ten minutes or so, since I have an appointment at the barbers at 10:00.

Fritz receives a number of compliments on his haircut—but this process started only two minutes after our leaving St. John's Pets yesterday when we ran into Liz outside the St. John's Wood Starbucks (where last week she met Ozzy Osbourne). Inspired by Fritz's spiffy appearance, she immediately called to ask if they could give Roxy a bath and five minutes later the Beagle was also a customer—and Liz had bought a new diet food for her chunky pet. Dan says that he is taking Winnie off her dietary regime today; she has lost a lot or weight but her pooing regime is way off. Oscar penetrates our sanctum and Fritz and the others chase him off—he takes this in good stride and even leaps atop a brick wall as he makes his escape.

Dorothy comes in to relieve me and I head off for Boundary Road. But half an hour later the group is just finishing their coffee and I am able to accompany the gang on a back passage walkround. The bushes have been planted outside the picnic area now and all of the dirt is still in place. We meet Albert sitting on a bench; he has just had a cataract removed from one eye and the second will have surgery as well. We also pass Natasha with Leila and I have to tell her that they were spotted by me in Regents Park yesterday, as I was walking back to pick up Fritz, and that this constitutes the doggy equivalent of whoring after strange gods—since they belong in Paddington Rec. Fritz does a final poo just as we are about to leave the park and this is when I learn that the trash barrel that always used to be at this spot is now missing and I have to backtrack some distance to find a place to dispose of this gift.

Thursday, March 29:

A run of sunny days comes to an end, and this morning we have a slight mist, grey skies and cooler temperatures. I pass Denise with Rizzo just as we enter the park and just as she is being shouldered aside in a narrow corner by an impatient jogger. We make our way out to the green where there are a number of dogs at play in the centre: Rufus and Chica are gnawing at one another while Jess, the Labrador puppy, is content to gnaw on a stone. Also present is a chocolate Lab named Maya (that means we have a Rya, a Maya and a Baija among the dogs these days) though only the first two are present today. Maya's owner says that her pet likes to sit on her little girl's head. You can tell that this worries mom just a bit but the little girl thinks it's fun.

Fritz is soon off by himself near the Grantully exit and so I make a beeline for the spot, not trusting my lad with such an open opportunity. He is soon content to follow Hanna and her dogs, but when we reach the Randolph roadway he begins to disappear into the bushes, acting on some independence imperative that has lead to a wild period of puppy naughtiness already. (As Dorothy tried to make one side of the bed this morning he would undo the other side—or snatch a pillow and give it a good beating.) Now I try to bribe him by producing my goody bag but he merely stares at me knowingly. What I have done is attract the attention of the giant Poodle, Charlie, and he now wants a biscuit, indeed he wants to be my friend forever. We follow him, his mistress and Hanna over the top of Mt. Bannister. Fritz agrees to come along but on the other side he wants to explore the junction of the parking lot and the Carlton roadway and I have to put him on lead.

We have only a small turnout at coffee this morning, just Dan and Liz, with Albert riding shotgun. Dan reports that his bird feeder has attracted a tribe of sparrows—very good news since this species has almost disappeared from these parts. Toast is offered to Albert for Saffy and Tinkerbelle—and as they scarf it down he says, "They act as if they hadn't eaten in a fortnight." Roxy the Beagle begins to bay hysterically at one of the baristas, who is standing inside the café door, and Liz explains that her dog has no tolerance for idle men. I can see that Fritz is shivering without the coverage provided by all that recently clipped fur and so I join the others in a retreat to the Morshead gate.

Friday, March 30:

The rain has lifted, temporarily it turns out, as Fritz and I make our visit to the park on a cold and damp Friday morning. Overhead a Canada goose is honking to itself as it flies north. Fritz pays no attention, even though he has a stuffed plush replica of this animal in his toy basket—it honks too. Near the playground we can see that a second line of bushes is being planted up against the picnic ground fence—soon there won't be any dirt for the odd dog to kick around on his way to the green.

I venture to the centre of this gloomy space today, mostly so Fritz can say hello to David the dogsitter. The latter is a true Skye pilot this morning, having both the Alsatian and the Cairn in his charge. We are kept busy trying to kick the tennis ball to Michaela's dog, who, disappointed in the efforts of one designated kicker, brings the ball to another foot, hoping for an improved effort. Fritz is chortling in delight as David lofts him for a cuddle, but down on the ground things are taking a more violent turn. Kate's Skye is wrestling with Buddy the Golden Retriever and it doesn't seem as innocent as such scrambles usually are. Saskia says that today they are behaving like brother and sister, only one of them has borrowed the other's CDs without permission and must now pay the consequences. Not only are these big dogs gnawing at one another's fur but they are uttering fearsome growls and there is a park policeman who feels that things have gone far enough. I refer to my own dog, who now charges forward with a growl of his own, chasing Skye away from her buddy. (That's all right—Fritz soon has to chase both Cosmo and Oscar after each has committed the serious crime of existing.) I take the thug with me as we head in for coffee, a process that allows us to catch the first glimpse of a returned Ziggy, back in the park after almost two months on the Continent.

Again we have a small turnout at coffee, just Hanna with a new hair colour, Liz, Georgie, and Albert. The latter receives a call on his mobile phone and it's nice to see that a guy in his mid-eighties knows how to answer this contraption. Georgie says she can't make up her mind whether to go to Glasgow or not. Liz says that her India visas have arrived. I announce that I will be travelling to Paris on Monday. We get up to begin a back passage walkround. Hanna believes that the park keepers are planting the bushes too close to one another. Albert, overfaced by the oppressive fencing that surrounds us now, says, "A tank couldn't get through that."

Saturday, March 31:

We enter the park under cool, grey skies and almost immediately we encounter Jean-Baptiste and Suzanne. They see at once that I am wearing a new pair of hiking boots, recently arrived from Hawkshead and getting their initial outing. Fritz is far less dilatory than usual and we make rapid progress toward the green, where the barking pupils in the Saturday morning obedience class are being infiltrated by our ill-disciplined lot. Fritz soon turns his back on all this and I have to follow him out the Randolph walkway, along the back of the tennis courts, up to the top of Mt. Bannister and back to the café—where the breakfast club is just foregathering.

I can see Bailey and Sparkie tied to one chair and Winnie and Roxy with their noses pressed up against the glass of the café door so I know that Dan, Georgie and Liz are already at the counter. While I am waiting for them to return I am surprised by the sudden reappearance of Ronnie! It has been over six weeks since our friend went down with pneumonia and though we have often seen Rosie here in the care of Georgie, it is really good to have owner and dog reunited in their old kinship. I am able to hand Fritz off to Ronnie but by the time I get inside Dan has already bought him his usual espresso. One by one the other park regulars come in to greet our long-missing member. Ronnie looks tired but he seems in good enough spirits.

We have a very pleasant session over our coffees and for some reason there is much conversation about birds today. Liz says that when her pet bird escaped from the house in Bermuda her kids cried and she reassured them that the bird would be just fine—the next day, however, there was a hurricane. "You *should* have told them the bird is just fine," I said, "it's just that he lives in New Jersey now." Hanna tells the tale, again, of the time her cockatiel, Num-num, escaped—and the entire neighbourhood was mobilized in his recapture. There were frequent sightings; she tried to pluck him off window ledges of the flats of strangers; when he at last came down near the BBC studios there was a round of applause. Dan says that his first pet was a budgie but that he came home from school one day to be informed that the cat had captured the loose bird and eaten its tail feathers off. Dan says he tried to comfort the poor thing but it suddenly took fright, flew directly into a wall, and broke its neck. I tell the others about the time we had a bat take up residence on the wall of our kitchen in Michigan. We didn't know what to do—so someone succeeded in placing a cardboard box over the animal. This still left us in a what-to-do-next position, and the solution was to tape the box to the wall!

These tales have taken a long time to tell but at last we are ready for a back passage walkround. The playing fields are surprisingly empty for a Saturday morning, but perhaps this is to be explained by the beginning of a half-term holiday. Hockeyettes are active on one of the fields and the Saturday morning exercise class is getting instruction in a corner of the running track. Observing a few of these pupils on their knees, literally, when they are supposed to be doing push-ups, Albert says, "Some of them are cheating, you know."

April, 2007

Sunday, April 1:

Fritz begins his day in the park with an obligatory growl in the direction of Buddy, who is walking along the back passage with Paddy, the interior decorator's dog. Indeed we seem to be following Saskia and Kathy, but by the time we have reached the five-a-side courts we are once again alone. The courts, rarely used these days in spite of their novelty, are littered with juice cartons and drinks bottles. This will certainly continue to happen until someone remembers to put a trash bin out here—and it may continue even after that.

Fritz briefly joins a pack that includes Bailey, Sparkie, Winnie, Ziggy, Roxy, Spadge and George. Then I see him taking off for the Randolph roadway and I have to follow him as well, coaxing him at last to accompany me to the forecourt of the café—when it is coffee time. As yesterday the topic was birds, so today the topic is discipline. Conversation moves in this direction because Dan is just placing Winnie into the naughty corner after another unprovoked attack on his own hand. She wanders off almost immediately and he makes her sit behind a bush, but she manages to extract herself from this open prison before long. Perhaps she has grown jealous of Fritz, who is sitting in Dan's lap, getting a big cuddle (I notice that since his haircut everyone wants a piece of Fritz). In Winnie's case her retaliation is to jump into *my* lap, sitting there contentedly until she spots someone who needs chasing on the other side of the fence, a barrier that is missing just a tiny portion at the bottom of *one* picket—big enough to permit the egress of one small Pug. Perhaps Dan needs to use the technique devised by his mother when he was a small tot: Christine would take to her bedroom, climb under the covers, and pretend to weep until little Dan ventured a tear-filled apology. It is unclear if Winnie has ever apologized for anything, but then she may be cross today because Dan has received a telling off from the vet—for taking his dog off her diet before the twelve weeks is up.

There is a curious sequel to the breakfast session today. As Hanna, Georgie and Dan depart, their seats are taken by Faz, Celine, Yasmina (who has the custody of Sasha) and the owner of the little King Charles, Maddy. I hang around for a bit of this session too, but when Celine gets up I accompany her toward the Morshead gate. She announces that Ziggy, perturbed by tummy trouble during his recent sojourn on the Continent, is soon to undertake the same anti-allergenic diet that Winnie has been enduring. Somehow, however, it is hard to imagine dizzy Ziggy turning nasty over this regime.

Thursday, April 6:

Four days have passed while Dorothy and I, accompanied by our friend David Oswald, have undertaken a brief trip to Paris. Fritz was evidently not a stranger to Paddington Rec during this period, since he was in the care of Linda and her family, and not only visited his old haunts in the morning but Regents Park in the afternoon as well. We return to the park on a marvellous and warm sunny Thursday morning and this time I bring David with me. Almost immediately, coming out of the cypress walkway on the back passage route, we encounter Jean-Baptiste and Dan. This makes for a fortuitous encounter since David, like Dan, has a background in box office management, although for many years David has been head of the Theater Arts Department at Cardinal Stritch University in Milwaukee.

I introduce David to the rest of the park as we continue our walk. Opposite the café Blake, even though muzzled, has managed to tear open a garbage bag awaiting collection—much to the annoyance of the park keeper who has just been getting these bags ready for removal. This is not the only instance of puppy naughtiness. After I have diverted Fritz from his walk along the Randolph roadway I have a lot of trouble getting him to follow my route and at one point he dashes ahead and turns left at the beckoning gap that is the Grantully entryway. When I dash up to this spot myself I head immediately for the gate, from which I can see my dog sitting in the middle of the street, a car idling at the curb! Nor is he at all interested in answering my urgent summons, moving forward only when the biscuit bag comes out. Sucker! I hand this goody bag to David and give my dog an admonitory smack on the bottom. I can see we are in a Mexican standoff. He must be punished for such a violation of the rules; I must be punished for abandoning him to another loving home for four days.

We continue around to the café, where a large group is sitting around two conjoined tables celebrating Hanna's birthday. Today we have, at our table, Kate, Dan, Georgie, and Ronnie. Their dogs are very much in evidence as are Ziggy, Buddy, and Frank (wearing his Superdog cape). Linda also comes in with Pepper—but here he and Fritz haven't much to say to one another. I pass around my camera, which still contains photos of a dog sitting at the table of a Paris café and a poster with a Pug bearing the label "Villain"—which I snapped in the Gare du Nord. The warm weather has everyone in a cheery mood, though Hanna complains that as a Master of Reiki *she* could offer for no fee at all a treatment she has seen advertised for £70 in Primrose Hill. We use the Morshead walkway to return home and, a few minutes later—and to the cries of distress of an abandoned dog feeling very sorry for himself—we begin a day of errands.

Saturday, April 7:

Weak sunshine still presides in Paddington park today, but it is a bit chillier than yesterday. I have persevered in my style of dress and I am wearing only a sweatshirt and my tan summer-weight trousers. Today David and I guide Fritz toward the Morshead gate, an entryway we have to share with dozens of little football players who are arriving en masse for a day of competition on the playing fields. As we near the Grantully gate there are echoes of yesterday's contretemps. Fritz runs, in fact, into the play area for a few minutes but it is easy to tell that he would really like to run out of the park next—though he manages to make do with a continuation of our grand circle.

I can see some of our lot heading for the café and so we meet them there. Faz, whom we have not seen in some days, is bursting to share some wonderful news: Dianah is three and a half months pregnant! We spend the first few minutes of our session reminding our friend of all the changes that a new arrival will bring to the life of this couple but you can tell that Faz is looking forward to all of them. We have brought some macaroons purchased Thursday at the Grande Epicerie of the Bon Marché and these delicious comestibles go down well with our coffee. Of course my tan trousers do not survive this session, as Sparkie lands almost immediately on my empty lap with his muddy feet. Ziggy also insists on imitating a lap dog, though his long, thin limbs sprawl over the sides of Celine's chair.

For once all eight of those present participate in a back passage walkround. There is still much discussion over the close proximity in which the trees and bushes have been planted next to the picnic ground. As we pass the football pitch on our left we notice that Jasmine and Winnie have joined the game. The reason for this incursion is that a sliding fence door has been left wide open. It takes a while for the missing dogs to come under control, but at least the players and coaches take this incursion in good spirit. Hanna has to remind these chaps on the need to keep the door closed—and then we can complete our walk.

Sunday, April 8:

Sunny skies are again dominant and it is a little warmer today than yesterday. I take Fritz out somewhat earlier than usual and we make slow progress along the back passage, where I notice that the footy lads have again left the gate open. On the green there is a large turnout of animals in all sizes, with much attention devoted to a tiny mixed terrier named Summer, a rescue puppy making her first visit to the park. A bit over-faced by all the other dogs, particularly a manic Sparkie, Summer keeps trying to jump into the arms of her owners. Another dog seldom seen here is Sally, a small terrier belonging to a neighbour of Peter, who brings the lively animal on the long ribbon lead formerly used by his new Gypsy.

Dan, who is taking photographs of all participants this morning, has brought an orange rubber bone with a mild squeak for Winnie to play with, but all the other dogs have a go at commanding its ownership, especially Fritz—who roars in protest if another dog comes near the prize. Buddy and Sparkie do succeed in making off with the toy but Fritz is distracted by the appearance of our houseguest, David, who now appears on the margin of the green as coffee time beckons. To me today's morning session is truly a throwback to all those days spent out here—especially when our dogs were a bit younger and craved such exercise.

At coffee we are presented with a large chocolate egg into which Dan has inserted a variety of smaller eggs. He tells us that he is bringing biscuits to a house warming that Kate will host at her new house this afternoon—because that lady has just discovered that Sainsbury is closed today. (We have an extended Easter serenade from the bells of St. Augustine's as we drink our coffee.) Little Summer is walking on the top of the nearby table, Winnie is attacking all the other dogs in her jealousy over their receiving treats that are again denied *her*, Sunny is barking again at all the shadows, and Pepper makes a sudden appearance under our feet as well. We begin a back passage retreat and this time Winnie manages to infiltrate the five-a-side field since *its* gate is open as well.

Wednesday, April 11:

Although I have penetrated the park on the last two mornings, a heavy head cold has prevented me from observing anything other than my dog's processes of elimination—and so two days have passed without a report. I am not in much better shape today but I soldier on, just getting Fritz into the Rec before he comes to a sudden halt and prepares to repel boarders. Somehow he has sensed that Scamp and Oscar are coming in behind him and he has to have a word on the subject of his own eminence. These three circle around a tree listening to Fritz's growls and trying to piss on one another's heads—and then they happily run down the walkway together in tandem. At the corner of the cypress trees there is a brief traffic jam as Frank barks hysterically skyward—no doubt having seen a squirrel hereabouts.

We pass Kate on her way home with Skye the Alsatian and reach the green where David the dogsitter has Skye the Cairn. That chap stations himself in front of my shoes—which he associates with a good kicking—but I am too unfocussed to be of much use. Blake, in the care of Sasha's mum today, is chasing Charlie, the little black poodle, and Fritz gets to growl at this innocent creature too. Dan spends the session on his mobile phone and soon departs for the café—so I follow suit, looking forward to sitting down as soon as possible.

We are eventually joined by our houseguest, David, but there is only a small turnout at coffee—Dan, Georgie, and Hanna being the only other participants. Hanna and I note that we are surrounded by two Chinese dogs (Winnie, Frank), two Germans (Fritz, Blake) and a Romanian (Gypsy). Peter has brought with him a rubber chicken bone with a pronounced squeak and, having discovered this object sitting atop the next table, Fritz moans in lust for the next fifteen minutes. The weather is warm but skies are clouding over—truth to tell we need some rain—and, with Frank having to put on his Superdog cape, no one is in the mood for a back passage walkround today.

Thursday, April 12:

Fritz and I enter the park an hour or so after seeing our David off in his minicab for Heathrow—and before long we have reached the green, where there is a knot of dog owners occupying the centre. Today is Fritz's fourth birthday and the birthday boy distinguishes himself by making off with Gypsy's rubber chicken bone. There is a roar of surprise from the other owners accompanying this audacious theft and then the sound of happy squeaking as Fritz settles down to munch on his prize. Young Timmy is barking hysterically and has to go on lead and I succeed in putting my own animal on lead as well—so that we can head in for coffee, the rubber bone still in his jaws.

Liz, just back from a week in India, buys the coffees this morning, even ordering up some sausage and toast for the birthday boy—though orders get confused and these treats never arrive. Spadge is far less likely to bark if he is allowed to wander around off lead in the confines of forecourt and this is where I discover him today. "Hmm," I tell Hanna, "I see we have free range Schnauzer in here today." Hanna is in tears with the advent of the hay fever season. Fritz is in tears because I have had to return the rubber chicken bone to Peter.

We are enjoying our coffee when there is an incident at our feet. Winnie, resentful as ever because she is restricted to health pellets, while George is gorging on toast, attacks our Hannibal Lecter—rolling him over on his back in a moment of madness. The contestants are separated but Winnie, her rage boiling over, continues around the table attacking any dogs in her way including Roxy and the sulking Fritz. My dog is not phased by this behaviour but poor Roxy is unnerved by this unprovoked assault. Her tail down, she trots over to the gate and Liz says she has to take her pet home. Dan has a quiet chat with Winnie on the subject of anger management and then he and I and our dogs undertake a back passage walkround.

Friday, April 13:

I suppose it is fair to say that the birthday celebrations continued well into the night for our Schnauzer, if not for his exhausted owners. This is because Pepper arrived for a three-night sleepover and the two dogs had their usual riotous wrestling matches for several hours. The evening ended with a long walk at 11:00, Fritz on Dorothy's lead and Pepper on mine, as we attempted to extract any unwanted waste products from these chaps before bedtime. (The score: Pepper two pavement poos; Fritz one tree well poo.) But at 4:30 in the morning Pepper began to fret in the hallway, waking us up with a series of insistent chirps—and I had to get up, get dressed, and take him out for a third pavement poo.

Somewhat under the weather from a less than restful night of sleep (Dorothy goes back to bed shortly after rising) I take the chaps out again at 9:15. I can actually manage with both of them on lead, twisting and turning so that I don't get these lines entangled, but once we reach the park I can let Fritz run free anyway. Here Pepper manages three more poos to my dog's two. (How much has Pepper had to eat in the last 24 hours?) Oscar makes a third Schnauzer in our party but Sabina explains that her dog can't leave the fragrant Pepper alone and, indeed, she has to drag him off. When we reach the green most of the usual animals are present and we stand around under cloudy skies with temperatures so surprisingly cool that Kate has to leave us almost as soon as we sit down for coffee.

There are quite a few people about today (both of the large tables in the forecourt are already occupied) but Liz, Hanna, Davide and I find another one outside the café's front door. I attach Pepper to one leg of my chair, Fritz to another. Liz brings me some English language papers from India and much of the conversation is devoted to her recent trip—which she enjoyed tremendously. Davide has also brought some cigarettes from Bahrain for Hanna. Everyone keeps an eye on Winnie, fearing a repetition of yesterday's brainstorm, but she contents herself with chasing after other loose dogs here and out on the green. I then begin my march home, exiting via the Morshead gate, both dogs back on lead but behaving themselves tolerably well—if you don't count Pepper's barking at everything and everybody.

Saturday, April 14:

Pepper has spent a much more relaxed night—and so, consequently, have we. Dorothy accompanies me as we enter the park this morning, Fritz off lead, Pepper on. Heading toward us are Hercules and a Westie named Charlie. As in the case of Oscar yesterday, these two gents want to hit on Pepper and it takes a while for us to make an escape—Charlie even following us around the corner and practically back to the café before being hooked by his mystified owner.

There is a lively scene out on the green, with Saturday scholars on one side and our lot fifty yards away. Pepper now has to endure mounting charges by Sparkie and Bailey while Fritz, who might be expected to protect his pal under other circumstances, is preoccupied by a squeaky ball that Buddy is brandishing in the face of all comers. Jean-Baptiste has by now completed a circle and rejoins us with Hercules. The Frenchman is clearly upset, since his flat has been burgled and several of the art pieces in which he deals have been taken by thieves—who kicked down two doors. We have left Ronnie sitting alone at a table in the café forecourt, however, and it is time to rejoin him.

In fact we need two tables, drawn together, to find enough room for us, Faz, Janet, Ronnie, Hanna, Dan, Albert, Liz, and, making her return after several weeks in Israel, Ofra. Bailey is overjoyed to be reunited with his mum; Georgie, who has been away for two days because of the funeral of the pensioner she used to keep an eye on (Tom, a.k.a. "Gummy") will now have just a noisy Sparkie to contend with. Many of this morning's participants are looking a bit rough for last night they had started off at the Greek restaurant on Marylands Road (Janet wanting a way to spend some of the insurance money that she was awarded after the death of Koko) and then ending up at Dan and Davide's—where they succeeded in breaking the karaoke machine. Faz, who was not a member of these revels, reports that he has passed the second part of his sergeant's exam.

It is rather pleasant in the morning sunshine but at last we begin a back passage walkround. This is a ramshackle affair as Dorothy, letting Fritz off lead again, hangs back with Hanna and a slow-moving George, while I am in the middle, cleaning up Pepper's mess, and the others get far ahead. The latter group includes a loose Fritz and I have to call him back and hang on to his collar so that he doesn't start a second circle or exit the park on his own. By this time Dorothy has at last drawn level and he can be reattached to his lead for the walk home.

Sunday, April 15:

It is another lovely sunny morning as Dorothy and I edge into the park with the two Schnauzers. Fritz waits for us as I clean up Pepper's poo and then his own—by this time we are able to access the green, where there is a lively Sunday scene in progress. Pepper, still on lead, is hectored by both Hercules and Sparkie again; in his spare moments *he* boards his old pal, Skye the Cairn. Fritz is mesmerised by a squeaky toy that a boy is using to attract his own dog, and my dog makes a real pest of himself—jumping up on this lad's bare legs until Dorothy has to put him on lead.

There is a very large turnout at our table in the sunny forecourt, for joining us are Jo Lynn, Hanna, Faz, Janet, Georgie, Albert, Ofra, Dan, and Kate. The café is crowded and, with Bouzha trying to break in some new staff members, orders are long in coming and often confused. "What are they doing back there?" our frustrated senior barista asks Dorothy—who is waiting in the queue. "Well," Dorothy replies, "one of them is fiddling with her pony tail and the other is adjusting the sleeves of her t-shirt." Janet reports that she won a little money when her horse came in third at yesterday's Grand National. Dan is getting up an expedition to the Clifton Nursery—a fatal mistake because he is now bombarded with advice on how he can get any plant he wants cheaper elsewhere. I suggest he can shop at Clifton for a water feature for his new backyard. Janet tells Faz, who is also smartening up his garden, that—with the new arrival on the way—he will soon have a permanent water feature.

We begin a back passage walkround, though by this time Dorothy has headed off to buy the Sunday papers and I have to manage both dogs on my own. This isn't such an easy task since they both have one more poo that needs to be cleaned up and there are lots of others dogs, strollers, joggers and jocks in the back passage by now. Fortunately Fritz keeps well in touch and I am able to hook him well before we reach our gate. By this time Dorothy is just returning from the store with her purchases and can open the door for us. We only have the goofy one for another hour or so—as both Fritz and Pepper are soon trying to climb Linda when she returns to claim her pet.

Monday, April 16:

For the first time in several days I am able to enter the park with only one dog at my side. There is a distraction, however—as Natasha is heading our way, a mobile phone in one hand, a coffee cup in the other, and dancing at her feet is little Leila. Fritz always seems to welcome Leila's presence and the two are soon inseparable as they make their way along the back passage. The Schnauzer and the Miniature Pincher disappear into the cypress trees, they have to put their heads together to sniff the same patch of grass, they trot along in tandem as we near the green.

Here, although it is not quite 9:30, the rest of the dog owners are already seeking the comforts of the café—leaving only Saskia with Buddy in the middle of a vast green emptiness. Fritz wanders around a bit longer, pausing to add a poo at the feet of some men in suits, and then we join Hanna, Ronnie, Liz, Georgie, Ofra and Albert at coffee. Ronnie notes that Albert has abandoned his coat on this very warm morning; I add that the old gentleman, even more unusually, is wearing no head covering. David the dogsitter enters the forecourt in an attempt to give Skye the Cairn a drink of water from one of the abandoned ice cream trays. This causes Fritz great consternation because he is on a short lead attached to my chair and David doesn't see or greet him. A few minutes later this foray is repeated—mostly because Skye has lost his ball, but—while it is being located afloat in the water dish—I let Fritz off the hook so he can greet his pal. David is supposed to be watching Pasha as well as Skye, even though Pasha's mom, the heavily pregnant Tanya, only six weeks away from her delivery date, is having coffee with Natasha, who is now holding baby Isabella.

When Ofra goes in to complain about the watery nature of her coffee I tell the others that the missing bag of jewellery store goodies, which she had lost months ago, has been recovered behind a drawer—where she hid it before forgetting she had done any such thing. This was a hot topic of conversation at the time, but she has forgotten to tell the others of this happy outcome. Nicholas comes in and sits down with Tanya and Natasha and this gives Liz a chance to seek the measurements for her curtains—which the furnishings entrepreneur has taken some weeks ago. The others are making plans to crash Nicholas' wedding, scheduled for August. Every time we see him the venue for the honeymoon changes—"Is

Cabo posh enough?" he now wants to know. When coffee is over for the day the participants scatter and so Fritz and I are on our own to make our way towards the Morshead gate.

Tuesday, April 17:

Temperatures have dropped considerably as Fritz and I make our way into the park on a cloudy, grey morning. As earlier in the week, Fritz now has to turn almost immediately to defend his territory against the presence of Rizzo, Scamp and Oscar—who are coming up behind us. "Fritz, just listen to you," Denise says, as my dog unleashes his patented rumbling growl. The air is cleared by this assertion of primacy, however, and these four dogs can now trot happily together toward the café.

Out on the green there is a knot of dog owners discussing canine diseases, with Franca urging all the others to make sure that their pets are immunized against parvo virus. Winnie is playing at our feet with a clear plastic detergent ball (first they won't let her eat toast, then they make her play with the cheapest toy available). Sparkie also has a ball, a somewhat scaled-down red soccer ball. He barks repeatedly at it until someone gives it a kick, but when Fritz shows an interest in this object the little Yorkie gives it a proprietorial pee.

At coffee Albert shows us just how much his eyesight has been improved by cataract surgery by spotting Bailey, half a park away. Dan is complaining about the rudeness of another theatre employee and Ofra is complaining about the difficulties of organizing Guy's *bar mitzvah*. Janet is making a rare weekday appearance but she tells us that sometime next year she may retire—though her boss wants her to stay on. I tell the others that *our* Janet made the same announcement to her boss, the Governor of Michigan, who urged her to stay on because she only had a year or so to go before the end of her term and didn't want to hunt for a replacement in the interim. Our Janet agreed to stay on—and then the Governor got herself elected to another four-year term. Hanna comes in with George and Spadge, the latter having just had a tooth extracted, and I yield my seat so that I can go pay my taxes to the Feds in Grosvenor Square.

Wednesday, April 18:

On these clear and bright mornings my dog duties do not begin with our arrival in Paddington Rec. This is because I have an overview of this burgeoning green scene from my study window and this means that Fritz does too—if he can obtain the right purchase on my lap as I sit at my desk. This is not an altogether happy posture for me—since he insists on putting his back legs or his bum on my chest in order to get the maximum height for his keen-eyed survey of the doggy scene already under way—and this position makes it rather hard for me to do anything else at the same time. I usually put him down after a few minutes, during which I try to convince him that the larger animals, those that have incited a gutteral protest, are actually on their way over to our house, where they are certain to take up a position on the middle of his bed. He neither believes me nor relinquishes his post without protest. This morning he leaps into my lap whenever I am not in a defensive position and there are hurt feelings when he is unceremoniously rejected.

Compared to this performance life is much simpler when we actually enter the park itself and head resolutely for the green, where there is the usual lively scene. I have to kick the tennis ball for Skye again but Fritz keeps up the pressure on Peter and Gypsy, coming away with a tattered rubber bone that once boasted a squeak of its own. Fritz will have to make do with this prize now but later, when I try to put it in my pocket in order to return it to its proper owner, the object takes on a mythic aura and he climbs my leg in pursuit of its wonderfulness. Placed on a table in the café forecourt this rubber fetish exerts its magical influence still, and eventually Ronnie gives it back to him in order to escape from all the whining. My dog is not finished with his naughtiness, however. He now sticks his head into Georgie's plastic shopping bag—always on the lookout for something worth stealing—but this time he manages to get his head stuck on one of the straps and when he pulls away he takes the entire bag with him (Sparkie has just done the same thing). Fritz is soon distracted by the arrival of Nicholas with Monty and a young blonde woman who has a Yorkie puppy, a miniature Sparkie, again named Jack. Nicholas wants Liz's phone number—are the curtain measurements at last going to make it over to the owner of the windows in question?

Today we have Hanna, Albert, Dan, Georgie, Ofra and Ronnie. You can tell that Ronnie is feeling better because he is smoking one of his big cigars. One of the waitresses brings out a tub of water and Ronnie offers this to Saffy and Tinkerbelle—but Albert says they actually prefer beer. The conversation, not surprisingly, turns to the shooting massacre at Virginia Tech University, a story that had dominated the news for the last few days, and you can measure the shock and disbelief of these island dwellers, especially over the comments of gun lobbyists who have argued that perhaps *every* student should have had a gun. Dan has been spending a lot of time getting his garden ready for spring and everyone has a lot of advice; indeed Hanna, having made a passing visit, has discovered a withered basket of pansies on Dan's front porch and taken them home for some emergency treatment. "Let me get this straight," I say, getting up to leave, "You went by Dan and Davide's and discovered that these pansies have at last dried out?"

Thursday, April 19:

Another beautiful day beckons. Rizzo is just being placed in his bicycle basket for the ride home as Fritz and I make our way into the park. A Papillion is heading our way, but Fritz is on his best behaviour. Not so, a minute later, when the approaching Hercules gets a peremptory growl; so does Skye the Cairn. Out on the green there are a dozen or so dogs at play—well I don't know if Sunny's barking at shadows counts as play or paranoia. Among the cast list today we have Zara and Dash, the King Charles Spaniels, who have made a rare visit with the now teen-aged Lisa. Much of the discussion out here is devoted to the search for another dog-groomer—the closure of All Dogs of Finchley having lead to some displacement in this category.

I follow Fritz on a solo quest for a suitable poo poo place—though I would not say that the side of a giant leaf bag really qualifies. Near the loos Fritz has to investigate the presence of two sturdy but quiescent Bulldogs, Wilma and Oscar. Then we head in for coffee, where I sit down at a table also occupied by Dan, Liz, Ofra, Georgie, Hanna and Albert. The dogs get through a mountain of toast (well, not you, Winnie) and Elian the chef even *offers* a plate of sausages on the house—but since he really means for this treat to go to his favourite, Miss Winnie herself, we have to decline. Crime is again a topic of conversation since Dan has observed an unsavoury collection of youths lounging on a corner near his new flat in classic drug dealing mode (Rhianne, who lives around the corner, says she is moving because of such neighbours). I note that an article in the *Wood and Vale* of March 24th has noted an instance of dog theft here in Paddington Rec—the larceny of an expensive Staffordshire puppy by a gang of youths, each armed with an adult version of the same breed.

A number of visitors drop by. Dan has a reunion with a neighbour from his old flat. Angie drops by to discuss the latest efforts to get Michael to pay us a visit. And Rowena drops by to report on her progress with the new Timmy. The latter, fitted with a collar that she can trigger to emit a spray of inert gas when there is any misbehaviour (in his case a need to chase motorcycles as well as a penchant for barking), had been so traumatized by the initial uses of this device that he has retreated into his pre-Mayhew shell again. He seems fine this morning—messing it up with Saffy and Tinkerbelle. On our back passage walkround, where we encounter the chocolate Lab Milo, I bring Dan up to date with Rowena's intifada against pigeons, one in which her balcony, alone on its street, has been napalmed in order to eliminate any cover for the flying rats. After we part I discover, all too late, the obvious solution: Rowena needs to get some of those collars around the necks of the pigeons.

Friday, April 20:

As we are about to cross the street a family, on their way to the kiddies' playground, are getting out of a red car, and the little girl's attention is drawn to the doggy, waiting at the curb. Fritz is cautious in the presence of such youngsters but he is also quite patient and so he remains in place while the toddler wanders over to stroke his whiskers. Once launched on our own entry into the park itself, things go fairly rapidly for once, and Fritz is soon making his entrance onto the green, where there is a substantial turnout on a grey and chilly morning. Fritz is immediately approached by Bianca and Ché, but the presence of these large dogs is unsettling and he issues a gigantic roar which sends them scattering. A half-term boy in wrestling on the grass with Chica, but the dog owners in general are about to be displaced by a school group who have commandeered the green for games.

Fritz and I decide to climb Mt. Bannister, where a woman is exercising two dogs, including one with only three legs, a brave chap who dashes all over the hillside with a stick in his mouth. On the other side we drop down to the café and take our places at a table from which Peter and Ellen are just leaving—but at which Davide, Ronnie, Georgie and Liz remain. Fritz wants to jump into Ronnie's lap this morning and manages to do so, spending most of the session here happily. However when Chica rushes in Fritz protests on the grounds that you can't just make *occasional* visits to the group—if you want to keep up your membership in his pack you have to appear on a regular basis. Liz says that her oldest son is obsessed with golf and hit 600 balls at the driving range in one session last week.

I join Davide and Georgie on a back passage walkround. Davide says that he is having to endure his annual cabin crew examination ritual and that today it is the medical exam—not an evaluation of his own health but a test of his medical knowledge, including CPR on a dummy. Georgie says that she has to go through the same ritual as part of her job with special needs students. The subject of medical emergencies reminds her that her husband has special insurance if he dies on the job. "I told him that if he has a heart attack at home, I'm putting on the work boots, rolling him into a wheelbarrow and dropping him off at the site."

Saturday, April 21:

The sun has returned, I am able to abandon my jacket again, and I am wearing my dark over-glasses as well; in fact, that is all I am wearing on my nose—since I have absent-mindedly forgotten my specs. I do have plenty of time to ponder this fact since Fritz is dilatory in the extreme today, pausing to sniff every patch of grass, choosing to nibble at a few strands here and there, inching along as the spirit moves—until I am beside myself with boredom.

Out on the green there is a lively Saturday scene, though only a few class members are present, and Fritz and I trot out here to see what's going down. Peter, with Sally on lead and Gypsy in tow, is sporting a badge from the Mayhew Home because he is about to participate in a sponsored walk round Wormwood Scrubs. (Is there something symbolic in this choice of site?) At breakfast he circulates a sponsor sheet that most of the other dog owners sign as well. Faz says that 200 policemen have signed a similar sheet to assist a fellow officer in his London Marathon run—in aid of a cancer-stricken daughter, who is being treated in the United States.

Today we have Dan, Georgie, Janet, Liz, Kate, Celine, Faz, and Albert at breakfast. Both Ziggy and Winnie are still on health pellets but every now and then someone forgets and slips one of these animals a real treat. Fritz decides he wants to sit in Janet's lap this morning and then, a little later, in Dan's. Buddy and Skye the Alsatian begin to mix it up in the background and Fritz takes umbrage over these shenanigans, jumping down in order to break it up. We begin a back passage walkround, creeping past the oldest soccer field—where the dads are lined up, one or two with forbidden dogs on the sidelines, shouting instructions at their toddlers. Someone notices that, high above us, a flight of four geese is crossing the heavens.

Sunday, April 22:

The unseasonal warm weather persists and today I could have entered the park without wearing even a sweatshirt, if I had wanted to. The sun is beaming down on a tribe of joggers, on and off the track, and Fritz seems to make better progress toward the green, encountering only the Cockers, Jake and Domino, in the process. There are again lots of dogs on the green itself, and Fritz manages to find sufficient amusement among them. First he has to accept greetings from the owners of Rex, the Springer Spaniel—as they loll on the grass. Then he has to chase a seven month-old Cavalier named Barney. He has a go at chasing Sparkie's red football as well, though Skye the Alsatian also makes a claim on this toy.

We have a large group at coffee, including Ronnie, Albert, Hanna, Georgie, Dan, Janet, Jo Lynn, Kate and Ofra, who has brought her son Guy today. I share with them a little local lore—adduced recently by Dorothy, who has read in her *Shepperton Babylon* book that the lyricist for Ivor Novello's World War I anthem, "Keep The Home Fires Burning," was killed in a zeppelin raid on Maida Vale! It takes forever for our coffees to arrive and in the interim I am surprised to see half of our table rise ("Is it something I said?") and move to a new one bathed in the direct light of the sun. Our old table is taken by Peter and this means that Fritz gets to moan over a bag that may or may not contain a squeaky toy but which, under any circumstances, he cannot get his snout into. Quite a few members of the Sunday crowd are staring over the fence at our strange group—we seem to be something that will keep children amused for several minutes at a time. Also on the other side of the fence is Trudy with her Dachshund Freddy. It does my heart good to see that this little fellow is being petted by a Moslem mom and her little girl—a rare sight.

As we get up to begin a back passage walkround people are discussing their Sunday plans. Jo is going to trundle her granny trolley over to the market on Marylebone Lane. Dan is heading for Homebase to buy a trellis for his burgeoning wisteria. And Kate is going to a paella party. Our progress in the narrow fenced defile is slow, as one after another of us has to pause to pick up a poo—though I do notice that they have at last emptied the long-barricaded red poo box that used to stand at the turnoff for Mt. Bannister. Sparkie jumps onto the benches as we continue, just for the hell of it, and Skye's head has to be extracted from a baby carriage in which a newborn is demonstrating well-developed lungs. "Winnie likes to bring up the rear these days," Dan says—and, as we make our exit, this means that our last view of this caravan comes as the Pug teeters by on her bowlegged pins.

Monday, April 23:

Skies are overcast and even weeping a bit—though hardly with vigour sufficient to dent the drought that we have been enduring for some time. After its Sunday workout the park seems very quiet this morning and our only company for the first few minutes is provided by joggers—on the track and off. Those on the track are dominated by Middle Eastern women and I suppose it is fair to say that most of them don't actually jog—they just walk purposefully in endless circles, sometimes pushing their baby carriages in front of them. Today a few clutch umbrellas.

Out on the green Winnie is still chasing her laundry ball and Sparkie is still pursuing his red football. The unfriendly weather leads to an early departure for the café, where we hunker down at a table under the overhang. At the next table Chica, in season for the first time, is chewing on a stick. None of the other dogs, even the intact Ziggy, pay any attention to her. At our table we have Ronnie, Celine, Georgie, Liz and Dan. The topic of conversation is again ill-discipline among the young. Several of the coffee drinkers report that life in the aisles of Sainsbury's has become less than pleasant as a consequence of temper tantrums and anti-social hi-jinks. Dan reports that yesterday there was a scene when one youngster became distraught because the store had run out of crustless bread.

I accompany Dan and Georgie on a back passage walkround but half an hour later I am making my way back through the park as Fritz has an appointment at the Hamilton surgery for his rabies booster shot. Dr. Seddon reports that our lad now weighs almost ten kilos. He may have to return later in the week, not for any further treatment, but because Tara wants to try out some clothes which Fritz may model in a fashion show at Clifton Nursery on May 2nd. If Fritz appears on the catwalk, and Winnie does not, there will be ructions.

Tuesday, April 24:

It's another warm morning in the park and, truth to tell, we already have patches of grass turning yellow in the drought. Around the corner we can see the familiar trio of Rizzo, Scamp and Oscar but, unusually, I notice that Oscar is on lead. The explanation for this restraint involves that seductress, Chica. Oscar, as an intact male, is evidently out of control in her vicinity and, after a merry chase, he has had to accept the leash. Someone suggests that perhaps the owner of Chica needs to be reminded of the ancient park tradition—no bitches in season in these precincts. But whom to entrust with this mission? Where is Hanna when you really need her?

Fritz and I soon reach the green and he is off on his ramblings. I tell Dan about Fritz's new role as a fashionista. He covers Winnie's ears as I complete my recital. I notice that my dog has joined the party of Peter and Ellen and is following them around the green in the company of Holly, Sandy and Jack. The latter gets into a scrap with another white Jack Russell, in this case Chelsea. Fritz then switches his affections to Rizzo, Scamp and Oscar (the latter off lead again as Chica has left the theatre) and he follows this group on a second loop. Indeed I have quite a time getting his attention when it is time to go in for coffee—"Biscuits" being the magic word in this case.

It is Kate's birthday and she has laid on coffee and toast for the crew. Not surprisingly the topic is age. There is a good deal of reverential nostalgia on the subject of youth—but Dan says that he thinks that there are pleasant memories to be derived from every stage of life. Kate says there isn't a single thing about her life that she would change now—a remarkably optimistic utterance after the year that she has had. It is a sentiment that Dorothy would assent to as well, minus her cough and her vocal problems, but I now get up to prepare for her first appointment with her new ENT consultant. Out on the green Buddy and Skye are chewing one another in a spirited wrestling match.

Wednesday, April 25:

I seem to be on the same schedule as Sabina and Denise because once again our dogs meet just after I enter the park and turn left. Oscar is not on lead this time but this could change at any moment because these sharp-eyed women have spotted Chica, off-lead, a hundred yards or so ahead of them. Sabina is afraid that her pet could easily follow the siren out of the park and is just about to hook him when we see that Chica is herself now under restraint.

Out on the green there are a dozen dogs at play, quite a turnout for midweek, and Fritz is soon part of a trio of Schnauzers, including Oscar again, and the visiting Butter, a two-year old slightly browner and larger version of the common type, a playmate of Ziggy's belonging to a colleague of Celine. For his part, Ziggy also has a new playmate, a six month-old slightly larger and darker female version of himself (that is part Bedlington, part Lurcher) named Flea. Before long the moms have cooked up a romance between these two animals, but no one has mentioned doggy dowry yet. Another newcomer is Charlie, a fluffy Bichon Frise, who is running in delighted circles. I am kept busy kicking the tennis ball to Skye the Cairn—while the slim-downed Winnie is still pursuing her laundry ball.

At breakfast there are ten of us at an outdoor table under glowering skies: Dan, Georgie, Liz, Kate, Ronnie, Albert, Hanna, Ofra and, enjoying a rare sit-down, a heavily pregnant Tanya. Again we return to the local crime blotter. Dan begins by suggesting that the crack-swapping gang of black youths who were displaced by the installation of a CCTV camera at their original site have now rounded the corner to take up residence on the steps of his own building! The police have had to be called, though Dan has bravely marched through this hostile crowd in order to enter his own flat.

Various instances of assaults on motor vehicles are then mentioned but, as usual, the last word belongs to Liz, for yesterday, in front of her own house, she was beaten up!

The incident began when, while chatting with a neighbour, the latter noted that a local youth (described as a twelve year-old from QK) was systematically spilling sugar over the back of her car. When the neighbour's request for a clean-up session was answered only with repeated use of the F-word, the neighbour, a tough cookie indeed, pulled the miscreant over to the car and forced him to face his own mischief. The sequel came when he used his mobile phone to call in the help of his parents and his auntie who arrived (straight from the pub, evidently) and preceded to throttle Liz and her friend, without a moment's interest in the behaviour of their lad—who was now putting on a tearful Oscar-winning performance as victim. Soon local shopkeepers and estate agents were rushing out to separate the combatants—though the police were evidently not called. "Liz," I conclude, "we expect this kind of carry-on in Brixton. We do not expect it in St. John's Wood."

Thursday, April 26:

Even before we reach our entry gate I have to pass a spare poo poo bag through the fence to Liz, who has dropped hers somewhere during her round with Roxy. As we reach the cypress trees we encounter Jean-Baptiste and Michaela. Fritz has just hunkered down for his own poo behind the cypress trees when Hercules pokes his nose in—and there are words. There is one unexpected dividend, however—as Hercules, for some reason, kicks earth and leaves all over Fritz's pile, obviating the need for a poo poo bag of our own.

Out on the green there is a gathering of dog owners surrounding Liz, who is just launching into her recital of "Slugfest in St. John's Wood, Part II." It seems that yesterday Liz was having coffee at an outdoor table at Starbucks with two friends, including the owner of the sugar-strewn car. Upon this party there fell with great ferocity the aggrieved mom of the little mischief-maker—who not only punched Liz's friend, but, with her own parents baying her on, indicated that she would continue to do so whenever given the opportunity. Leaping into this fray, however, was an undercover policeman, a chap who was soon joined by more cops coming out of Tesco. They managed to restrain the enraged one but they refused to affect an arrest, even though they had witnessed an unprovoked attack—or to take down the woman's name. This meant that when the victim, making her way down to the police station, reported the assault, there was no name to complain against. Liz now concludes her recital with a question, "Is this craziness going to be my fate forever?" "Yes," I replied, "because Things Happen to Liz!"

Our group now heads in to coffee—Kate, Ronnie, Georgie, Ofra, Liz and Dan. Nicholas, who has finally managed to drop off an egregiously expensive quote for Liz's humble curtains, arrives, and, without having any of the details of the incident, has many suggestions on what should happen next on Wisteria Lane—as Liz now calls her street. Then he spills his coffee on Roxy's back and manages to get Dan's up over an ill-timed remark about putting on weight.

We now begin a back passage walkround, accompanied by Saskia and Albert and their dogs. Fritz, the park policeman, growls at Buddy and Skye the Alsatian—who are making a disorderly progress of our route with their wrestling. The topic now switches to supermarket shopping. Saskia says that she has always avoided Sainsbury's Ladbroke Grove because when she was an infant her mother was told she couldn't bring her pram-bound baby inside an earlier version of this store. As this incident happened over thirty years ago, I tell Saskia that it is perhaps time to get over this insult. A few hours later Dorothy and I are again in the park as we take Fritz the fashionista up to Boundary Road for his fitting. Four outfits are chosen, including one coat clearly marked "Police."

Friday, April 27:

The weather has turned grey and chilly and I am back in wool hat and leather jacket for today's excursion. As usual we encounter Rizzo, Scamp and Oscar on our in-lap and then we face a real menace as we reach the cypress trees. One of the park keepers is riding his tractor in the narrow space between the foliage and the playing field. Fritz slips into the greenery but I almost get my toes squashed as the vehicle squeezes by. Fritz seems more perturbed by the high speed of a second tractor inside the field, one which seems to be massaging rubber pellets into the artificial turf. Next we pass a woman on her mobile phone—"So I said to him, if you feel that way, why are you treating me like shit?"

Just as we reach the café Blake and Ché are arriving from the Carlton gate and John is dismounting from his bicycle. Stuck between the pickets of the forecourt fence are a series of tennis balls, no doubt rescued from the bushes by the gardeners. I select one for Fritz and we head out to the green, where I am astonished to discover not a soul. Liz, who soon appears around a corner with Roxy, is also unable to explain the total absence of activity—though she speculates on the unfriendly weather. I ask her if there have been any developments in the War of Wisteria Lane and she says that a detective has questioned her about the most recent incident. "We're having a little trouble identifying who this undercover policeman is," the tec admits. "That's funny," Liz replies, "I just saw him in uniform on the High Street." There is still no reasonable explanation for the failure to note the assailant's name, but later in the day Liz and her friend have spotted this woman driving down the street, presumably looking for more trouble, and noted down her license plate number.

The two of us now head for the café, where we sit at a table beneath the overhang—in case it starts to rain. It's pretty quiet here too, though one little boy on a scooter is sporting a serrated Mohawk that has been teased into attention with lots of hair gel. After a while we are joined by John. He is excited by the recent behaviour of Saturn and tells us that he has been making a close observation of the weather reports on the Beeb, only to discover that they are not telling us the whole truth. He adds that he'd be afraid to go to the United States because, with his outspoken opinions and long hair, he'd no doubt end up in Guantanamo Bay. "Anyway," he concludes, "the only thing that would get me to America is a chance to commune with the medicine men of the Hopi Indians."

Saturday, April 28:

The sun has returned to the Paddington scene but it is still fairly cool in the park. The toddlers are charging about during their football lesson in the central field—about half of them in Chelsea colours and the rest in Arsenal livery. I can see a knot of dog owners on one side of the cricket crease and the pupils of the Saturday morning obedience class on the other. I have brought with me the tennis ball obtained in yesterday's giveaway and Fritz has a go at chasing this while I tell the others that we expect written excuses from them if they expect to be readmitted to our coffee circle after their derelictions of duty yesterday.

I can see that Fritz is having trouble securing the tennis ball because he already has something in his mouth. The object in question turns out to be one of those squishy red rubber balls with a mild squeak; it belongs to Sparkie and I can see that the little Yorkie is not happy to see it purloined in this fashion. A moment later Sparkie has reclaimed his toy and is dashing about, brandishing it in the faces of any other comers. When it is time to head for the café he and Fritz actually have a snarling match over possession of the ball, with Fritz arriving at our table with the prize in *his* teeth. I manage to return it to Georgie a few minutes later and Sparkie's red football—which has been nicked (in this case by Ché) is also returned.

There is a rather small group at breakfast this morning: Davide (Dan has gone off to work), Janet, Ronnie, Celine, Georgie, and Faz. The latter announces that he and Dianah are looking for more space and are interested in buying the next-door flat and knocking these two properties together. And that, with the prospects of a baby on the way, Miss Jasmine is being discouraged from jumping up on their bed. Janet says that she has received a letter from St. Mary's with her admission date—a somewhat unsettling moment since she is not under treatment at this time. Georgie says that at the same hospital the medicos mistook her husband for another patient and were just about to insert something in his stomach when he convinced them that he was here for quite another procedure. Ronnie passes on to Faz the number of his gardener—since the latter has received an email from his own chap announcing the dissolution of his business because his partner has succumbed to paranoid delusions after chewing on some African root. We undertake a back passage walkround—everyone is kidding Faz about picking up poo: Jasmine's in this case, baby's in the offing.

Sunday, April 29:

Dorothy, back from buying her Sunday papers, warns me that it is still quite cold outside and this means that I am back in leather jacket when Fritz and I enter a quiet park scene a few minutes later. Only joggers, some on the track, some on our walkways, one even running around the central playing field, provide any sign of activity. Fritz makes it as far as the café, where Peter and Ellen are usually the first to take seats in the forecourt, but thereafter I lose track of him for several minutes. Eventually

I spot him over on the walkway that descends from Mt. Bannister and here I head myself.

Out on the green there are two sets of Frisbee slingers and this may explain why the dog owners have settled for the foothills of the mount. Here we have Faz with Jasmine, Georgie with Sparkie, Ofra with Bailey, and Kate, who has not only Skye but also Mercedes, the four year-old daughter of a friend. Also present is Janet, now at last beginning to talk about making a visit to a Shih-tzu puppy farm in Colchester. She is on the phone as I arrive, saying her farewells to Dan and Davide, who are at Luton Airport at the outset of a week in Sardinia. Linda also arrives with Pepper and I have to call Fritz down from the heights so that he can greet his old pal. The latter proves an irresistible object for the lusts of young Sparkie, and a few minutes later, when the little dogs are contesting ownership of a ball on a string, there are words.

Ronnie joins us at breakfast. Both Faz and Georgie note that his Rosie, seemingly the most docile of pets, can be quite fierce on her home territory and that, while they have been visiting Ronnie, both Sparkie and Jasmine have found themselves pinned beneath the re-assertive King Charles. Faz, carried away by talk of a new Shih-Tzu claims, "Shih-Tzus rule the world." I respond, "The only world in which Shih-Tzus might possibly dominate would be the world of Rodeo Drive." There is now a quarrel over Primark—Ronnie denouncing every item on sale as "crap," while Janet, who is wearing a turquoise Primark jumper bought for two quid, defends the downmarket emporium.

John comes in with Ché, who immediately craps in the bushes—Janet makes sure that John cleans it up. Twice Fritz objects to the Alsatian's big head at the tableside and the larger dog backs off after receiving the customary growl. Ofra is upset because her Guy has lost his uniform jacket (with an expensive mobile phone in it) at his school—and she wants this institution to pay for any replacement. The others say that this is not going to happen. The heretofore very poised Mercedes, after completing her chocolate croissant and her still water, bumps her head on a chair and there are tears. When Kate picks the child up to comfort her, Skye has a jealous fit and jumps on Kate's back. Never a dull moment.

Monday, April 30:

There is a crisp wind but you can tell that warmth is on its way as Fritz and I make our way into the park on a sunny Monday morning. Spotting the Corn Star catering lorry making a three-point turn, I attempt to arrest Fritz's progress as we near the Carlton roadway. I do succeed in getting him to Sit!!! But when I praise him for this gesture he assumes that he is free to move on, and he is soon across the roadway and into the empty confines of the café.

There is not much activity on the green, which perhaps explains why a Japanese gentleman is doing exercises and yoga on the felt of the cricket crease (assisted by an unnamed white Jack Russell, who finds it great sport to leap onto the sedentary body). We meet the lovely long-haired Dachshund Snoopy and pass Gypsy, who is chewing a stick. Peter reminds me that he has completed his sponsored walk for the Mayhew Home and he needs the cash I have pledged. Truth to tell, I have forgotten even my coffee money this morning. Fritz keeps edging toward the eastern end of the green and I follow as he sidles toward the Grantully gate—but I am on to him, and I manage to steer him beyond this peril. I have not spotted any of the other regulars but I can see a dog owners' conclave at the east end of the green, so we head this way, finding yet another new tennis ball on the way.

In addition to Gypsy, Snoopy and Ziggy the group now has Rufus, Jack the Yorkie, Tara the Rhodesian Ridgeback, and—dashing in at great speed—Jess the Labrador puppy. Everyone wants a piece of Jess, who lies on her back so that everyone can have a sniff. At one point Fritz chases the other dogs away from the puppy, but when she takes refuge between my legs he objects to this too. Having seen not a single member of the coffee club, I keep my dog out on the green for an extra half hour and then we make our way toward the Morshead gate. On the way I peek over the café fence—some interlopers have claimed our table!

May, 2007

Tuesday, May 1:

We have another lovely morning in the park as Fritz and I enter through the Essendine gate. There is a roar of disapproval as my dog encounters the nose of Hercules again, but after being called "grumpy" by Jean-Baptise, my dog trots off happily toward the cypress trees. On the green we again have a lively turnout, though I never get a chance to count noses in the distant pack since there is so much activity at my feet. Pepper arrives and he and Fritz both manage to get hold of the same tennis ball in their teeth. This makes for a nose-to-nose tug-of-war which Fritz, displaying his alpha dog credentials, insists on winning. On our way to the café I pause to give Peter the five pounds I had pledged for his sponsored walk.

We are sitting at a table in the shade today, and I am a bit chilled, but at least there is a better turnout. No Liz today (jail or emergency ward?) but we do have Hanna, Georgie, Linda, Albert, Ronnie and Ofra. Tinkerbelle and Gaffy have had really short haircuts from a groomer who works out of her home on Shirland Road and some of the other dog owners want her number. There is a lot of toast for the dogs today and it is a delight to see Pepper, dressed in his new harness, lining up in the queue as though he does this all the time. Ofra is wearing her New York Yankees sweatshirt and I have to tell her that if she gets any dirty looks it is because half of America hates New York and almost all of it hates the Yankees—the Evil Empire of baseball. She says she doesn't care—she loves New York.

I walk with Linda along the back passage. Today she is fulminating against Culture Secretary Tessa Jowell, who has sited a new super casino in East Manchester where, far from providing work for the local residents, it will soon exist to empty their pockets of any hard-earned cash. We reach Linda's car eventually and here I say goodbye to Fritz for a while—since I have to accompany Dorothy to a doctor's appointment at

St. John and St. Elizabeth in St. John's Wood. Linda, our saint, is not only going to look after Fritz for the next few hours but take him to his fashion show rehearsal at Clifton Nursery. By the time we see him again, shortly after 3:00, he has even had his afternoon walk. I repeat: "Saint!"

Wednesday, May 2:

Another lovely day—this recent run of wonderful weather has lead the climatologists to conclude that we have just had the warmest April since such statistics were first recorded. Out on the green a park keeper is diligently chalking in the boundaries of the cricket field, though every now and then his efforts on the crease itself are interrupted by the flight of charging dogs. Foremost among these are Rufus and Ziggy, though Fritz, assuming the role of Ziggy's protector, chases Rufus away on several occasions. I try to keep my dog occupied in ball chasing but, truth to tell, I have better luck with Skye the Cairn, who presents his own ball to me on several occasions, hoping for another good kicking. As we cross the green we meet the ever enthusiastic, tail-wagging Beano. As the Tibetan Terrier dances in circles around Fritz, his mommy says, "He always loves any dog he remembers from when he was six months old."

At breakfast this morning we have Ronnie, Hanna, Ofra, Nicholas and Georgie. Ronnie is a bit shaken, since Rosie had earlier wandered off while he was in conversation, and he had lost track of his pet for about ten minutes. She is all present and accounted for now and just as eager to sample whatever treats may be going as any of the other dogs. Hanna accompanies me on a back passage walkround. She is reminded of a cold winter morning on the same stretch of walkway, just beyond the cypress tree that we have reached now, for here she discovered a most unusual object. I say unusual because her keen-eyed patrol of the park has lead to the discovery of lost passports, credit cards, hammers, and knives. On the day she recalls now the object in question was a crawling mud-splattered baby! Not knowing what to do with this creature and needing to get to work, Hanna picked it up at last—though at arms length since it stank—and carried it into the park office. Here the cantankerous Reg responded, "What the hell do you expect me to do with a fucking baby?" It seems that the child in question had crawled under the fence from her back yard on Kilburn Park Road—without anyone noticing that she was missing. Hanna says she was reminded of this incident by the sighting of the first leaves on the little tree that was planted on the edge of the green as a memorial to Reg last year.

Of course doggy matters are not over for the day because at 5:40 Dorothy and I set out for the Clifton Nursery, the setting for Frank Seddon's fashion show extravaganza. Organized chaos reigns. There are seven or eight canine models, their outfits tugged on in a shed in the back. Then the tall Tara, herself outfitted in a costume provided by a shop in Brent Cross, leads them down a catwalk that usually serves as the walkway to the indoor plants conservatory. Many of the outfits are on the verge of ridiculous—Fritz has to wear a white bathrobe with a hood and a yellow duck on its back; other animals are dressed in skirts or dungarees. There are too many Chihuahuas and Pomeranians and they can't even walk properly so that Tara has to carry them; others have never been on a lead in the hands of anyone other than mommy. Fritz does look nice in a red coat; he should, since it retails at £82.50. At any rate he is now down to two outfits since one of his has been passed on to a dog belonging to a woman who writes for the *Evening Standard* (sometimes) in a shameless instance of you scratch my back, I'll clothe yours. There are lots of photographers around and Fritz has his picture taken often—though we never see any of these. Dorothy has the best view of the proceedings and she says that our dog was the only animal who completed his task with any show of personality or interest. I note, as we walk home with our goody bag containing some doggy treats and a jar of organic marmalade, that this was an interesting instance in the micro-geography of canine populations—for we were only a fifteen minute walk from Paddington Rec and yet I did not recognize *one* of the other participants, canine or human.

Thursday, May 3:

We have a chilly grey morning for our walk in the park today and I am back in leather jacket and wool hat for the adventure. Fritz manages to let Hercules pass without protest—Skye the Cairn using the same moment to drop his ball at my feet, a gesture I pretend I have not noticed. A second later, however, the eternally optimistic Oscar receives the full blast of Schnauzerish disapproval for the crime of getting too close to the grumpy old man. I now follow my dog into the precincts of the café, where Peter and Ellen are sitting down with Ronnie.

Out on the green, our next stop, only Celine is present—though I can see Georgie on the periphery. Fritz pals around with Ziggy while I give a report on yesterday's doggy show to his mom. Off to one side Charlie the little black Poodle (deluded chap) is attempting to hump a surprisingly patient Oscar, while at our feet Charlie and Simon, Cockers, are attempting to engage Ziggy in some spirited play. School groups are filing in and out of the park on the Carlton roadway but otherwise it is rather still in here—we have been spoiled by April's unusual weather and perhaps we are not ready for a return to winter.

Celine and I join the others at coffee. Everyone here is complaining of the cold and Celine insists on having Ziggy in her lap as a defence against the chill temperatures. I distribute some organic doggy treats that were among the rewards Fritz received for participation in yesterday's fashion show. Ronnie is telling us about a gala concert he attended in the refurbished Royal Festival Hall. "We had Mozart 41," he begins—"Mozart 41," I interrupt, "what did the other team score?" Saskia comes in with Buddy and Fritz gives the Golden Retriever the obligatory growl. I explain that this is because Buddy has failed to present his membership card when questioned by the boss of the park. Albert comes in with his Yorkies and tells us an interesting tale. He was so bored when he retired that he and a friend decided to see if they could pick up some work as labourers on a building site in Hampstead. They were taken on by one of the big construction firms and, although Albert's mate lasted only a week, our veteran persisted for the better part of two years. But there was very little actual work. When inspectors were due crews would be collected in a van and ferried to the site in question—just so it would look like activity was under way. Albert says he got so bored that he gave up on work a second time.

Friday, May 4:

It's still chilly as Fritz and I make our way into the park. Though the sun is trying to come out, it is not making much of a success of this venture and I am glad I am still wearing my leather jacket. Under any circumstances I cannot be cocooned from the winds of change that are blowing their evil ways into our lives—for yesterday we learned that Dorothy almost certainly has lung cancer—and we know now that she faces a long period of investigation and treatment. The park scene fades in and out in my consciousness, unable to compete with the enormity of circumstances that now dominate our lives.

When Fritz and I reach the green this morning it is, perhaps fittingly, completely empty. I can see some activity on the slopes of Mt. Bannister—Ziggy, Rufus and Sasha at play, but I don't go there. Heading toward us are Charlie the little Poodle and Leila—today in the company of Maggie. Leila dashes forward to greet her pal, Fritz, and they spend some time trotting around together. A chap is bringing in from the Randolph gate a sixteen week-old mostly white Staffordshire puppy, a timid little fellow (so far) named Governor. Even though the pup flops down meekly (while the other dogs give him a sniff) I can tell that Charlie's mom is almost in tears—such is her fear of the menace to other animals presented by this breed.

I have a look around for any of our crew—but there is no sign of Hanna, Ronnie, Georgie, Liz or Ofra—and we know not to expect Janet or Dan and Davide these days.

I sit down with Peter and Ellen at their little corner perch and Ellen does the honours in taking in our orders and bringing out a trough of water from the caff (vandals have done in the men's room toilets, where we usually get water). Albert comes to join us, tying his dogs to the fence and producing some crunchy kibble for the others to nibble. Fritz tries to stick his nose into Ellen's purse, where he can sniff out a squeaky toy. The subject of retirement comes up and Peter says that he worked as a mechanical draftsman for most of his career, but computers made his skills redundant and he finished his working life behind the post office counter. Nicholas comes in with Monty—"Where is everybody?" is his first question too. David the dogsitter then arrives with Yoyo; I have to hold her lead in order to avoid a jealous fit when Fritz leaps into David's lap. For his part my dog is mightily interested in Yoyo's pink Frisbee ring and, on our return along the back passage, he carries it in his teeth for a while. For just a few minutes the antics of the dogs have driven other thoughts from my troubled mind.

Saturday, May 5:

It's still grey and cold outside as Fritz and I make our way, at a glacial pace, past all the miniature Ronaldos and Henrys on the Saturday morning practice pitch. My dog does agree to join me out in the middle of the green, where, as usual, we have the typical Saturday morning divide between obedience class pupils and all the rest. Today it is Ziggy's turn to have a go at disrupting the scholars. Janet has brought with her the picture of a female puppy that she and her friend Lyndon will check out tomorrow. Janet is already calling the little Shih-Tzu Daisy-Mae, but the latter is unlikely to make her home with her new mom until the end of the month.

No one wants to linger for long on the green so there is a determined march toward the café at 9:30 exactly. Today there is a much better turnout—with Kate, George, Faz, Albert, Ronnie, Janet and Celine circling our table. Kate, however, complains of the cold and makes an early departure, but not before her Skye has fallen in love with the organic savoury dog treats, Fritz's reward for his fashion show efforts—which I have again brought today. Ziggy also seems to like them. Fritz seems indifferent; he is much more interested in seeing if he can winkle Sparkie's squishy red rubber ball out of Georgie's pocket. Faz says that he and Dianah are looking at a neo-Gothic house in Highgate today, another housing option if they can't buy the flat next door and knock through an archway. This is a sobering idea for the rest of us—because such a move would clearly rob our group of one its vital members.

Not that I am in a cheerful mood under any circumstances. Janet asks me about Dorothy as we begin our back passage walkround. To this point, I just say she is unwell. An hour later and we have taken a cab to Sainsbury's (we take cabs everywhere these days, since Dorothy hasn't enough energy to walk). Here a more complete reaction to my wife's condition is manifest, for, as we are strolling between the cauliflowers and the aubergines, I begin to sob like an infant. Dorothy says not to worry, that she still has a lot more money she wants to spend in this life.

Sunday, May 6:

There is no sign of the sun yet, and so Fritz and I have the park pretty much to ourselves as we stroll toward the green under grey and chilly skies. I don't much care at what speed we travel this morning and I am just as happy to inch along, Fritz in his diligent sniffing, me in my thoughts. For once we encounter not a single soul from the time we enter the park to the moment we reach the café—not a dog, not a jogger, not another slow moving stroller. This is not to say that our passage is untroubled, because just as we reach the sharp corner near after the cypress tress Fritz pulls up in fright. The source of his anxiety is an unmanned piece of navy blue luggage, a suitcase on wheels that has reached this point at the end of its journey from its owner's hand to that of the thief who purloined it. Fritz finds its solitary presence ominous and tries to run in the opposite direction, resuming his normal progress only at my repeated urging, skirting the object in terror and proceeding on to less threatening precincts.

I can at once see that Dan has returned from his travels and that Winnie has returned to her proper home. She it is who now steals Sparkie's red squishy ball, causing hysteria in the Yorkie department. The little madam makes matters worse for the real owner by leaving it on the grass between her paws, where she tauntingly licks at it very slowly and pointedly. Only when Bailey broadsides her is she distracted long enough for Sparkie to claim his prize. Thereafter it is Fritz who waits for his chance and the object heads for the café, after several chilly moments, in his mouth. Here Georgie retrieves it but if she thinks putting it in her purse is going to be the end of the matter she is sadly mistaken—for pretty soon Fritz had fished it out of this bag and is happily gnawing at it under our feet.

We are well represented at table this morning, much closer to our usual strength—though Faz reports that Bouzha is still talking about the morning, earlier in the week, when *I* was the only member of our gang present. Today, in addition to those already mentioned, we have Davide, Ofra, Janet, Kate, Albert, and Ronnie. Janet and Georgie seem vastly amused with the report of a fight they got into here the previous afternoon—just a verbal one this time—when two seniors with a Pomeranian had a hissy fit just because Bailey was off lead. They seem to be understaffed at the café this morning since first Ofra and then Dan have to make the journey from the counter to our table with well-loaded beverage trays. The dogs share out the treats but an empty paper plate flies off the table in the wind and Davide traps it on his chest. Faz announces the beginnings of a back passage walkround and I warn him that he will be visiting a crime scene—the empty bag is still guarding its corner. Fritz, of course, is still clutching the ball in his mouth and we decide to let him borrow it for the night. This works well for only a short period, for when he is not knocking it under the sofas he is worrying it in his jaws and after an hour or so of this torture my frazzled nerves can't take it any more and the toy has to go into the naughty fridge.

Monday, May 7:

A light rain has been flecking the surfaces with moisture this morning and I am wearing my rain jacket as Fritz and I return to the park on a brisk and unpleasant morning. I can't see anybody out on the green but as I reach the foot of Mt. Bannister I find Georgie, her back up against the sheltering wall of the ladies loo. This becomes a place of refuge for other dog owners as well and we soon have Kate, Janet, Dan, Jean-Baptiste and Celine here as well. Janet has new photos of Daisy-Mae, the Shih-Tzu puppy she will take delivery on nearer the end of the month—pictures taken during a visit to a puppy farm near Lakeside yesterday. While she is standing with her back to the wall Janet finds an old two Shilling piece at her feet. I find a second one a few seconds later.

We round the corner and head for the café, where we join Peter and Ellen at a table under the overhang. Out in the forecourt we can see great changes in the offing. Metty has installed a fleet of round wooden picnic tables, each surrounded by a flight of four two-bum benches. There are immediate objections among the dog fraternity. It takes only a little rain for us to recognize that water will collect on these surfaces on many a night and that, if the tables are not dried off properly by the staff, there will be a lot of wet bums. Also, we can easily squeeze in twelve chairs around the old metal tables, but—unless more chairs are added to the present arrangement—there is room for only eight customers here. Worst of all, there is no way to lean back while enjoying one's coffee; it isn't a solution for old backs—of which there are many among the café's customers. There is no way of testing any of these theories as the whole forecourt is cordoned off and no one would want to be out there in the occasional blast of wet weather that is still blowing in from the west.

I tell Dan that, with her new trim appearance, Winnie has regained her old swagger. It soon becomes obvious, however, that her temper has not improved as she nips her master's fingers as he tries to wipe moisture off her face. Returned to the ground she walks around the table and takes a bite out of Hanna's hand just for the hell of it. Hanna is telling us that one of the Elgin Avenue college scholars has brought a puppy to class in his knapsack, one so young that its eyes were not even open yet, and, in brandishing this poor animal, has been having the time of his life scaring his female classmates. (Who is the biggest idiot seems to be the question here.) Hanna then tells us that she has rescued another animal—a stunned blackbird that she found off the Golborne Road, taken to the vet and home for a night of recuperation, then (at a minute past Congestion Charge time) returned to the spot where the little fellow had been plucked from the gutter. We begin a back passage walkround and I tell her that I won't be in the park tomorrow morning, as I will be taking Dorothy to the Royal Free Hospital for yet more tests. I haven't had the heart to tell any of the park people the whole story so far.

Thursday, May 10:

My return to the park comes in fragments. While Fritz was still in the care of Linda and Rob, I did return very briefly on Wednesday—as I made my way through the park on my way to the Royal Free—I knew that, at certain times of the day, I could make it there faster on foot than on public transportation. I found Dan, Ronnie and Michaela on the green and told them what I knew so far: Dorothy has a tumor (or perhaps two) attached to the left-hand branch of her windpipe. This helps to explain not only her cough but the swelling of nearby lymph glands and the collection of fluid in her left lung. The doctor says this is not a condition in which a cure can be definitively promised, but that it is not necessarily a terminal condition either. Dorothy is having fluid drained from her lung and undergoing additional tests and will be in the hospital for several days. Chemotherapy and perhaps radiation treatment are being discussed.

When I did reach the hospital Dorothy and I discussed the position of the dog. He was evidently having a grand time with Linda, whom he adores, but at the same time it was also very lonely in our house and so that afternoon his second mommy brought him home. He was exhausted after a march through Regents Park and a day of wrestling with Pepper, and so he mostly wanted to sleep—though he did brighten a bit when I made some microwave popcorn. But he slept by himself in Dorothy's study—until a rattling rainstorm at 2:00am brought him back to our bed.

This morning I again find Dan on the green and give him an update. A young woman brings in a four month-old white Staffie puppy named Pico. He seems to be a delightful chap with an adorable black eye but it is hard to imagine this bruiser as the happy playmate of our pets for much longer. Fritz takes an instant dislike to the newcomer and chases him away on a number of occasions. I tell Dan that I won't come in for coffee because I want to make an early start for the hospital and after about fifteen minutes on the green I head for home. Naturally my dog considers my departure a betrayal and no sooner have I closed the door than he begins an almighty howl of protest (Ginsberg had nothing on Fritz); the postman is entering the building as I head for my mini-cab. "Just ignore the singing Schnauzer," I tell him.

Saturday, May 12:

It appears that another day has passed without a report on park progress—this in spite of the fact that I did make a brief appearance here, though an hour earlier than usual, yesterday. The reason for this unusual entry time is that I had to head for the Royal Free at 8:30 in order to retrieve my wife. It did take three and a half hours for her to receive her discharge meds, but we were home by the early afternoon and Fritz was at last reunited with mommy number one.

Today thus marks the first time since Monday that something like our usual morning schedule can be attempted. The rainy weather that has dominated affairs for the last few days is in temporary abeyance as Fritz and I make our way out to the green—where the dog owners are congregated next to the cricket crease. Today we even have Humpty the Basset Hound baying in the background, with Winnie, Jasmine, Sparkie, and Bailey all in action. Ziggy is present too, but he has had a brief dietary relapse, one requiring a 3:00am emergency exit. (Celine suspects that Christopher may have slipped the fellow some forbidden biscuits.) Janet is set for a 10:00 departure for the puppy farm and she and Dan, who is driving her there, head in for coffee as soon as the café doors are open.

I have to answer many questions about Dorothy's health and spirits, and everyone asks me to pass on their good wishes. I hand Fritz's lead to Janet when I go in to order my cappuccino, and this is just as well because my dog wants to sit in her lap and receive his toast morsels on high. There is continued discussion on the subject of the new wooden picnic tables, still cordoned off in the forecourt, with universal apprehension expressed—but someone says that Elian has promised that a metal table will be set out here each morning just for the dog owners, and everyone hopes he is not just kidding. We end the morning with a series of conflicts that are typical of park life. First a mom tries to push a baby carriage around our table, only to encounter Ziggy's lead, which has been attached to one of the new hooks screwed into the forecourt wall. Then, on our back passage walkround, we are jostled several times by impatient joggers, particularly in the narrow defile between the playing fields. I conclude that some degree of normality has returned.

Sunday, May 13:

It's is an intensely grey morning as Fritz and I head for the park today and shortly after we have reached the green a light rain begins to fall. Joining the group for the first time in almost two weeks is Liz, whom I discover as she walks in from the parking lot with Roxy. In fact the Beagle has been under the care of a friend while Liz has been entertaining family from Ireland, but it is clear that there are also lots of domestic problems, plus lots of anxieties over the lady battlers on Wisteria Lane. Dan, seeing her close to tears, takes her off to one side. It hasn't helped her mood that I have just told her about Dorothy's illness.

Full marks to our dog owners, who in spite of the wet, are here in force this morning. One newcomer is an oversized terrier named Leo, the latest in a long string of mistaken studs who want to mount poor Pepper. Later Leo does an unattended poo on the far side of the green and there is a long debate over whether someone should chase after the owner or pick up the poo themselves. David arrives with Campbell the Westie, and he is immediately besieged by former clients—including Fritz, of course, and also a leaping Skye the Alsatian, whose boisterous antics are deeply upsetting to my dog. (And as well to Dan, who has suffered the indignity of a chomp on his family jewels from this same source yesterday.)

We are eventually driven from the green by the intensity of the rain and soon we are surrounding a table in front of the café's front door. Janet has new pictures of her puppy-to-be, and these are passed around. Kate, staring out at the downpour, reports that it's 30 degrees and sunny in Cannes, where she is heading next week. ("Shut up!" Dan and I respond in unison.) Fritz II has arrived with Richard and Christine and is setting up a deep-throated colloquy on the periphery. Pretty soon I see Faz springing into action as a man arrives bearing up a young jogger—who now collapses at a little table to the right of the café doors. The girl is a whiter shade of pale—tinged with green—and the decision is soon made to call an ambulance. It arrives about fifteen minutes later and the stricken girl is taken off. Faz says he suspects that drugs have had something to do with this incident and evidently the paramedics agree. We have to squeeze around their vehicle as we begin a back passage walkround in the rain. Out on the central playing field the Thai population of London is gathering for some sort of athletic extravaganza. They don't have a good day for it.

Monday, May 14:

For the second day in a row a light rain is falling when it is time for us to make our way into the park. Heading toward us, yoked by a chain, is a mismatched pair made of the lively Ziggy and a smaller but equally robust Manchester Terrier named Biscuit. Ziggy pauses for a greeting, but this means that Fritz has to tell Biscuit just who is the only boss in this park. A minute later we cross paths with what looks like a miniature Husky; this is another Elvis (a Shiba Inu, actually) and he wants to mount my dog—a gesture that is rejected with some vehemence.

As we reach the Carlton roadway there is a small convention of dogs including Leila, with Maggie, and Campbell and Yoyo, both with David. David says that it is not easy watching this pair, since Yoyo—on lead—is such a prima donna. I continue out to the green, where I spend some time with Michaela. Her Skye has a bright green tennis ball which I have to kick in a variety of directions, when he is not stationed an inch in front of my toe (yesterday he was clipped on the schnoz by Jean-Baptiste's boot because of this habit—but he chased the ball anyway). There is an extra tennis ball lying in the grass of the green (where a chap is adding chalk to the cricket boundary) and I keep both Fritz and Flash the Border Terrier active.

My dog wanders up to the top of Mt. Bannister, where I encounter Ofra with Bailey. She is the only member of the breakfast club present this morning and she is thus heading home, without any coffee, dropping down to the parking lot at this point. I get Fritz to return to the green for some more ball chasing. A woman has brought a lively long-haired mostly Jack Russell, a Mayhew rescue dog named Sid, and he is soon mixing it up so boisterously that Fritz has to break it up. The woman is delighted with Paddington Rec, where she is making her first visit after a disappointing outing in Queen's Park—"Imagine, they don't let dogs off lead there. How is a dog supposed to get any exercise?" The rain is coming down even harder out here, however, and, as there is no one at coffee at all today, I put Fritz on lead and we head for home.

Tuesday, May 15:

A few drops are again falling as Fritz and I head for the park on a grey Tuesday morning. A lone shirker, dressed in school jacket and tie, is seated on a bench at the head of the track. He stares balefully at us as we head for the cypress trees. Then Fritz puts on some speed and I lose track of him as he races out to the green and the company of quite a few members of the canine crew, including Gypsy, Winnie, Bailey, Sparkie, Rosie, Campbell, Sandy and Jack. Into this mix bounces the inky black silhouette of Charlie the Toy Poodle, but this incursion is not acceptable to my dog—who believes that Charlie's membership card has expired. Unusually, Fritz's efforts to expel the interloper are seconded by a number of the little dogs and together they chase the Poodle to the margins of the green.

As the rain intensifies we have to move our table closer to the front door of the café. Remembering Sparkie's real name, I tell Georgie that a boxer named Steve Spartacus will contest the British light-heavyweight championship this weekend. A number of the dog owners admit that they have had to rekindle the central heating this last week, though Peter (of Peter and Holly) says that he has never turned his off. Tanya comes by with baby Isabella, who is having a bad morning because she doesn't like being encased in the anti-rain plastic wrap of her buggy. She brightens a bit when she gets to share some of the dogs' toast. Tanya, who is expecting baby two in two and a half weeks, is kept busy keeping track of Pasha—who seems to have developed a new friendship with Gypsy.

We have to begin our back passage walkround in the rain, but we get no further than the Carlton roadway—where Leila and Charley the Bichon Frise are waiting. Charley is a bundle of energy and she kisses Fritz on the head as she dashes about. As often happens these days, I leave with the good wishes that the other dog owners are directing towards Dorothy. We pass the shot put launching pad, where youthful athletes are trying to heave their missiles from a turning circle that is brimming with water.

Here Dan tells me that Dorothy's get well card is in Davide's car, which is safely parked at Heathrow Airport. Davide is in Australia.

Wednesday, May 16:

Well, at least there is no rain. Still, we have grey skies once again and chilly temperatures to accompany our entry into the park. Fritz takes forever to make any progress along the back walkways, nibbling at all the really tall grass shoots and paying no attention to any of the other dogs or to the ubiquitous magpie—who seems to make his home in the cypresses. I have to wash my hands as soon as we reach the green and I think that Fritz is sitting expectantly at Peter and Ellen's table all this time, but when I return he has gone off and I have to retrieve him from the Carlton roadway.

Out on the green Buddy is playing tug-of-war with Sparkie's flattened red football. Winnie still has her laundry ball and Sid, back for a second day, is barking manically at all this canine activity. David is here and we have a fantasy on the subject of the oft-repeated question, "Who are you with today?" David wants a t-shirt that reads, "Today, I am with . . . ." and then a series of Velcro strips, each with the name of another client. I suggest that he ought to have a t-shirt bearing the likeness of every dog on his list—"You could make such a shirt part of your fee-structure," I add, "new clients have to begin by presenting you with a new shirt." Today David is with Campbell.

We go in for coffee and Dan shows me Dorothy's get-well card, one that the others have commissioned from one of Janet's handy friends. It has a picture of Fritz inside and some beautiful lettering in relief. Ofra is offended that the signatures are on a separate sheet of paper and wants Dan to add an inscription to the card itself. Today Ofra is full of details regarding Guy's bar mitzvah, which will take place in Israel in August. Georgie, who has been looking after Winnie, says that the little Pug is offended by the sight of her husband in his own bed and sits at the foot of this piece of furniture and barks until James gets up. Ronnie says that when he fell down on Maida Vale Parade a gent stopped to help him up and that Rosie barked hysterically at the Samaritan.

Thursday, May 17:

The mist has returned but the moisture is so slight that I am quite comfortable in my leather jacket; indeed it is quite mild today. For once Fritz makes quick work of his progress toward the green, perhaps encouraged by the alien presence of a park keeper, who is smoking a cigarette and blowing the ubiquitous leaf (singular) along the walkway at the head of the running track. The park seems to be a hive of such activity this morning, no doubt because the suits have arrived for an inspection. It unnerves the rest of us—having so many strangers walking around with clipboards at the ready.

Almost in the category of stranger is Tanya, the animal warden, who is making a rare morning appearance in her van. She says that she works mostly in Bromley now, having switched posts with Lee, whose patch this used to be. He, in turn, has to spend most of his mornings on a local estate where there are serious dog problems. This will explain why we have all been so desperate for poo poo bags—the portions they dole out at the clubhouse office being pretty meagre. Today we all stock up and then Georgie and Ofra have a contest to see who can fold one faster—since Ronnie brings carrots and biscuits for the dogs in such bags—and each day Georgie refolds the green plastic, now reduced to the size of a postage stamp, ready to slip into his pocket. I tell the women that they have done so well with this task that tomorrow they can demonstrate their skills with some poo poo *in* the bag.

It looks like you could actually sit at the picnic benches in the forecourt this morning but, as predicted, the seats are covered in sheets of rainwater and, since there is still mist in the air, we choose a metal table under the eaves. An obvious topic is the conflict between Chelsea manager Jose Mourinho and the police over allegations that his Yorkie, Gullit, had been travelling back and forth to the continent without proper papers—an impasse that has lead to the disappearance of the dog and the arrest of the manager. It is noted that the incident, a readymade festival for the media, has produced a plethora of awful puns: "Jose in Dog House," "War on Terrier." Dan says that Vanessa Feltz, whom Dorothy saw getting out of a cab on Marylebone High Street on Tuesday, is discussing whether or not a Yorkie *is* a real dog on her radio show today. Georgie covers Sparkie's ears during this conversation. He has just spent a night at Dan's house—much to Winnie's disgust. He did not, however, bark at anyone in bed.

Friday, May 18:

I am probably a bit overdressed today, but it is still grey and no doubt I have in the back of my mind the long series of rainy mornings we have been experiencing lately. By the time we reach the green the sun is trying to come out and this is a most welcome presence. There is a small knot of dog owners near the cricket crease and Fritz soon finds David the dogsitter and before long my dog has rolled over onto his back in order to receive a tummy rubbing tribute. No one can explain the diabolical squeals that now issue from Fritz's throat; he sounds like a stuck pig but he is actually enjoying himself. Georgie is complaining that she is dying for a cup of coffee so we soon head for the café. We have just about reached this oasis when we notice that Winnie has missed the signal to head off and, discovering herself all alone on the green, has now begun to streak after us in exaggerated panic.

Georgie, Dan and I take to a metal table outside the café's doors. For the first time ever I actually see someone utilizing one of the new wooden picnic tables, but, as I hang my leather jacket over the back of my *chair*, I discover yet another reason why the *benches* on these tables are no substitutes for chairs. Fritz is trying his luck over at Peter and Ellen's table but he has arrived too late—"You better put a new battery in your watch, mate," Peter is saying. Sparkie has spent more time at Dan's place and the guest had to have a shower this morning after rolling in poo. He needed a bath anyway as he will accompany Georgie to Scotland this weekend.

We begin a back passage walkround. I notice that a mother is pushing her baby on the swings with one hand and clutching a mobile phone to her ear with the other—this is what we call multi-tasking. As usual these days Winnie hangs back and Dan has to pause several times before the little Pug will agree to catch up with the rest of us. Shot-putting kids are at the head of the track, facing us since their turning circle is still full of water. "Let's taunt them," I suggest, "their attempts to strike us with these cannon balls will lead to much greater distances if they are properly motivated."

Saturday, May 19:

Today we have nice bright sunny weather, the first time in a number of days, and I have been able to leave my jacket behind me. Fritz makes quick work of his progress toward the green but here he has his work cut out for him, since Gus the Schnauzer makes a return visit and Fritz, forgetting for a short while that this is really not permitted, at last breaks into a run and sees his cousin off. In the dog owners' group in the middle (a slight displacement due to the supine body of a late riser who is trying to sleep on the grass) there is also a newcomer who needs chasing, a Winnie-like Pug named Monty. It is quite uncanny how much these two dogs resemble one another, though Monty is slightly larger and has a bit more black on his face than Dan and Davide's dog. Winnie seems to like the new fellow but perhaps she is just showing her snobbish side—trying to impress a visitor whose real home is Eaton Square.

When we go in for coffee I claim our old metal table in front of the café's front door but Dan says that, as it is sunny, Janet wants to try out one of the new wooden picnic tables. We take the one in the prow of the forecourt ship and the objections begin almost immediately: no convenient way to tie your dog to a chair leg, no place to hang your coat, the rather close proximity of bums who must now share a bench, no back rest. There is also the problem of what to do with Albert, who always sits as a satellite to our table—here Dan goes and gets a chair. A second is brought out for Ronnie, but he has a go at sitting on a picnic bench as well. Faz says that there is no way he would ever spend an hour in such an uncomfortable setting.

Janet tells us that she will be picking up her new puppy a week from today. Dan says he has been doing some research on her behalf, searching for a dog gate in the Argos catalogue. He found one for £39 in the dog section, then a similar gate in the baby section for ten quid less—and that this same discrimination was reflected in the price of blankets. There is a good deal of discussion on the topic of the missing four-year old, Maddy, who was kidnapped in Portugal two weeks ago. Faz says that he has no doubt that the local police are doing everything possible to recover the child, and there is some concern over the media's feeding frenzy and the general public's need to get involved in a situation where there is little they can do. It is noted that the same thing happened when Princess Diana died—an all-but forgotten ex-royal who was considered a bit of a trollop until she was suddenly killed—whereupon she became a heroine and a saint whose cult everyone had to join.

We head for the Morshead gate, stepping over an abandoned pair of teal-coloured lace knickers. Janet and Dan want to show me that in the gnarly twists and turns of a recently lopped tree they can see what looks like a little bear on his back. An hour or so later they are at our front door, bringing with them the famous card and some flowers for Dorothy, who begins chemotherapy on Thursday. I take them to my front window. In the twists and turns of a recently lopped tree outside my front window I show them what looks to me like the head of a dog.

Sunday, May 20:

If we make our way slowly along the walkways today it is down to me this time, not Fritz. This is because I have pulled a calf muscle in my left leg and progress is slow for me these days, inside or out. Outside we have a radiant spring morning, with gentle breezes and glorious sunlight to cheer us on our way. There are lots of people and their dogs about and on the green I can see a dozen animals at play. Fritz is soon joined by Pepper, who is his usual manic self. Out of the corner of my eye I can see a strange courtship ritual involving Monty and Winnie. It all ends in tears when Monty becomes just another in a lengthy line of suitors licking Bailey's tummy. Dan says that Ofra ought to take her dog to the vet, since there must be something that veterinary medicine can do to discourage such attentions. Davide says that Monty's preference for Bailey is of no concern to Winnie—since she's a lesbian anyway.

A number of dogs are paying court to David the dogsitter, including both of the aforementioned Schnauzers and Buddy, who is the loudest barker in the mix. Saskia says that Buddy will soon be accompanying the family on a holiday in France and that she has asked the landlady of their hotel in the Pas de Calais if they can eat in their room—since she fears that Buddy will bark the establishment into submission if left to his own devices. "He will take his place in the restaurant," was the response—score one for France. A lively Fox Terrier named Ruby now joins the mix. She's eager to mount Bailey too, but when she hits on Pepper, Fritz drives her away.

After yesterday's experiment the group returns to a metal table in the shadows: Dan, Davide, Linda, Ofra, Janet and Ronnie. Janet is getting up a group expedition to the puppy farm, where there will be a final visit with her new puppy before she picks Daisy-Mae up for good. Dan warns Ofra to bring her chequebook, since there is one unclaimed male in the litter, and he is adorable. I note that our animal warden, Lee Nash, has been in the news of late (even getting his picture on this week's *Have I Got News For You*) as one of the principal pursuers of the missing Yorkie, Gullit. "Anyway, now that Chelsea have won the FA Cup, Gullit can come out of hiding," I conclude. Linda gets up and her place is taken by John. He complains that the country seems to be without a prime minister since it will be almost six weeks before Tony Blair steps down and Gordon Brown replaces him. "Why not say the country has two prime ministers, then, rather than none," I add. After a few more moans from John, I conclude, "It's a thankless job anyway—I can't think of any more difficult task than trying to please the English." To their credit, the citizens of this country at our table do laugh in agreement.

We begin a back passage walkround, not easy with all the competition provided by Sunday parents who want to push their strollers at great speed through our lot as they hurtle toward the five-a-side courts, where their kids are at play. One competitor in a red shirt is being lead into the bushes by his dad for an emergency pee. I have let Fritz off the lead for this return journey, something I do not ordinarily do, since it is easier for me to limp homeward (angel) without his tugging. He disappears behind the cypress trees and I lose track of him altogether for the next two minutes (which is why I usually keep him *on* lead), spotting him at last at the head of the queue, far ahead of me. To his credit he now waits and even puts his bum on the grass when I command, "Sit!" What a good dog.

Monday, May 21:

The grey weather has returned as Fritz and I make our way into the park on a gloomy Monday morning. Almost immediately I am cornered by Jean-Baptiste, who wants to know how Dorothy is getting on, a frequently asked question in the park these days. "I mean," he concludes, "does she have a fighting spirit?" "Yes, she does," I reply. "And what about you?" "I have a fighting spirit too."

This conversation puts me well behind Fritz, who races ahead to the green for once, and soon takes his place among the small turnout near the cricket crease. Back, after a flying visit to Glasgow, is Georgie, somewhat spacey after two six hour train rides in about 48 hours. I ask her about the eightieth birthday celebrations held in her mom's honour. She says that no sooner had she presented the birthday girl with a beautiful bouquet then the old lady turned to another sister and said, "Who is that then?" "That's Georgie," was the explanation. "Well I don't like her hair."

I join Peter, Ellen, Davide, Ronnie, Georgie and Albert at coffee. Davide is recovering from a major case of jet lag after last week's long haul to Australia—where he was under instructions to buy a pair of Ugg boots for Ofra. In two days he will be flying off for his first visit to Calgary. Winnie is sitting in his lap contentedly when, spotting a park keeper she doesn't like, she flies off in pursuit and has to be chased down by Davide before she causes any mischief. Then there is considerable discussion of the burning of the *Cutty Sark*, which went up in flames this morning. I tell the others that I have to leave early. I have a workman in my house this morning—which means I have to go the market for milk and biscuits.

Tuesday, May 22:

One could fairly call this the first day of summer, for I am overdressed in my purple sweatshirt and the sun beams down warmly on the park scene. Again Fritz sees no reason to dally on his way to the green and when we reach the latter I can see that we have a bountiful weekday turnout near the cricket crease. Some of the bigger dogs, including the Boxer Sid, are giving chase to a wonderful but overfaced Tibetan Terrier puppy named Izzy. Fritz intervenes to chase the larger dogs off, and the owner of the puppy, who also has a little white Poodle named Sweep, says, "I can't deal with boisterous dogs today. I have a neurotic little girl at home and I don't want that Boxer turning my dog into a neurotic as well."

I am about to follow the others (and their dogs) toward the café when Richard Dunkley crosses the green, pushing his bicycle. As the famous photographer is about to have his first game of tennis after his own bout with cancer, I have to bring him up to date on the condition of my wife, who starts chemotherapy the day after tomorrow. This conversation lasts about five minutes and I lose track of my dog, who, looking for me, has evidently twice penetrated the sacred precincts of the café. I join the others at last, that is Dan, Georgie, and Ofra. The latter tells us that it is Shavuot, a Jewish holiday that requires the creation of a cheesecake. I am honoured when Winnie chooses to sit in my lap, but I soon enough realize that she really has her eyes on a small bag of biscuits I have placed on the table. Our dogs have to see off a number of casual visitors who appear at our side—including the other Sid and the lanky Phoenix.

I begin a back passage walkround with Dan and Georgie. Fritz, as usual, manages to hang back, even further back than Winnie, and I soon trail the others. A low-slung stretch version of a brindled Staffie, Mimi, comes up to have a sniff at my dog's bum, and she has to be rudely expelled. Half an hour later I walk through the park on my way to get my hair cut in St. John's Wood. I am surprised to see that a number of the dogs who populated the green an hour earlier are still here—taking advantage of the pleasant weather.

Wednesday. May 23:

I am better prepared for the sunny weather, which will climb to 75 degrees today, and thus I am wearing only a short-sleeved shirt as Fritz and I make our way toward the green. Denise again pronounces Fritz a grumpy old man as we pass the trio of Rizzo, Scamp and Oscar. I am grumpy at the sight of an over-stuffed poo poo box, one of the new generation of red plastic stations whose design I question and whose prompt evacuation is necessary in hot weather. This one has yesterday's contributions, in white plastic, still hanging from its crammed mouth.

As we reach the green we encounter Bailey, heading for the exits at a great pace; this is because he is getting a grooming from Ofra, a process which continues when he is captured. For some reason the dog owners have congregated at the northeast corner of the green and they have done so in outstanding numbers: I count fifteen at one time. Fritz is soon bored and I have to follow him on his perambulations; he likes to sneak into underground passages in the bushes but this time he is a bit surprised when, anticipating his wanderings, I have stationed myself on the other side when he at last emerges.

I order only a bottle of still water, which I share with Fritz, a capful at a time, when we are seated. Today we have Ofra, Albert, Dan, Ronnie, Georgie, Peter, Ellen and Nicholas. The latter asks after Dorothy's health and I try not to be too judgmental when, seeing that he is clutching a pack of cigarettes, I tell him that she has lung cancer. (Hours later, Linda having delivered my dog to the beauty parlour in St. John's Wood, I run into the kitchen entrepreneur a second time shortly after reclaiming Fritz—and Nicholas is therefore the first to tell Fritz just how handsome he looks.) Meanwhile our table is approached by Ronnie's next-door neighbour, the famous rocker Paul Weller (ex-The Jam, Style Council, etc), who has brought his little boy over to the playground. With his iron-grey hair he looks well preserved for a musician of his vintage. His little boy, who can't read yet, of course, is wearing a t-shirt with the legend, "The war is over, if you want it to be."

Thursday, May 24:

The warm weather persists and I enter the park under cap and dark glasses, again wearing only a short-sleeved shirt. Fritz doesn't dawdle and he is soon racing far ahead of me as we reach the kiddies' playground. Here I find him exchanging sniffs with a little black dog who has come into the park with a chap on a bicycle. The latter explains that he is only minding Monty today and that the latter is a Patterdale Terrier. I can see the resemblance to Jasper; a year ago I hadn't even heard of Patterdale Terriers, now I have met two. I have been telling the others, incidentally, that Charlie is the most popular dog name this year, with seven entries, but Monty, with five, is certainly next. Poppy (with four entries) would seem to be the most popular female name.

There is not much activity on the green itself, only Oksana with Rufus, but over in a corner, squatting in the bright sunlight, I find Dan and Georgie. Hanna, George on lead, is standing with them and this is a reminder that we have not seen her in about a week—since Spadge has had to spend five days on a drip at the vets after a serious case of gastro-enteritis. Fritz wanders off for his second poo and I follow, plastic bag at the ready. When I return I sense that there has been a subtraction from our little group and it is explained to me that Dan has gone off to work, leaving Winnie in Georgie's charge for the day. (No one is brave enough to break the news to Sparkie.) Ofra arrives with Bailey. She says that Fritz knows how handsome he looks in his new haircut and that he is prancing around, showing himself off.

We take up our usual position at a table in front of the café doors. I put some water in the cap of my bottle and both Sparkie and Fritz try to insert a tongue at the same time. Elian brings out a bonus portion of chopped sausage and the dogs, even including Winnie again, enjoy a rare treat. Nicholas, in shorts and a Bob Marley t-shirt, arrives with his Monty and orders a sausage sandwich for himself. There are lots of questions about the progress of Dorothy's treatment and I tell the others that shortly I will retrieve her from her first chemo session. When I leave the house to do so a spoiled Fritz howls in rage over the abandonment.

Friday, May 25:

It is still quite warm in the park; pity that they have *still* not emptied the red doggy bin next to the cypress trees. I persist in getting my contribution entered—today I have forgotten poo poo bags and I have to empty all the biscuits out of their bag, depositing these goodies in my front pocket, in order to scoop up Fritz's entry. We encounter Sid the Boxer, still a puppy really, and Fritz makes his protest known. His Italian owner puts him on lead, suggesting that Fritz is about to beat him up and that his dog will squeal like a little girl. The green itself seems deserted but soon I discover our group sitting on the grass at the foot of Mt. Bannister. Today we have Dan, Georgie, Janet (just a day away from picking up her new puppy) and, again back after almost a week's absence, Liz.

When we sit down for coffee at a picnic table in the sun Liz holds forth on her ongoing sagas, foreign and domestic. She tells us that she has refused to make a statement that might be used in court in matters relating to the Battle of Wisteria Lane, since police themselves witnessed the assault at Starbucks, it would seem unnecessary to involve third parties—especially as the feuding ladies are refusing to meet for a mutual apology session. In other news, Liz says that she has been having breakfast recently with Sir Paul McCartney, who frequents the same St. John's Wood patisserie as our Liz. This gossip has so enflamed the other American School moms that a phalanx of ten showed up to observe the next rendezvous and Sir Paul, making Liz's day, week and year, waved our friend over for a chat. These activities would seem to have only a tangential relationship to Paddington Rec, though we do remember Paddy McCartney—the Irish rescue dog whom Paul's daughter Mary sometimes brings to the green. But Hanna says that in happier times Paul and the soon-to-be-jettisoned Heather used to stroll around our park.

There are lots of complaints this morning about parking tickets—many of which have been issued erroneously in the wake of ad hoc Thames

Water projects on our streets. Janet says that her most recent one has been cancelled. Hanna gives us an update on the ailing Spadge, who got her up for a wee wee at four this morning. John arrives with Ché, who finds a use at last for the uncomfortable bench we are sitting on—storing a tennis ball on its surface. (Winnie, who is quite naked today, jumps up on the same bench—and then continues onto the tabletop.) John has brought with him a copy of today's *Metro*, with a cover page story about the murder of a teenager in Blackpool and the suggestion that her dismembered body ended up in the day's kebabs. The dog owners are deeply offended by this tale (more media misdeeds) and in high dudgeon we begin our back passage walkround.

Saturday, May 26:

The weather has now turned back to grey, overcast and cool, and I am back in sweatshirt for this morning's session. I think that Fritz is making a lively progress among the heavy-footed joggers but at one point he turns back to greet Billy the Bearded Collie. These two dogs join one another in a sniff-a-thon around some bushes at the head of the track and Nix and I have a hard time getting them moving. Fritz and I are a bit behind times in our entry today anyway, since I have paused at the last minute to lay out Dorothy's morning pills, and the consequence of all this delay is that no sooner have we reached the café then the other dog owners arrive from the opposite direction—ready to sit down for their morning coffee.

Today we have Ronnie, Dan, Georgie, Janet, and Liz. As usual, the tabletop is piled high with biscuits and mobile phones, but only Ronnie senses that one of the latter is vibrating. As Liz picks up her phone, I ask, "Did the table move for you, too?" Meanwhile Dan is experiencing another kind of vibration. Winnie (again naked) has been experiencing tummy rumbles as a consequence of her return to a more normal diet. First Dan has to endure a really smelly fart from his pet, who is sitting calmly on his lap, and then he can actually feel the next entry bubbling forth from the little madam's bottom, whereupon she is returned to the ground.

Liz puts down the phone in order to chide her Roxy, who has set up a howl of protest over the presence of an orange-clad maintenance man, who is emptying a bin right behind us. Liz is a bit worried that this carry-on will be taken as a sign of racial prejudice, but in fact Roxy dislikes all men in uniform, and the guy laughs off the insult. Elian arrives with white toast and Dan, tongue in cheek, says he actually ordered brown. Two minutes later Elian arrives with a plate of brown toast, having taken our Essex Man seriously. "He's so good-natured, always smiling," Dan says. "Yes," I add, "he even smiles when Ofra calls him Eliot." The dogs are soon agitated by the arrival of a twelve-week old mostly Staffie puppy named Socks. They all have a good sniff; Socks, on lead, is a bit shy.

We begin a back passage walkround. The football players, adults this time, are active on both sides of the fenced isthmus. "Fucking cunt!" one of them is shouting at no one in particular. (Sorry to be so explicit, but this is what we have to endure from footie society.) On the other side, a geriatric warrior is whining, "Stop shoving me!" Janet, meanwhile, is bursting with excitement—her next stop will be at the puppy farm, where she will at last bring home Daisy-Mae.

Sunday, May 27:

A steady rain means that both Fritz and I have to wear our rain jackets as we brave the sodden streets of Maida Vale this morning. There is not much activity in the park, though, to their credit, the Sunday football players are foregathering for another session of kicking and cursing in foreign tongues. Fritz is not at all happy with the rain, or perhaps he just hates his coat, and it takes forever for him to find a comfortable spot for a squat. Indeed, it seems to me that he would just as soon head for home on a number of occasions, and I have to keep him on lead (and moving forward) in order to prevent just such an eventuality.

By the time we do reach the café, and the safety of its overhang, the hardiest dog walkers are already in residence and the doors of the establishment are just being unlocked. This presents an opportunity for entry to a number of sodden pooches, Winnie and Gypsy among them, but such incursions are strongly resisted by their owners. I leave Fritz in Hanna's care while I make my order but he is soon squealing in delight as David appears with Skye the Cairn in tow. At the counter we discover that the café is out of sweetener—just as well that I have my own and can share this with Peter (of Peter and Gypsy) and Dan.

At our well-protected table Dan and David are discussing Helen's summer wedding in Holland, where both will be guests. Dan says that Helen has a second dog in Washington, a half Pug, half French Bulldog, and that her Cleo is not best pleased. Peter says that his Gypsy was part of a posse of Romanian street dogs scheduled for execution before being rescued and shipped back to the Mayhew. Gypsy himself is curled in a tight circle, a posture that he must have adopted many a time when he was out in the cold. I follow Dan toward the Morshead gate, the quickest way out of the wet park. (This route would be even faster if Fritz had not insisted on smelling Winnie's pee spots in the grass.) Dan says that, believe it or not, he is going shopping for a barbeque this morning. I say they ought to offer him a big discount.

Monday, May 28:

It isn't actually raining as Fritz and I venture forth on this grey and windy Bank Holiday Monday, but it has rained for over twenty-four hours (we got drenched every time we went out yesterday) and it looks like there might be more moisture on the way. There is tree litter everywhere and we have to step over leaves, twigs, chestnut buds and even small limbs which pepper the walkways. Fritz and I are both wearing our rain jackets; Fritz doesn't really need his, though perhaps it preserves some extra warmth; mine is inadequate to the task and I am quite chilled by the time we sit down for our coffee.

Today we have Dan, Georgie, Faz, Hanna, Ofra, David and John. The coffee orders get mixed up a bit and I get the small cappuccino while Ofra gets the medium. She sulks—"I hate big coffee." "You don't have to drink it all," I respond. Hanna is also cross with the number two cook—because her scrambled eggs have been overcooked. He disagrees. Dan says that the recent bad weather has had the happy effect of dispersing the street gang that has been hanging around his flat. Faz says that his father has had a dream, which can be interpreted as a prediction that he and Di will have a boy. Both Winnie and Bailey spend a lot of time in my lap, perhaps because this puts them close to Hanna's scrambled eggs.

Coming into the café now is Janet, who is carrying her new puppy, Daisy-Mae, in a basket. All attention is now riveted on this delightful creature, who resembles a flat-faced guinea pig. The other dogs are not allowed to get too close to the newcomer, who should have her last set of shots on Friday, but their owners are playing pass the parcel with the Shih-tzu puppy—Ofra even buttoning Daisy-Mae into her jacket. Janet is the subject of some good-natured kidding since, in spite of all her preparations and plans, the puppy has *not* spent her first two nights in the doggy crate, but cuddled up in her new mom's bed. Georgie, David (again with Skye the Cairn in tow) and Janet are part of the back passage posse today. There is a little moisture in the air but the icy winds are the chief problem as we edge our way through the tree debris. My teeth are chattering.

Tuesday, May 29:

There has been a good deal of sun about this morning, but it is still pretty chilly, and I am back in my leather jacket as Fritz and I make our entry into Paddington Rec. A large Weimaraner, ominously muzzled, dances up, and he and Fritz circle one another before the stranger is enticed to follow his jogging mistress with cries of "Barney!" Next we encounter Oscar and Scamp, and Sabina stops to cuddle Fritz, whose recent haircut is still earning accolades. I think we are making smart progress toward the green but this soon bogs down in a sniff-a-thon and my dog even seems to retreat a bit before I can coax him to resume the right direction—though he does so behind the cypress trees—which means that I lose track of him more than once. Our corner rounded at last, Fritz then breaks into a run, completing a dash toward the Carlton roadway at a speed that my sore calf muscle can not duplicate, and I even have to endure the anxiety caused by a speeding catering truck before discovering my dog safely on the other side of the café.

There is a lively scene on the green and we head for the cricket crease just as Dan, Georgie, and Hanna are heading for the café. Also coming out to greet us is a mostly white mostly Poodle named Kelly. At one end of the crease Sasha and Rufus are having a titanic wrestling match. Oscar and Scamp have arrived here too and when Oscar and Fritz are sniffing the same patch of grass I see why it is really hard to tell them apart at any great distance. Fritz spots two ancient Labs on the hill above the tennis courts and crosses the green to check them out, me limping in pursuit. By the time he has deposited a second gift I have turned him in the direction of the café itself. We are a good ten minutes behind the others—whom we discover sitting with Peter, Ellen and Ronnie at a table outside the front doors.

It's half term again and there are a lot of little girls around. One, in a pink tracksuit, is weaving her bike carefully through the obstacle course of dogs. A second, with bright red hair, is gazing out the café window as the canines pass in parade below her. A third, a Chinese lass named Leslie, is accompanying David the dogsitter. She is carrying Skye the Cairn's ball sling and David introduces her to each of our dogs—she thinks Winnie is ugly so it is just as well that Dan has headed home because of a crisis involving his boiler. Ronnie wants to discuss the recent TV program we have both seen, the one involving the efforts of the Bloch-Bauer family to recover five Klimts appropriated first by the Nazis and then by the Austrians (with the Bush administration siding with the Austrians, though unsuccessfully). Little Jack, the tiniest Yorkie, bustles up and this time the little red-haired girl gets to pick up one of the dogs and give him a nice cuddle. On our back passage walkround Georgie reminds us that Faz and Di begin a week's holiday on Crete on Friday. I ask her who will be looking after Jasmine, but Georgie's bemused expression is a reminder that there is no need for me to ask that question.

Wednesday, May 30:

We have grey skies, with rain threatening, as Fritz and I head for the park today. Our progress toward the cypress trees seems to be speedy enough, but just before we reach this sacred waymark my dog suddenly decides to reverse directions. He did the same thing yesterday, but today, for some mysterious reason, he continues at some speed almost back to our entry point. I have to follow him, of course, and soon it is obvious that we will not be heading for the green along our usual route. Meanwhile a little boy is pedalling past us on a low-slung wagon and he stops to ask if Fritz wouldn't like a large stick which has been lying next to the walkway. I suggest that my dog is not really into sticks and that he much prefers balls. "But we don't have any balls," is the peevish response.

The dog owners are gathered over at the northeast corner of the green again and here we head at last. Lying in wait for his pal is Pepper, and there is soon a raucous recognition scene. Buddy also seems to have an interest in Pepper's presence and barks hysterically for most of the session. I can see Fritz following Georgie into the café and so I head this way myself but Linda calls me back, "Fritz is here!" This is something of a puzzle—until I turn around and see that the Schnauzer in question is Oscar, not Fritz.

Rain begins to spit a bit as we gather around our table in front of the doors of the café. Today we have Ofra, Ronnie, Peter, Ellen, Georgie, Dan, and Albert, though Linda and Liam join us after a while as well. Ronnie is walking around the table, showing us a picture on his mobile phone. The scene represents the orchid that we bought him when he got out of hospital some time ago. It now has fifteen blossoms and Ronnie is obviously delighted. Ofra is happy too, having taken Bailey for his first grooming at St. John's Pets. Liam buys some toast for the dogs and carefully parcels these treats out to all comers, including Winnie, who will spend the morning with Georgie again.

We begin a back passage walkround, the dogs managing to tangle their leads more than once as we make desultory progress. Just as we near our exit we encounter the veteran pair of Asher the Rhodesian Ridgeback and Blue the Weimaraner. It has been some time since we have seen these chaps, or the blonde mom accompanying them. Blue seems a bit weakened in his rear legs this time—is age catching up with him too?

Asher and Blue bring the total number of dogs whose names I have recorded during my hour or so in the park this year to 225. This would seem to be a somewhat smaller number than the 250 or so I recorded in the first year of my observations here in Paddington Rec, but the difference is explained by the total absence of Michael this year. His role, as the master of ceremonies of all things canine, meant that everyone's name (owners' too) was elicited, and that proper greetings and introductions were made to all newcomers. There is no one to perform this role now, but this doesn't mean that the Rec is any less welcoming to its special clientele, or that its role in our lives is in any way diminished.

I also realize that today is my last day here—at least the last day I can report on doggy activities in the calendar year framed by my journals, which, in the case of the present volume, began last June 1 and must end today—since tomorrow I have to take Dorothy down to the oncology lab on Harley Street. I shall miss my day in the park, a place where the folkways of our pets enliven any moment and the friendship we owners have waiting for us here brightens any day. Soon we can see what adventures await us in the next year.

INDEX: THE DOGS OF PADDINGTON REC

In the following list I have tried, by date, to note every time one of the dogs of Paddington Rec has been mentioned in the text. If they have *only* been mentioned, though not actually seen by me, I have listed the date in italics. Of course many dogs share the same name, so I have tried to indicate (in parenthesis) which animal is being referred to. Apologies for the occasional misspelling of a dog's name, but this is inevitable in our environment. Dates begin with June, 2006 and conclude with May, 2007.

ABOUT THE AUTHOR

Anthony Linick was born in Los Angeles in 1938 and educated in the city's schools, including Alexander Hamilton High School. In 1955 he entered the University of California at Los Angeles where, majoring in history, he completed his BA in 1959 and his PhD. five years later. While still an undergraduate he began work on the little magazine *Nomad* (1959-1962)—which he co-edited with Donald Factor. This background also contributed to his choice of doctoral dissertation topic, *A History of the American Literary Avant-Garde Since World War II.*

In 1964 he and Dorothy were married in Los Angeles and the following year they moved to East Lansing, Michigan, where Anthony took up a post as Professor of Humanities at Michigan State University. He taught a variety of courses in Western Civilization, literature and contemporary culture here, and published a number of articles on popular culture topics, American and British. Indeed, the Linicks began to spend more and more time in England, including a sabbatical year begun in 1979; in 1981 they moved to London.

Here Anthony began a twenty-year teaching career at the American School in London, in St. John's Wood, offering many courses, first in the high school social studies department and then in the English department—where he served as department head from 1994 to 2002, the year he retired. Dorothy also worked at the American School as a special projects coordinator; she had also held the post of director of student services at the American College in London. She died in July, 2007.

Since his retirement Anthony has been at work on a number of writing projects, including two earlier volumes in the dog people of Paddington Rec cycle, *Strictly Come Barking* and *Have I Got Dogs For You!*—as well as *The Lives of Ingolf Dahl*, a biography of his stepfather, and *A Walker's Alphabet, Adventures on the long-distance footpaths of Great Britain.* All of these books are available from the publisher at Authorhouse.com or Authorhouse.co.uk—or from any of the other online booksellers. He can be contacted at AnthonyLinick@compuserve.com.